Performing with

Word Processing Applications

Iris Blanc

New York City Department of Education

COURSE TECHNOLOGY
25 THOMSON PLACE
BOSTON MA 02210

Australia • Canada • Denmark • Japan • Mexico • New Zealand • Philippines • Puerto Rico • Singapore
South Africa • Spain • United Kingdom • United States

Performing with Computer Applications

by Iris Blanc

Senior Vice President
Chris Elkhill

Managing Editor
Chris Katsaropolous

Sr. Product Manager
Dave Lafferty

Development Editor
Thompson Steele, Inc.

Marketing Manager
Kim Ryttel

Directors of Production
Becky Herrington
Patty Stephan

Production Manager
Doug Cowley

Associate Product Manager
Jodi Dreissig

Print Buyer
Laura Burns

Cover and Internal Design
Ann Small
A Small Design Studio

Illustrations
Ferruccio Sardella

Compositor
Kellee LaVars

Printer
Banta

Printed in the United States of America

1 2 3 4 5 6 7 8 9 BM 07 06 05 04 03

For more information, contact Course Technology, 25 Thomson Place, Boston, Massachusetts, 02210.

Or find us on the World Wide Web at: www.course.com

For permission to use material from this text or product, contact us by
Tel (800) 730-2214
Fax (800) 730-2215
www.thomsonrights.com

ISBN 0-619-05595-2

Give Your Best with this new addition to the Performing Series!

This is a new text for the Performing series and provides a comprehensive word processing applications text that can be flexibly used in many situations. Using a unique approach to learning, this text offers a means of learning about computers, thinking critically, solving problems, communicating effectively, applying technology to task, and working in teams.

- **NEW! Performing with Computer Applications, 2nd Ed.**
  Over 200 exercises for word processing, desktop publishing, spreadsheets, database, presentations, and web design
  0-619-05596-0 Textbook, Hard Top-Spiral, Easel-Backed Cover, 75+ Hours
  0-619-05597-9 Instructor's Resource Kit (IRK) CD-ROM Package
- **NEW! Performing with Word Processing Applications**
  0-619-05595-2 Textbook, Hard Top-Spiral, Easel-Backed Cover, 35+ Hours
  0-619-05597-9 Instructor's Resource Kit (IRK) CD-ROM Package
- **Performing with Microsoft Office XP,**
  Introductory Course by Iris Blanc and Cathy Vento
  75+ hours of instruction for beginning through intermediate features
  0-619-05853-6 Textbook, Hard Spiral Cover, Core MOUS Certification
  0-619-05854-4 Instructor's Resource Kit (IRK) CD-ROM Package
  0-619-05931-1 Annotated Instructor Edition
- **Performing with Microsoft Office XP,**
  Advanced Course by Blanc, Vento, and Thompson Steele
  75+ hours of instruction for intermediate through advanced features
  0-619-05855-2 Textbook, Hard Spiral Cover, Expert MOUS Certification
  0-619-05856-0 Instructor's Resource Kit (IRK) CD-ROM Package
  0-619-05932-X Annotated Instructor Edition
- **Performing with Microsoft Word 2002,** Comprehensive Course
  0-619-05857-9 Textbook, Hard Spiral Cover, Expert MOUS, 35+ Hours
- **Performing with Microsoft Excel 2002,** Comprehensive Course
  0-619-05859-5 Textbook, Hard Spiral Cover, Expert MOUS, 35+ Hours
- **Performing with Microsoft PowerPoint 2002,** Comprehensive Course
  0-619-05861-7 Textbook, Soft Spiral Cover, Comprehensive MOUS, 35+ Hours
- **Performing with Microsoft Access 2002,** Comprehensive Course
  0-619-05863-3 Textbook, Soft Spiral Cover, Expert MOUS, 35+ Hours
- **Performing with Microsoft FrontPage 2002,** Comprehensive Course
  0-619-05880-3 Textbook, Soft Spiral Cover, 35+ Hours
- **Performing with Publisher 2002,** Comprehensive Course
  0-619-05970-2 Textbook, Soft Spiral Cover, 35+ Hours
- **Performing with Microsoft Office XP and 2000,** Projects for the Entrepreneur
  by Iris Blanc and Cathy Vento
  0-619-05865-X Textbook, Soft Spiral Cover, 50+ Hours, 512 pages
  0-619-05866-8 Instructor's Resource Kit (IRK) CD-ROM Package

Join us on the Internet at

The workplace of today requires its workers to use computers, understand how they interface with other technologies, think critically, solve problems, communicate effectively, apply technology to task, and work in teams. To prepare students for this changing workplace, we must provide learning activities that support the development of these skills.

Performing with Word Processing Applications includes a variety of learning activities and projects that are interesting, engaging, and skills-rich to help the student develop the competencies and skills needed for today's workplace. Students will study how software tools are used with each other for business, personal, and school purposes. Applications throughout the text are integrated with Internet activities to develop research, problem solving, and communication skills. The exercises proceed from basic to intermediate level. This book can be used with Word 2000 or 2002 for the PC and Word for the Macintosh.

ORGANIZATION OF THIS TEXT

Performing with Word Processing Applications will introduce the student to concepts on *The History of Computers, The Computer System, Parts of a Computer, The Internet, Telecommunications,* and *Computers and Society.* The text continues with the following three software application units—word processing, desktop publishing, and Web sites. Each unit introduces the student to generic software concepts. Students then apply the concepts through sequential, developmental, and *integrated* application exercises. Internet activities are included in each unit after students are introduced to World Wide Web concepts in the Word Processing unit.

End-of-Lesson Skills Review Exercises include integrated applications using the Internet to challenge and reinforce the concepts learned in the lesson. *End-of-Unit Projects* provide activities that allow the student to demonstrate mastery of unit concepts as well as communication, research, and critical thinking skills. Many of the exercises may be used as **portfolio-work samples** and are identified as such (see Directory of Documents and Portfolio Work Samples). A final *Capstone* exercise provides the student with an opportunity to apply all the concepts learned throughout the text.

SPECIAL FEATURES

- **A Keyboarding Reinforcement Unit** (found on CD) contains 18 exercises of drill and practice material covering the entire alphabet for those who wish to learn the keyboard or improve their keyboarding skills quickly.
- **A Speech Recognition Unit** (found on CD) provides basic concepts and activities to develop skills in the use of voice recognition software.
- **End-of-lesson summary skills review exercises** reinforce the concepts and applications learned in the lesson.
- **End-of-unit integrated projects** apply the concepts learned throughout each unit.
- **A Capstone project** applies all the skills learned throughout the text.
- **Data files** (found on CD) allow students to complete many of the exercises without keyboarding lengthy text.
- **An Exercise Log** lists file names in exercise number order.
- **A Directory of Files** lists file names alphabetically with corresponding exercise numbers.
- Clear, simple exercise directions.
- **Generic concepts** for each lesson (*Concept Builders*).
- **Marginal Boxes** include *Concept Builders, Hot Tips,* and *Did You Know?* information.
- **Vocabulary words** relating to each exercise, which are defined in the Glossary.

- **Key words for using the Help Index** provide search words for getting Help.
- **Portfolio-building exercises.**
- **Appendices** that include:
  - A. Microsoft Office Specialist Correlation
  - B. Using the Mouse
  - C. Toolbars, Menus, and Dialog Boxes
  - D. Proofreaders' Marks
  - E. Leading and Line Spacing Illustrations
  - F. Letter Styles
- **Multiple-choice, true/false, and performance-based test bank.**

WORKING WITH DATA AND SOFTWARE-SPECIFIC PROCEDURE FILES

Data files are provided for many of the exercises so that the student need not keyboard lengthy text. Exercise directions include a CD-ROM icon to direct the user to open a document from the separate Data CD.

ACKNOWLEDGMENTS

Many people play a role in the production of a quality book, and I owe them my gratitude and appreciation. First and foremost among them are Dave Lafferty, Senior Product Manager, Chris Katsaropolous, Managing Editor, Doug Cowley, Production Manager, Kim Ryttel, Marketing Manager, Kellee LaVars, Compositor, and Jodi Dreissig, Associate Product Manager, for their professionalism, guidance, and support throughout this project.

My heartfelt thanks go to those who have made significant contributions and assisted me with the production of this book:

- To my contributing writer: Jaime Blanc, thank you for your creative input and assistance.
- To the production team at Thompson Steele: Sally Steele and Karla Maki, who kept everyone on track and on time, and did so with support and guidance all along the way.
- To Deb Thompson, of Thompson Steele, with whom I interacted on a daily basis. I thank you for your patience, support, direction, and follow-through. Your professionalism and temperament made working with you on this project a pleasure.
- To Marie Michal, designer, New York City, for her outstanding illustrations.
- To Lauren Slutsky, graphic design consultant, New York City, for her direction and design of the desktop publishing exercises.
- To the Donnelly family for permission to adapt the Keyboarding Reinforcement Unit from the work of the late Frank Donnelly.
- To my family, Alan, Jaime, Pamela, and Matthew Chasin: Thank you for your encouragement, your love, your inspiration, and above all, your patience.
- To the newest member of our family—my grandson, Benjamin Howard Chasin, I dedicate this book.

Lastly, I wish to thank my assistant and contributing writer, Jaime Blanc, who has been a guiding light on this project—her fresh view of the world helped to create fun and relevant material; her keen eye for detail assisted in the review process. She is a talent beyond words, and best of all, she is my daughter.

ABOUT THE AUTHOR

Iris Blanc is currently the Director of Virtual Enterprises, International™, a New York City Department of Education school-to-career program. Formerly, Ms. Blanc was Assistant Principal/Department Chair of Business Education at Tottenville High School, a New York City Public High School.

Ms. Blanc has taught business education and computer applications at the high school and college levels for over 25 years. In 1989, The Business Education Association of Metropolitan New York presented Ms. Blanc with the "Outstanding Educator of the Year" award.

Ms. Blanc gives seminars, workshops, and short courses in applied learning strategies and methods of teaching and integrating technology at business education conferences nationwide.

Ms. Blanc is the author of numerous computer application texts and reference guides.

HOW TO USE THIS BOOK

Exercise Objectives
Objectives are listed at the top of each lesson.

End-of-Unit Test Questions
Provides assessment of the concepts covered in the unit.

Portfolio Work Samples
Identify critical thinking applications, which may be included in a learner's portfolio.

Directions
Clear, step-by-step directions help students complete the exercise.

Vocabulary
Vocabulary words introduced in the lesson are indicated and are defined in the Concept Builders or in the Glossary.

EXERCISE 2

Create a Document; Correct Spelling; Use Smart Tags; Save and Close a Document

SCANS

Directions

1. Create a new document.
2. Use the default settings.
3. Begin the exercise at the top of your screen.
4. Key the paragraphs shown below, allowing the text to word-wrap. Press the **Enter** key twice to create a new paragraph.
5. Correct spelling errors, if necessary.
6. **Word 2000 Users:** Skip this step.
   Position the insertion point over the phone number, click the **Smart Tag Actions** button, and view the actions.
7. Save the file; name it **1.2thankyou**.
8. Close the document window.

Thank you for taking time to meet with me last Monday. I have enclosed three copies of my résumé and writing samples.

If I can provide you with any information or materials, please contact me at (212) 555-5555. I admire the work you do at WEB-ONE Interactive, and I hope I will have the opportunity to work with you in the future.

VOCABULARY

Smart tag

CONCEPT BUILDERS

- Press the Enter key at the end of a short line or to begin a new paragraph.
- Smart tags appear as purple dotted lines beneath names, addresses, phone numbers, dates, and times. Resting the insertion point over a smart tag displays a Smart Tag Actions button, which gives you access to e-mail and Outlook. **This feature is not available to Word 2000 users.**
- A smart tag below a phone number gives you access to Outlook's Contacts list.

NOTE

Smart Tags
To check to see that smart tags are turned on and will appear below names, addresses, phone numbers, dates, and times, click Tools, AutoCorrect Options. Click the Smart Tags tab and click all the check boxes below Recognizers.

Use the Help Index

How do I...?	**Enter the keyword(s)**
Use smart tags	Smart

Lesson 1 • Exercise 2 Unit 2 • Word Processing – 44

Concept Builders
These marginal boxes explain generic concepts presented in the exercise.

SCANS
(Secretary's Commission on Achieving Necessary Skills) The U.S. Department of Labor has identified the school-to-careers competencies. The five workplace competencies and foundation skills are identified in the exercises throughout the text.

End-of-Unit Projects
Provide activities that integrate the use of software tools and applies the concepts learned in the unit.

Marginal Boxes
These boxes provide Hot Tips, additional information for the Internet, and facts (Did You Know?).

Illustrated Exercises
Models for students to apply the concepts learned.

Appendices
These include information, illustrations and reference material including Using the Mouse, Toolbars, Menus, and Dialog Boxes, Proofreaders' Marks, and Leading and Spacing.

Using the Help Index
Search words are provided for getting Help on new features through menus within the software.

End-of-Lesson Skills Review Exercises
Provide critical thinking review exercises that reinforce all the concepts covered in the lesson.

TABLE OF CONTENTS

UNIT 3: DESKTOP PUBLISHING

UNIT 4: WEB SITES

CAPSTONE

APPENDIX

START-UP CHECKLIST

PC HARDWARE

Minimum Configuration

- PC with 90 MHz processor
- 32 MB RAM for Windows 98
- 64 MB RAM for Windows NT, Windows 2000, or Windows XP
- 4 MB available space in the registry for Windows NT
- Hard disk with 350 MB free for typical installation
- CD-ROM drive
- VGA monitor with video adapter
- Microsoft Mouse, IntelliMouse, or compatible pointing device
- 28,800 bps or higher modem
- Printer

Recommended Configuration

- Pentium PC with greater than 32 MB RAM
- Super VGA 256-color monitor
- 33,600 bps modem
- Multimedia capability
- For e-mail, Microsoft Mail, Internet SMTP/POP3, or other MAPI-compliant messaging software

PC SOFTWARE

- Windows 98, Microsoft Windows NT 4 with at least Service Pack 6, Windows 2000, Windows Millennium Edition, or Windows XP
- Internet Explorer Browser 5
- Word 2000 and 2002

MACINTOSH HARDWARE

- Mac OS-based Apple Computer with a PowerPC processor
- 150 MB to 250 MB for an easy install (though a universal install can be up to 400 MB) of free disk space, depending on options selected, and drive size and format
- 40 MB of RAM (32 MB of physical RAM, with virtual memory set to at least 40 MB)
- CD-ROM drive
- Monitor that can display 256 colors and a resolution of 800 x 600 or higher
- Modem: 14.4 Kbps or higher
- Internet access: Internet connections through either an Internet service provider (ISP) or a network

You can use the Apple System Profiler program included with Mac OS X to determine whether your computer meets these requirements.

MACINTOSH SOFTWARE

- Mac OS 9
- Word 98

DIRECTORY OF FILES

Directory of Files, Word Processing

Unit - Lesson	Exercise	Data	Solution
2-1	1		s1.1begin.doc
2-1	2		s1.2thankyou.doc
2-1	3		s1.3net.doc
2-1	4		s1.4policy.doc
2-1	5		s1.5hr.doc
2-1	6		s1.6bp.doc
2-2	7	d2.7begin.doc	s2.7begin.doc
2-2	8	d2.8thankyou.doc	s2.8thankyou.doc
2-2	9	d2.9bp.doc	s2.9bp.doc
2-2	10	d2.10net.doc	s2.10net.doc
2-2	11	d2.11hr.doc	s2.11hr.doc
2-2	12	d2.12bp.doc	s2.12bp.doc
2-2	13	d2.13eq.doc	s2.13equity.doc
2-2	14	d2.14off.doc	s2.14offer.doc
2-3	15		s3.15confer.doc
2-3	16		s3.16party.doc
2-3	17		s3.17eat.doc
2-3	18	d3.18confer.doc	s3.18confer.doc
2-3	19	d3.19eat.doc	s3.19eat.doc
2-3	20	d3.20montreal.doc	s3.20montreal.doc
2-3	21		s3.21cclet.doc
			s3.21run.doc
2-3	22	d3.22bp.doc	s3.22bp.doc
2-3	23	d3.23party.doc	s3.23party.doc
2-3	24		s3.24tennis.doc
2-3	25		s3.25mylet.doc
			s3.25problem.doc
2-3	26		s3.26schoolad.doc *
2-4	27		s4.27present.doc
2-4	28		s4.28ad.doc
2-4	29		s4.29citation.doc
2-4	30		s4.30biblio.doc
2-4	31	d4.31ad.doc	s4.31ad.doc
2-4	32	d4.32citation.doc	s4.32citation.doc
2-4	33	d4.33present.doc	s4.33present.doc
2-4	34	d4.34db.doc	s4.34dbase.doc
2-4	35	d4.35phone.doc	s4.35phonecharges.doc
2-4	36	d4.36travel.doc	s4.36travel.doc
2-4	37	d4.37run.doc	s4.37run.doc
2-5	38	d5.38voicetech.doc	s5.38voicetech.doc
2-5	39	d5.39dance.doc	s5.39dance.doc
2-5	40		s5.40memo.doc
2-5	41		s5.41resume.doc
2-5	42		s5.42intro.doc
2-5	43		s5.43altech.doc
2-5	44	d5.44intro.doc	s5.44intro.doc
		d5.44altech.doc	s5.44altech.doc

Directory of Files, Word Processing

Unit - Lesson	Exercise	Data	Solution
2-5	45	d5.45newtips.doc	s5.45newtips.doc
2-5	46	d5.46organize.doc	s5.46organize.doc
2-5	47	d5.47ad.doc	s5.47ad.doc
2-5	48	d5.48organize.doc	s5.48organize.doc
2-5	49		s5.49myown.doc *
2-5	50	d5.50confer.doc	s5.50confer.doc
2-6	54	d6.54memohr.doc	s6.54memohr.doc
			s6.54rights.htm
2-6	55	d6.55dctourlet.doc	s6.55tour1.doc
			s6.55tourinfo.htm
2-6	58		s6.58nymemo.doc *
2-6	59		s6.59mystatement.doc *
2-7	60	d7.60cclet.doc	s7.60ocr.doc
2-7	61	d7.61ad.doc	s7.61ad.doc
2-7	62		s7.62dtp.doc
2-7	63		s7.63history.doc
2-7	64		s7.64www.doc
2-7	65	d7.65animate.doc	s7.65animate.doc
2-7	66	d7.66ocr.doc	s7.66ocr.doc
			s7.66ocrmerged.doc
2-7	67	d7.67history.doc	s7.67history.doc
2-7	68	d7.68dtp.doc	s7.68dtp.doc
		d7.68run.doc	
		d7.68bp.doc	
2-7	69	d7.69confer.doc	s7.69conferad.doc
2-7	70		s7.70compute.doc
2-7	71	d7.71dctourlet.doc	s7.71tour1.doc
		d7.71tour1.doc	s7.71tour2.doc
2-8	72		s8.72news.doc
2-8	73		s8.73zoo.doc
2-8	74		s8.74repair.doc
2-8	75		s8.75virus.doc
2-8	76		s8.76jbminutes.doc
2-8	77		s8.77cash.doc
2-8	78		s8.78donate.doc
2-8	79		s8.79itinerary.doc
2-8	80		s8.80payperiod.doc
2-8	81	d8.81contributions.doc	s8.81giving.doc
2-8	82	d8.82cash.doc	s8.82cash.doc
2-8	83	d8.83cclet.doc	s8.83newsites.doc
2-8	84		s8.84application.dot
			s8.84myapplication.doc *
2-8	85		s8.85jborderform.dot
			s8.85ord1004.doc
2-8	86		s8.86careers.doc
2-9	88		s9.88protect.doc
2-9	89	d9.89cclet.doc	s9.89doctor.doc

Directory of Files, Word Processing

Unit - Lesson	Exercise	Data	Solution
2-9	90	d9.90will.doc	s9.90willfinal.doc
2-9	91	d9.91present.doc d9.91newtips.doc	s9.91pretips.doc
2-9	92	d9.92doctor.doc d9.92virus.doc	s9.92doctor.doc
2-9	93		s9.93release.doc
2-9	94	d9.94investment.doc d9.94investad.doc	s9.94investor.doc
2-10	95		s10.95jobdata.doc s10.95jobform.doc * s10.95jobfin.doc
2-10	96		s10.96sordata.doc s10.96sorform.doc s10.96sorfin.doc
2-10	97		s10.97joydata.doc s10.97joyform.doc s10.97joyfin.doc
2-10	98	webcomputerassn.mdb 10-98accountant (query)	s10.98seminaracct.doc s10.98acctlabels.doc
2-10	99	d10.99sordata.doc	s10.99sordata.doc s10.99sorfin2.doc s10.99sorenv.doc s10.99sorlabel.doc
2-10	100	d10.100joydata.doc	s10.100joydata.doc s10.100joyfin2.doc s10.100joyenv.doc
2-10	101	d10.101joydata.doc	
2-10	102	d10.102joydata.doc	s10.102joyemail.doc
2-10	103	d10.103memo.doc d10.103sales.xls	s10.103memosales.doc s10.103sales.xls
2-10	104	d10.104jacksmith.doc d10.104bonus.xls	s10.104jacksmith.doc s10.104sales.xls
2-10	105	d10.105jbanalysis.doc d10.105jboctsales.xls	s10.105jbanalysis.doc s10.105jboctsales.xls
2-10	106	d10.106ad.doc d10.106grow.xls	s10.106adgrow.doc s10.106grow.xls
2-10	107	d10.107dbase.doc equipinv.mdb d10.107eqprice (query)	s10.107eqprice.rtf s10.107dbase.doc
2-10	108	d10.108funddata.doc	s10.108funddata.doc s10.108fundfin.doc s10.108fundlabel.doc
End-of-Unit Projects	Project 1		swkfmdata.mdb swkfmfinal.doc swkfmformlet.doc swkfmlabels.doc swkfmlethd.doc
End-of-Unit Projects	Project 2	dproj2careers.doc	scareerbiblio.doc scareerreport.doc scareertitle.doc
End-of-Unit Projects	Project 3		scomputermanuf.doc

Directory of Files, Desktop Publishing

Unit - Lesson	Exercise	Data	Solution
3-1	1	d1.1montreal.doc	s1.1montreal.doc
3-1	2		s1.2bblet.doc
3-1	3	d1.3news.doc	s1.3news.doc
3-1	4	d1.4dtp.doc	s1.4dtp.doc
3-1	5	d1.5party.doc	s1.5party.doc
3-1	6		s1.6food.doc

Directory of Files, Desktop Publishing

Unit - Lesson	Exercise	Data	Solution
3-1	7	d1.7zoo.doc	s1.7zoo.doc
3-1	8		s1.8travelad.doc
3-1	9	d1.9sccbrief.doc	s1.9sccbrief.doc s1.9chinamap.gif
3-1	10	d1.10intmenu.doc	s1.10intmenu.doc
3-2	11		s2.11shapes.doc
3-2	12		s2.12layer.doc
3-2	13		s2.13objects.doc
3-2	14		s2.14gcc.doc
3-2	15	d2.15eat.doc	s2.15logo.doc s2.15eat.doc
3-2	16		s2.16caflogo.doc s2.16neweat.doc
3-2	17		s2.17backyard.doc
3-3	18	d3.18practice.doc	s3.18merci.doc
3-3	19	d3.19news.doc	s3.19news.doc
3-3	20	d3.20present.doc	s3.20present.doc
3-3	21		s3.21sanbar.doc
3-3	22	d3.22confer.doc	s3.22conferdtp.doc
3-3	23	d3.23bblet.doc d3.23release.doc	s3.23pressrelease.doc
3-3	24		s3.24makefilm.doc s3.24makefilmweb.html
3-3	25	d3.25protect1.doc d3.25virus.doc	s3.25protect1.doc
3-3	26		s3.26manual.doc
3-3	27		s3.27reportcover.doc
3-3	28	d3.28brochure.doc	s3.28brochure.doc
3-3	29		s3.29cdcover.doc
End-of-Unit Projects	Project 1A		sdtp.proj1a.newsletter.doc
End-of-Unit Projects	Project 1B		sdtp.proj1b.flyer.doc
End-of-Unit Projects	Project 1C		sdtp.proj1c.certificate.doc

Directory of Files, Web Sites

Unit - Lesson	Exercise	Data	Solution
4-1	1	d1.1guidelines for eating healthy.doc d1.1energy.doc d1.1fiber.doc d1.1fruit.doc	s1.1pyramid.doc s1.1foodnewsletter.doc s1.1foodwebpage.htm
4-1	2	d1.2jbmarketweb.ppt	s1.2jbmarketweb.htm
4-1	3		s1.3formweb.htm
4-1	4		s1.4ski.htm
4-1	5		s.1.5recipeweb.htm
4-2	6	d2.6foodwebpage.htm d2.6recipeweb.htm d2.6formweb	s2.6foodfantasymagazine .htm
4-2	7	d2.7healthtext.doc d2.7nutritiontext.doc d2.7exercisetext.doc	s2.7healthweb.htm
4-2	8		s2.8cakes.htm
4-2	9	d2.9ski.htm	s2.9goaway travelweb.htm
4-2	10	d2.10pricing table.doc	s2.10niftytees.htm
4-2	11		s2.11resumeweb.htm* s2.11mywebpage.htm*

* Denotes student-specific exercise; solution file not provided.

Introduction to Computers

NOTE TO STUDENTS Read this section carefully so you have an understanding of the computer, its history, hardware and software applications, the Internet, telecommunications, and related topics.

INTRODUCTION

Thirty-five years ago, few people handled computers. Computer users were limited to specially trained operators and engineers.

No one ever anticipated that today every office worker must work with computers and that most people use computers in their everyday lives—both at home and at school.

Therefore, it is important to learn about the parts of a computer, how a computer operates, some of the tasks a computer can perform, and the many responsibilities of being a computer user. It is also important to understand how the computer you are using today evolved and how this incredible tool can give you access to one of the greatest sources of information—the Internet.

BRIEF HISTORY OF COMPUTERS

Although the microcomputer, or *PC* (personal computer), was developed in the early 1980s, computers have been around for a long time. A major step in computer technology was the development in the early 1800s of machines that could be programmed. The operation was controlled by cards with holes punched in them. In 1886, an electric punch-card machine was developed that could be used with electricity. In 1890, the U.S. Census results were tabulated for the first time with this new electrically driven punch-card tabulator.

In 1944, engineers from IBM and Howard Aiken of Harvard University developed a 50-foot-long, 8-foot-high machine that was able to add, subtract, multiply, divide, and refer to data tables using punched cards.

In 1945, a team from the University of Pennsylvania developed a machine for the U.S. Army's Ballistics Research Lab. This machine could make calculations a thousand times faster than earlier devices. The machine weighed in at approximately 30 tons and covered about 1,000 square feet of floor space.

In 1947, a method was developed for storing programs electronically. This invention of storing programs led the way for the development of today's computers. Before this invention, computers were wired to perform only certain tasks. If you wanted to change the task, the computer had to be rewired.

The first machine to be called a computer was completed in 1948. In 1951, the first commercial computer was completed. Eight of them were sold.

Besides becoming more versatile, computers were becoming faster, cheaper, and smaller. Computers were designed to perform tasks that responded to machine instructions. One of the original IBM computers could perform about 2,000 instructions per second. By the mid-1970s, operating speed had increased by more than 2,000%, to 43,000 instructions per second. By the late 1980s, computers had begun to be rated in ***MIPS (millions of instructions per second).*** Today's fastest supercomputers can handle well over a billion instructions per second.

The development of tiny silicon chips led the way for desktop microcomputers, or PCs. Microcomputers were

Sheet 1, Page 2, Inside Left

Insert the following text:

```
Welcome to the 12th annual Santa Barbara Women's
Business Conference!!

Once again, we have an overwhelming turnout of enthusi-
astic attendees. Based upon last year's evaluations, we
have added workshops in Web page design and interna-
tional business etiquette.

This year's keynote speaker, Jaime Lund, will share with
us how she started her company—out of the trunk of her
car!

Thirty local businesses are displaying and selling their
products and services, including designer eyewear, home
improvement, health and fitness, telecommunications, and
financial planning.

Relax and visit with friends at the luncheon and fashion
show. Our chef has prepared a delightful menu.

Finally, enjoy local anchorwoman Carol Thomas as she
recaps her success in climbing the corporate ladder.

Don't forget!! Enter your name in the drawing for a free
weekend at the Fess Parker Double Tree Hotel and
Conference Center.

...And enjoy your day!
```

Sheet 1, Page 7, Inside Right
Insert the conference sponsors and conference exhibitors.

Sheet 2, Page 6, Inside Left
Insert the room layout.

Sheet 2, Page 3, Inside Right
Insert the conference schedule.

Sheet 2, Page 4, Left Center Spread
Insert five breakout sessions and room assignments.

Sheet 2, Page 5, Right Center Spread
Insert remaining breakout sessions and room assignments.

- Save the conference program as **capstone.sbconference program**.

first introduced in the mid-1970s. At that time, these small computers had limited memory and storage ability. Two major developments occurred in the early 1970s that led the way for the incredible growth of the computer industry. In 1975, Steve Jobs and Steve Wozniak started Apple Computer in the Jobs' family garage and, also in 1975, Paul Allen and Bill Gates established their own company, Microsoft.

Today's modern PC is the direct result of the advancements made by Apple Computer and IBM in hardware and software development, Microsoft in software development, and chip manufacturers such as Motorola and Intel in processor development. These advancements have brought us computers that have thousands of times the capability of those much larger computer systems of years ago—and at a fraction of the cost.

THE COMPUTER SYSTEM

A ***computer*** is an electronic device that can perform tasks and calculations based on the instructions that have been given to it.

How a Computer System Works

Although computers amaze us with their apparent "intelligence," all of their functions are based on these three very simple tasks:

- Compare numbers or symbols to see if they are the same
- Add two numbers together
- Subtract one number from another

Computers can perform these tasks with great speed, accuracy, and reliability. Data is entered into the computer, the computer processes the data, and displays the desired information. How does the computer know what to do with the data? A ***software program,*** a detailed set of computer instructions installed in the computer, tells the computer what to do.

There are two types of computer software programs. One is *system program software,* which controls the way computer parts work together. The other is *application program software,* which tells the computer to perform a specific task. (See later section on software.)

Types of Computers

Computers vary in type, size, speed, and capability. The most common type of computer used in homes, offices, and schools is the ***personal computer*** (more commonly known as the ***PC***), a computer that is small enough to fit on a desk, is relatively inexpensive, and is designed for an individual user. ***Laptop computers*** (also called *notebooks*), which are portable, also fall into this category.

Other types of computers include the following:

- *Supercomputer*
  The ***supercomputer*** is the fastest type of computer. It can store data and perform numerous tasks simultaneously at incredible speeds. This type of computer is used for specialized tasks that require vast amounts of mathematical calculations such as weather forecasting and medical and weapons research. Usually comprising many computers working in unison, the supercomputer is used only by government agencies, educational institutions, and large corporations.

- *Mainframe*
  Mainframe computers are less powerful and less expensive than supercomputers, but they are still capable of storing and processing large amounts of

G. The Conference Program

- Now that the conference details have been established, you can design the conference program to distribute to all conference attendees. The program should be in the form of an eight-page brochure. Prepare the program using two sheets of 8 ½" x 11" paper set to landscape orientation. After creating the front and back of each sheet, print them back-to-back and fold them in half to create the brochure. Plan the pages as follows:

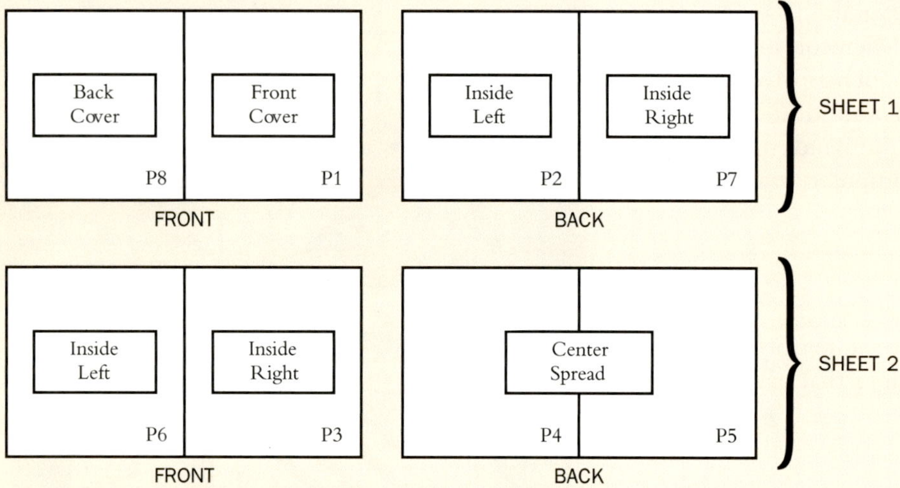

Each page should contain the following information:

Sheet 1, Page 8, Back Cover

- Insert a map of Santa Barbara showing the location of the Fess Parker Double Tree Hotel and Conference Center. To find a map of the hotel's location, go to: http://maps.yahoo.com Enter the following address in the appropriate text boxes, and click **Get Map:**
  `633 East Cabrillo Blvd.`
  `Santa Barbara, CA 93103`

  A copy of this map is also located on the Data CD 
  under the file name **dcapstone.sbmap**.
  OPTIONAL: *Include a list and brief description of cultural events taking place in Santa Barbara at the time of the convention. Search the Internet to find this information.*

Sheet 1, Page 1, Front Cover

- Insert the name of the conference (using the conference logo), the conference date, and the conference location.

data. Several hundred individuals can use a mainframe, with their own terminals, at the same time. These computers are used most often by universities, medical institutions, and large companies such as banks and brokerage houses, where it is necessary to complete millions of daily transactions and save corresponding amounts of data.

- *Minicomputer*
  The ***minicomputer***, also called a ***server,*** is smaller than a mainframe, is larger than a microcomputer, and can support multiple users, with their own terminals, at the same time. Medium-sized companies, such as accounting, advertising, and manufacturing firms, use these computers.

Computer Memory

Computer memory is composed of circuits that are contained in tiny computer chips. The number of memory locations is stated in terms of bytes. A ***byte*** is a unit of storage capable of holding a single character. A byte is equal to 8 bits. Large amounts of memory are indicated in terms of ***kilobytes*** (K or KB), ***megabytes*** (M or MB), and ***gigabytes*** (G or GB). A ***kilobyte*** is equal to 1,024 bytes, a ***megabyte*** is equal to 1,048,576 bytes, and a ***gigabyte*** is equal to 1,073,741,824 bytes. Twenty megabytes of memory can hold data equivalent to what could be saved on one box of floppy disks.

Every computer comes with a certain amount of physical memory, usually referred to as main memory or ***random access memory (RAM)***. Think of main memory as an array of boxes, each of which can hold a single byte of information. A computer that has 1 megabyte of memory, therefore, can hold about 1 million bytes (or characters) of information.

Read-only memory, or ***ROM,*** is computer memory on which data has been prerecorded. Data recorded on a ROM chip can only be read; it cannot be deleted. Unlike RAM, ROM preserves its contents even when the computer is shut down. Personal computers contain some ROM memory that stores critical programs, such as those needed for system start-up, for example.

Processing Power

A computer's procesing speed (also known as clock speed) is measured in ***megahertz*** (mHz) and ***gigahertz*** (gHz). In 1993, the average computer processing speed was 25 mHz. By the end of 1994, processing speed increased to 66 mHz for the PC. The 486DX2 chip was new, and there was talk about two new revolutionary chips from Motorola and IBM—the PowerPC and Pentium chips.

The PowerPC chip's speed started at 60 mHz and was capable of running at 120 mHz—unheard of in 1996. The Pentium matched these speeds. Within a year, chip speeds increased exponentially. Today, the PowerPC can run up to 1 gHz, and the current speed for a Pentium 4 runs at 2 gHz.

Although processor speed is one of the major factors of computer speed, several other significant factors give a computer a greater operating speed. In addition to faster RAM (the memory chips that hold data when the computer is running), computers now take advantage of a data buffer called ***cache*** (pronounced "cash"). Cache is a series of superfast RAM chips that allow the processor to communicate more quickly and efficiently with the rest of the computer.

As for the future, both Motorola and Intel are working on the next-generation processor, again exceeding current processing speeds. These advancements in technology will be a step toward computers 100 billion times as fast as today's most powerful personal computers.

PARTS OF A COMPUTER

A computer system is made up of two principal components: hardware and software.

Computer hardware

Hardware

Hardware refers to the physical parts of the computer and includes four main components: input devices, processing unit, output devices, and storage devices.

E. Merge the Letter

Merge the form letter with the **Women** database table to produce your mailing. Save the merged letters as **capstone.sbletfinal**. Create mailing labels for your letters.

F. The Web Site

Create a home page for the Santa Barbara Women's Business Conference. You may use a Web template, if you want. Include the following:

- Date/Time
- Exhibitors
- Schedule of Events
- Contact Information

  For general information:
  Jennifer Rogers, Conference Coordinator
  Santa Barbara Chamber of Commerce
  jrogers@sbcc.org
  (805) 555-3838 extension 27

  For exhibitor information:
  Janet Brice, Event Coordinator
  Santa Barbara Chamber of Commerce
  jbrice@sbcc.org
  (805) 555-3838 extension 32
- Registration Information
- A link to the Fess Parker Double Tree Hotel and Conference Center's home page, as well as any other links you feel would be appropriate.
- If you want to create a more elaborate Web site, you may work with other memers of your class to plan and develop it.
- Save the Web site as **capstone.sbweb site**.

Input Devices *Input devices* transport data into the computer.

- *Keyboard*
  The ***keyboard*** is the most commonly used input device. It contains typewriter-like keys as well as specialized keys for entering data.

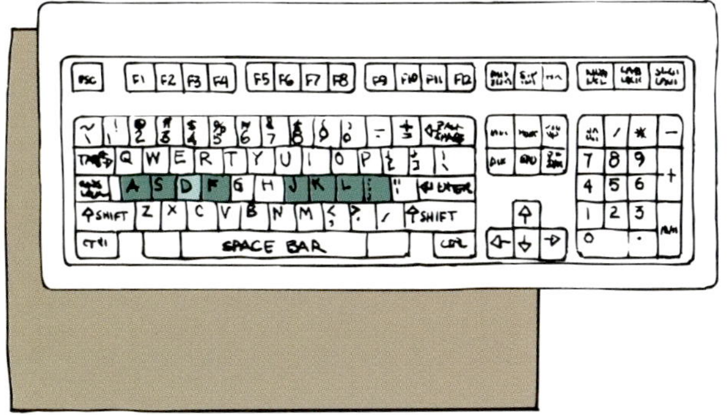

- *Mouse, pointing stick, trackball, light pen, puck, and touchpad*
  These small alternative input devices direct the movement of the insertion point on the screen.

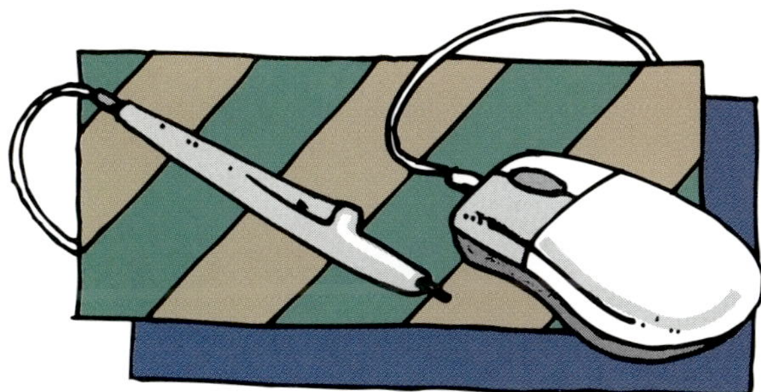

- *Optical character recognition (OCR) system*
  This device scans the printed page and translates characters and images into a computer file that can be edited (by a word processing application, for example).

- *Scanner*
  A ***scanner*** is a device that can read text or illustrations and transmit them in a digitized format to the computer screen. Scanners can be handheld or as large as a photocopy machine.

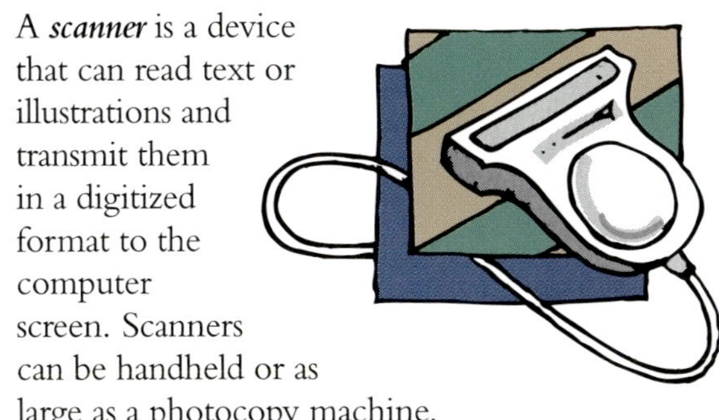

- *Digital camera*
  This is a filmless camera that captures images into memory storage. A ***digital camera's*** images can be transferred to a computer and edited or inserted into a document.

- *Video input camcorder*
  A ***video input camcorder*** is a digital video camera that can record live audio and video, which can then be downloaded into a computer for multimedia applications.

- *Microphone*
  A ***microphone*** accepts voice input to enter data or execute commands.

Processing Unit The processing unit, also referred to as microprocessor or *CPU (central processing unit),* is the "brains" of the computer. This piece of hardware contains the computer chips and circuits that control and manipulate data to produce information.

Output Devices *Output devices* allow the user to see or hear the information the computer compiles.

- *Printers*
  Printers are devices that print text or graphics on paper. Printers come in a variety of types and are categorized as either impact or nonimpact. An *impact printer* uses a device that strikes a

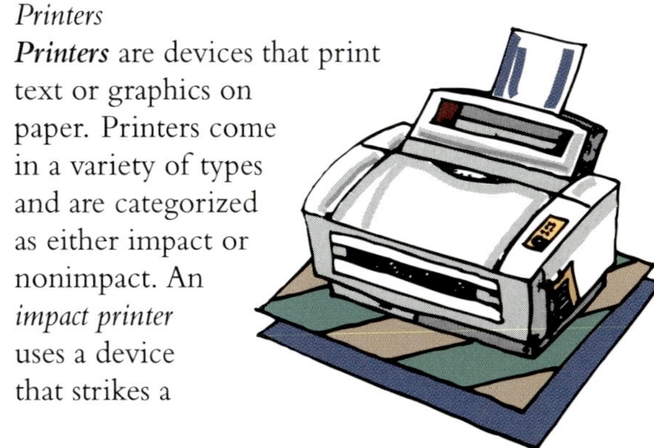

Project Details

A. The Logo

Create a colorful logo to use on the flyer and the conference program. Save the logo as **capstone.sblogo**.

B. The Press Release

The press release should announce the Santa Barbara Women's Business Conference and indicate highlights of this year's program. The press contact is Jennifer Summers from the Santa Barbara Chamber of Commerce. See Unit II, Exercise 93 and/or Unit III, Exercise 23 for the proper press release format. Save the press release as **capstone.sbpress release**.

C. The Flyer

This one-page document will be mailed to businesses in the Santa Barbara area to attract prospective attendees. (It will also be enclosed with the letter to the female members of the Santa Barbara Business Association.) The flyer should include the conference logo, the conference date, the breakout session titles, and the keynote and closing speakers. The flyer should also include a tear-off, so people can register by fax or mail. The mailing address and fax number are:

Jennifer Rogers, Conference Coordinator
Santa Barbara Chamber of Commerce
110 Anacapa Street
Santa Barbara, CA 93103

FAX: 805-555-2727

Be sure to indicate that the registration fee is $60. However, members of the Santa Barbara Business Association only have to pay $45. Also include a check box for payment type as follows:

❑ Check enclosed
❑ Credit Card (Amex, Visa, or MasterCard)
Acct #______________ Exp. date________
Signature____________________________

Save the flyer as **capstone.sbflyer**.

D. The Letter

- A form letter has been created to invite the female members of the Santa Barbara Business Association to the Conference. The letter can be found on the Data CD under the file name **dcapstone.sbletter**. However, the letter does require that you insert merge field codes.
- The data file comes from the Santa Barbara Business Association database, which contains the names of the female members. The database is found on the Data CD under the name **dcapstone.sblist**.

ribbon on paper; *nonimpact printers* use laser and inkjet technology. The quality of the print and the printing speed determine the cost of a printer.

- *Monitor*
  A ***monitor,*** also known as a ***display, CRT*** (cathode ray tube), *VDT* (video display terminal), or simply ***computer screen,*** allows the user to view computer information. Computer screens vary in size and cost depending on their ***resolution,*** which is the clarity and sharpness of an on-screen image. If you look closely at a computer screen, you will see that it is made up of a series of ***pixels,*** which is a series of dots. The more closely packed the pixels, the higher the resolution of the image.

- *Speakers*
  Speakers are devices that amplify sound. Speakers can be internal or external to the computer.

Storage Devices *Storage devices* allow instructions and data to be saved. Some storage devices are housed within the computer; others are removable and thus allow data to be transported from one computer to another.

- *Hard drive*
  A ***hard drive,*** an internal storage device, is also known as a "fixed" disk. Hard drives can hold huge amounts of information. The size of the drive, that is, how much information it can save, affects the price of the computer. A computer that has one "gig" (gigabyte) of storage capacity can hold 1 billion bytes of information.

- *Floppy disks*
  Floppy disks (often called *diskettes*) are bendable, oxide-coated, magnetic plastic with a hard cover that can be inserted and removed from a disk drive. The 3½" floppy disk can store 1.4 MB of data.

- *Zip disks*
  Zip disks are larger versions of floppy disks. Each Zip disk holds as much information as 80 floppy disks (about 100 megabytes). Zip disks require a Zip drive, which can be connected inside or outside of the computer.

- *CD*
  These disks can store huge amounts of data (approximately 650 megabytes, or about 500 floppy disks). Because of their large storage capability, ***CD-ROMs*** are often used to save graphics, video, and audio. CD-ROM discs require a CD-ROM drive.

- Corporate sponsors, whom you should credit in the conference program that you will create, are noted below:

Santa Barbara News-Press	Santa Barbara County Lemon Growers' Association
Gottschalk's Department Store	Jim Lund Ford
Workforce Employment Agency	Santa Barbara Title Company
Santa Barbara Business College	

- The conference schedule and room assignments are as follows:

7:30 a.m. – 8.30 a.m.	Conference registration and continental-style breakfast	Conference Center Patio
8:30 a.m. – 9:15 a.m.	Keynote address—Jaime Lund	Grand Ballroom
9:30 a.m. – 10:30 a.m.	Breakout Session #1	Various
10:45 a.m. – 11:15 a.m.	Breakout Session #2	Various
12:00 p.m. – 1:30 p.m.	Luncheon and fashion show	Banquet Room
1:45 p.m. – 2:45 p.m.	Breakout Session #3	Various
3:00 p.m. – 3:45 p.m.	Closing speaker—Carol Thomas	Garden Room
4:00 p.m. – 5:00 p.m.	Networking and cocktail party	Grand Ballroom

- The layout of the conference facility is as follows:

GARDEN ROOM

STATE ROOM

BANQUET ROOM

GRAND BALLROOM

EXHIBITORS

CONFERENCE LOBBY REGISTRATION

PATIO

CABRILLO ROOM

COLD SPRINGS ROOM

MISSION ROOM

ANACAPA ROOM

EL CAMINO ROOM

VISTA ROOM

HOLLISTER ROOM

CACHUMA ROOM

- *DAT (digital audio tape)*
  Digital audio tape is a standard magnetic tape that resembles basic audiocassettes. DATs have the ability to hold tremendous amounts of information on a tape much smaller than an audiocassette. DAT devices can hold up to 10 separate DAT tapes, each of which can hold up to 26 gigabytes of information.

Software

Software is a set of instructions written by programmers in a machine (or programming) language that tells the computer what to do, how to do it, and how to perform tasks based on input from the user. The numerous ***programming languages*** include FORTRAN, COBOL, BASIC, C, C++, Java, JavaScript, Visual Basic, Visual C++, and RPG.

The words "software," "program," and "application" are used interchangeably. There are two types of software: operating system software and application software. Application software (like Microsoft Office) can run only when operating system software (like Windows XP) is installed and running on a computer. Operating system software can be compared to the foundation of a house; application software can be compared to the rooms within the house.

Operating System Software The basic operation of the computer is controlled by ***operating system software.*** This type of software manages the computer's files and programs and acts as a graphic interface that translates mouse and keyboard actions into appropriate programming code. There are many types of operating systems, each having different capabilities. Some operating systems can run only a single application at a time; others can multitask and run several at once. The most popular operating systems include Microsoft Windows and Apple Computer's Mac OS. Others include IBM's OS/2 Warp, Microsoft DOS (Disk Operating System), and UNIX, a text-based command-line interface operating system.

Some operating systems were created specifically for use on a network. These include Novell NetWare, AppleShare IP, Microsoft Windows for Workgroups, and Microsoft Windows NT Server.

Application Software Sometimes referred to as "tool" software, ***application software*** provides the tools needed to complete a task. Tool software is widely used by business, government, schools, and individuals for anything from financial management, Web surfing, and word processing to sound engineering, graphic design, and cooking.

These are the most common types of application software:

- *Word processing*
  Word processing software is used to create and print documents such as letters, memos, and reports. This type of software allows for easy editing of text. Microsoft Word is an example of word processing software.

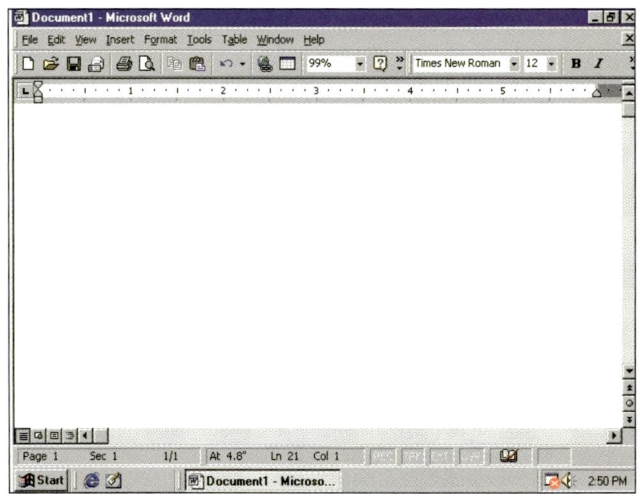

- *Spreadsheet*
  Spreadsheet software is used for analysis and reporting of statistical or numerical data to complete such tasks as preparing budgets, payroll, balance sheets, and profit and loss statements. Spreadsheet software can create charts from statistical information. Microsoft Excel and Lotus 1-2-3 are examples of spreadsheet software.

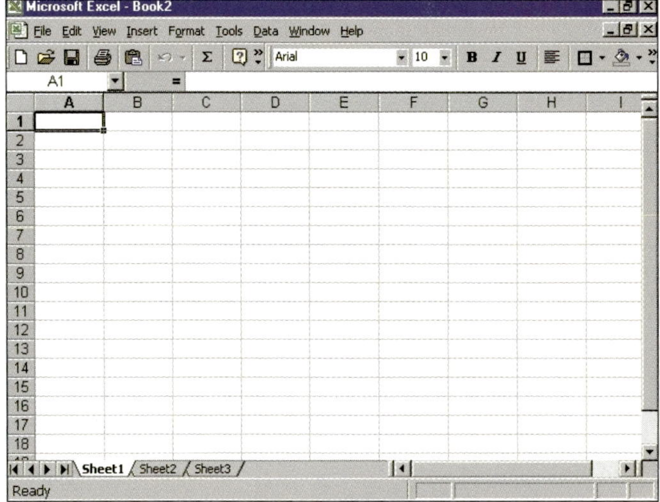

Hairstyles and Fashion for Women On-the-Go (State Room)
Speaker: Dennis LeBrock
Throw away that curling iron and gel! Get dressed and get out of your house in the morning in less than 20 minutes! Quick tips for busy women.

International Business Etiquette (Hollister Room)
Speaker: Mary Ann Sada
Avoid those faux pas when doing business in foreign countries. Learn how to conduct business internationally.

Is There Really a Glass Ceiling? (Vista Room)
Speaker: Sheryl Barber
Have you been overlooked for a promotion? Share experiences and strategies for climbing the corporate ladder.

Networking (El Camino Room)
Speaker: Sonia Rand
What are the most effective ways to make business contacts? Learn to network!

Starting a Business Franchise (Cachuma Room)
Speaker: Lyle Lancaster
Interested in business franchising? Learn what to look for in starting your own franchise.

Web Page Design for the Small Business (Cold Springs Room)
Speaker: Robert Maroni
Keep up with the competition and get on the Web! Learn the basics of creating your company's very own Web page and the advantages of doing so.

- Thirty local businesses will be exhibiting their products and services. These businesses include companies that deal in designer eyewear, home improvement, health and fitness, telecommunications, and financial planning. Conference exhibitors are indicated below:

Computers Plus!
Christine's
The French Connection
Dr. Hulsey's Fashion Eyewear
Betty Lee, Esthetician
Carats & Crystals
Laguna Designs
Santa Barbara Beach Wear
Handbags by Lisa
The Back Massagers
Katie's Kitchen
Santa Barbara Salsa
Santa Barbara Tourist Bureau
The Enterprise Fish Company
Los Padres Winery
Sea Breeze Fragrances
Santa Barbara Business College
Community Connection for Children
Bel Air Modeling Company
Custom Gourmet
Rutherford's Books
Mary Kay Cosmetics
Kathy Frankhouser Fitness, Inc.
Cynthia's Herbal Vitamins
Workforce Employment Agency
D'Nails
Hair Decors by Lil
Santa Barbara Cellular
Laguna Travel Bags
Oceanview Travel Agency

- *Database*
  Database software allows the user to collect, store, organize, modify, and extract data. Microsoft Access is an example of database software.

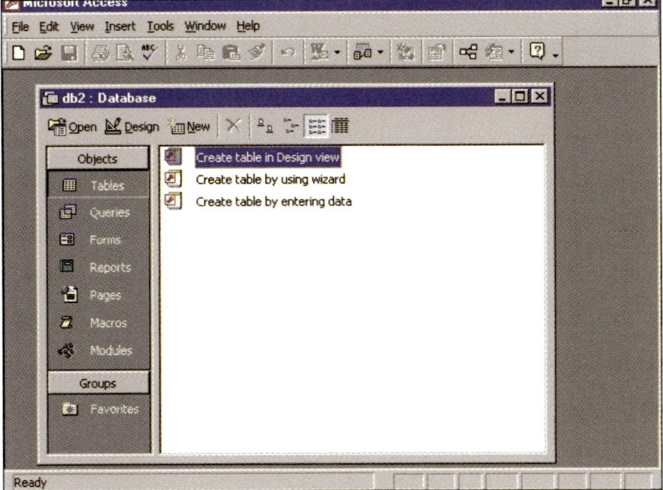

- *Accounting*
  Accounting software is used for organizing and managing money and finances. QuickBooks is an example of this type of software.

- *Groupware*
  Groupware is software that helps groups of users communicate and organize activities, meetings, and events through one common interface. For example, group software is used within corporations so all employees can share the same common screens on their computers. Lotus Notes is an example of groupware.

- *Communication*
  Communication software is used to transmit and receive information from one computer to another. For the transfer to take place, both the receiver and the sender must have the software installed.

- *Internet browser*
  Internet browser software is used to locate and display Web pages. The most popular Internet browsers are Netscape Navigator and Microsoft Internet Explorer.

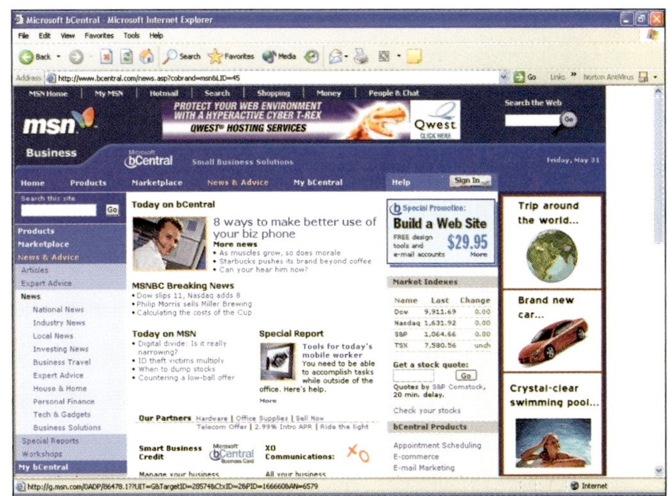

- *E-mail programs*
  E-mail programs are used to send and retrieve e-mail from a mail server. Outlook is an example of an e-mail program. Many e-mail programs (like Outlook) are now part of other software applications. For example, you can now e-mail from within all Microsoft Office XP applications.

- *Online service*
  Online service software provides subscribers with the ability to communicate with one another, through e-mail, for example, as well as connect with unlimited third-party information providers, such as news, weather, and sports bureaus. America Online and MindSpring are examples of online service software. Access to this information also requires communications equipment. (See section on Telecommunications.)

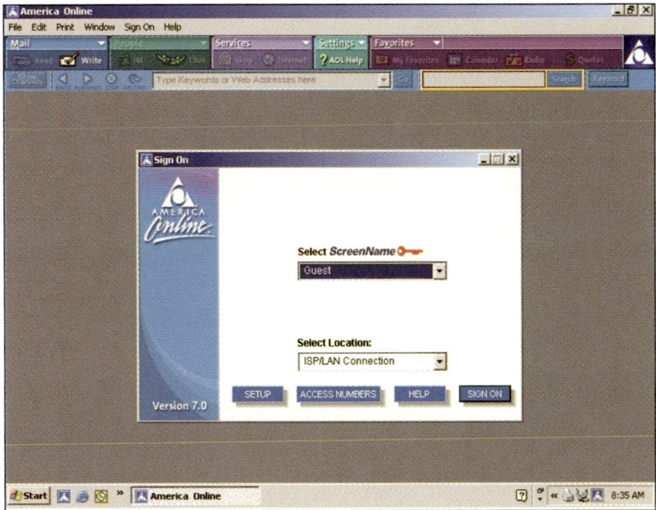

Directions

1. Read the Conference Details section. You will use this information to complete many of the projects, which are explained under the Project Details section. ***NOTE:*** *The Conference Details (such aslocal business names, session titles, and corporate sponsors) can be found on the Data CD under the file name* ***dcapstone.sbconference details****. You may copy this information and paste it into the project(s) where appropriate.*
2. Include your first and last names as a header on each project.
3. Complete each project; keep all first drafts.
4. Print each project.
5. Place all first drafts and final projects in a folder. These may be used as portfolio work samples.

Conference Details

- The conference will open with a keynote address by Jaime Lund, CEO of the well-known local business consulting firm, Self Esteem, Inc. Local anchorwoman Carol Thomas will make closing remarks and recap her success in climbing the corporate ladder.
- The luncheon will include a fashion show with models from the Bel Air Modeling Agency.
- Throughout the day, there will be numerous one-hour breakout sessions. Attendees may choose to attend any one of the 10 sessions listed below and on the following page. Each session will be repeated three times throughout the day.
- Each session listing includes the room in which the session will be held, the speaker's name, and a brief description.

Balancing Family, Home, and Career (Cabrillo Room)
Speaker: Nancy Chan
Do you need a 48-hour day? Learn how to organize your time and even have some time left over for yourself and your family.

Dress for Success (Mission Room)
Speaker: Fran Shaw
Learn how to create a new wardrobe with clothes already in the closet.

Financial Planning (Garden Room)
Speaker: Jean Christiansen
Plan for retirement by learning smart investment strategies.

Fitness and Health (Anacapa Room)
Speaker: Kathy Frankhouser
You don't have to go to the gym to be healthy! Learn how to incorporate fitness and health into your busy lifestyle!

- *Presentation*
  Presentation software is used to create slides that can be shown while an oral report is given. The slides often summarize report data and emphasize report highlights. Microsoft PowerPoint is an example of presentation software.

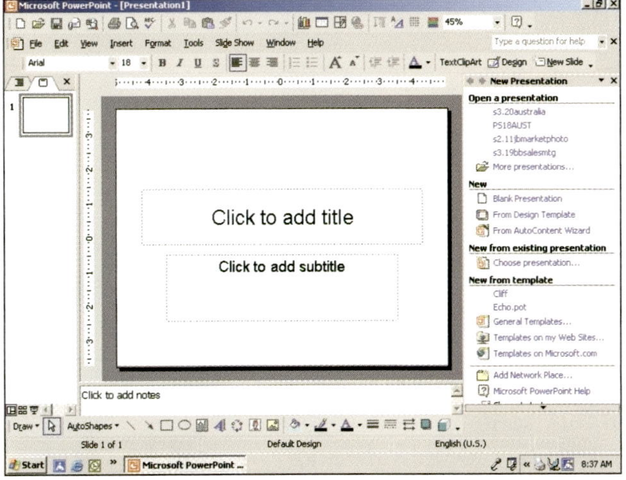

- *Voice recognition*
  Voice recognition software is used to create, edit, and format documents by speaking into a microphone (which is attached to the computer). The dictation is transcribed directly on the computer. Dragon Naturally Speaking and Point and Click are two popular voice recognition software products.

- *Web page*
  Web page software is used to create and manage professional-quality Internet Web sites. Microsoft FrontPage and Adobe PageMill are examples of Web page design software.

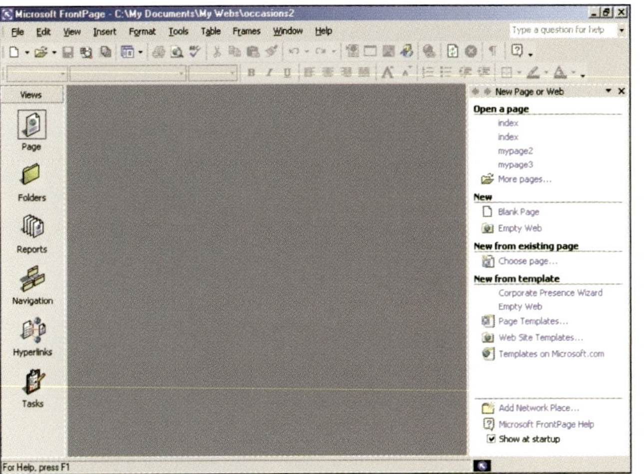

- *Graphics*
  A variety of ***graphics*** software packages are used to create charts, pictures, illustrations, drawings, and 3D images. Included in this category are the following types of programs:
  - Paint
  - Illustration/design
  - Photo-editing
  - Desktop publishing

THE INTERNET

The ***Internet*** is a worldwide network of smaller computer networks all linked together by unique *IP* (***Internet Protocol***) addresses. These computers may be located in businesses, schools, research foundations, hospitals, and/or individuals' homes. The Internet has unlimited uses. Businesses use the Internet to share information and to advertise their services and products. Students use the Internet for research and to share information with fellow students and professors. The Internet can be used to book airline flights, buy movie tickets, check your savings account, buy and sell stocks, order a pizza, shop for a gift, apply to a college, find a job, and buy a home. Internet users can also share personal information about themselves through chat groups, bulletin boards, and e-mail.

To access the Internet, a user must sign up with an ***Internet Service Provider (ISP)***, which sells access to the Internet for a monthly charge. Some popular ISPs include the Microsoft Network, America Online, EarthLink, net.com, MindSpring, and AT&T Worldnet. Connecting via modem to an ISP allows a user access to the ***World Wide Web,*** a service of the Internet on which pages, or ***Web sites,*** display information. These Web sites are created by companies, individuals, schools, religious institutions, government agencies—just about anybody.

By subscribing to an ISP, a user is offered much more than access to the Web. Other ISP services include e-mail, news on demand, personal Web site hosting, and much more.

Some ISPs offer specific online content such as Dow Jones News Retrieval and Lexis/Nexis. These ISPs provide financial and business news that is updated daily. The cost to use these services depends on how long a user stays online and how much of the information is downloaded.

Planning a Conference

CAPSTONE PROJECT

Introduction

- You are the assistant to Jennifer Rogers, the conference coordinator of the Santa Barbara, California Chamber of Commerce. Your office has been contacted by the Santa Barbara Business Association to assist in planning the 12th annual Santa Barbara Women's Business Conference, to be held on April 20, 2004, from 7:30 a.m. to 5:30 p.m., at the Fess Parker Double Tree Hotel and Conference Center. The purpose of this conference is to give businesswomen in the Santa Barbara area the opportunity to network and share issues that relate to being a woman in the business world.
- In preparation for this conference, you will need to complete the following projects. The next few pages will provide detailed information to assist you with finalizing these projects.

  A. Create a *logo* for the 12th annual Santa Barbara Women's Business Conference to use on the flyer and the program.

  B. Prepare a *press release*.

  C. Prepare a *flyer* with registration information to mail to local businesses in the Santa Barbara area.

  D. Prepare the *letter* inviting the female members of Santa Barbara Business Association to the conference.

  E. Merge the letter with a database table that contains the name of the Sanat Barbara Business Associationsd female members.

  F. Create a *Web site* for the 12th Annual Santa Barbara Women's Business Conference with relevant information about the event.

  G. Prepare the *conference program* for distribution to attendees on the day of the conference.

Web sites reside on a ***Web server,*** a dedicated computer that delivers Web pages. Every Web server has an IP address and possibly a ***domain name.*** Domain names are used in URLs (Uniform Resource Locators), to identify particular Web sites. (A URL is also referred to as a Web address). For example, in the URL http://www.microsoft.com, the domain name is ***microsoft.com***. A domain suffix identifies the Web site as commercial (.com), noncommercial (.org), government (.gov), educational (.edu), U.S. military (.mil), or network (.net) organization.

Information on the Web is created using a programming language called ***HTML (hypertext markup language)***. A Web browser translates HTML into a readable format. The Internet user can choose to use one of several dozen different Web browsers. Some popular Web browsers include Netscape Navigator and Microsoft Internet Explorer. Certain Web sites have a different look when viewed with different Web browsers due to translation inconsistencies. A Web browser can locate a specific site by its ***uniform resource locator (URL)***.

You can transmit files between a computer workstation and a file server (a dedicated computer) or a Web server. File transfer protocol or FTP is a format for transmitting data from one device to another in order for the files to be available on the Internet. When "ftp" appears in a URL, it means that the user is connecting to a file server and not a Web server.

HTTP is a protocol used to transfer files from a Web server onto a browser in order to view a Web page that is on the Internet. Using FTP, entire files are transferred from one computer device to another; HTTP only transfers the contents of a Web page into a browser for viewing. When "http" appears in a URL, it means that the user is connecting to a Web server and not a file server.

TELECOMMUNICATIONS

To transmit data over a phone line, you need a modem. A ***modem*** (modulator/demodulator) is a device that connects a computer to a phone line, allowing data to be transmitted from one computer to another. For the transmission to work, both computers must have modems and the appropriate communications software. A modem can be internal (inside the computer in the form of a circuit board) or external.

Modems have various speeds at which they transmit data. Downloading files and transmitting data requires fast modem speeds. Otherwise, tasks can be very time consuming. Traditional dial-up modems provide online access through telephone lines at speeds up to 57.6 bits per second (bps). A cable modem, however, gives users high speed Internet access through a cable line at more than 1 million bits per second. A bit is a single binary unit of measurement.

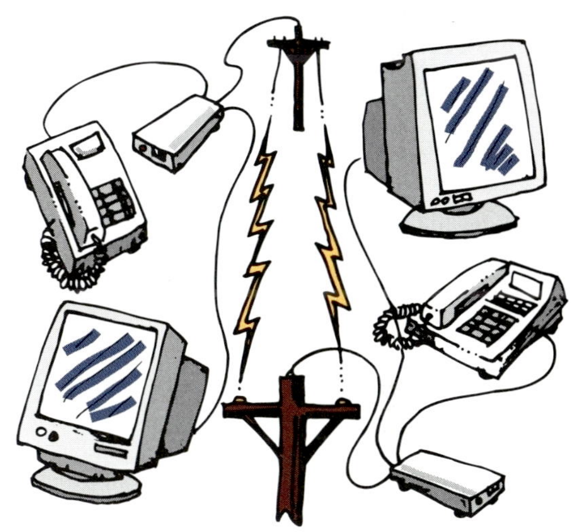

A *fax modem* not only transmits data, but allows graphics and documents to be sent as well. In this respect, the modem is similar to a real facsimile machine; however, the computer, unlike the fax machine, can receive faxes while it is turned off. To transmit faxes via the computer, you need to have the appropriate communications software package installed.

There are various ways to transmit data, sound, and video electronically. Here are some of the more common options:

- *Electronic mail (e-mail)*
  This method of transmitting electronic messages does not necessarily use a telephone line or assistance from

Planning a Conference

an ISP. It may use a ***network system*** also known as an *intranet.* Users are able to send messages to one or more Internet mailboxes simultaneously. They can also retrieve messages. Access to an electronic mailbox is exclusive and limited. Generally, users of the mailbox must know a ***password,*** or code, to send or retrieve messages 24 hours a day to anyone around the world who has an e-mail address. E-mail addresses are usually formatted in a specific way: user@domain.com. For example, John Doe works for the Pixie Soda Company. His e-mail address might be: john.doe@pixiesoda.com

- *Fax*
  A term derived from the word "facsimile" (which means "duplicate" or "copy"), a ***fax*** is a machine connected to a telephone, that scans a document and translates the visual image into electronic impulses. These impulses are then transmitted along telephone lines to another fax machine at a different location. The remote machine receives the electronic impulses, reconstructs the visual image of the document, and prints out an exact copy of the original document.

- *Electronic bulletin board*
  Information on a variety of topics can be placed on or accessed from an ***electronic bulletin board.*** Through a computer connected to a telephone line, it is possible to "talk" with other users, "discussing" or exchanging information on topics ranging from zoology to taxes, stocks and bonds to medical issues. Access to some bulletin boards is free; others charge a subscription fee.

- *Teleconferencing*
  Teleconferencing allows persons in different locations to see and hear one another. A videoconference is accomplished by using a television camera and microphone to transmit voice and video signals through satellite networks.

WIDE AREA NETWORK

Networks

A computer ***network*** is a linked group of computers. Networks allow computers to share information, programs, printers, or scanners, or to facilitate communication between people via e-mail. There are two principal kinds of networks: ***intra*** networks and ***inter*** networks. An ***intranet*** refers to an internal network confined within a specific location, usually one particular office or building. An intranet is sometimes referred to as a ***LAN (local area network).*** An intranet can also include several interlinked LANs.

The main purpose of an intranet is to share files and records within a company. An intranet can also be used to facilitate group collaboration and for teleconferences. For example, a law office might set up its own intranet so that every computer in the office can access the same files and case information and every computer prints to the same printer. An intranet can connect users to a common *file server* (minicomputer) that allows all of the computers connected to the network to access the same hard drive or the Internet, or to go outside the company to a *WAN* (wide area network).

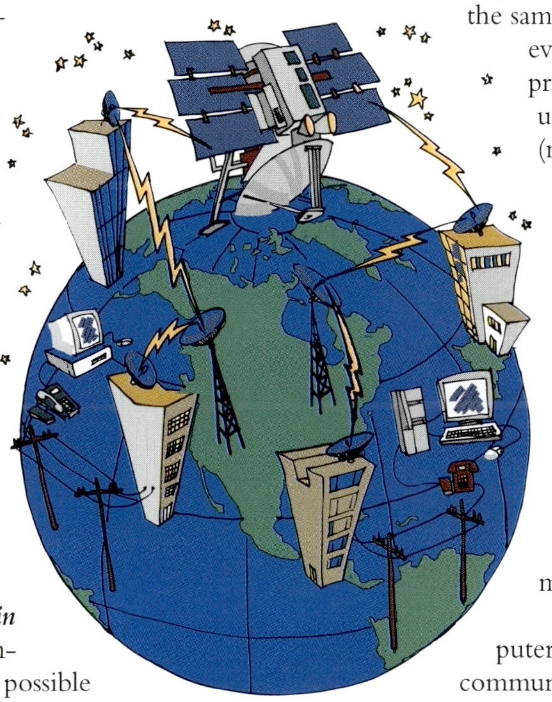

Regardless of whether you are connected to a LAN or a WAN, you must always enter a password to access, or "log in to," the network. Network connections transmit data at a much faster speed than does a modem or a telephone line.

In addition to networked computers, businesses have the ability to communicate with workers outside the office as well as with overseas co-workers through telecommunication and access to the Internet. Developing computer video and sound technology makes it possible for business meetings to take place entirely through computers (video conferencing). This is known as the "virtual office." Because the Internet provides 24-hour access to information, businesses that operate in multiple locations and time zones can continue to work even when one workday is ending and another is just beginning. Workers no longer need to share office space or have a networked computer to share important information and accomplish team projects.

Directions *continued*

6. If you are using FrontPage, do the following:
   a. Open the Personal Web template in your home directory; name it **2.11mywebpage**.
   b. Enter your own information into the categories to complete the site.
   c. Use photos of yourself to create the photo gallery (if they are available to you). Or, you can use photos from clip art that you feel create a "picture" of who you are, or you can delete the page entirely.
   d. Create a link where you feel it is appropriate to do so to the résumé file **2.11resumeweb**.
7. View the page in your browser and test the links.
8. Close the browser.
9. Close and save all files.

Many households with more than one computer are establishing networks so that the computers can share an Internet connection, printers, and data files. There are four main technologies that allow a user to set up a home computer network:

Ethernet technology requires an Ethernet card that slips into one of the computer's slots. Each computer must be linked with cables to its Ethernet connectors. If you have more than two computers in your network, you need to connect them all to either a hub (a common connection point for devices in a network) or, for a little more money, a router (a connection device that connects any number of LANS, or local area networks). The advantage of a router is that it lets each computer in the network connect to the Internet without having to have another computer turned on. The disadvantage of this type of setup is cabling, which can involve running cables through walls and ceilings.

Phone line technology uses your home's existing phone wires to link computers. Each computer connects to the network via a phone jack.

Power line technology uses your home's electrical wiring to link computers. Each computer connects to the network through an electrical wall outlet.

Wireless technology works like a cordless phone. A wireless base station broadcasts to a special card inside, or to a small device attached to, each desktop or laptop. Heavy walls, aluminum siding, or brickwork can block transmissions.

To summarize, the major components needed to assemble a home network include the following:

- *Ethernet cable*—connects computers to networking devices such as routers or hubs.
- *Hub*—connects several computers so they can "see" each other.
- *Network card* (also known as an Ethernet card)—provides an outlet for networking or for directly connecting to a DSL or cable modem. (DSL, an acronym for Digital Subscriber Line, is a high-speed transmission line used for sending data).
- *Printer server*—resides near a printer and connects the printer directly to the network so you can use the printer without having to keep any particular computer turned on.
- *Router*—has outlets for computers, high-speed modems, and print servers. Once a router is connected to the Internet, any computer connected to it can go online, even if other computers are turned off.
- *Wireless access*—lets you wirelessly connect multiple devices, such as laptops or printers, to a network that is otherwise connected by wires.

Telecommuting

Telecommuting is a term used to describe employees using technology to perform regular work activities from a remote location. Telecommuting moves the work to the worker instead of vice versa, almost completely eliminating the need for a downtown business office.

The typical telecommuter has a personal computer (usually a laptop) with a fax/cellular modem. Once dialed into the company network as a remote user, the telecommuter has full use of the company's intranet, including the e-mail system, server files, and, in some cases, Internet capability as well.

Wireless Computing

Wireless computing allows you to work from almost anywhere, and gives you access to all kinds of information when you are on-the-go by maintaining a data connection with a remote network. Some popular wireless communication devices are the PDA (personal digital assistant), cellular phones, and mobile e-mail devices.

The PDA is a handheld device that combines computing, telephone/fax, and networking features. Information can be input into a PDA using a keyboard, a stylus (a pen-like device), or your own voice. Today, Palm Pilots are one of the most popular PDA brands.

Cellular phones allow for text messaging. Text messaging can be used for short messages, which are usually sent between two or more mobile devices.

Mobile e-mail devices provide access to e-mail accounts, allowing users to read and send e-mails, as well as view calendars and contact information, which exist on their Internet-connected PCs. Blackberry is a popular line of mobile e-mail devices that includes airtime and software.

COMPUTERS AND SOCIETY

At home, computers perform many functions. Application software can be used to calculate an individual's taxes, the household budget, and interest on a personal loan, or to determine an amount owed on a mortgage. More and more banks, through the use of ATMs (automatic teller machines), offer individuals the opportunity to do their banking without ever having to leave their homes. Financial transactions can be performed on one's personal computer which, through the Internet, can be linked with a bank's computers.

Skills Review

EXERCISE 11

You are about to graduate from high school and attend college in another city. You have decided to create your own personal Web page so that your friends and family can learn of your accomplishments and interests. You may use Word or FrontPage to create this project.

SCANS

Directions

1. Open the **5.49myown** file you completed in Exercise 49 of the Word Processing unit.
2. Delete your address and phone number from the document.
3. Save the file as a Web page; name it **2.11resumeweb**.
4. Open Word (or FrontPage).
5. If you are using a Word template, make the following changes to the template headings:
   a. Use the Personal Web Page template.
   b. Change "Work Information" to `School Information` in the Contents section and in the subtext.
   c. Change "Job Title" to: `School`
   d. Change "Key responsibilities" to: `Date of Graduation`
   e. Change "Department or workgroup" to: `Major`
   f. Delete the "Current Projects" category in the Contents section and in the subtext.
   g. Select the subtext "Biographical Information" and create a hyperlink to the résumé file **2.11resumeweb**.
   h. Enter your own information into the categories to complete the page.
   i. Apply a theme to the page.
   j. Save the file; name it **2.11mywebpage**.

PORTFOLIO

Include this exercise in your portfolio.

DID YOU KNOW?

You can use a personal Web page as the Start page on your browser so that you can easily access your favorite sites each time you go online.

In addition, many home computers have Internet access and more and more home users are able to use the World Wide Web to shop. Internet credit card purchasing has increased significantly. Now you can book a flight to Walt Disney World, reserve a hotel room, order a pizza, and buy books, clothing, vitamins, or even concert tickets with very little effort.

Tired of television? Then play games! Computer-based video games have become increasingly popular among young and old alike. The types of games available range from traditional games—such as chess, backgammon, and poker, which are adapted to video screens—to more complex, interactive games, such as flight simulation and strategy games in which the computer is a challenging opponent.

Computers are often present in the household in less visible ways. Home heating thermostats, watches, cars, and even children's toys all contain complicated computer systems. Washing machines, microwave ovens, answering machines, and dishwashers are just a few of the household appliances containing small computers that greatly reduce manual household labor.

Future Technologies

Computer technology is developing at an extraordinary rate. It has been said that the state of technology doubles in efficiency and speed every year. Computer hardware and software become obsolete within months of their initial development, while at the same time new products with extraordinary capabilities become available to the general market. For example, ***DVDs (digital versatile or video discs)*** have seven times the storage capacity of CD-ROMs without taking up any more space. In addition, DVD players are backward compatible and thus able to support the soon-to-be-outdated CD-ROM technology. DVD will eventually replace laser discs, CD-ROMs, and traditional VHS videotape.

Another example of a rapidly developing technology is virtual reality. ***Virtual reality*** (***VR***) software uses three-dimensional graphics and special devices such as a data glove and VR goggles to allow the user to interact with a computing environment in "real space." Although many people are familiar with VR in relation to computer simulation games, the development of VR technology has had a significant impact on many professions and fields of research.

Voice recognition software technology is making incredible advancements in perfecting the computer's ability to carry out voice commands and take dictation. It is now possible to purchase software for as little as $200 that allows the user to speak naturally into the computer up to 160 words per minute without pausing between words. The words appear immediately on the computer's screen.

An up-and-coming technology known as ***intercasting*** is the merging of the personal computer with the television. Web TV is a television that can be used to surf the Internet. Computer data must still be converted into signals that can be understood by the television. With the development of digital television and cable modems, however, complete intercast, with high-quality resolution, will be a definite reality.

Your Responsibility Using a Computer

In business, workers mostly deal with public information; however, a great deal of private information (e.g., phone numbers, social security numbers, tax records, credit card information, medical histories, and legal records) is also stored on computers. Access to this information usually requires knowledge of passwords and/or codes. Therefore, a computer database may be a secure place to keep private, extremely important, or secret records. Computer databases can be a more secure storage medium than a piece of paper. Some of the U.S. government's top secret records and research are entered into computers. In the wrong hands, such information could do great damage.

When irresponsible or unethical individuals, sometimes referred to as ***hackers,*** discover ways to break codes and gain access to classified files, not only personal but also national security may be threatened.

A great deal of responsibility goes along with personal computing. Working in an office allows you to obtain confidential information only when you are authorized to do so. It is a criminal offense to retrieve or view information from a private or limited-access computer or database without permission. It is also illegal to make copies of software programs. In addition, information provided on the World Wide Web is usually copyrighted and protected by the creators and Webmasters of the site. Copying software or duplicating information from the Web for public business is a violation of U.S. copyright infringement regulations. Violators are subject to prosecution and imprisonment. Finally, when using information from the Internet for independent research, cite the Web site, author, and original source where applicable. Failure to do so is considered plagiarism.

CARE OF YOUR COMPUTER, PERIPHERALS, AND DATA

To maximize the use of your computer, take steps to maintain its operation. Some maintenance is required periodically; other care is required each time you use your computer. It is also critical to take positive, proactive steps to reduce the risk of data loss.

Directions *continued*

- `Pricing: $10 per shirt in any color`
- `Silk Screening Colors and Prices:` (insert **d2.10pricing table**)

4. Design the page using any elements you have learned.
5. Link the home page to the Newsletter you created in Project 1A of the Desktop Publishing End-of-Unit exercises.
6. Save the file; name it **2.10niftytees**.
7. Preview the file in a browser and test the links.
8. Make any necessary adjustments.
9. Close the Web; save the changes.

Care of Computer and Peripherals

System Care The system case should be cleaned, both inside and out, on a regular basis to prevent buildup of dust.

- Wipe the outside case clean with a damp cloth. Never spray liquids directly on the casing.
- The inside of the computer can be cleaned by using a compressed-air can to blow out dust, or by using a small handheld vacuum to remove the dust.
- Check the power supply fan periodically to be sure that it has good ventilation and is free of dirt and dust buildup.

Monitors

- Clean monitors using a soft, damp cloth to remove the dust, which accumulates rather quickly. This should be done at least once a week.
- Be sure to check that the monitor's cooling vents are never blocked.
- Do not keep monitors turned on for extended periods of time, and certainly not overnight. This will minimize safety risks and increase the monitor's life span.

Floppy Disk Drives Unlike hard disk drives, which are sealed within the central processing unit of the computer, floppy drives are exposed to the outside air. The drive's read/write heads should be cleaned every few months using alcohol or special cleaning kits.

Keyboards Keyboards are somewhat resistant to abuse, but over time they will develop keys that stick or repeat if they are not maintained. To avoid these problems, keep food and liquids away from the keyboard.

- Develop a "no eating and drinking" policy while using the computer. Should liquids spill into the keyboard, it is likely you will need to replace it.
- Clean the key caps at least once every six months, and use compressed air to blow out dust from between the keys.

Mice Like keyboards, mice are handled all the time and tend to accumulate a good deal of dirt. If the ball becomes dirty, it will not roll properly and the pointer will not react on the screen's surface. Using a damp cloth, clean the mouse and the rollers inside the mouse unit at least once a month.

Care of Media

Floppy Disks

- Do not subject disks to temperatures above 120°F, because they will warp and all data on them will be lost. Keep disks in a cool, dry place.
- Do not touch the surface of the disk, because fingerprints or dirt can cause problems reading the disk.
- Do not expose disks to moisture or liquid.
- Do not expose disks to magnetic fields (magnets, stereo speakers, home appliances). This too can cause data loss.
- Although disks are called "floppy," the magnetic tape within the jacket should not be bent. Doing so will damage the disk.
- Airport X-ray machines do not affect disks.

Compact Discs (CDs) Compact discs are more durable than floppies and they do not require as much special care.

- CDs should not be subjected to temperatures above 100°F.
- Do not handle the surface of a CD. Doing so causes the surface to become scratched, which will interfere with the computer's ability to read the disc.
- Moisture and liquids will not harm a CD. If a CD becomes wet, simply wipe it off with a soft cloth.
- CDs are not affected by magnetic fields.
- CDs can be cleaned using a damp, soft cloth.
- Airport X-ray machines do not affect CDs.

Care of Data

To prevent data loss, perform daily backup of your data from your hard drive to a floppy disk, Zip disk, or tape drive.

To avoid losing data in an unexpected shutdown of your computer, be sure to:

- Save data frequently in all applications.
- Close all open applications.
- Shut down your operating system according to the instructions given to you by the system.

Install a virus-scan program on your computer to protect data from becoming infected.

Delete unwanted files from your hard drive monthly to increase hard drive performance.

Skills Review

EXERCISE 10

As part of its marketing strategy, Nifty Tees, a T-shirt company, plans to advertise on the Internet. Your boss has asked you to create a Web site for the company. The company contact information is as follows:

720 Ash Street
San Diego, California 92101
P: 1-800-555-TEES
F: 1-800-666-TEES
E-mail: nftyt@mind.com

To get ideas of what your site might look like and what information it should include, search the Internet and look at competitors' Web sites. Note the information presented, as well as the design, layout, and navigation of the page. Then create a Web site for your firm.

Directions

SCANS

1. Using either FrontPage or Word, create a Web site for Nifty Tees.
2. Include a home page that describes the company, the products it offers, and the benefits of owning a Nifty Tee.
   - Design the page using any elements you have learned.
   - Insert a scrolling marquee that includes: `Mission Statement: To Make Today's Business People Look and Feel Better About What They Wear`
   - Apply any theme and color scheme you prefer.
   - Include a hit counter (if this is available in your software).
3. Create a page (using a template, if you prefer) that links to the home page and contains color selections and silk screening pricing information as follows. (The table, which you can use on the Web page, is found on the Data CD under the file name **d2.10pricing table**.)
   - `Color Selections: White, Blue, Purple, Red, Yellow, Black, Orange, Dark Blue, Pink`

PORTFOLIO

Include this exercise in your portfolio.

UNIT ONE ORIENTATION

LESSON 1
Get Started

LESSON 2
Use Settings, Displays, Help, and File Management

Directions *continued*

8. Display the home page. Apply any theme you prefer to the Web site.
   - Create hyperlinks on the text in the second paragraph as follows:
     Cruise = Cruises page
     Ski Vacations = Ski Vacations page
     Vacation Highlights = Vacation Highlights page
   - Save the page.
9. Switch to Navigation view.
10. Add **Cruises**, **Ski Vacations**, and **Vacation Highlights** to the navigation structure below the home page, making sure that the pages are linked to the home page.
11. Switch to Page view and be sure all pages in the Web are open (**index**, **Cruises**, **Ski Vacations**, and **Vacation Highlights**).
12. Insert a left and top shared border on all the pages.
13. In the left shared border, click **Insert, Navigation** and insert a link bar based on the Web site's navigation structure. Use the following options: Use Page's theme, vertical orientation, Child pages under Home, and Additional pages: Home page.
14. In the top shared border, insert a page banner.
    NOTE: *The page banner will automatically insert each page's title. You can format the banner text and background as you prefer.*
    - Add `Contact Us` within the banner, format it as you prefer, and link it to this e-mail address: goaway@net.net (not an actual address)
15. Insert a hit counter.
16. Save all the pages.
17. View the pages in your browser and test the links.
18. Make any necessary adjustments.
19. Close the Web and the pages.

LESSON 1

Get Started

EXERCISE 1

Start a Program; Use the Mouse; Identify Screen Elements; Close a Document; Exit a Program

EXERCISE 2

Use Menus and Toolbars; Work with Dialog Boxes; Hide/Display the Task Pane

Directions *continued*

6. Create a new Web page using the One-column Body with Staggered Sidebar template; save the page as **Ski Vacations** with a page title of: `Ski Vacations`
   - Enter the text shown in Illustration C.
   - Insert a hyperlink on "Italy" to the file **1.4ski**, which you created in Exercise 4. If this file is not available to you, you can find it on the Data CD under the file name **d2.9ski**.

> Go Away Travel provides customized individual and group ski and snowboard trips to the Western U.S., Canada, Italy, South America, and New Zealand. We have been developing our programs for over 15 years, and pride ourselves on the level of professional service we provide to each of our clients.
>
> All the destinations that we offer have been visited by at least one of our travel consultants in order that we may provide you with the first-hand information and insights that you seek. All of our sales team are skiers and snowboarders who share a love of the mountains and the outdoor activities they inspire.
>
> Our custom ski vacations can include any or all of the following: discounted contracted airfare on major carriers, hotel and condominium accommodations, lift tickets, and ski school reservations. Our sales staff will also be happy to assist you with recommendations for restaurant selections, shopping ideas, and many other insights to make your vacation as enjoyable as possible.

Illustration C

7. Create a new Web page using the Photo Gallery template; save the page as **Vacation Highlights** with a page title of: `Vacation Highlights`
   - Insert photos of vacation destinations or use the photos that are part of the template. Enter the following text at the top of the page:
     `Enjoy the scenic beauty of these destinations. We can take you there. Go away with us!`

Start a Program; Use the Mouse; Identify Screen Elements; Close a Document; Exit a Program

EXERCISE 1

Directions

NOTE: *Illustrations in this book are shown using Microsoft Office XP and Windows XP. References are made to the component parts of Office XP, which are known as Word 2002, Excel 2002, Access 2002, PowerPoint 2002, FrontPage 2002, and Outlook 2002. However, illustrations are also provided for Office 2000/Windows 2000 users, where significant changes have been made to the upgraded software. Some of the screen elements and icons may differ if you are using different software.*

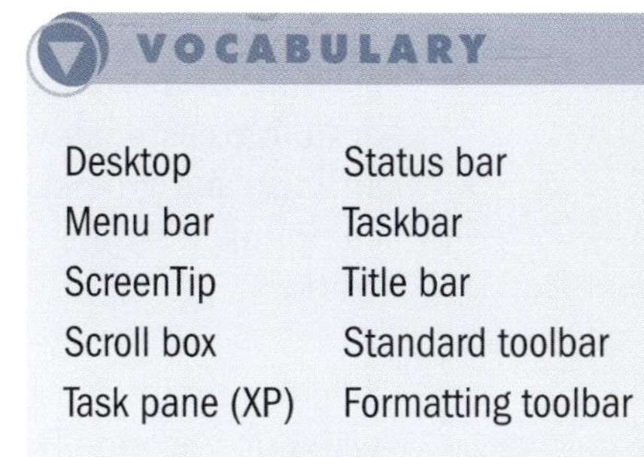

VOCABULARY

Desktop	Status bar
Menu bar	Taskbar
ScreenTip	Title bar
Scroll box	Standard toolbar
Task pane (XP)	Formatting toolbar

1. Identify the following desktop elements, as shown in Figure 1.1:
   - Taskbar
   - Shortcut Bar
   - Quick Launch toolbar
   - Shortcut access icons to programs or files

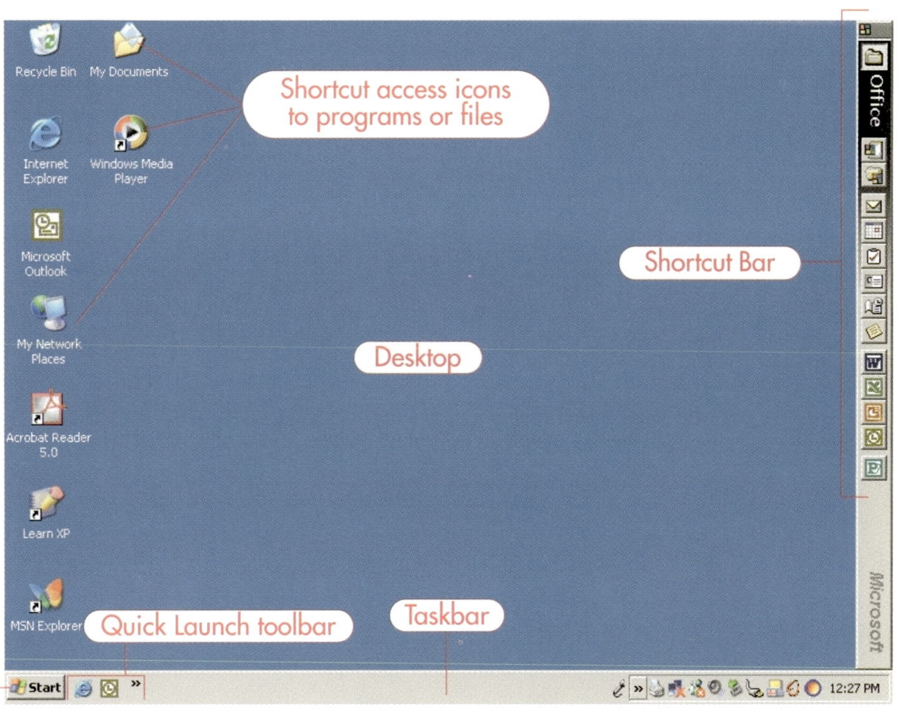

Figure 1.1 Desktop

4. Save the Web page as **index.html** with a title of: `Welcome to Go Away Travel on the Web`
   - Enter the text shown in Illustration A.
   - Insert relevant graphics.
   - Save the page.
     NOTE: *Click OK if you are prompted to save embedded (graphic) files.*

We at Go Away Travel are a proud member of the DreamVacations Travel Group, an exclusive network of travel specialists. Our combined multi-billion dollar business makes you a valuable, desirable customer with the world's leading hotels, resorts, cruise lines, tour companies, rail lines, airlines, and ground operators. Our alliance with DreamVacations enables us to offer you complimentary upgrades, outstanding amenities, privileged access, and private events all over the world.

While we will plan any dream vacation for you, we specialize in cruises and ski vacations. Just visit our Vacation Highlights page to view some spectacular destinations.

Illustration A

5. Create a new Web page using the One-column Body with Two-column Sidebar template. Save the page as **Cruises** with a title of: `Cruises`
   a. Enter the text shown in Illustration B.
   b. Insert relevant graphics.
   c. Save the page.

Leisure
Relaxation
Luxury
Welcome to a state of utter calm and total relaxation. It begins the moment the wind sweeps under the crisp, white sails of your Windstar ship, carrying you out to sea. Schedules, obligations, and daily dramas are all left behind. Ahead of you lie the timeless shores of Europe and the joy of traveling there aboard Windstar.

Count yourself among the few privileged guests who look forward to day after day of endless pampering. Stretch out in your ocean-view stateroom. Have a massage in the spa. Relax on the deck, favorite cocktail in hand, as your ship glides into scenic Portofino, colorful Marseille, and ancient Dubrovnik. Later, a quiet table for two and a beautiful meal await you onboard.

Illustration B

Directions *continued*

2. Start Word.

a. Click **Start** on the taskbar.

b. Select **Programs.**

c. Select and then click **Microsoft Word,** as shown in Figure 1.2.

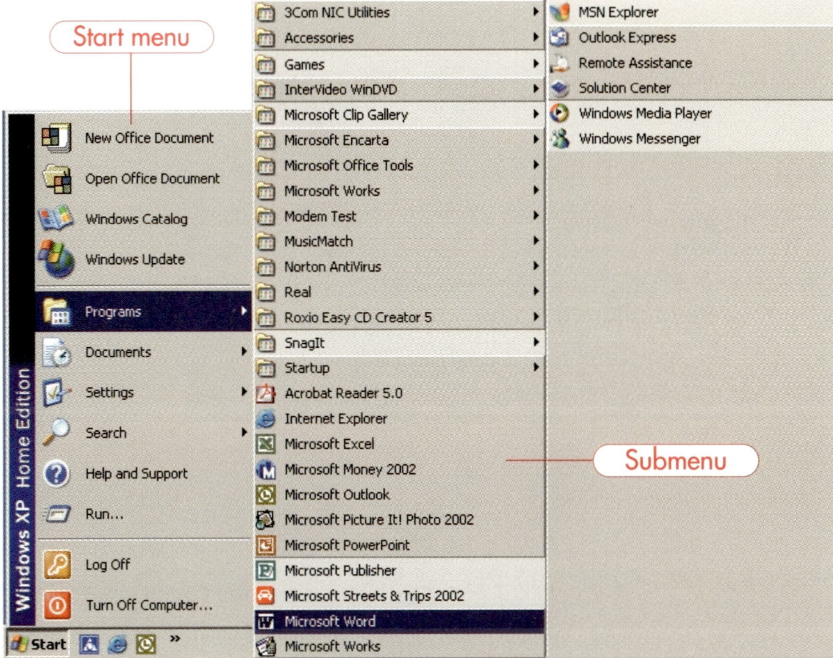

Figure 1.2 Start menu

3. Roll the mouse on your table or mouse pad in all directions.

a. Notice the corresponding movement of the pointer on your computer screen.

b. Observe how the mouse pointer changes its shape, depending on where it is pointing.

4. Identify the following parts of the Word window, shown in Figure 1.3a on page 18 for Word 2002 users, and in Figure 1.3b for Word 2000 users:

- Title bar
- Menu bar
- Toolbars
- I-beam
- Insertion point
- Ruler
- Text area
- Status bar
- Scroll box
- Scroll buttons
- Start button
- Taskbar
- Task pane (XP)
- ScreenTip
- Minimize, Maximize, Restore, Close buttons

CONCEPT BUILDERS

Most mouse actions require the use of the left mouse button.

Create and Enhance a Web Site Using FrontPage; Add Web Pages and Navigation

EXERCISE 9

SCANS

Directions

1. Open FrontPage.
2. Create a new Empty Web in your home directory; name it **2.9goawaytravelweb**.
3. Create a new Web page using the Narrow, Right-aligned Body template.

VOCABULARY

Hit counter
Photo gallery

INTERNET CONCEPT BUILDERS

- You can create a Web site from scratch using FrontPage. To do so, click File, select New, and click Page or Web, as you did when you started the Web Site Templates Wizard.
- In the Web Site Templates dialog box, you can choose page templates, a wizard (which you used in the previous exercise), or the Empty Web option. This option creates a Web site without pages. Think of an Empty Web as a folder for your pages.
- Once you have selected the Empty Web and indicated where you want to save your new Web site, you can begin to add page templates or blank pages to the "folder."
- To add pages to your site, click File, select New, and click Page or Web. Then click the Page Templates (or Blank Page) link in the task pane. Each new page appears as a page tab, as it did when you created a Web site using a wizard.
- You save Web pages as you do with any other file in Office. Remember that FrontPage automatically assigns "index" as the first page in a Web site to identify it as the home page.
- After you have added pages to your site, you must create a structure in Navigation view for the pages. The only page that will appear in this view is the home page. You must drag each page from the Folder List window on the left onto the document area and connect it to the home page.
- You can use the structure that you create in Navigation view to create link bars for all your pages. To insert a link bar, click Insert, Web Component, and click Link Bars. Choose Bar based on navigation structure and then follow the prompts to choose a style and orientation for the link bars. You should insert a link bar in a shared border so that the link bar appears on all pages of your site.
- A ***hit counter*** displays the number of visitors to your Web site. FrontPage provides numerous styles of hit counter formats, which you can select in the Web Components dialog box. When you insert a hit counter on a page, only a placeholder will appear until you publish the Web site, at which time the formatted hit counter will appear.
- A ***photo gallery*** is a Web page that contains placeholders for graphics, which are arranged in a specific layout. You can choose a photo gallery template page or you can choose to insert a photo gallery from the Web Components dialog box. FrontPage provides four different layouts to arrange your graphics.
- When you close a Web site, you will be prompted to save each page that is part of it, if you have not already done so.

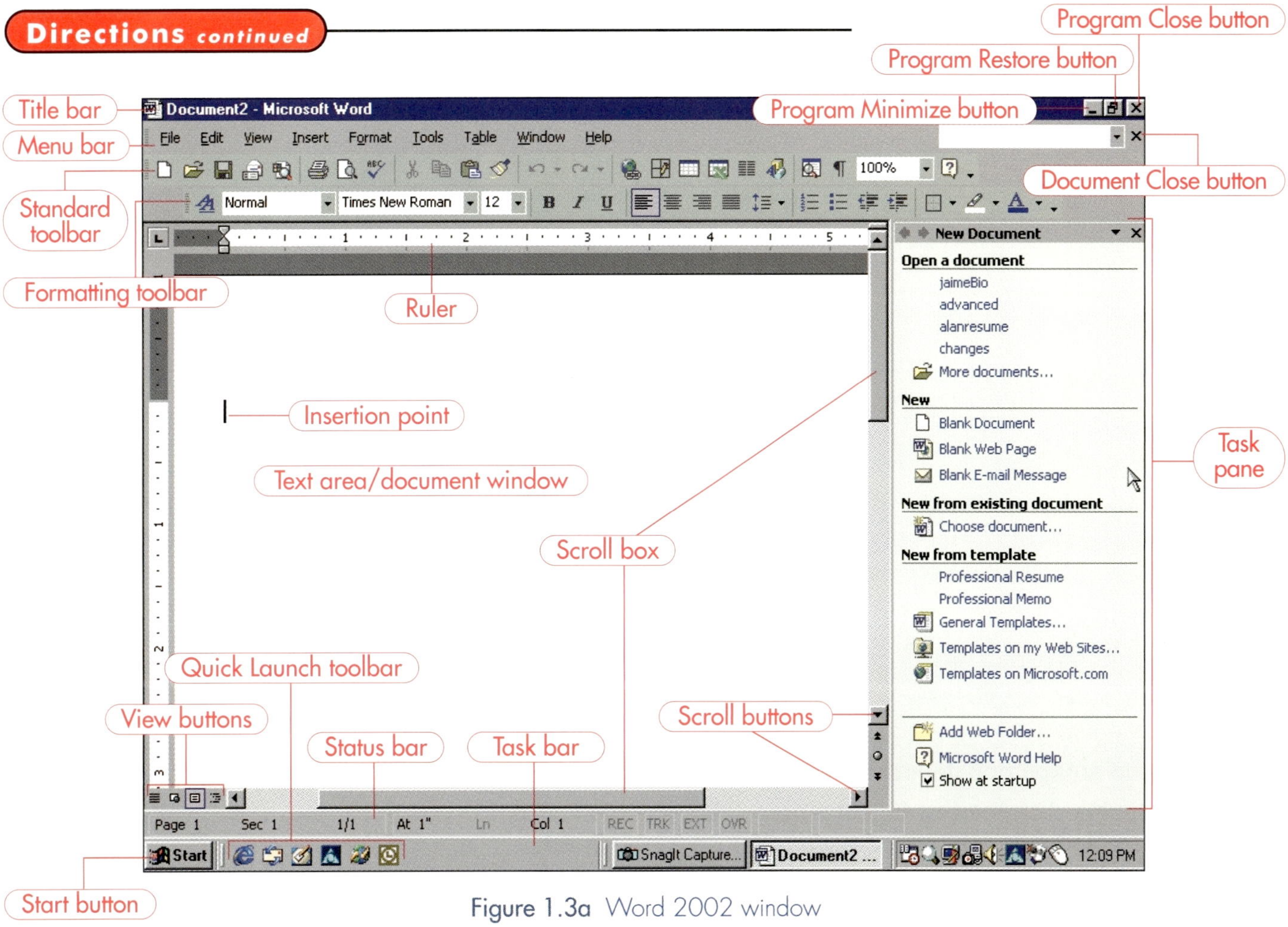

Program Close button
Program Restore button
Title bar
Program Minimize button
Menu bar
Document Close button
Standard toolbar
Formatting toolbar
Ruler
Insertion point
Text area/document window
Task pane
Scroll box
Quick Launch toolbar
View buttons
Scroll buttons
Status bar
Task bar
Start button
Document2 - Microsoft Word
New Document
Open a document
jaimeBio
advanced
alanresume
changes
More documents...
New
Blank Document
Blank Web Page
Blank E-mail Message
New from existing document
Choose document...
New from template
Professional Resume
Professional Memo
General Templates...
Templates on my Web Sites...
Templates on Microsoft.com
Add Web Folder...
Microsoft Word Help
Show at startup

Figure 1.3a Word 2002 window

Document1 - Microsoft Word

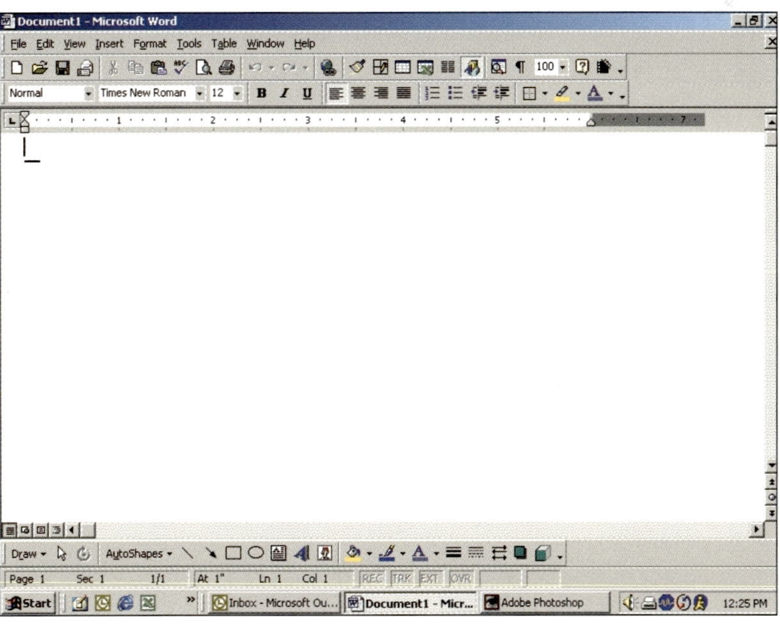

Figure 1.3b Word 2000 window

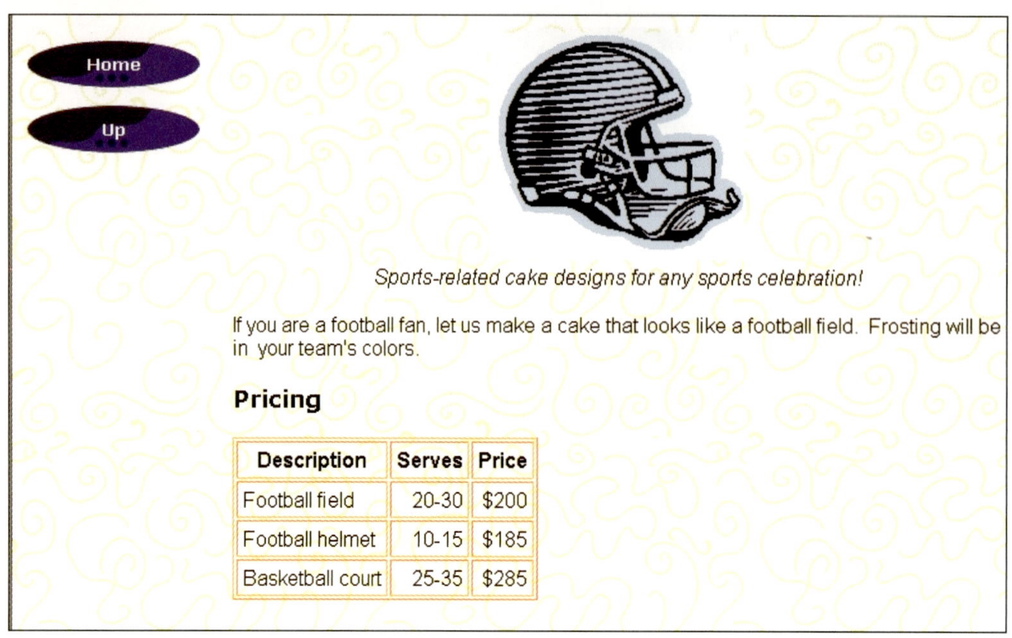

Illustration F Sports Cakes

b. Add an appropriate graphic to each page.

c. Double-click the text **Edit the properties for this link bar to display hyperlinks here,** which will open the Link Bar Properties dialog box.

d. Click the check boxes for **Home page** and **Parent page** under Additional pages, and then click **OK.** This will add navigation buttons that link back to the home and parent pages.

e. Save each page after entering the text and graphic. Do not provide a page file name at this time.

25. Click the **Preview** button at the bottom of the screen and test the links.

26. Preview the file in your browser.

27. Make any adjustments necessary.

28. Close the Web site; save the pages, if prompted.

Directions *continued*

5. Move the mouse pointer over each toolbar button to display its ScreenTip, as shown in Figure 1.4.

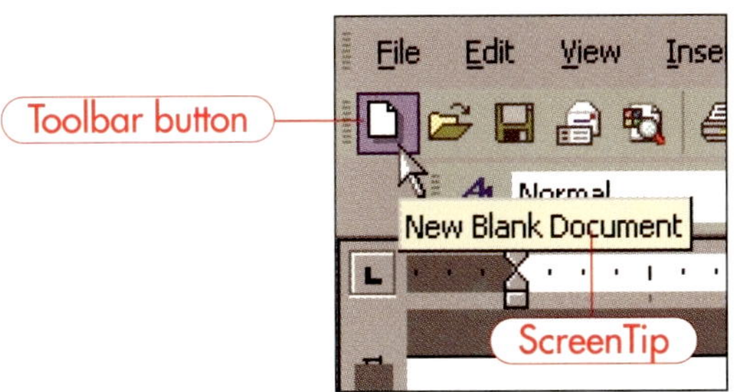

Figure 1.4 ScreenTip

6. Point to and click the **New Blank Document** button on the toolbar.
7. Drag the vertical scroll box down and then up.
8. Close the task pane. **Word 2000 Users:** Skip this step.
9. Click the **Document Close** button to close the document window.
10. Click the **Program Close** button to close the program window.

NOTE: *The button that closes the program is sometimes called the Close Window button.*

NOTE

See Appendix B, Using the Mouse, to review mouse terms and actions.

CONCEPT BUILDERS

- The ***desktop*** is the first window you see when your computer is started and displays program and file icons.
- The ***menu bar*** is located below the title bar and displays items that you click to execute commands.
- When you point to a toolbar button, a pop-up window known as a ***ScreenTip*** displays the full document and application name.
- Scroll bars are located at the right and bottom of the window. You can click and drag a vertical or horizontal ***scroll box,*** which is located on a scroll bar, to display areas of the screen that are not in view.
- A ***task pane*** is located on the right side of the screen and appears when the application is started. A task pane contains hyperlinks or shortcuts with links to other information.
- The ***status bar*** is located at the bottom of the window and displays information about the current status of the document. The information shown on the status bar depends on the application that is open.
- The ***taskbar*** is located at the bottom of the Windows screen and displays the Start button and the Quick Launch toolbar, as well as open documents and programs.
- The ***title bar*** is located at the top of the application window and displays the document name, followed by the program name. An application-specific generic name appears until you provide a name during the Save process.
- Toolbars provide quick access to frequently used features. The ***Standard*** and ***Formatting toolbars*** appear in every application. These toolbars contain common buttons, as well as application-specific buttons.

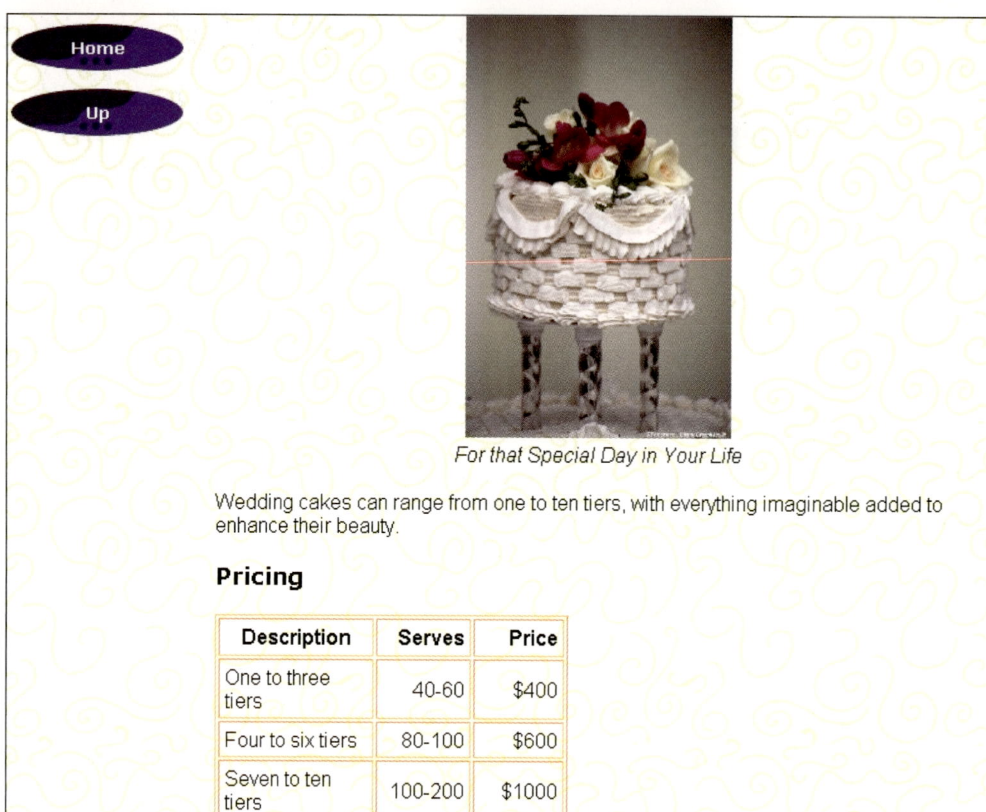

Home

Up

For that Special Day in Your Life

Wedding cakes can range from one to ten tiers, with everything imaginable added to enhance their beauty.

Pricing

Description	Serves	Price
One to three tiers	40-60	$400
Four to six tiers	80-100	$600
Seven to ten tiers	100-200	$1000

Illustration D Wedding Cakes

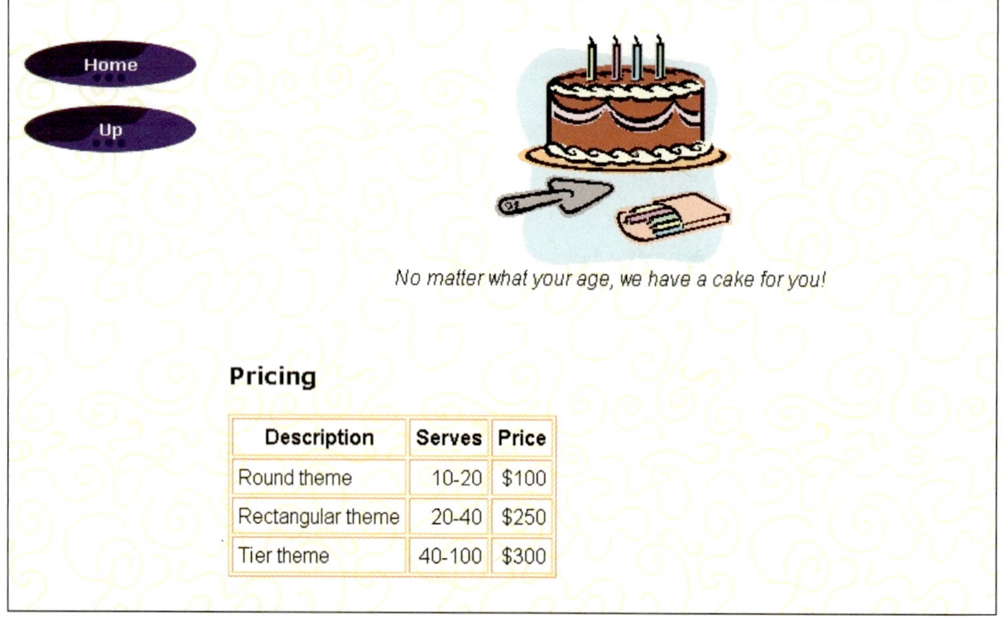

Home

Up

No matter what your age, we have a cake for you!

Pricing

Description	Serves	Price
Round theme	10-20	$100
Rectangular theme	20-40	$250
Tier theme	40-100	$300

Illustration E Birthday Cakes

Use Menus and Toolbars; Work with Dialog Boxes; Hide/Display the Task Pane

Directions

1. Start Word.
2. Click each menu name and view its menu and submenu (if applicable), as shown in Figure 2.1.

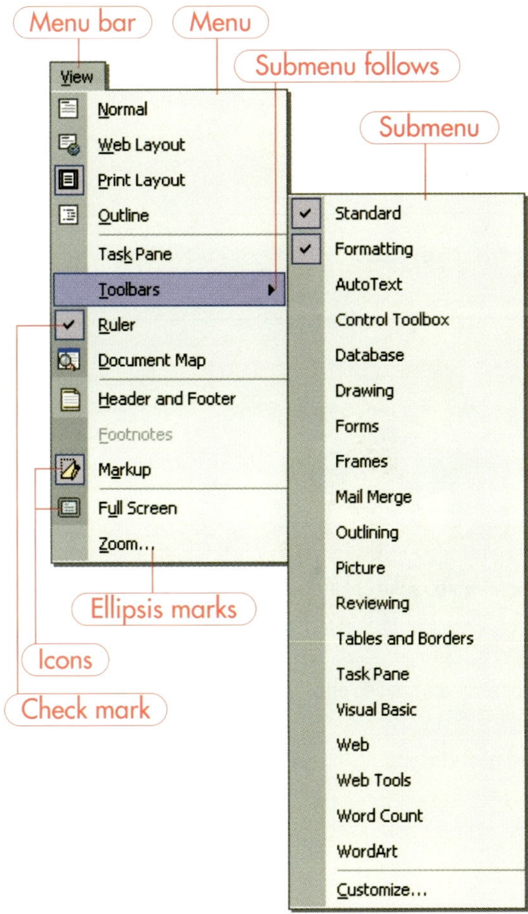

Figure 2.1 Word View menu

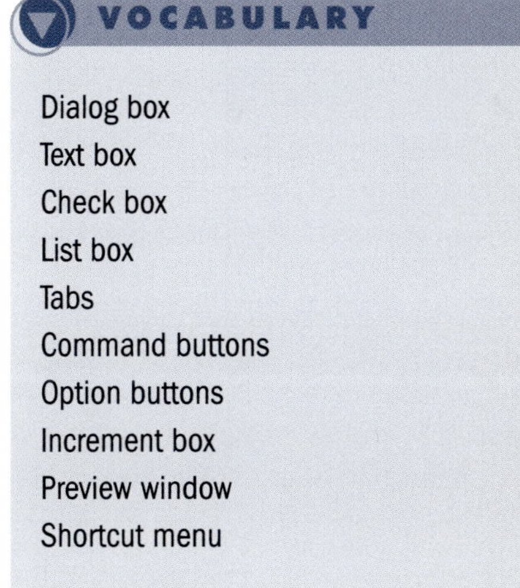

VOCABULARY

Dialog box
Text box
Check box
List box
Tabs
Command buttons
Option buttons
Increment box
Preview window
Shortcut menu

Directions *continued*

24. Press the **Ctrl** key, click the link to each page, and do the following:
    a. Enter the text as shown in Illustrations B (Cake Ideas), C (Kids' Cakes), D (Wedding Cakes), E (Birthday Cakes), and F (Sports Cakes).

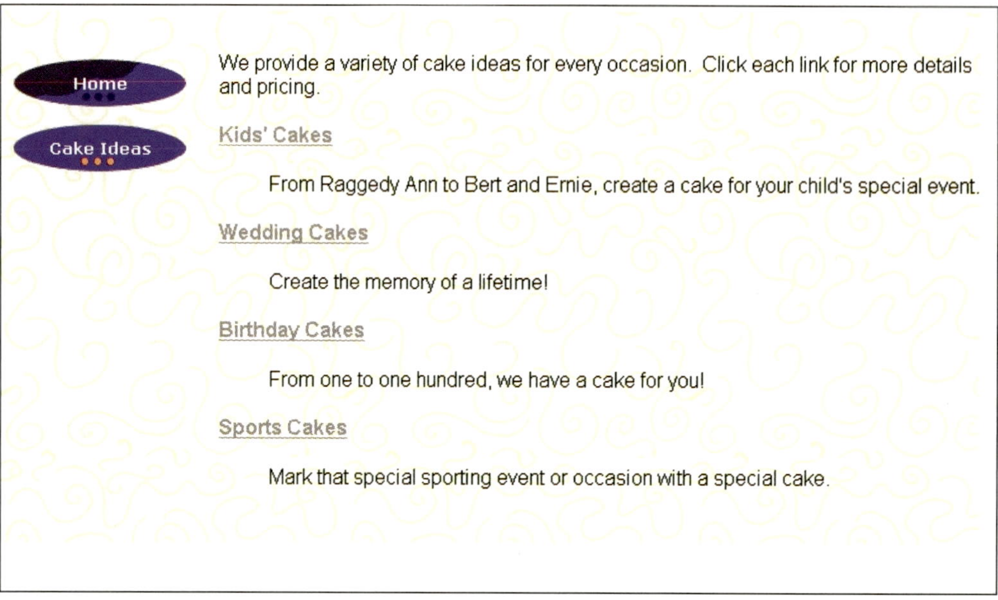

Illustration B Cake Ideas

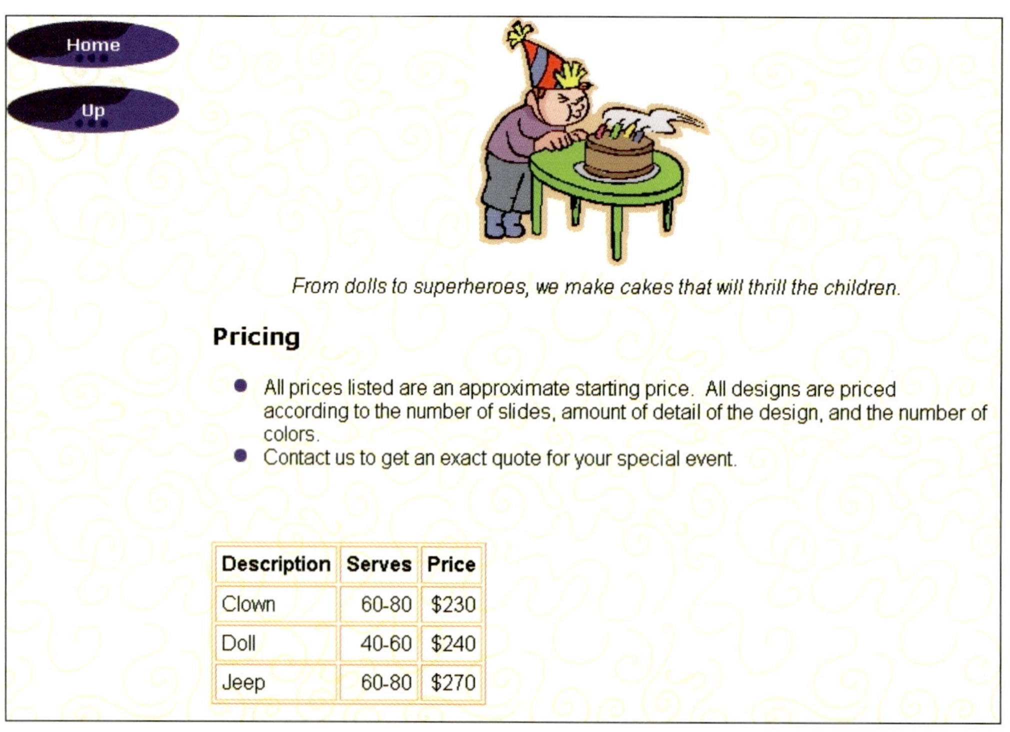

Illustration C Kids' Cakes

Directions *continued*

3. Notice the following about menu items:
   - Dimmed menu items are not available for selection at this time.
   - A check mark next to a menu item means the option is currently selected.
   - An icon to the left of a menu item means you can access this command from a toolbar button.
   - An item followed by ellipsis marks (...) means a dialog box is forthcoming.
   - An arrow to the right of the menu item means a submenu follows, as shown in Figure 2.1.

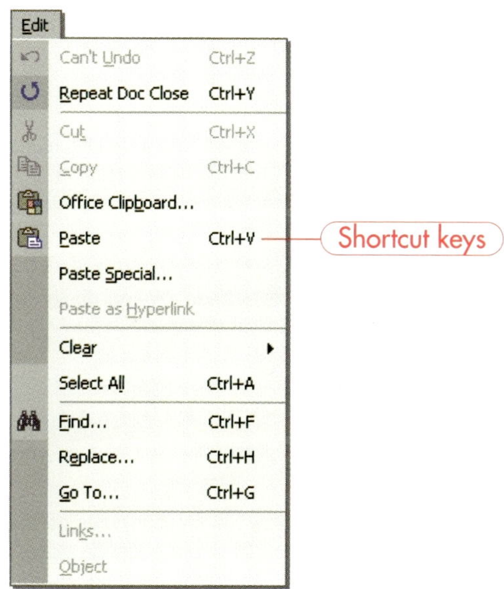

Figure 2.2 Word Edit menu

4. Click **View** on the menu bar and select **Toolbars** on the submenu.
5. Click the check mark or check box to deselect a toolbar that is currently selected.
6. Click **View** and select **Toolbars** again. Reselect the toolbar.

HOT TIPS

- Learn the keyboard shortcut commands (which appear next to some submenu command names) for easy command access, as shown in Figure 2.2.

CONCEPT BUILDERS

- When you click a menu bar item, a drop-down menu appears with additional options.
- You can access menu bar items by clicking the menu name or by pressing the Alt key plus the key of the underlined letter in the menu name.
- You can access menu items by clicking the option, by pressing the key of the underlined letter in the command name, or by using the up or down arrow key to select the command and then pressing the Enter key.

Directions *continued*

19. Repeat Step 16 for each product page. Edit the page banner for each product page as follows:

a. Product 2 = `Wedding Cakes`

b. Product 3 = `Birthday Cakes`

c. Product 4 = `Sports Cakes`

20. Return to the home page.

21. Enter the text shown in Illustration A for the home page.

Illustration A Home page

22. Add the Marquee Dynamic Effect Web Component (scrolling text) to the bottom of the home page that reads: `One-of-a-Kind Custom Cakes`

- Format it as you prefer.

23. Save the page.
NOTE: *When you save a Web page with images, you may be prompted to Save Embedded Files. Click* ***OK*** *to ensure that the graphic files are part of the page.*

Directions *continued*

7. Click **Format** on the menu bar; click **Font** on the menu. Notice the following dialog box elements, as shown in Figure 2.3:
   - Title bar
   - List box
   - Check box
   - Drop-down list box
   - Tabs
   - Scroll bar
   - Command buttons

NOTE

See Appendix C, Toolbars, Menus, and Dialog Boxes.

CONCEPT BUILDERS

You can close a dialog box without making changes to it by clicking the Cancel button or by clicking the Close button.

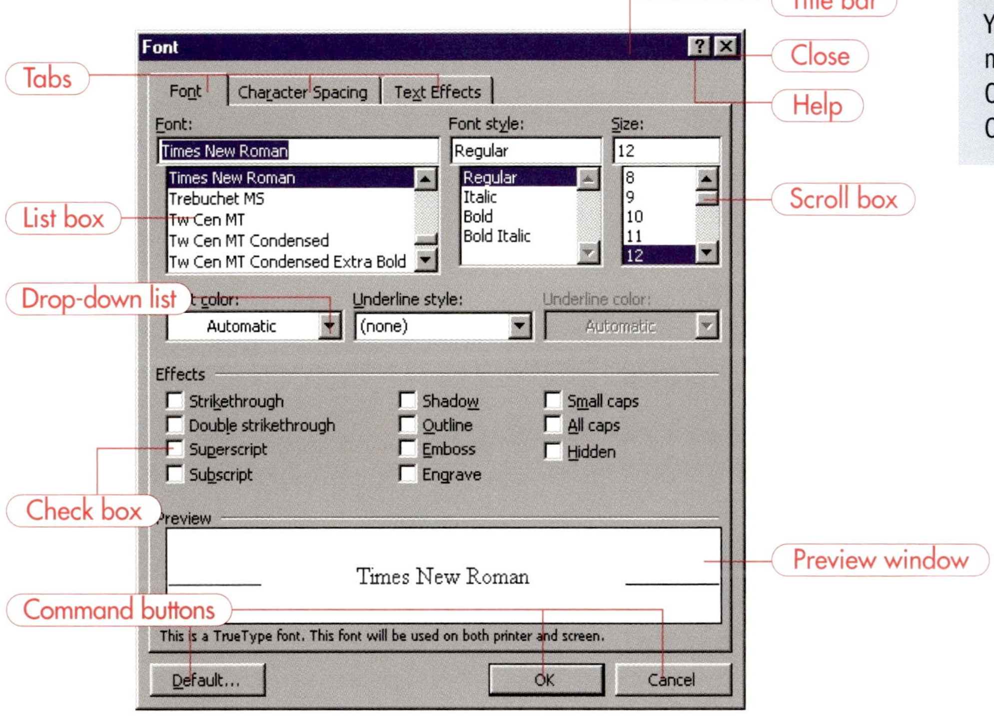

Figure 2.3 Font dialog box

CONCEPT BUILDERS

- A ***dialog box*** presents information about the current settings for a command and allows you to change the settings, if necessary. The title bar identifies the title of the dialog box. Dialog boxes let you enter information in a variety of ways.
  - A ***text box*** is a space where you enter information.
  - A ***check box*** is a small square box where you can select or deselect an option. A ✓ in the box indicates the option is selected. If several check boxes are offered, you may select more than one.
  - A ***list box*** displays a list of items from which you can make selections. A list box may have a scroll bar that you can use to show hidden items in a list, or the list may be displayed by clicking a down arrow.
  - ***Tabs*** display options related to the tab's name in the same dialog box.
  - ***Command buttons*** carry out the actions described on the button.
  - ***Option buttons*** are small circular buttons that indicate options in a set. You can choose only one option from the set. A selected option contains a dark circle.
  - An ***increment box*** provides a space for entering a value. Clicking the up or down arrow (usually to the right of the box) allows you to display the incremental value.
  - A ***preview window*** allows you to see a sample of the selection you made.

Directions *continued*

10. Enter your company information on the next two screens as follows and click **Next.**

`CreativeCakes Company` (CreativeCakes is one word.)

`1075 Madison Avenue, New York, NY 10128`

`Phone: 212-555-5555`

`Fax: 212-555-6666`

`Webmaster: someone@creativecakes.com`

`General Information: someone@creativecakes.com`

11. Click **Choose Web Theme** and select the **Waves** theme. Then select **Active Graphics** and **Background picture,** click **OK,** and click **Next.**

12. Click **Show Tasks View after web is uploaded** and click **Finish. NOTE:** *Your pages will assemble in Tasks view, a convenient feature that keeps track of the level of priority to complete each task.*

13. Click **Navigation** view. Note the structure of your Web site, as shown in the Concept Builders, which the FrontPage Wizard automatically creates for you.

- Double-click the **home** page in Navigation view.

14. Right-click the "Home" page banner and select **Page Banner Properties** from the shortcut menu; edit the banner to read `CreativeCakes` and click **OK.**

- Insert a relevant graphic in the page banner as the company logo.

15. Press the **Ctrl** key and click the **Products** link to take you to the Products page.

16. Right-click the Products page banner and select Page Banner Properties; edit the banner to read `Cake Ideas` and click **OK. NOTE:** *This will cause the link bar name to change on the home page.*

17. Press the **Ctrl** key and click the **Product 1** link, which will take you to the Product 1 page.

18. Edit the page banner to read `Kids' Cakes` and click **OK.**

DID YOU KNOW?

- You can access FrontPage templates by clicking File, selecting New, and clicking Page or Web on the menu, which will display the task pane. Click Web Site Templates and choose a template.
- FrontPage contains Web site template wizards that have a specific purpose. As you go through the Web site creation process, you will be prompted to add many of the elements that relate to the theme of the Web site. The Corporate Presence Web site, for example, allows you to create a Web site for your organization that gives it an Internet presence.

8. Click each tab in the Font dialog box; then click the **Cancel** command button.

9. Click **File, Print.** Notice the following additional dialog box parts, as shown in Figure 2.4:
   - Option buttons
   - Text box
   - Increment box (sometimes called a spin box)

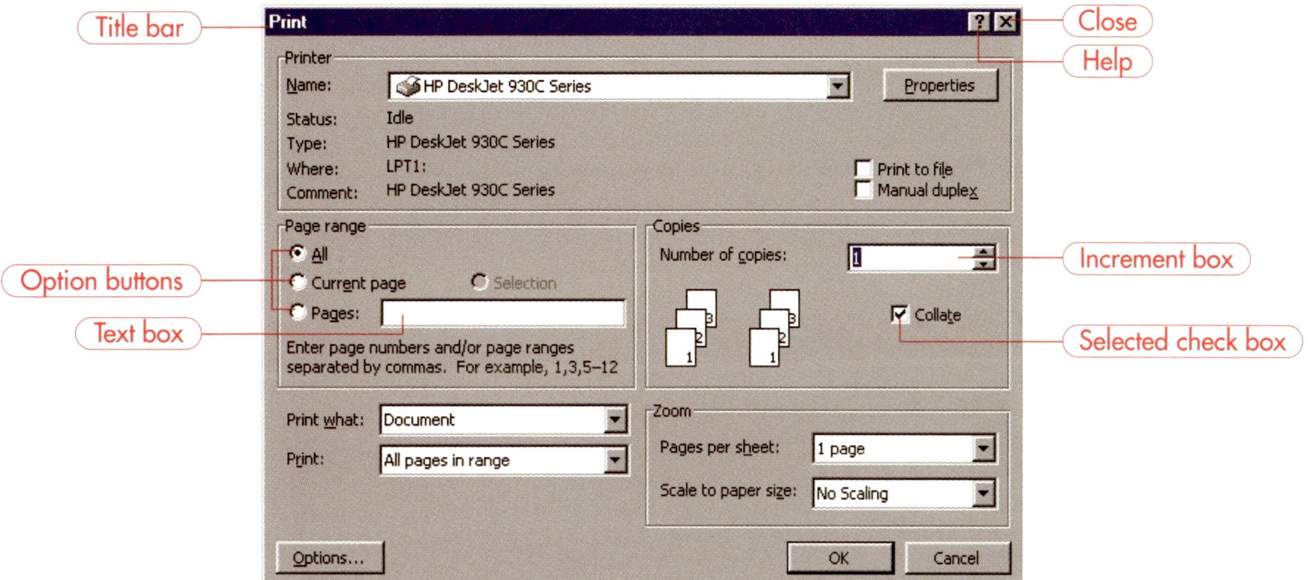

Figure 2.4 Print dialog box

10. Click the **up** increment arrow to increase the number of copies to print. Then click **Cancel.**

11. Place the mouse pointer in the document text area. Click the right mouse button and notice the shortcut menu that appears, as shown in Figure 2.5.

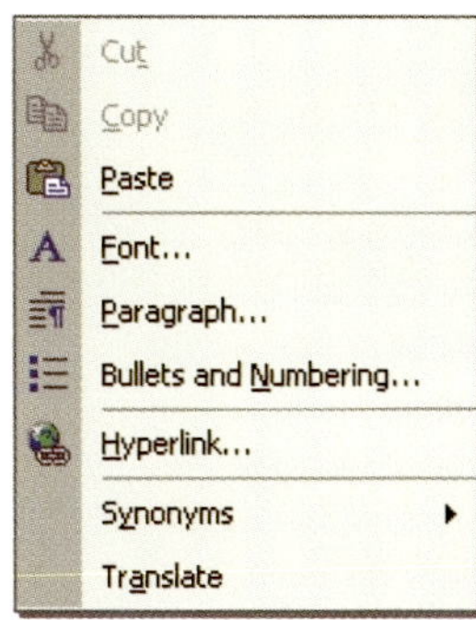

Figure 2.5 Shortcut menu

CONCEPT BUILDERS

- A ***shortcut menu*** appears when you click the right mouse button. The menu items that it contains may vary, depending on where the mouse is pointing and what task you are performing.

HOT TIPS

- Click the right mouse button when the pointer is on a screen item to display a shortcut menu. This allows you to access useful commands for working with that item.

Directions *continued*

3. Start the Corporate Presence Web Wizard in your home directory; rename the Web site folder (My Web) **2.8cakes**. Click **OK.** Click **Next** to start the Wizard.

   NOTE:
   - *If FrontPage is unavailable to you, you may use Word to create this Web site; however, you will have to modify some of the directions.*
   - *In the options area of the Web Site Templates dialog box, you must choose the location, or path, in which to save your new Web site. FrontPage sets the default as C:\My Documents\My Webs\My Web. You should change the folder name for each new Web site you create.*

4. Select the following main pages to include in your Web and click **Next.**
   - Home (required)
   - Products/Services

5. Select the following topics to appear on your home page and click **Next.**
   - Introduction
   - Mission Statement
   - Company Profile
   - Contact Information

6. Enter 4 to indicate the number of pages you will need to describe your product; enter 0 for the number of pages for Services. Then click **Next.**

7. Select the following items to display for each product and click **Next.**
   - Product image
   - Pricing information

8. Click the following to appear at the top and bottom of each page and click **Next.**

   Top:
   - Your company's logo
   - Page title
   - Links to your main web pages

   Bottom:
   - Links to your main web pages
   - E-mail address of your webmaster

9. Click **No** to identify pages under construction and click **Next.**

INTERNET CONCEPT BUILDERS

- In FrontPage, a ***page banner*** is any text or graphics that you add to the top of your Web page and it usually contains the page's title. If you add the page banner within a shared border (an area common to all pages in a Web site), it will appear on every page of the site. (In Word, you were able to create text and graphics to appear on all pages of the site by inserting them into a frame.) Page banner is a term associated with FrontPage and other Web-creation programs.
- Page banners use the styles and graphics associated with the theme that you applied to the site during the Web-creation process.
- To insert a banner, open the page in Page view, move the insertion point to where you want to place the banner, and click Insert, Page Banner. In the Page Banner Properties dialog box that opens, you can change the banner by entering new text. (You can also right-click the banner and choose Page Banner Properties to open the dialog box.)
- ***Web components*** are different elements that you can add to your Web site. Examples include dynamic effects (marquee, hover button, banner ad manager), spreadsheets and charts, a hit counter, a photo gallery, link bars, and a table of contents, as well as other items.
- A ***marquee*** is the same as scrolling text used in Word.
- When you close a Web site, you will be prompted to save each page that is part of it.

Directions continued

12. Click off the menu to close it.
13. Click **View, Task Pane** to display the task pane (if not already displayed), as shown in Figure 2.6. Otherwise, close the task pane and then click **View, Task Pane. Word 2000 Users:** Skip this step.
    - Click the **More documents** link to open the Open dialog box. Then click **Cancel.**

The New Document task pane lists the last four files you saved.

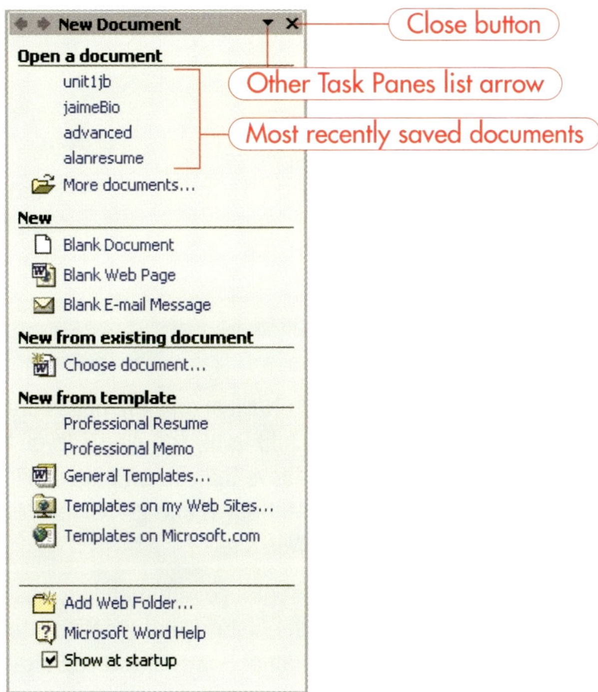

Figure 2.6 New Document task pane

14. Click **File, Close** to close the document.
15. Click **File, Exit** to exit the program.

Create and Enhance a Web Site Using a FrontPage Wizard

EXERCISE 8

SCANS

Directions

1. Open FrontPage.
2. Click **File,** select **New,** and click **New Page or Web** to access Web Site Templates in the task pane.

VOCABULARY

Page banner
Web component
Marquee

INTERNET CONCEPT BUILDERS

- FrontPage contains several different wizards to help you build a Web site and also contains Web page templates that you may include in the site.
- FrontPage provides three views, Normal, Preview, and HTML. Normal view is used for entering and editing text. Preview mode is used to see your Web page as it will look when viewed in a browser and to test the links. HTML view allows you to see the HTML codes that were used to create the page.
- FrontPage provides six different ways to view your Web site as you develop it. The Views bar appears alongside of your Web page. Page view allows you to edit, preview, or view the HTML code for individual pages. Folders view allows you to see the individual files and folders that make up your Web site. Reports view allows you to analyze and summarize your Web site. Navigation view (shown in the illustration) displays the navigation structure of your site (similar to using a diagram when working with Word). Hyperlinks view shows you all the hyperlinks that are on each of your Web pages. Tasks view provides you with a "to do" list for your Web site and is commonly used when more than one person is working on the development of the site.
- In Navigation view, pages are identified as parent level, child level, and global level. Parent level is a link to a page above the current page; child level is a link below the current page; and global level links to the highest level of the Web site.
- FrontPage automatically assigns the file name "index" for the first page of the Web site. Do not change this file name; however, you can change the page title and you can name subsequent pages. Remember, the index.htm file identifies the "home page," the first page that you see when you open a Web site.

Views bar

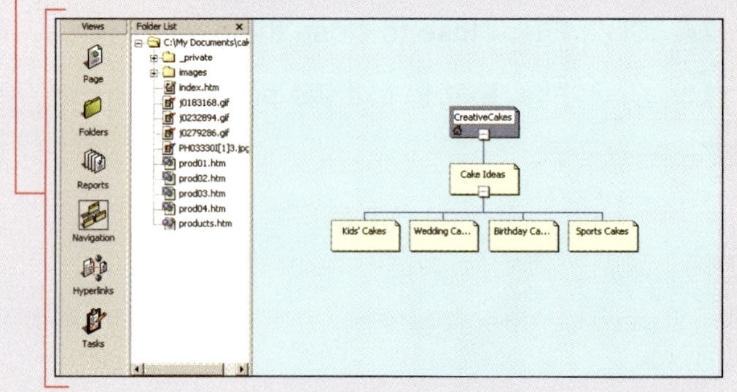

Continued on next page

LESSON 2

Use Settings, Displays, Help, and File Management

EXERCISE 3
Use Default Settings; Use Zoom

EXERCISE 4
Change Window Displays

EXERCISE 5
Get Help

EXERCISE 6
Use Windows Explorer to Manage Files; Search for Files

Directions *continued*

14. Click the **Nutrition** link, which will bring you to the page template.

a. Delete the sample text.

b. Insert the text found on the Data CD under the file name **d2.7nutritiontext**.

c. Format the text and the page as you prefer.

d. Replace the existing graphic with one that relates to the text.

e. Enter a caption that complements the graphic and relates to the text.

f. Save the file.

g. Click the **Home** page link.

15. Click the **Exercise** link, which will bring you to the page template.

a. Delete the sample text.

b. Insert the text found on the Data CD under the file name **d2.7exercisetext**.

c. Format the text and the page as you prefer.

d. Replace the existing graphic with one that relates to the text.

e. Enter a caption that complements the graphic and relates to the text. Apply a Square wrap and center alignment option.

f. Save the file.

g. Click the **Home** page link.

16. Preview the file in your browser and test the links.

17. Make any necessary adjustments.

18. Close the file; save the changes.

Use Default Settings; Use Zoom

EXERCISE 3

IMPORTANT: *The exercises in this book were created using a 12 pt, Times New Roman font. Because defaults and fonts vary, your line endings may not appear like those in the exercise. Do not be concerned at this time. In a later lesson, you will learn to change default settings.*

The AutoCorrect feature in Word automatically replaces common spelling errors and mistyped words with the correct text as you enter it. It may capitalize the first letter of a line, even if you do not want it capitalized. If you find this feature annoying, turn it off.

Directions

1. Start Word.
2. Create a new document.
3. Click **Format, Font.**
   a. Notice the default font and font size.
   b. Close the dialog box.
4. Enter the letter j twice.
5. Click **View, Zoom.**
6. Change the magnification to **200%,** as shown in Figure 3.1. Click **OK.**

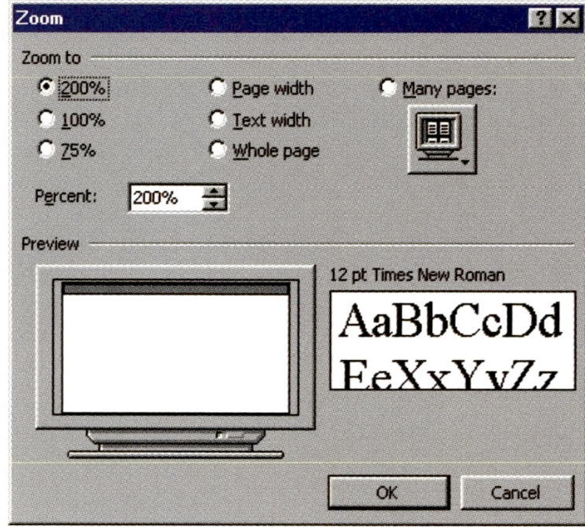

Figure 3.1 Zoom dialog box

VOCABULARY

Default settings
Zoom

CONCEPT BUILDERS

- ***Default settings*** are pre-established settings within the software. For example, when you start a program, margins, font size, and text alignment are already set. You can, however, change these settings to suit your needs.
- If you change a default setting, each time you open the file the settings will be in effect until you make another change.
- Selecting the ***Zoom*** option from the View menu allows you to set the magnification of data on screen by a specific percentage. You can also set the magnification with the Zoom list arrow on the Standard toolbar.

Directions *continued*

11. Add a frame to the bottom of the page as shown in Illustration A on page 381.

a. Enter and center the text shown (Privacy Policy) using an 8 pt font.

- Format the text as you prefer.

b. Link Privacy Policy to a blank page. Name the page **2.7privacypolicy** and enter the following text. Then link http://www.today'shealthonline.com back to the home page.

`Thank you for visiting Today's Health Online. Today's Health Online is committed to providing our visitors with content and services characterized by outstanding quality and customer service. Our online Privacy Policy continues our commitment to serve you and to protect your privacy online.`

`BY USING OUR WEB SITE, YOU AGREE TO THE TERMS OF THIS PRIVACY POLICY. Accordingly, please review the following carefully so that you understand our privacy practices in regards to:`

`Children Under Age 13`

`How We Collect Information`

`How Your Information Will Be Used`

`If you have questions about this Privacy Policy, please contact us at: http://www.today'shealthonline.com`

12. Add a scrolling text enhancement below the top frame that reads: `Healthy Minds and Bodies Live Longer` Use any font face and background color.

13. Click the Health link, which will bring you to the page template.

a. Delete the sample text.

b. Insert the text found on the Data CD under the file name **d2.7healthtext**. 

c. Format the text and the page as you prefer.

d. Replace the existing graphic with one that relates to the text.

e. Enter a caption that complements the graphic and relates to the text, if you want.

f. Save the file.

g. Click the **Home** page link.

Directions *continued*

7. Click **View, Zoom.**
8. Change the magnification to **75%.** Click **OK.**
9. Click **File, Page Setup,** and click the **Margins** tab.
   a. Notice the default margins.
   b. Close the dialog box.
10. Click **Tools.**
    a. Click the **AutoCorrect** tab.
    b. Notice the options for correcting text as you type it.
    c. Close the dialog box.
11. Click **File, Close** to close the document.
12. Click **File, Exit** to exit the program.

If you are using an IntelliMouse, you can zoom in or out by 10% increments. Simply press the Ctrl key while rotating the center wheel.

Directions *continued*

10. Replace the text on the home page template with the text shown in Illustration B.

a. Format the text in each section of this page as you prefer, using any font, font color, and font size. Add a graphic to the page.

b. Create a link on the text in the left column to the sections in the middle column.

c. Create a link on the text in the right column to the pages noted as follows:

- Choosing the Right Gym = Exercise
- Our Vitamin Guide Will Make You Feel Strong = Nutrition
- Summer Health Issues = Health

d. Add background color to each section of the page as you prefer.

Illustration B

Change Window Displays

EXERCISE 4

Directions

1. Start Word.
2. Start Excel.
3. Click the Word document button on the taskbar to switch to Word, as shown in Figure 4.1.

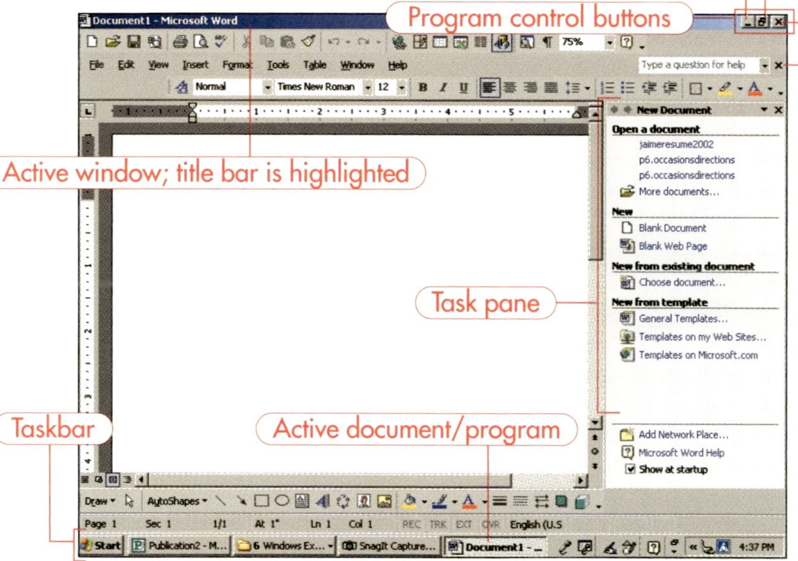

Figure 4.1 Word window

4. Click to minimize the program window.
5. Click to maximize the window.
6. Switch to Excel.
7. Click to minimize the window.
8. Click to maximize the window.
9. Click to close Excel.
10. Click to close Word.

VOCABULARY

Minimize button
Maximize button
Restore button
Close button

CONCEPT BUILDERS

- You can use the Minimize, Maximize, and Restore buttons to change the size of the window display.
- The ***Minimize button*** shrinks the window to a button on the taskbar.
- The ***Maximize button*** sizes the window to fill the screen (and then changes to a Restore button).
- The ***Restore button*** restores the window to its previous size.
- The ***Close button*** closes the document or program window.

DID YOU KNOW?

The active window displays an active title bar; the active program or document is selected on the taskbar.

Directions *continued*

5. Click **Next** to access the Organize Pages option. Rename the pages as follows:
   - Simple Layout = `Home`
   - Left-aligned Column = `Nutrition`
   - Right-aligned Column = `Health`
   - Column with Contents = `Exercise`
6. Click **Next** to access the Visual Theme option and choose **No visual theme.**
7. Click **Next** and click **Finish** to end the Wizard.
   NOTE: *The Web Page Wizard will automatically assemble the pages and add navigation link bars with the names of the pages in the top horizontal frame.*
8. Save the Web site as **2.7healthweb**.
9. Format the navigation links as you prefer. The format shown in Illustration A is merely a guide.
   - Add `Today's Health Online` above the links as shown. Set the font style and size as you prefer.

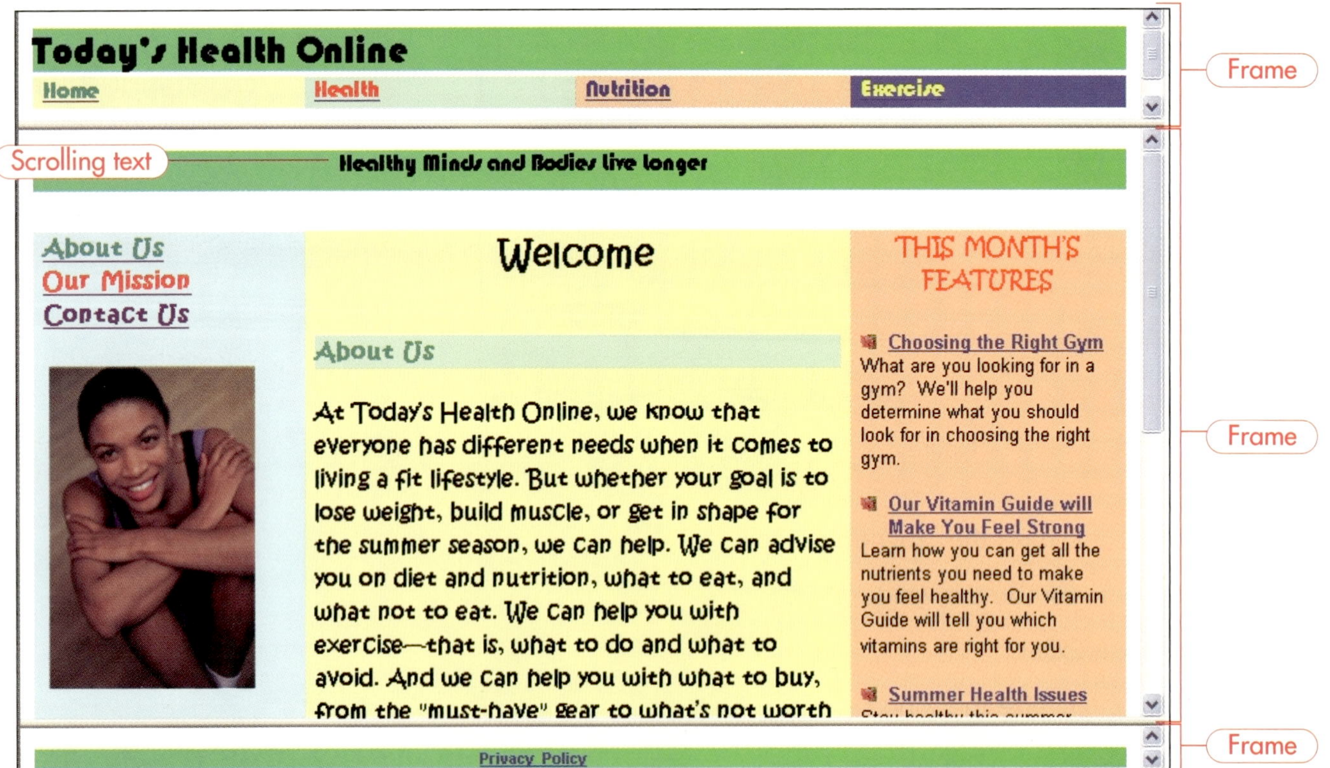

Illustration A

EXERCISE 5

Get Help

Directions

1. Start Word.
2. Open a new document.
3. Click **Help** on the menu. Click **Microsoft Word Help.**
4. Click the **Contents** tab, as shown in Figure 5.1, to display a listing of the Help contents in the current program by topic.

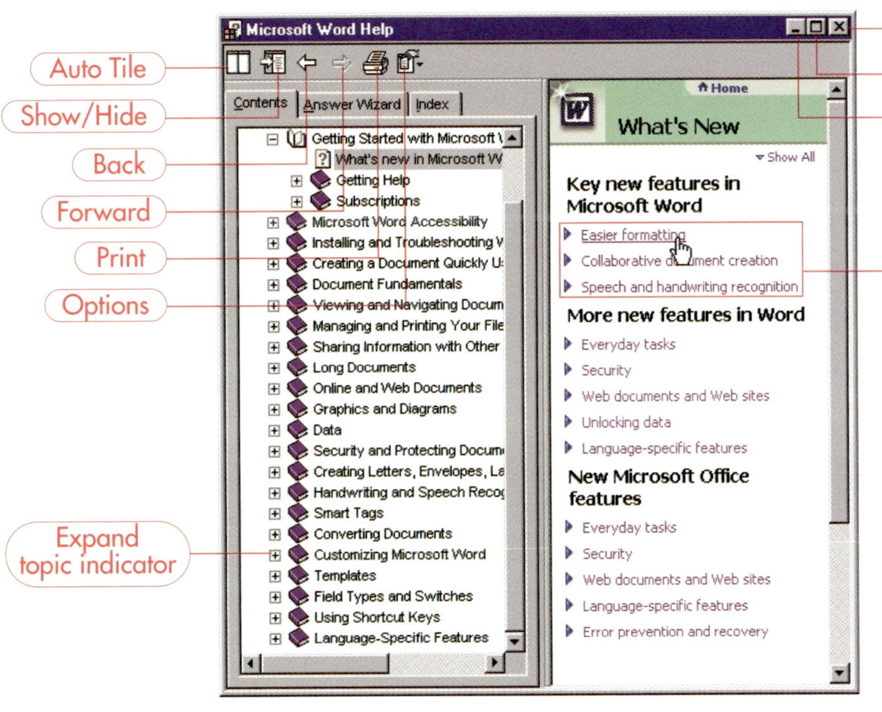

Figure 5.1 Microsoft Word Help window

5. Double-click an entry to expand the topic (or click the **expand topic indicator,** if this is available).

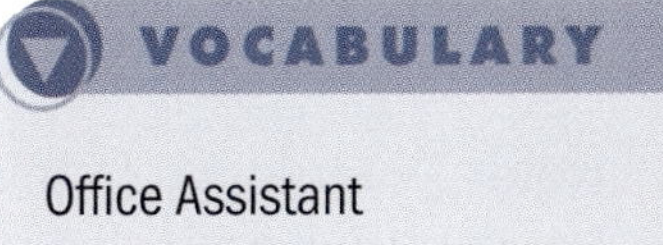

VOCABULARY

Office Assistant

HOT TIPS

- Help is available from a variety of sources in your software.
- Pressing the F1 key from within any application accesses Help.
- You can get help on the Web from within any Office application by clicking Help on the menu bar and clicking Office on the Web.
- You can print Help results.
- The Type a question for help box appears in all Office applications.

Create and Enhance a Web Site Using a Word Wizard; Add Enhancements

EXERCISE 7

Directions

1. Note the structure of this site as illustrated in the Concept Builders.
2. Using Word, start the Web Page Wizard.
   a. Click **Next** to access the Title and Location option.
   b. Enter `Health` as the Web site title.
   c. Enter the location where the Web files will reside.
3. Click **Next** to access the Navigation option.
   - Choose **Horizontal frame.**
4. Click **Next** to access the Add Pages option.
   a. Remove all current pages listed in the Web site.
   b. Add the following page templates:
      - Column with Contents
      - Left-aligned Column
      - Right-aligned Column
      - Simple Layout

VOCABULARY

Frames
Scrolling text/Marquee

INTERNET CONCEPT BUILDERS

- ***Frames*** are regions of a Web page, which you can scroll and size. Word allows you to add frames to any Web page; FrontPage provides frames page templates which display frames in different formats.
- Frames remain in the same place when you move from page to page. Therefore, enter text in a frame that you would like to remain constant on every page. Frames behave like headers and footers.
- You can insert an entire file from another application into a Web page by clicking Insert, File on the menu bar. The file is converted to HTML code when it is inserted into the page.
- In Word, you can add ***scrolling text*** to your site as an enhancement. To do so, click in the place to insert the scrolling text and then click the Scrolling Text button on the Web Tools toolbar. In FrontPage, scrolling text is referred to as a ***marquee.***
- The structure of this site is shown below. Refer to it when constructing the Web site.

6. Click the **Index** tab, as shown in Figure 5.2.

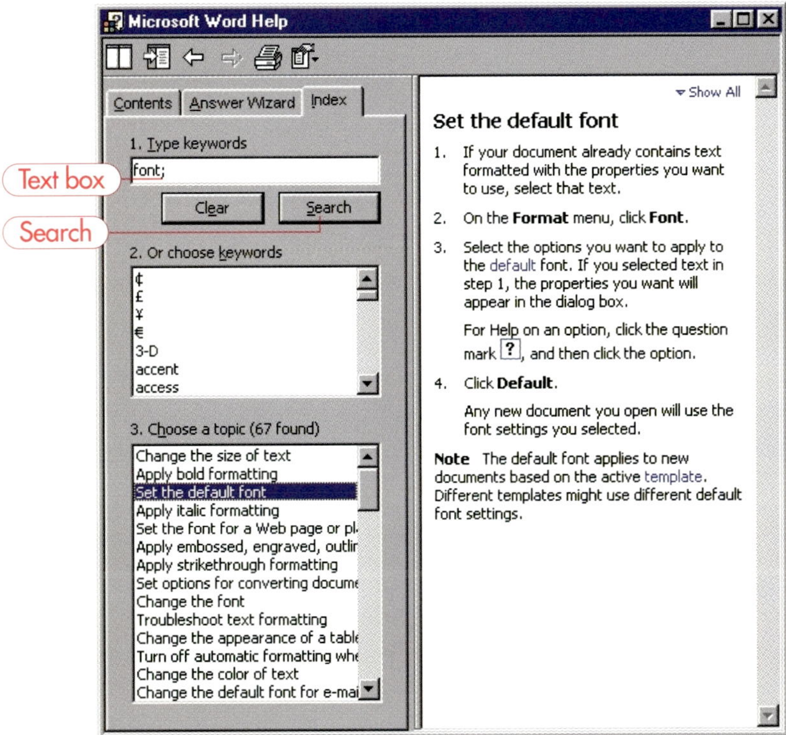

Figure 5.2 Microsoft Word Help window, Index

7. Enter the word `Font` in the keyword text box and click **Search.** ***NOTE:*** *You can enter the first few letters of the topic on which you need help in the text box provided.*
8. Click any topic about fonts to display the Help screen.
9. Print the topic.
10. Click the **Close** button to close the Help window.
11. Press the **F1** key to access Help.
12. Enter the word `Toolbar` in the keyword text box.
13. Display the information **About toolbars.**
14. Print the topic.
15. Close the Help window.

NOTE

- Microsoft Office provides many Help windows containing hyperlinks. Hyperlinks are underlined words that provide shortcuts to Help information. Click a hyperlink to access the information indicated.
- If the tabs are not visible in the Help dialog box, click the Show/Hide button on the Help toolbar.

Directions *continued*

11. Create a link on the text "Contact the Editors" to: www.foodfantasymagazine.com (This is not an authentic address.)
12. Preview the page in your browser and test the links.
13. Make any necessary adjustments.
14. Close the file; save the changes.

Food Fantasy Magazine

Your Online Source for Food and Entertainment

www.foodfantasymagazine.com

Eat Healthy for Long Life

Welcome to Food Fantasy Online

Each month, we will bring you highlights online from our magazine.

This month, learn about foods for eating healthy, which can be found in our newsletter.

Our Recipes section will provide you with this month's favorites.

What's Coming Next Month

Tune in next month for an expanded online edition. You will find the following new sections:

- Great Neighborhood Restaurants
- Every-Night Cooking: Great Recipes from Monday Through Friday
- Feature Articles

Contact the Editors

We always appreciate hearing from our readers! Your questions will be answered as quickly as possible. If you wish to subscribe, click the appropriate link on the left of the page and submit the subscription form to us.

16. Click in the **Type a question for help** box, as shown in Figure 5.3.

Figure 5.3 Type a question for help box

17. Enter the words `Office Assistant` and press the **Enter** key.

18. Click the **About tips and messages from the Office Assistant** topic.

19. Print the topic.

20. Close the Help window.

21. Close Word.

The ***Office Assistant*** is an animated graphic that answers questions, offers suggestions, and provides help unique to the Office program you are using. You can turn this feature off if you find it annoying.

HOT TIPS

Keywords for finding help on keystroke procedures and other information are provided at the end of each exercise throughout this book. Enter these keywords in the appropriate text box in the Index tab within the Help menu.

Use the Help Index

How Do I...?	**Enter the keyword(s):**
Change a toolbar	Toolbars
Show/Hide Office Assistant	Office Assistant

Directions *continued*

4. Click **Next** to access the Navigation option.
   - Choose **Vertical frame** (the default).
5. Click **Next** to access the Add Pages option.
   a. Click **Remove Page** to remove all current pages listed in the Web site.
   b. Click to add a template page and choose **Left-aligned Column.** Click **OK.**
   c. Click **Add Existing File** and add **1.1foodwebpage**, which you created in Lesson 1. If this file is not available to you, find it on the Data CD under the file name **d2.6foodwebpage**.

   d. Repeat Step c to add each of the following files, which you created in the previous lesson:
   - **1.3formweb**
   - **1.5recipes**

   If these files are not available to you, find them on the Data CD under the file names **d2.6recipeweb** and **d2.6formweb**.

6. Click **Next** to access the Organize Pages option. Rename the pages as follows:
   a. Left-aligned column = `Home`
   b. **d2.6foodwebpage** = `Newsletter`
   c. **d2.6recipeweb** = `Recipes`
   d. **d2.6formweb** = `Subscribe`
7. Click **Next** to access the Visual Theme option.
   - Click **Browse Themes** and choose a theme that complements the color scheme of the other pages. Click **OK.**
8. Click **Next** and click **Finish** to end the Wizard.
   NOTE: *The Web Page Wizard will automatically assemble the pages and add navigation link bars with the names of the pages.*
9. Save the Web site as **2.6foodfantasy magazine**.
10. Replace the text on the home page template with that shown in the illustration on page 379.
   a. Format the left frame that contains the link bars as you prefer. You may add a background to the frame as shown.
   b. Format the text in the main section as you prefer using any font color and size that complements the theme of the other pages.

CONCEPT BUILDERS

- A ***shared border,*** a term used in FrontPage, is a region of the Web page that is common to all pages. The link bars that appear in this Word Web site appear in a shared border, although Word does not use that term to describe it. The border remains in the same place no matter what page of the site you access.

DID YOU KNOW?

- Word allows you to create basic Web sites but provides few enhancement options. It is, however, simple to use.
- FrontPage allows you to create high-quality, professional, and user-friendly Web pages and sites, and also contains Web management tools and numerous enhancement options.
- FrontPage is included in Office XP.

NOTE

Only the basic elements of creating a Web site using Word and FrontPage will be covered in this unit.

Use Windows Explorer to Manage Files; Search for Files

EXERCISE 6

Directions

1. Start Windows Explorer.
   a. Click **Start.**
   b. Click **Programs.**
   c. Click **Windows Explorer.** The Windows Explorer screen opens, as shown in Figure 6.1a (Windows XP) and Figure 6.1b (Windows 2000) on page 33.

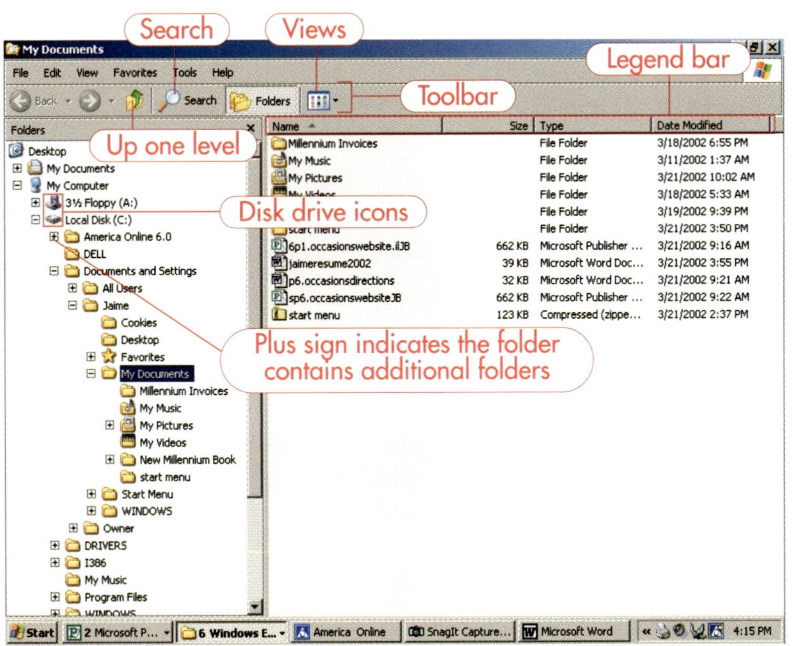

Figure 6.1a Windows Explorer (Windows XP)

VOCABULARY

Windows Explorer
File extension

NOTE

The left pane displays folders in the currently selected drive. The right pane displays the contents of the drive or folder selected in the left pane. A plus sign (+) to the left of a folder indicates that the folder contains additional folders. A folder that does not display a plus sign indicates that the folder contains only files.

DID YOU KNOW?

- Every program allows you to create and save files. Files are stored inside your computer in folders. Sometimes folders contain other folders.
- Windows contents are organized by drive letter, folder name, and then file name.
- In this exercise, you will display folders using different views, you will open folders, and you will create and rename a folder.

Plan a Web Site; Create a Web Site Using a Word Wizard; Add Web Pages and Navigation

EXERCISE 6

SCANS

Directions

1. Note the structure of this site as described and illustrated in the Concept Builders.
2. Open Word. In the New Document task pane, click **General Templates;** in the Web Pages tab, select **Web Page Wizard.**
3. Click **Next** to access the Title and Location option.
   a. Enter `Food Fantasy Magazine` as the Web site title.
   b. Enter the Web site location where the files will reside.

VOCABULARY

Web site
Home page
Link bars
Navigation
Shared border

INTERNET CONCEPT BUILDERS

- A ***Web site*** is made up of many Web pages connected by hyperlinks. The hyperlinks allow visitors to jump back and forth between the pages in the site.
- Before developing your site on the computer, it is important to create a plan first that includes the site's objective or goal, and its content, structure, and design.
- Use a diagram to plan the structure or hierarchy of the site. Draw arrows from page to page to show how the pages will link or interact with each other.
- The hierarchy of the site in this exercise is illustrated here. Refer to it when you are constructing this Web site.
- The first page of a Web site is the home page. The ***home page*** is the introduction to the site and contains hyperlinks to key pages within the site. Each page within the Web site usually contains a link back to the home page. The home page is identified in the Web folder by the name "index.htm."
- Word contains a wizard to help you build a Web site. It also contains Web page templates that include font formatting, bulleted lists, and tables to align text on a page.
- Web sites usually contain ***link bars,*** which are hyperlinks that appear in the same place on every page of a Web site. This ***navigation*** tool provides the visitor an easy and consistent way to view and move around the site. Link bars are automatically created when you build a site using a wizard.

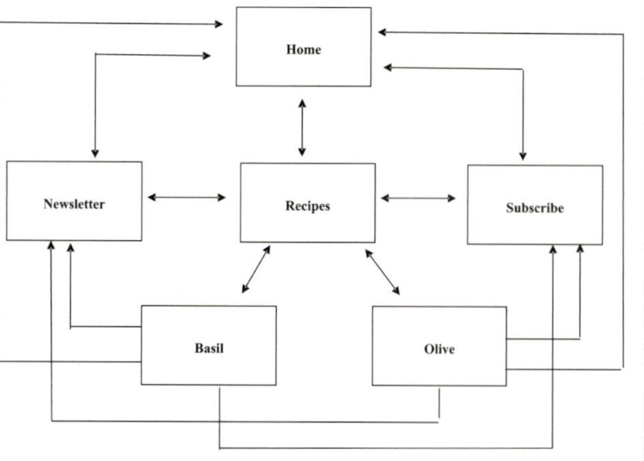

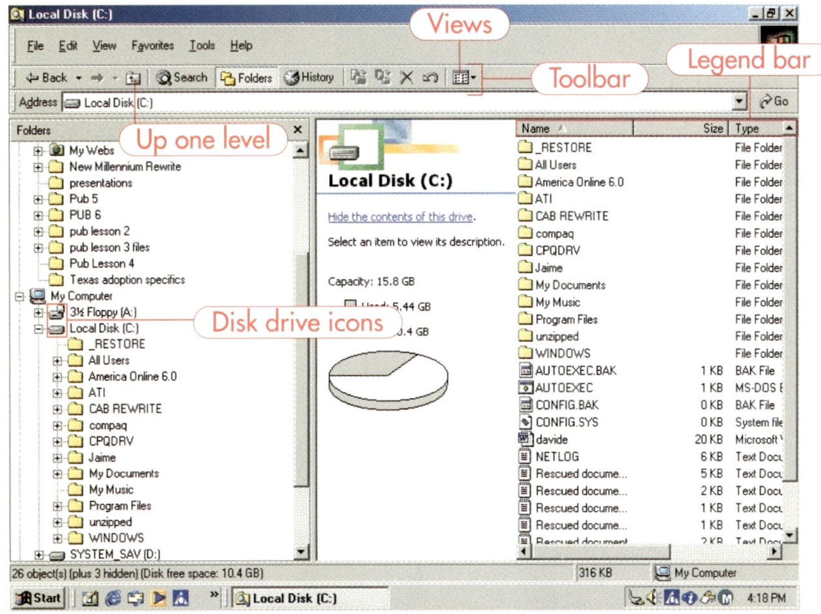

Figure 6.1b Windows Explorer (Windows 2000)

2. Double-click the **C** drive in the left pane and notice the folders contained in that drive. (If the C drive is not showing, double-click **My Computer** to display it.)
NOTE: *The plus sign has turned into a minus (–) sign. A minus sign indicates that the contents of the folder are displayed.*

3. Scroll down the left pane. Double-click **Program Files.**
NOTE: *The program files listed in the right pane are the application files contained on your computer.*

4. Double-click the **My Documents** folder in the left pane.
NOTE: *The folder opens and displays its contents in the right pane.*

5. Change the way the folders are displayed.
   a. Click the **View** button on the toolbar.
   b. Click **Tiles.** (**Windows 2000 Users:** Click **Large Icons.**)
   c. Click **Icons.** (**Windows 2000 Users:** Click **Small Icons.**)
   d. Click **List.**
   e. Click **Details.**

CONCEPT BUILDERS

- ***Windows Explorer*** is a Windows tool that allows you to look inside your computer and view its contents—that is, you can easily see files and folders.
- The menus within Windows Explorer help you to manage files and folders. You can create a new folder, as well as move, copy, delete, search for, or rename a file or folder.
- The Windows Explorer toolbar provides quick access to frequently used features.
- The icon to the left of a file name identifies the file's type. For example, a file that displays a "W" icon next to its name is a Microsoft Word file.
- File types are also identified by a three-character ***file extension.*** The file extension .doc indicates a Word file; the file extension .xls indicates an Excel file.

HOT TIPS

- You can start a program from Windows Explorer.
- When entering a file name for the search, you may use a wildcard symbol for characters you do not know. For example, if you are looking for a file with a name that ends with the word "memo," but you do not know the full name, you can enter *memo.doc. The asterisk replaces any number of unknown characters before the word memo.

LESSON 2

Create and Enhance Web Sites

EXERCISE 6
Plan a Web Site; Create a Web Site Using a Word Wizard; Add Web Pages and Navigation

EXERCISE 7
Create and Enhance a Web Site Using a Word Wizard; Add Enhancements

EXERCISE 8
Create and Enhance a Web Site Using a FrontPage Wizard

EXERCISE 9
Create and Enhance a Web Site Using FrontPage; Add Web Pages and Navigation

EXERCISE 10
Skills Review

EXERCISE 11
Skills Review

6. To sort folders and files alphabetically by name, click the **Name** button on the Legend bar in the right pane. (Notice that folders are sorted separately from files.)
   NOTE: *You can also sort files by size, type, or date by clicking the Size, Type, or Modified button.*

7. To create and name a new folder in the C drive:
   a. Double-click the **C** drive.
   b. Click **File, New.**
   c. Select **Folder.** The new folder is created and positioned at the bottom of the list of folders in the right pane, as shown in Figure 6.2.

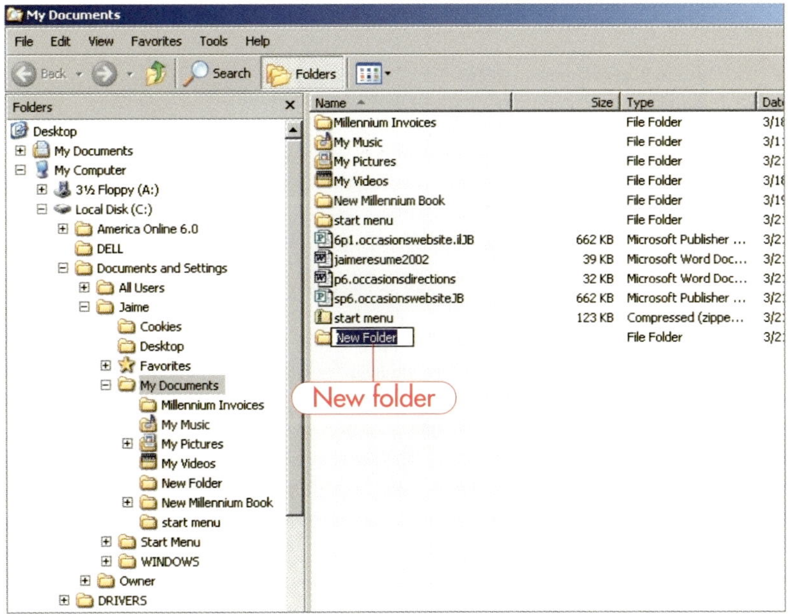

Figure 6.2 New folder

   d. Enter `My Files` in the new folder box and press the **Enter** key.
   e. Click the **Name** button on the Legend bar to list the new folder in the correct alphabetical order.

CONCEPT BUILDERS

- If you know the name of a file but do not know where it is located, you can use the Search feature in Windows Explorer to find it. You can search for a file by its file name or, if you do not remember the file name, you can search for it using unique text that you know is in the file. When you click the Search button, a Search Companion pane appears in which you can specify a search criterion.

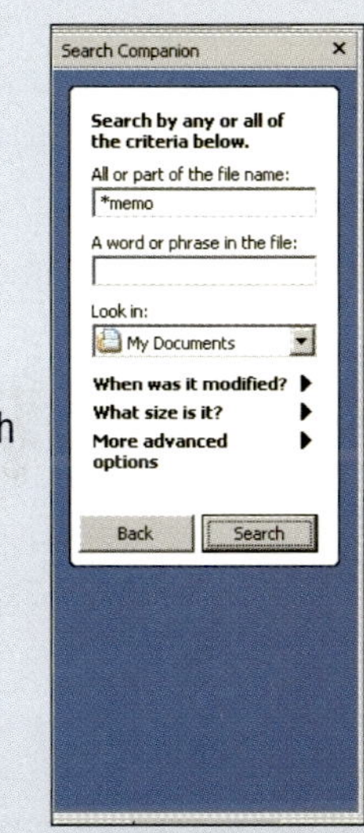

- You can also search for a file from within an Office application. To search for a file, click File, Search on the menu, or click the Search button on the Standard toolbar. This displays the Basic Search task pane, where you can specify a search criterion.

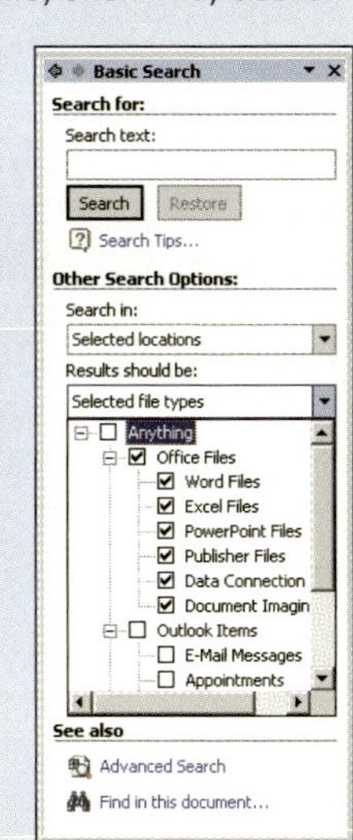

Directions *continued*

10. Return to Web page view.

11. Save the file; name it **1.5recipeweb**; change the page title to: `Recipes`

12. Print one copy of the page.
    NOTE: *The illustration shown is a printed Web page. Printed pages will differ from those viewed in a browser.*

13. Close all files.

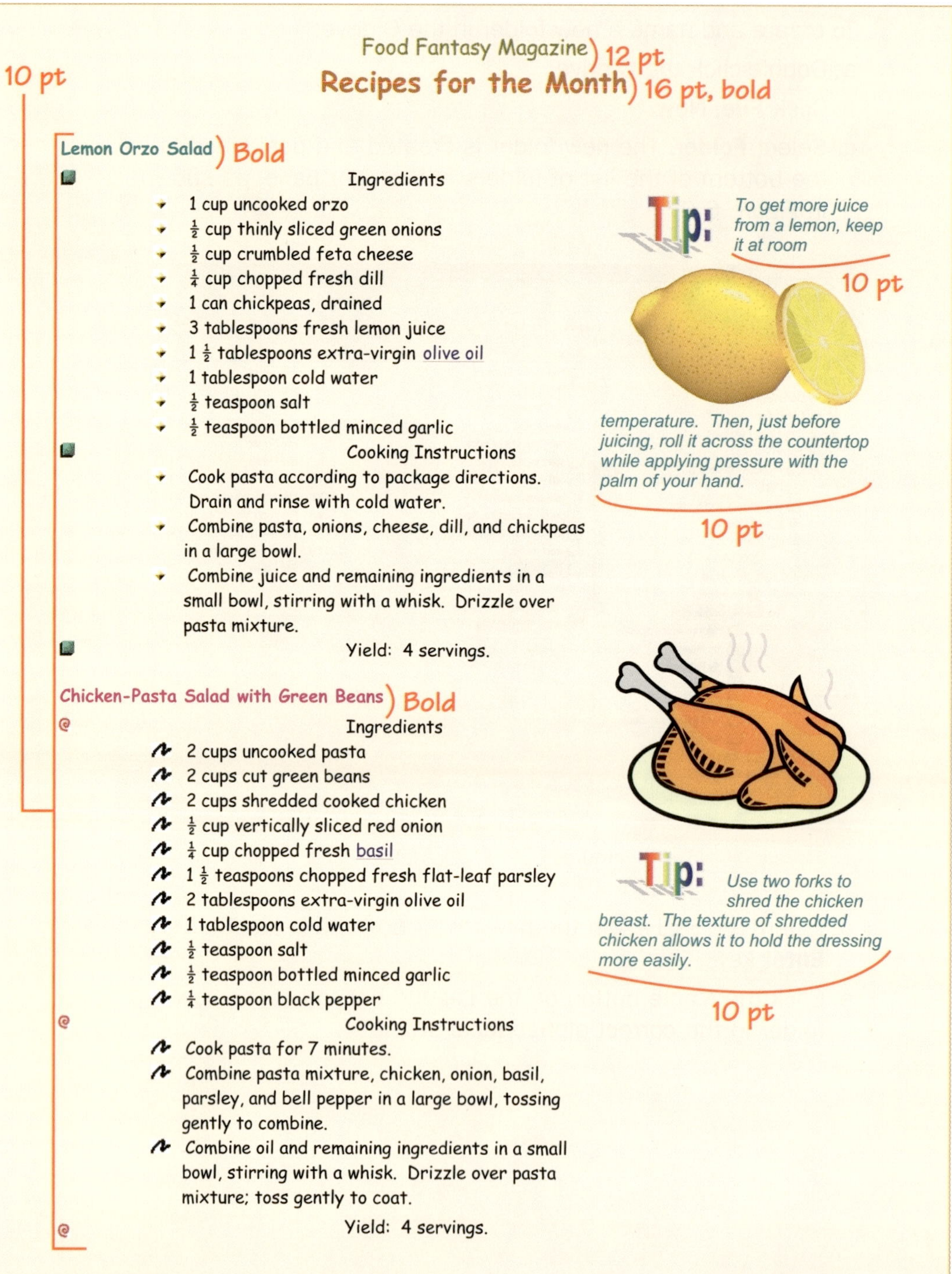

Directions *continued*

8. Rename the new folder you just created.
   a. Scroll up to find the folder.
   b. Place your mouse pointer on the new folder icon and right-click.
   c. Select **Rename.**
   d. Enter your name and press the **Enter** key.
   e. Click the **Name** button on the Legend bar to list the folder in the correct alphabetical order.
9. Click **My Computer** in the left pane.
10. Click the **Search** button.
   a. Click to search for **All files and folders.**
   b. Enter your name in the All or part of the of the file name box.
   c. Click the Look in list arrow and click Local Hard Drive (C:). **NOTE:** *If you have not updated to Windows XP, click the Look in list arrow and click Local Disk (C:).*
   d. Click Seach and notice the search results.
11. Close Windows Explorer.

Create a Web Page Using a Word Web Template; Link Files

EXERCISE 5

Directions

SCANS

1. Open a new blank Word document.
2. Access the Web templates and select the Right-aligned Column layout.
3. Set the left and right margins to .5".
4. Create the Web page shown in the illustration on page 375.
5. To create the left column, do the following:
   a. Set the font to Comic Sans.
   b. Set the font sizes as shown.
   c. Enter the text as shown, using any graphic bullets you prefer.
   d. Apply any color you prefer to the heading text.
   e. Apply a color scheme that complements those you used in Exercises 1 and 3.
   f. Insert a hyperlink on the words "olive oil" to: www.oliveoilsource.com
6. To create the right column, do the following:
   a. Insert two graphics that support the recipes' content. Apply a Square text-wrap and position the graphics as shown.
   b. Enter the caption text as shown.
   c. Create any WordArt design you prefer in 18 pt for the word `Tip`. Apply a Square text-wrap and position the graphics within the text as shown.
   d. Insert a hyperlink on the word "basil" to: http://www.gardenandhearth.com/Gardening/Growing Herbs/basil.htm
7. Apply an attractive textured background to the page.
8. Preview the page in your browser.
9. Make any necessary adjustments.

CONCEPT BUILDERS

While each template is formatted differently, all templates use a table format.

NOTE

- You can add attractive graphic bullets to your Web page, which you can find in the clip art collection.
- To change a bullet style, click Format, Bullets and Numbering, click Customize, and select Picture from the Customize dialog box. Then enter `Bullets` in the Search box. You can choose a bullet style from those that appear, and it will become a bullet style choice in the Bullets and Numbering dialog box.
- You can also add attractive graphic lines to your Web page, which are also part of the clip art collection. Enter `Lines` in the Search box. You can choose a line style from those that appear.

Orientation

END-OF-UNIT ASSESSMENT

MULTIPLE CHOICE

Make the selection that best responds to the following statements:

1. Most mouse actions require the use of the ______ mouse button.

A. Left
B. Right

2. A dimmed menu item indicates:

A. The option is currently selected.
B. A dialog box is forthcoming.
C. Another submenu follows.
D. Menu items are not available for selection at this time.

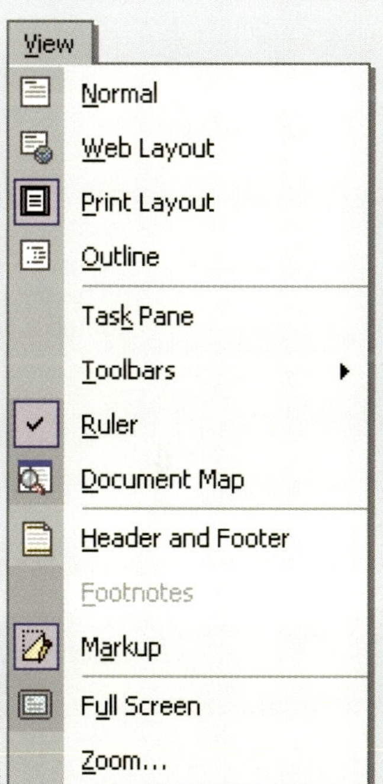

3. An ellipsis mark (. . .) means:

A. The option is currently selected.
B. A dialog box is forthcoming.
C. Another submenu follows.
D. Menu items are not available for selection at this time.

4. A check mark or bullet next to a submenu item means:

A. The option is currently selected.
B. A dialog box is forthcoming.
C. Another submenu follows.
D. Menu items are not available at this time.

5. You can close a dialog box without making changes to it by:

A. Clicking the Cancel button.
B. Clicking the Close button (X) to the right of the title bar.
C. Right-clicking the dialog box and then clicking Delete.
D. A and B

Directions *continued*

12. Save the file; name it **1.4ski**.
    NOTE: *If you are not working with a Web page template, save your file in HTML format.*
13. View the page in your browser and test the links.
14. Print one copy of the page.
    NOTE: *The illustration is a printed Web page. Printed pages will differ from those viewed in a browser.*
15. Close the browser.
16. Close Word.

You must use graphics that are formatted as .gif or .jpg files in a Web page document.

TRAVEL TOURS AND ITINERARIES

Presents...

SKI ITALY

25% DISCOUNT for a limited time!

Winter is just around the corner. TRAVEL TOURS AND ITINERARIES is offering outstanding prices for a week long trip to SKI ITALY. If you book at any of the following Italian ski resorts by October 31, you will receive a 25% DISCOUNT!!! Dates for travel (for this special ONLY) are as follows:
December 1-7
December 14-21
January 15-22
February 2-8

CORTINA D'AMPEZZO

Famous for its extraordinary beauty, winter polo games, and sophisticated travelers, Cortina D'Ampezzo is a top-notch ski resort located just 25 miles south of Austria.

- Five days/six nights, including lift ticket
- U.S. $1,450-$2,100
- Accommodations at the Park Hotel Faloria

COURMAYEUR

Historic, charming, and located on the Italian side of Mont Blanc, Courmayeur not only offers impeccable skiing conditions, but local mineral springs as well.

- Five days/six nights, including lift ticket
- U.S. $1,180-$1,900
- Accommodations at the Palace Bron Hotel

For more information or to book your trip to Italy, call us at
1-800-555-TTAI — Insert a bookmark

6. Pre-established settings within the software are called:

A. Sizes.
B. Defaults.
C. Pitch.
D. Codes.

7. Selecting the Zoom option from the View menu allows you to:

A. Set the magnification of data on the screen by a specific percentage.
B. Maximize the window.
C. Restore the window.
D. Minimize the window.

8. Use the ____________ to change the size of the window display.

A. Maximize button.
B. Minimize button.
C. Restore button.
D. All of the above

9. The active window has a:

A. Darker text area.
B. Active title bar.
C. Brighter text area.
D. Dimmed title bar.

10. Press the______key in any software or within any application to access Help.

A. F1
B. Esc
C. F10
D. Alt

Create a Web Page Using a Word Web Template; Link Files

EXERCISE 4

SCANS

Directions

1. Open Word.
2. Click **File, New.**
   a. Click the **General Templates** link in the New Document task pane and click the **Web Pages** tab in the Templates dialog box. **Word 2000 Users:** Select a Web page template.
   b. Select a simple layout, if this is available.
   Or:
   - Create a new blank document.
3. Enter the text as shown in the illustration on page 373.
   a. If you are using a template, replace the existing text.
   b. If you are not using a template, set 2.5" left and right margins.
4. Use any font, font size, and color you prefer to create the heading text.
5. Select the text "CORTINA D'AMPEZZO." Create a hyperlink to: http://www.skiitaly.com/cortina/newpic/htm/pic4.htm
6. Select the text "Park Hotel Faloria." Create a hyperlink to: http://www.phfaloria.com/pf-frm_e.htm
7. Select the text "COURMAYEUR." Create a hyperlink to: http://www.courmayeur.com/socpic/htm/index.htm
8. Select the text "Palace Bron Hotel." Create a hyperlink to: http://www.igluski.com/property/propertyinfo.cfm?pid=3591
9. Insert a bookmark on the last line of the document; name it: `MAILPHONE`
10. Select the text "Travel Tours and Itineraries." Create a hyperlink to the MAILPHONE bookmark.
11. Apply a theme to the page.

VOCABULARY

Web page template

INTERNET CONCEPT BUILDERS

- Like other templates, Web page templates contain formatting that is applicable to the Web.
- You can apply a background color, theme, and/or style to a Web page template.
- Web page templates sometimes include text that is formatted as a hyperlink.
- You can test a Web document in your browser to be sure all the links work.

TRUE / FALSE

Circle **T** if the statement is true or **F** if the statement is false.

T F 1. A file's path is a specific location on the computer where the file can be found.

T F 2. Files are saved in folders.

T F 3. Most file names have four-letter extensions.

T F 4. Windows Explorer allows you to see the contents of each drive and folder on your computer or network.

T F 5. The icon next to a file name identifies the file type.

T F 6. File names and file extensions are separated by a period.

T F 7. Toolbars are used to access the most commonly used tasks.

T F 8. Click the right mouse button when the pointer is on an object to display a shortcut menu.

T F 9. You can access menu options only by clicking the name of the option with the mouse.

T F 10. If you change a default setting, each time you open the file the settings will remain in effect until you make another change.

Directions *continued*

8. Make any necessary adjustments.
9. Close all files.

INTERNET CONCEPT BUILDERS

- You must be in Web layout view and Design mode to create a Web form in Word. Once in Web layout view, click the Design Mode button on the Web Tools toolbar. Now you are ready to create your form.
- To insert a form control, position the insertion point at the location you want and click the appropriate control on the Web Tools toolbar. When you insert a form control, "Top of Form" and "Bottom of Form" boundaries are inserted above and below the control (if you clicked the Design Mode button). You create your form between these boundaries.
- After you insert a form control, click the Properties button on the Web Tools toolbar. The Properties dialog box opens, in which you can customize the form control. To display text to appear in the drop-down box, click in the textbox next to Display Values. Enter the text you want to display. Use a semicolon to separate the items.
- The boundaries appear only in Design view, not when the page is viewed in a Web browser.
- You must always have a Submit button (which you can create using the Submit or Submit with Image control) on a Web form. Without a Submit button, there is no way to send the information to the Web server.
- You can customize the name of the Submit button. After creating the form, click the Exit Design Mode button on the Web Tools toolbar.
- Once you create the form, you must save it as a Web page.

IDENTIFY

Identify common parts of a Windows screen. Write the letter of the screen element next to its name.

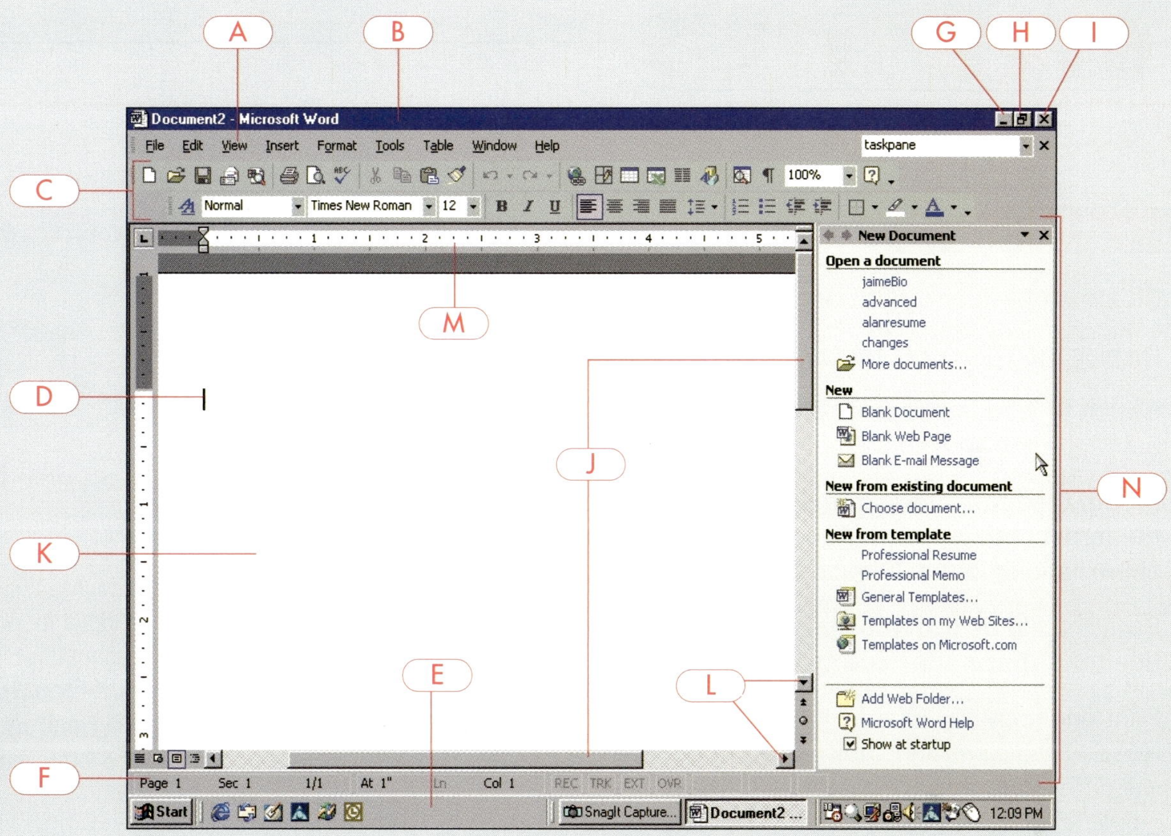

1.___Title bar
2.___Menu bar
3.___Taskbar
4.___Document text area
5.___Scroll buttons
6.___Insertion point
7.___Toolbars
8.___Task pane (not applicable to Office 2000 users)
9.___Status bar
10.___Minimize
11.___Scroll box
12.___Ruler
13.___Close
14.___Restore

Create a Web Form in Word

EXERCISE 3

Directions

SCANS

1. Create a new blank Word document.
2. Display the Web Tools toolbar.
3. Switch to Web layout view. Click to select the **Design Mode** button on the Web Tools toolbar.
4. Create the form shown in the illustration on page 371 using the form controls noted. Add the appropriate credit card abbreviations in the "Please charge my" drop-down box.
5. Save the file as a Web page; name it **1.3formweb**. Change the title to: `Subscribe today!`
6. Print one copy.
   NOTE: *The illustration shown is a printed version. Printed versions will differ from those viewed in a browser.*
7. Preview the page in your browser.

VOCABULARY

Form
Controls
Web Tools toolbar

NOTE

- The instructions in this lesson were developed for Word; however, you may adapt this lesson to FrontPage. A Form Wizard is available in FrontPage to guide you through the form-creation process.

CONCEPT BUILDERS

- A ***form*** is a document that contains fill-in blanks or fields that you use to submit information.
- Word allows you to create printed or online forms. Forms used on the Web allow you to collect information from those who visit your site.
- ***Controls*** are objects such as textboxes, checkboxes, scroll bars, or command buttons that allow a user to complete a form.
- The ***Web Tools toolbar*** contains standard Web form controls and other buttons that help you create a form. To display the Web Tools toolbar, click View, select Toolbars, and click Web Tools.

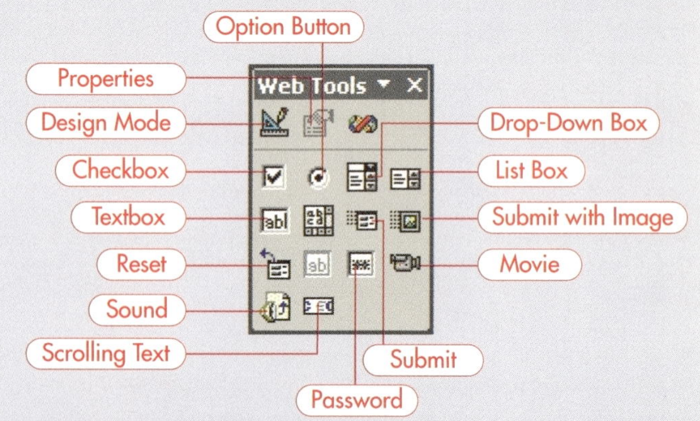

Continued on next page

IDENTIFY

Identify common parts of a dialog box. Write the letter of the dialog box part next to its name.

1.___Title bar
2.___List box
3.___Help
4.___Text box
5.___Tabs
6.___Command buttons
7.___Close
8.___Increment box
9.___Check box
10.___Drop-down list box
11.___Option buttons
12.___Preview window

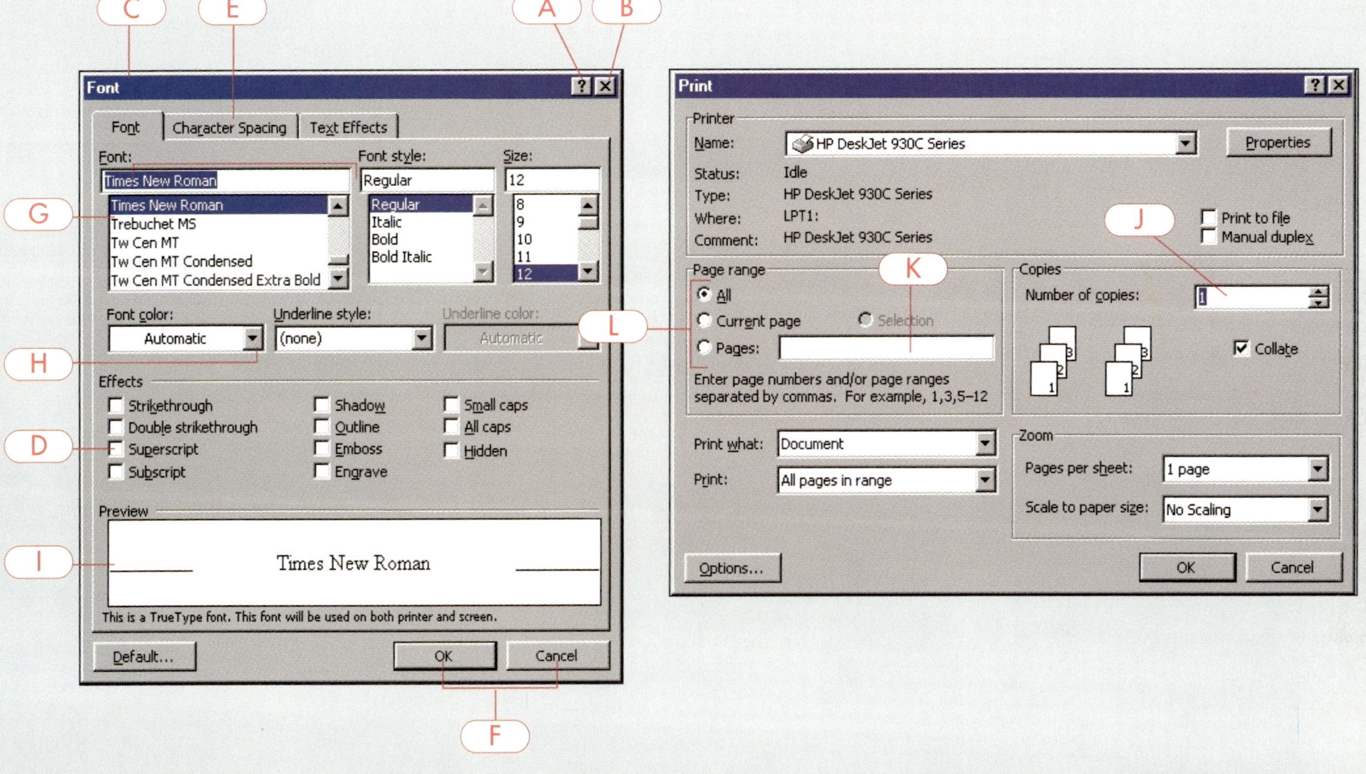

ESSAY

1. **Explain the purpose of Windows Explorer.**

2. **Explain the various ways you can get help.**

CONCEPT BUILDERS

- Navigation control icons always appear in the browser to help you navigate through a presentation.
- Action buttons allow you to navigate forward or backward through the slides when they are displayed in full-screen view. Action buttons are inserted on slides by the user as another navigation device.

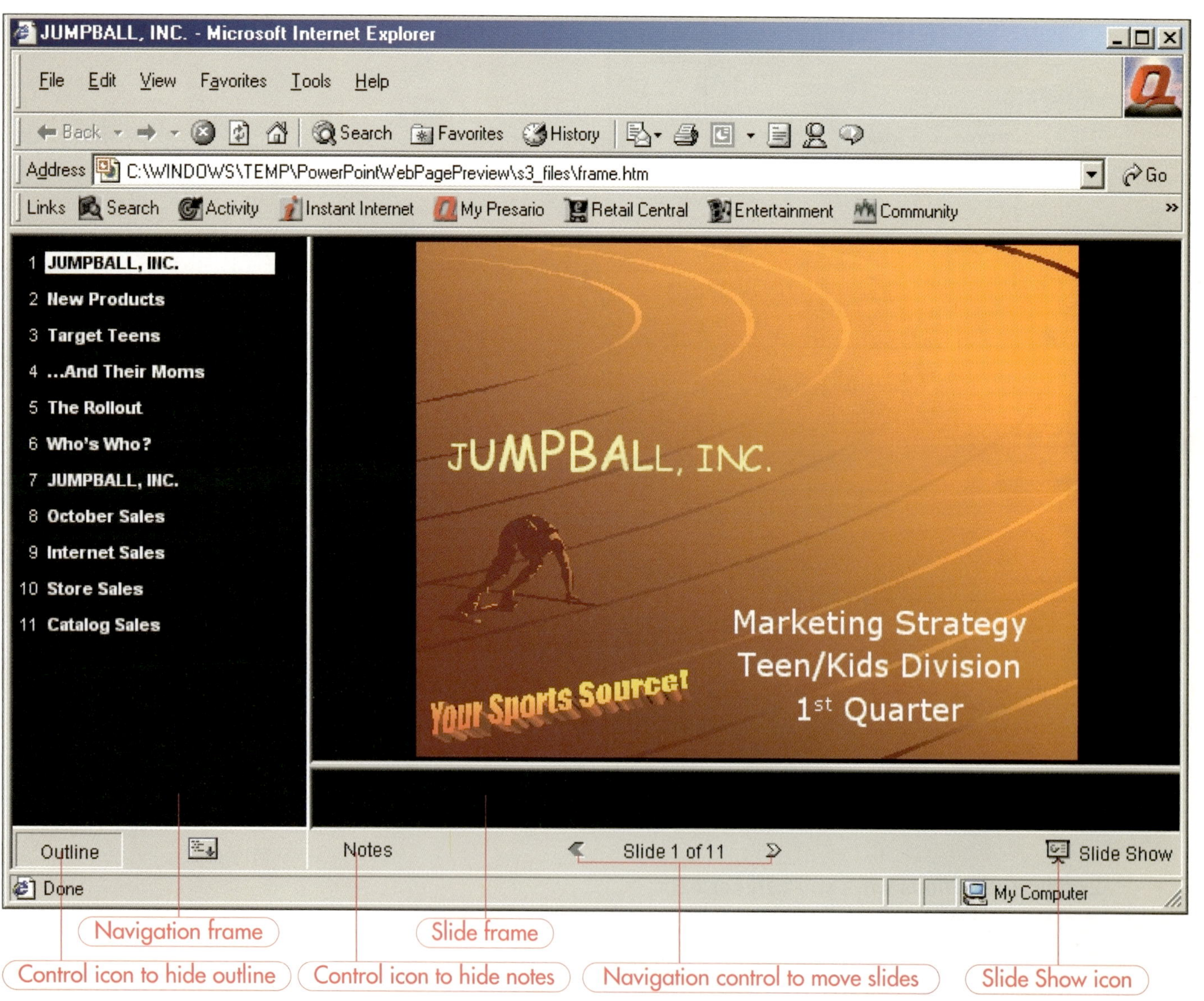

UNIT TWO
WORD PROCESSING

Save a PowerPoint Presentation as a Web Page; Use Action Buttons

EXERCISE 2

SCANS

Directions

1. Open **d1.2jbmarketweb** from the Data CD. 
2. Insert action buttons on the 1st and 7th slides for navigating through the presentation (action buttons were inserted on remaining slides in a previous lesson).
3. Save the file as a Web page; name it **1.2jbmarketweb**.
4. Preview the page in your browser.
5. Hide the outline.
6. Click the navigation control icon to display Slide 2.
7. Click the Slide Show control icon to display full-screen view.
8. Click the forward action button to view the slide show.
9. Test all the links.
10. Close the browser.
11. Close all files.

VOCABULARY

Frames

CONCEPT BUILDERS

- Web pages often display ***frames,*** which are regions or sub-windows on the page. You can size and/or scroll through a frame, and a frame can have a border.
- When you view a presentation saved as a Web page in a browser, the presentation automatically appears with the following:
  - A navigation frame, which is actually the outline of your presentation.
  - A slide frame, which contains the actual slide.
  - A control icon, which allows you to hide the outline of the presentation.
  - A Notes icon, which allows you to show or hide the notes pane.
  - Navigation controls, which allow you to move the slides forward or backward.
  - A Slide Show icon, which allows you to see the slide as a full screen, as it appears in slide show view.

Continued on next page

LESSON 1

Create and Save Documents

EXERCISE 1
Create a Document; Correct Spelling; Save and Close a Document

EXERCISE 2
Create a Document; Correct Spelling; Use Smart Tags; Save and Close a Document

EXERCISE 3
Create a Document; Use Spell and Grammar Check; Save and Close a Document

EXERCISE 4
Create a Document; Use the Tab Key; Use Spell and Grammar Check; Use Smart Tags; Save and Close a Document

EXERCISE 5
Create a Business Letter; Use Print Preview; Print

EXERCISE 6
Create a Business Letter; Use Print Preview; Print

Food for Thought

Spring 2004
Volume 1, Issue 10

A newsletter for food enthusiasts published by *Food Fantasy Magazine*

Guidelines for Eating Healthy

Eating a balanced diet is essential for you and your family to live a fitter and healthier life. Follow these guidelines and eat a variety of different foods using the food pyramid as a guide.

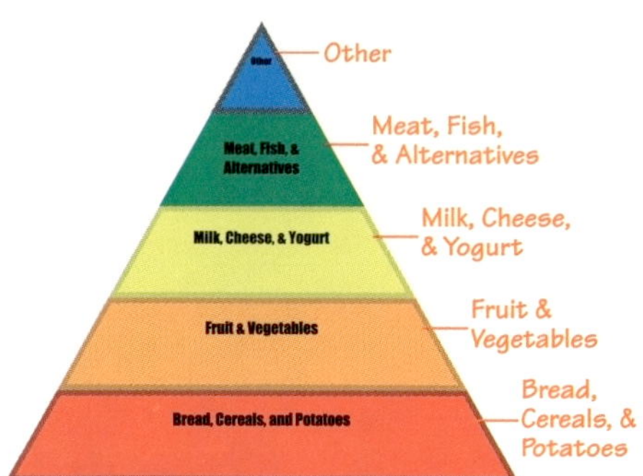

- Eat the right amount of food and exercise regularly.
- Eat four or more portions of fruits and vegetables every day.
- Eat foods rich in starch – bread, cereals, potatoes, pasta, and rice.
- Eat foods rich in fiber – bread, cereals, potatoes, fruit, and vegetables.
- Eat less fat, especially saturated fats. Make low-fat choices whenever possible.
- If you drink or eat snacks containing sugar, limit the number of times you have them throughout the day.
- Use a variety of seasonings – try not to rely on salt to flavor your foods.

Food and Energy

Balancing the energy you take in as food and the energy you use up through physical activity is the key to maintaining a healthy weight. Therefore, choose foods that provide lots of nourishment, but are low in fat, like breads, cereals, potatoes, rice, and pasta; low-fat milk and cheese, eggs, and yogurts; lean meat, fish, poultry; and peas and beans.

Eat as little as possible from the top shelf of the food pyramid, as these foods contain lots of energy but provide little nourishment. Look for low-fat and sugar-free choices when shopping.

Fruit & More Fruit

Fruit—yummy, high in fiber, and packed with Vitamins A, C, and E, and minerals. Fruit is also low in calories and virtually fat-free.

When making your shopping list, add up your fruit and vegetable choices and make sure that you have included at least four servings, each day, for all of your family.

Foods Rich in Fiber

It is very important to get enough fiber in the food you eat. There are two main types of fiber. Wheat fiber has a laxative effect and soluble fiber, such as oat fiber, may help reduce cholesterol levels and protect against heart disease. It is best to eat a variety of fiber-rich foods from bread, cereals (especially whole-grain), potatoes, fruit, and vegetables. Choose plenty of whole-meal breads and whole-grain breakfast cereals for added fiber. Eat whole-grain or bran-type breakfast cereals more often, instead of sugar or honey-coated cereals. Biscuits made with whole-grain flour, oatmeal, and raisins provide more fiber than other types. When you eat potatoes, try to eat them with their skins, which have added fiber. Dried fruits, such as prunes, apricots, raisins, and currants, are an excellent source of fiber, too.

Create a Document; Correct Spelling; Save and Close a Document

EXERCISE 1

Directions

1. Create a new document.
2. Use the default settings.
3. Begin the exercise at the top of your screen.
4. Key the paragraph shown below, allowing the text to word-wrap.
5. Correct spelling errors, if necessary.
6. Save the file; name it **1.1begin**.
7. Close the document window.

VOCABULARY

Word-wrap

CONCEPT BUILDERS

- As you enter text, the insertion point automatically advances to the next line. This is called ***word-wrap.***
- Space twice after punctuation that ends a sentence.

After creating a document, it is important to give the document a name so that you can identify it later. It is not necessary to press Enter at the end of a line of text. The words will "wrap" to the next line. Use Backspace to make an immediate correction.

NOTE

Spelling Corrections

- Correct immediate errors by pressing the Backspace key (or the Delete key).
- A red wavy line indicates a possible misspelled word. Correct these flagged errors using the shortcut menu (right-click the flagged error) and then select the correct spelling from the shortcut menu.
- You will learn to use the Spelling and Grammar option on the Tools menu later.

Use the Help Index

How do I...?	**Enter the keyword(s)**
Save a document (file)	Save
Check spelling	Spell check

Directions *continued*

7. Size it to 3.11" high by 3.11" wide.
8. Save the file; name it **1.1pyramid**.
9. Insert the article text and pyramid where appropriate. The article text can be found on the Data CD under the file names **d1.1guidelines for eating healthy**, **d1.1energy**, **d1.1fiber**, and **d1.1fruit**.

10. Use the headlines shown.
11. Use any font style.
12. Use a 48 pt font size for the newsletter title; use a 20 pt font size for the "Guidelines for Eating Healthy" headline; use a 12 or 14 pt font size for the other headlines; use a 10 pt font size for the article text; and use 10 pt for the newsletter date and volume information.
13. Apply any color to the table cells that supports your design.
14. Use any graphics or photos that support your design.
15. Apply a Square Left or Right wrap option.
    NOTE: *If you want to overlay a graphic on another graphic (as shown with the shaded circles and fruit), you must use the "In front of text" wrap option.*
16. Apply borders to the graphics (as shown in the bread photo), if you want.
17. Apply any background or theme that supports your design and/or color scheme.
    NOTE: *This may cause some of the text to shift. Make any adjustments necessary.*
18. Remove all border lines.
19. Save the file; name it **1.1foodnewsletter**.
20. Print one copy.
21. Save the file as a Web page; name it **1.1foodwebpage**.
    NOTE: *After the Save process, items on the page may shift. Make any adjustments necessary in Web layout view.*
22. Preview the page in your browser.
23. Close the file; save the changes.

NOTE

- Word automatically creates a folder containing any graphics associated with the Web page during the Save process and links these graphic files to the HTML document. Be careful when moving or renaming graphics associated with the Web document. Otherwise, the page will appear without the graphic components.
- If you know you want to use a Word document as a Web page, it is recommended that you create the document within a table format. This will insure that the graphics and text stay in place when the file is converted to HTML format.
- Creating a Web page does not mean the page has been posted to the Web. Publishing, or uploading a page to the Web, is an entirely separate process.

EXERCISE 2

Create a Document; Correct Spelling; Use Smart Tags; Save and Close a Document

Directions

1. Create a new document.
2. Use the default settings.
3. Begin the exercise at the top of your screen.
4. Key the paragraphs shown below, allowing the text to word-wrap. Press the **Enter** key twice to create a new paragraph.
5. Correct spelling errors, if necessary.
6. **Word 2000 Users:** Skip this step. Position the insertion point over the phone number, click the **Smart Tag Actions** button, and view the actions.
7. Save the file; name it **1.2thankyou**.
8. Close the document window.

Thank you for taking time to meet with me last Monday. I have enclosed three copies of my resume and writing samples.

If I can provide you with any information or materials, please contact me at (212) 555-5555. I admire the work you do at WEB-ONE Interactive, and I hope I will have the opportunity to work with you in the future.

VOCABULARY

Smart tags

CONCEPT BUILDERS

- Press the Enter key at the end of a short line or to begin a new paragraph.
- ***Smart tags*** appear as purple dotted lines beneath names, addresses, phone numbers, dates, and times. Resting the insertion point over a smart tag displays a Smart Tag Actions button, which gives you access to e-mail and Outlook. **This feature is not available to Word 2000 users.**
- A smart tag below a phone number gives you access to Outlook's Contacts list.

NOTE

Smart Tags

To check to see that smart tags are turned on and will appear below names, addresses, phone numbers, dates, and times, click Tools, AutoCorrect Options. Click the Smart Tags tab and click all the check boxes below Recognizers.

Use the Help Index

How do I...?	Enter the keyword(s)
Use smart tags	Smart

Save a Word Document as a Web Page; Apply a Background or Theme; Preview a Web Page

EXERCISE 1

SCANS

Directions

1. Open a new blank Word document.
2. Set the page size to 8.5" by 14".
3. Set the left, right, top, and bottom page margins to .5".
4. Create the newsletter shown in the illustration on page 367. **NOTE:** *The illustration shown is the printed solution before the theme is applied. This may not look like your final solution, particularly if you create your own layout design.*
5. Use a table format and design it as you prefer, using the illustration as a guide. You will need to merge cells where necessary.
6. Create the pyramid using the text shown. Format it in any way that supports your color scheme.

VOCABULARY

HTML (Hypertext Markup Language)
Web layout view
Web page preview

INTERNET CONCEPT BUILDERS

- Pages that you view on the Web must be in HTML format. ***HTML*** stands for ***Hypertext Markup Language,*** the language or code used to create documents for the Web.
- Once a document is saved as a Web page, the document automatically appears in Web layout view. ***Web layout view*** allows you to view a document as it appears in a browser. You can see how Word positions backgrounds, text-wraps, and graphics on a Web page (as opposed to the printed page). You can also edit the document and/or test any links in this view.
- You can use ***Web page preview*** to view a document saved as a Web page (or any .html file) in your default Web browser, even if you are not connected to the Internet. This is referred to as "working offline." You cannot edit a document in Web page preview; however, you can test the links to other pages, but not links to other URLs.
- The file name you used to save your Web page automatically appears in the title bar of the Web browser (for the entire world to see). You may not want to use the page file name as the page title. To assign a different name as the page title, click the Change Title button in the Save As dialog box and enter another name.
- Word documents generally have a white background. To add visual appeal to a document you want to use as a Web page, you can add a background or theme.
- A background allows you to apply a color, texture, pattern, or picture to the page; themes include a background with coordinated font formatting and specialized Web bullets and lines.

Create a Document; Use Spell and Grammar Check; Save and Close a Document

EXERCISE 3

Directions

1. Create a new document.
2. Use the default settings.
3. Begin the exercise at the top of your screen.
4. Deselect all AutoCorrect options.
5. Enter the paragraphs exactly as shown on page 46, including the misspelled words and grammatical errors that are circled. Allow the text to word-wrap.
6. Move the insertion point to the beginning of the document (Ctrl + Home).
7. Move the insertion point to the beginning of the first grammatical error in the second paragraph.
8. Use the shortcut menu to correct this grammatical error.
9. Move the insertion point to the end of the document using the express movement keys to do so.
10. Use the Spelling and Grammar option from the Tools menu to correct the remaining spelling and grammatical errors.
11. Save the file; name it **1.3net**.
12. Close the document window.

NOTE

Grammar Corrections

- A green wavy line indicates a possible grammatical error. Correct the first flagged grammatical error using the shortcut menu: right-click the flagged error and then select the correction from the shortcut menu.
- Use the Spelling and Grammar option from the Tools menu to correct the remaining spelling and grammatical errors.

LESSON 1

Work with Web Pages

EXERCISE 1
Save a Word Document as a Web Page; Apply a Background or Theme; Preview a Web Page

EXERCISE 2
Save a PowerPoint Presentation as a Web Page; Use Action Buttons

EXERCISE 3
Create a Web Form in Word

EXERCISE 4
Create a Web Page Using a Word Web Template; Link Files

EXERCISE 5
Create a Web Page Using a Word Web Template; Link Files

More than a million companies distirbute infromation on the Internet. Traffic on the Internet continues to grow, increasing exponentially each year.

Because of this astounnding growth in the number of users, businesses is rapidly tapping into the speed and cost savings of online communications. Therefore, it is important that you have some basic knowlege about computer's linked to the Internet.

Each computer linked to the Internet has its own addresss. To send a message to an Internet address, a special format must be used. An adddress may look something like this: msmith@sla.ohiostate.edu

Use the Help Index

How do I...?	Enter the keywords:
Check grammar	Grammar
Change AutoCorrect options	AutoCorrect

- The easiest way to move around a document is to place the insertion point where you want to be and click.
- The express movement keys can also help you move around a document quickly.
  To move to the:
  - Beginning of document: Ctrl + Home
  - End of document: Ctrl + End
  - Beginning of line: Home
  - End of line: End
  - Previous page: Ctrl + Page Up
  - Next page: Ctrl + Page Down
  - One paragraph up: Ctrl + ↑
  - One paragraph down: Ctrl + ↓

UNIT FOUR
WEB SITES

EXERCISE 4

Create a Document; Use the Tab Key; Use Spell and Grammar Check; Use Smart Tags; Save and Close a Document

Directions

1. Create a new document.
2. Use the default settings.
3. Begin the exercise at the top of your screen.
4. Press the **Tab** key once to begin each new paragraph. Enter the paragraphs shown below, including the misspelled words and grammatical errors that are circled. Allow the text to word-wrap.
5. **Word 2000 Users:** Skip this step.
   Position the insertion point over the date, click the **Smart Tag Actions** button, and view the actions.
6. Move the insertion point to the beginning of the document and then to the end of the document.
7. Move the insertion point to the end of the line and then back to the beginning of the line.
8. Correct spelling and grammatical errors.
9. Save the file; name it **1.4policy**.
10. Close the document window.

VOCABULARY

Tab

CONCEPT BUILDERS

- A ***tab*** allows the user to set a stopping point on the typing line. Each time you press the Tab key, the insertion point advances to the next tab setting. Tabs are set .5" apart across the page, which is the default. You will learn to change tab settings later.
- A smart tag below a date gives you access to the Outlook Calendar.

Tab ⟶ In an effort to maintain consistancy with our subsidiarry companies, we are revising our vacation policy.

Tab ⟶ The changes relates relates to a maximum accrual allowance of vacation days. As explained in the policy, your maximum accrual will be no more than two times your annual alllotment. This policy is effective starting September 1, 2004.

Tab ⟶ All other procedures and policies with respect to vacation and personal days remain unchanged. Of course, vacation and personal time off require your department supervisor's approval.

- HUMAN RESOURCES DEPARTMENT: Our employee of the month is administrative assistant Cynthia Gonzales. Cynthia is widely regarded, by both her peers and her supervisors, as one of the most dedicated employees at Nifty Tees. She always has a kind word to say, even when she is under deadline pressures. She always has a smile on her face and is a pleasure to work with.
- ADMINISTRATION DEPARTMENT: New medical insurance cards will be issued July 15. Please destroy your outdated card when you receive your new one. Your new cards cover both new and increased prescription drug charges. Your vision coverage remains the same. Please note that new medical claims must be sent to: Foundation for Medical Care of Kern County, 333 Palmer Street, Suite 200, Bakersfield, CA 93309.

Web-related Task: As an added incentive to read the newsletter, you have decided to add a section called IN AND AROUND SAN DIEGO. Here, you will list current cultural happenings (music and dance festivals, shows, or art exhibits). You will need to research these on the Internet.

PROJECT 1B

There will be a company BBQ on the Employees' Patio on July 7 at 12 noon. Create a flyer that will encourage all employees to attend. The Marketing Department will give away a free polo shirt to those who come. Save the file as **dtp.proj1b.flyer**.

PROJECT 1C

Create a certificate for the employee of the month, which will be presented to Cynthia Gonzales at the company BBQ. Save the file as **dtp.proj1c.certificate**.

PROJECT 2

To provide information on a variety of careers, your teacher is going to create a "Career Corner" library. The library will contain brochures and other materials on various career options.

After the completion of the Word Processing unit, you wrote a report on a career of your choice. Create a three-fold brochure on the career about which you wrote. If that file is unavailable to you, you can use **dcareerreport**, found on the Data CD. Include information that advertises or discusses the requirements, salary, responsibilities, and other interesting facts about that career.

You will deliver an oral presentation to the class on the content of your brochure. Everyone in the class will then contribute a copy of their brochure to the library.

Save the file as **dtp.proj2.brochure**.

Create a Business Letter; Use Print Preview; Print

EXERCISE 5

Directions

1. Create a new document.
2. Use the default settings.
3. With the insertion point at the top of the screen, press the **Enter** key eight times to begin the date 2.5" from the top of the page.
4. Create the full-block letter shown on page 49, including the misspelled words and grammatical errors that are circled. Allow text to word-wrap.
5. Press the **Enter** key between parts of the letter, as shown in the illustration.
6. Correct spelling and grammatical errors.
7. **Word 2000 Users:** Skip this step.
   Position the insertion point over Cathy Scruggs's name, click the **Smart Tag Actions** button, and click **Add to Contacts.** This will open Outlook's Contact dialog box with the addressee's name and address entered.
   a. Add the following e-mail address to the Contact dialog box: `cscruggs@home.net`
   b. Click **Save** and close the Contact dialog box.
8. Drag the vertical scroll box to the bottom of the scroll bar and then back to the top.
9. Click the **down** scroll arrow twice to scroll down two lines.
10. Click the up scroll arrow twice to scroll up two lines.
11. Save the file; name it **1.5hr**.
12. Preview the document.
13. Click the **Print** button on the toolbar to print one copy.
14. Close print preview; close the document.

VOCABULARY

Inside address
Salutation
Closing
Reference initials
Full-block style letter

CONCEPT BUILDERS

- The layout of a letter is called a format. There are a variety of letter formats, but most have the following parts: date, ***inside address, salutation,*** body, ***closing,*** name of sender, title of sender, and ***reference initials.*** (The first set of initials belongs to the person who created the document; the second set of initials belongs to the person who typed the document.)
- The ***full-block letter style*** is the most popular style because all parts start at the left margin.
- The dateline on most letters starts 2.5" down from the top of the page.
- To view text that is not visible in the document window, you must ***scroll*** the window up or down.
- Drag the vertical scroll box down to scroll the window up; drag the scroll box up to scroll the window down.

Desktop Publishing

END-OF-UNIT PROJECTS

PROJECT 1A

SCANS

You just moved to San Diego, California, and have landed a job as the public relations director and desktop publisher for Nifty Tees, a T-shirt company that has been in business for only two years. The company is located at 720 Ash Street, San Diego, CA 92101. It can be reached by phone and fax at its toll free numbers, 1-800-555-TEES (phone) and 1-800-666-TEES (fax). It can also be reached by e-mail (nftyt@mind.com) or the Web (www.niftytees.com).

The company would like to create a one-page company newsletter that it will publish monthly. Therefore, your first task is to design masthead for the company newsletter. Since this newsletter might be included on the Nifty Tees Web site, use a table format to create the newsletter. Save the file as **dtp.proj1a.newsletter**.

You should include the following information for this month:

- `ACCOUNTING DEPARTMENT: This month has been sensational! With the support of a great marketing and sales staff, Nifty Tees generated a net income of $17,940. An analysis of this month's sales and expenses is shown below:`

	A	B
1	Income Statement	
2	Nifty Tees	
3	June 1-30, 2004	
4		
5	Sales	$ 100,000.00
6	Less: Cost of goods sold	$ 30,000.00
7	Gross margin	$ 70,000.00
8	Less: Operating expenses	
9	Salaries	$ 25,000.00
10	Maintenance, insurance	$ 2,000.00
11	Office expenses	$ 3,000.00
12	Total operating expenses before depreciation:	$ 30,000.00
13	Operating earnings before depreciation:	$ 40,000.00
14	Depreciation expenses	$ 1,500.00
15	Operating expenses	$ 38,500.00
16	Interest expenses	$ 4,000.00
17	Earnings before income tax	$ 34,500.00
18	Income tax expenses	$ 16,560.00
19	Net income	$ 17,940.00

- `MARKETING & SALES DEPARTMENT: After a great deal of research, Nifty Tees has decided to expand its product line to include polo shirts and sweat suits. The new sales campaign will be launched with each Nifty Tees employee receiving a polo shirt at a kickoff BBQ on the Employees' Patio, to be held July 7.`

8x = 2.5"

Date — Today's date

4x

Inside address — Ms. Cathy Scruggs
67 Horatio Street
New York, NY 10003

2x

Salutation — Dear Ms. Scruggs:

2x

Body — THe Human Resources Department write job descriptions and determines salary ranges for those positions. Its the responsibility of the HR departtment to recruit the best applicants for open positions within the firm.

2x

HR staff is also responsible for dissemanating information regarding employee benifits and investment plans to staff members, for training employees, and for providing opportunities for advancement within the company.

2x

You must be an individual who like to interact with people if you want to work in the Human Resources Department.

2x

Closing — Sincerely,

4x

Name of sender — Janet Bass

Title of sender — Executive Vice President

Reference initials — jb/yo

Use the Help Index

How do I...?	**Enter the keyword(s):**
Scroll through a document	Scroll
Preview a document	Preview
Print	Print

- Drag the horizontal scroll bar left and/or right to view and move through a document that is wider than the document window.
- A smart tag below a name gives you access to Outlook's Contacts list.

ESSAY QUESTIONS

1. Explain the purpose of the drawing canvas and how you might use it.

2. Explain the difference between text boxes and paragraph borders. Give examples of when you might use each.

3. Explain when you would use a pull quote and the procedures you would use to create it.

4. Explain the difference between letter spacing and setting the width of characters, and the different effects these features have on text.

Create a Business Letter; Use Print Preview; Print

EXERCISE 6

Directions

1. Create a new document.
2. Use the default settings.
3. With the insertion point at the top of the screen, press the **Enter** key eight times to begin the date 2.5" from the top of the page.
4. Key the full-block letter shown on page 51, including the misspelled words and grammatical errors that are circled. Allow the text to word-wrap.
5. Correct spelling and grammatical errors.
6. **Word 2000 Users:** Skip this step.
   Click the **Smart Tag Options** button on the inside address and click **Add to Contacts.** This opens Outlook's Contact dialog box with the addressee's name and address entered. Add the following e-mail address to the Contact dialog box: `jthompson@mail.net`
7. Click **Save** and close the Contact dialog box.
8. Save the file; name it **1.6bp**.
9. Preview the document.
10. Click the **Print** button on the toolbar to print one copy.
11. Change the magnification to **200%.**
12. Change the magnification to **70%.** Use the IntelliMouse to do so (if it is available). Close print preview.
13. Close the document window.

HOT TIPS

- Rotate the center wheel of an IntelliMouse forward or backward to move through a document.
- Click the center wheel of an IntelliMouse to scroll down in a document automatically.

TRUE / FALSE

Circle the T if the statement is true or F if the statement is false.

T F 1. Drawing tools allow you to edit text.

T F 2. To create a shadow effect, you may stack or layer shapes.

T F 3. It is a good idea to use "dummy" text rather than real text to practice and experiment with formatting.

T F 4. Leading refers to the vertical space between lines of text as measured in inches.

T F 5. You can manipulate a text box like a graphic object.

T F 6. You can size an object by dragging a handle or by setting the size in the appropriate dialog box.

T F 7. Inline graphics move along with the text they are anchored to when you reposition text.

T F 8. Displaying gridlines allows you to place objects more precisely.

T F 9. The term "10 on 12" refers to a 12 pt font size with 10 pt leading.

T F 10. A drawn line is considered an object.

T F 11. Lines are often referred to as "rules" in desktop publishing.

T F 12. You can apply shadow and 3-D effects to lines and graphics, but not text boxes.

T F 13. You can fill both open and closed shapes with color.

T F 14. To draw a perfect circle or perfect square, hold down the Shift key as you drag the insertion point.

T F 15. Once you layer shapes, it is not possible to change their order.

Today's date

Mr. Jeffrey Thompson
500 West Lafayette Boulevard
Detroit, MI 48226

Dear Mr. Thompson:

A business plan is a desscriptive, detailed report of the business you want or intend to open. It describes the kind of products or services you want to sell and market. It also describes what it is that makes your business unique.

A good business plan also include a marketing plan, a management plan, a financial plan for the business, and financial projections (for at least five years).

The business plan play a critical role when applying for a small business loan package.

If you are planning to start your own business and need information about how to construct a business plan, you can go to the Small Business Administration's Web site where you can find detailed information about developing a business plan.

Sincerely,

Tyrone Simmons
Financing Department

ts/yo

6. **Text set off in a box, generally larger than the surrounding type, is called:**
   A. Boxed text.
   B. A hyperlink.
   C. A pull quote.
   D. Dummy text.

7. **Decorative or enlarged initial capitals are used to:**
   A. Draw the reader's attention to a paragraph.
   B. Enhance a flyer.
   C. Add dimension and richness to charts and graphs.
   D. Add a special effect to clip art.

8. **Which statement best describes desktop publishing?**
   A. Desktop publishing enables people to produce documents that look attractive.
   B. Desktop publishing is a combination of graphic design and electronic page assembly.
   C. Desktop publishing is a method of combining text and graphics to produce professional-looking documents.
   D. All of the above

9. **When wrapping text around a graphic, it is important to:**
   A. Select the object before selecting a text-wrap option.
   B. Adjust the object to avoid awkward line breaks within the text.
   C. Use a graphic from the Internet.
   D. Both A and B
   E. Both B and C

10. **The font face that would be most appropriate to use for a formal invitation would be:**
   A. Serif.
   B. Sans serif.
   C. Script.
   D. Symbol.

LESSON 2

Open and Edit Documents

EXERCISE 7
Open a Document; Insert Text; Use Print Preview

EXERCISE 8
Open a Document; Insert Text; Insert a Comment; Show/Hide Formatting Marks

EXERCISE 9
Open a Document; Delete Text; Insert a Comment; Undo an Action

EXERCISE 10
Open a Document; Insert and Delete Text; Insert a Date Automatically; Undo/Redo an Action

EXERCISE 11
Open a Document; Insert and Delete Text; Save As; Prepare an Envelope

EXERCISE 12
Open a Document; Insert and Delete Text; Save As; Delete a Comment; Prepare an Envelope

EXERCISE 13
Skills Review

EXERCISE 14
Skills Review

Desktop Publishing

END-OF-UNIT ASSESSMENT

MULTIPLE CHOICE

Make the selection that best responds to the following statements:

1. **The feature that creates one object out of individual parts is called:**
- **A.** Send to back.
- **B.** Stacking.
- **C.** Grouping.
- **D.** Layering.

2. **A logo is:**
- **A.** An object that you can flip or rotate.
- **B.** A symbol, picture, or saying that creates an image of a company.
- **C.** A screen capture.
- **D.** WordArt.

3. **An enlarged capital letter that drops below the first line of body text is referred to as:**
- **A.** An AutoShape.
- **B.** WordArt.
- **C.** A drop capital.
- **D.** A shadow effect.

4. **Any text or picture that appears behind regular text in a document is called:**
- **A.** A tint.
- **B.** A shadow effect.
- **C.** A watermark.
- **D.** None of the above

5. **The technologies available that support desktop publishing include:**
- **A.** Digital cameras.
- **B.** Scanners.
- **C.** Color printers.
- **D.** Pentium processors.
- **E.** All of the above.

Open a Document; Insert Text; Use Print Preview

EXERCISE 7

Directions

1. Open **1.1begin**, the file you created in Exercise 1, or open **d2.7begin** from the Data CD. 
2. Save the file as **2.7begin**.
3. Make the insertions shown below.
4. Correct spelling.
5. Preview the document.
6. Print one copy from the Print dialog box.
7. Close the file; save the changes.
   NOTE: *Some of the exercises in this lesson are double-spaced so edits are clearly visible. Print all final copies using the default line spacing, unless otherwise noted.*

After creating a ^any document, it is important to give the document a name so that you can identify it ^at a later ^time. It is not necessary to press ^the Enter ^key at the end of a line of text. The words will ^automatically "wrap" to the next line. ¶ Use ^the Backspace ^key to make an immediate correction.

Right-click words that display a wavy red line. Then select the correct spelling from the shortcut menu that appears.

Use the Help Index

How do I...?	**Enter the keyword(s)**
Open a file or document	Open
Resave a file or document	Save
Print a file or document	Print

CONCEPT BUILDERS

- You revise a document when you need to make corrections or adjustments to it.
- Before you can revise or edit a document, you must open it from the disk or hard drive where it is located.
- You can preview a document before printing it to see how the document will appear on the page.

DID YOU KNOW?

- Proofreaders' marks are symbols used to indicate what revisions need to be made.
  - The proofreaders' mark for insertion is: ^
  - The proofreader's mark for creating a new paragraph is: ¶
  - See Appendix D, which lists the most common proofreaders' marks.

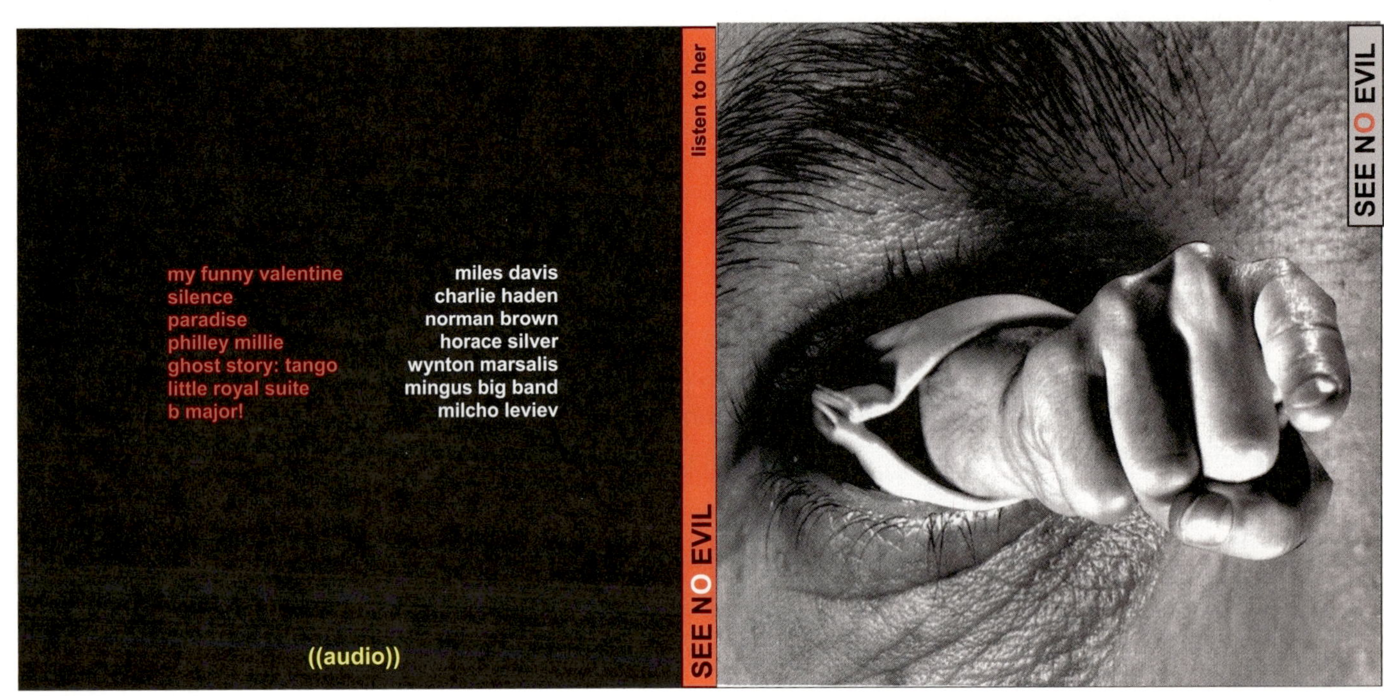

Sample solution

Open a Document; Insert Text; Insert a Comment; Show/Hide Formatting Marks

EXERCISE 8

Directions

1. Open **1.2thankyou**, the file you created in Exercise 2, or open **d2.8thankyou** from the Data CD. 
2. Save the file as **2.8thankyou**.
3. Display formatting marks.
4. Make the insertions shown below.
5. Use Overtype mode to change the phone number in the second paragraph. Return to Insert mode immediately following this step.
6. Press the **Tab** key once to begin each new paragraph.
7. Insert the following comment where indicated: `Check correct address before sending; be sure to enclose résumé and writing samples.`
8. Correct spelling errors.

VOCABULARY

Insert mode
Overtype mode
Comment

 DID YOU KNOW?

To insert international characters, click Insert, Symbol. Then select (normal text) from the Font list arrow and double-click the character you want to insert.

Tab ⟶ Thank you for taking ^[the] time ^[out of your busy schedule] to meet with me last Monday. ^[As you requested at the interview,] I have enclosed ^[Insert comment] three copies of my résumé and ^[two] writing samples.

Tab ⟶ If I can provide you with any ^[further] information ^[about myself] or materials, please ^[do not hesitate to] contact me at (212) 555-~~5555~~ [6666]. ¶ I admire the work you do at WEB-ONE Interactive, and I hope I will have the opportunity to work with you ^[and your outstanding staff] in the ^[near] future.

Skills Review

EXERCISE 29

Directions

SCANS

One of your friends loves jazz and is having a birthday. To create a special gift, you have decided to customize a CD with jazz by artists that you know he loves. You will use the Internet to find titles of songs to include on your CD. To make the gift even more special, you will design the CD cover and give it your own title. The illustration shown on page 356 is only an example. Use your creativity in designing your cover.

1. Create a new document.
2. Set the page orientation to landscape.
3. Save the file; name it **3.29cdcover**.
4. Create a CD cover using the design elements you have learned thus far.
5. Create a text box anywhere on the page.
6. Use the Internet to find seven jazz titles and artists to include on your CD. (These will be listed on the back cover of the CD.)
   a. Open your Web browser.
   b. Enter this URL: `www.cdnow.com`
   c. Review the jazz titles on this site (you can listen to them).
   d. Copy the title and artist's name that you want to include.
   e. Switch to Word.
   f. Paste the title and artist's name in the text box. (You will format and position it later. If you copied a link with the title, remove it.)
   g. Repeat Steps d – f for the remaining six artists.
   - If you do not have a live connection, use the artists and titles provided in the sample exercise illustration.
7. Complete the CD cover design.
8. Print one copy.
9. Close the file; save the changes.

HOT TIPS

- The CD cover dimensions are 4.6" high by 9.75" wide.
- The spine divides the front and back covers of the CD. It measures 4.6" high by .25" wide.

Directions *continued*

9. Hide formatting marks.
10. Print one copy.
11. Close the file; save the changes.

Use the Help Index

How do I...?	Enter the keyword(s)
Insert comments	Comment
Show/hide formatting marks	Paragraph mark
Change to Overtype mode	Typeover

CONCEPT BUILDERS

- When you insert text in ***Insert mode*** (which is the default on most word processors), existing text moves to the right.
- Press the Insert key once to change Insert mode to Overtype mode (or double-click OVR on the status bar). In ***Overtype mode,*** existing text does not move to the right; it is typed over.
- The ***Comment*** feature allows you to insert hidden notes or annotations that can be read on screen. They can be hidden when the document is printed, or printed within the document.
- In print and Web layout views, comments are entered in a comment balloon. In normal view, a Reviewing Pane opens at the bottom of the screen, in which you can enter your comment text.
- As you create a document, formatting marks are inserted. Formatting marks for paragraphs (¶), tabs (→), and spaces (·) are visible in your document (if you click Show/Hide ¶). These symbols do not appear when you print the document.

2.25" x 2.15"
6.15" x 2"
2.25" x 1.3"
.5 pt, aqua, 2.75"
Sans serif, 50 pt, yellow
jazz
.5 pt, aqua, 2.3"
Serif, 18 pt
El Rio
May 28, June 2
Music by Jorge Vasquez
Choreography by Sandra Lee and Adam Tam
Serif, 11 pt
Sans serif, 50 pt, dark red
ballet
.5 pt, aqua, 5"
Serif, 18 pt
Sundance
May 29, June 4
Music by Roger Levin
Choreography by Vanessa Powers
Serif, 11 pt
El Primavera del Sol
Serif, 18 pt
May 25, June 1
Music by Francis Herreros
Choreography by Michael Knotter
Serif, 11 pt
1.33", .5 pt, aqua
Sans serif, 50 pt, plum
tap
Van der Bek
Serif, 18 pt
May 26, May 31
Music by Rolf Wittink
Choreography by Cynthia Manning
Serif, 11 pt
Sound Factory
Serif, 18 pt
May 30, June 3
Music by Laura Belle
Choreography by Mark Cage
Serif, 11 pt
Levity
Serif, 18 pt
May 27, June 3
Music by Loren Piercy
Choreography by Alexis Regent
Serif, 11 pt
Lightening
Serif, 18 pt
May 25, June 1
Music by Latrell Melling
Choreography by Dameon Sanders and Jennifer Green
Sans serif, 11 pt
EVENT PRICES Price per event: $20, $30, $40 Entire Program: $100, $150
Serif, 11 pt

Inside page

Open a Document; Delete Text; Insert a Comment; Undo an Action

EXERCISE 9

Directions

1. Open **1.6bp**, the file you created in Exercise 6, or open **d2.9bp** from the Data CD. 
2. Save the file as **2.9bp**.
3. Change the magnification to **90%**.
4. Display formatting marks.
5. Make the indicated deletions and other changes shown on page 57.
6. Correct spelling errors.
7. Insert the following comment where indicated:
   `Check the SBA Web address.`
8. Preview the document.
9. Hide formatting marks.
10. Delete the last paragraph.
11. Undo the action.
12. Print one copy.
13. Close the file; save the changes.

Use the Help Index

How do I...?	**Enter the keyword(s)**
Delete text	Delete or edit
Undo an action	Undo

CONCEPT BUILDERS

- If you make a change to a document that you realize is a mistake, you can undo the action by clicking the Undo button on the toolbar. 
- Most software allows you to undo a series of actions–some software allows you to reverse up to 300 actions.
- Before you can delete a block of text, you must first select it.

HOT TIPS

- The quickest way to select text is by using mouse selection shortcuts. Try selecting text as follows:
  - A word: position the insertion point on the word and double-click.
  - A paragraph: position the insertion point anywhere in the paragraph and triple-click.
  - A sentence: hold down the Ctrl key and click once.

DID YOU KNOW?

- The proofreader's mark for deletion is: 
- The proofreader's mark for "Let the original stand" is: .... or "stet."

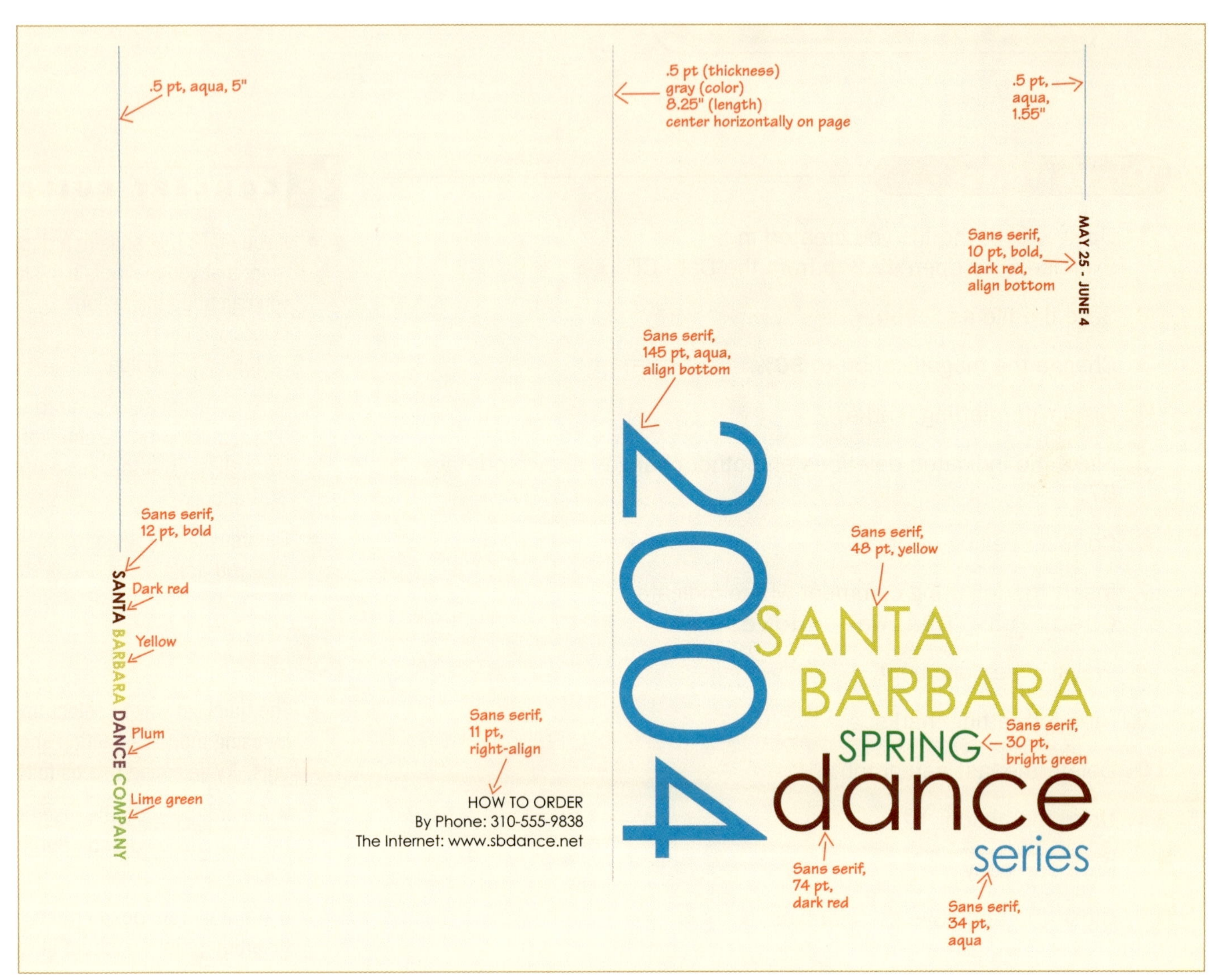

Back and front covers

Today's date

Mr. Jeffrey Thompson
500 West Lafayette Boulevard
Detroit, MI 48226

Dear Mr. Thompson:

A business plan is a descriptive, detailed report of the business you want or intend to open. It describes the kind of products or services you want to sell and market. It also describes what it is that makes your business unique.

A good business plan also includes a marketing plan, a management plan, a financial plan for the business, and financial projections (for at least five years).

The business plan plays a critical role when applying for a small business loan package.

If you are planning to start your own business and need information about how to construct a business plan, you can go to the Small Business Administration's Web site where you can find detailed information about developing a business plan.

Insert comment

Sincerely,

Tyrone Simmons
Financing Department

ts/yo

Skills Review

EXERCISE 28

SCANS

Directions

As the desktop publisher who works for the Santa Barbara Chamber of Commerce, you are often asked to create flyers, brochures, advertisements, and other literature that highlight the cultural events and attractions in your city. Because Santa Barbara is only one hour's drive from Los Angeles and has many cultural offerings, the Chamber of Commerce is very busy producing informative material to attract tourists. You have been asked to create a brochure that highlights the Santa Barbara Dance 2004 Series event.

1. Create a new document.
2. Set the page orientation to landscape.
3. Save the file; name it **3.28brochure**.
4. Create the brochure shown on pages 353 – 354, using the fonts, sizes, colors, and lines indicated in the exercise.
   NOTE: *The dotted lines around the text are for illustration purposes only to indicate that a text box was used. Remove all line borders from text boxes for the actual brochure.*
5. For the dance information for Panels 3 and 4, open **d3.28brochure** from the Data CD. 
   a. Copy the text from **d3.28brochure** and paste it into the appropriate text box.
   b. Remove any indents.
6. Insert relevant graphics where shown.
   NOTE: *If similar graphics are not available on your computer, you can download them if you have a live Internet connection.*
7. Print one copy of each page.
8. Close the file; save the changes.

Include this exercise in your portfolio.

When you fold 8½" x 11" paper in half, the first page (Panels 1 and 2) represents the front and back covers of the brochure; the second page (Panels 3 and 4) represents the inside text material. These two pages will ultimately print back-to-back and be folded in half.

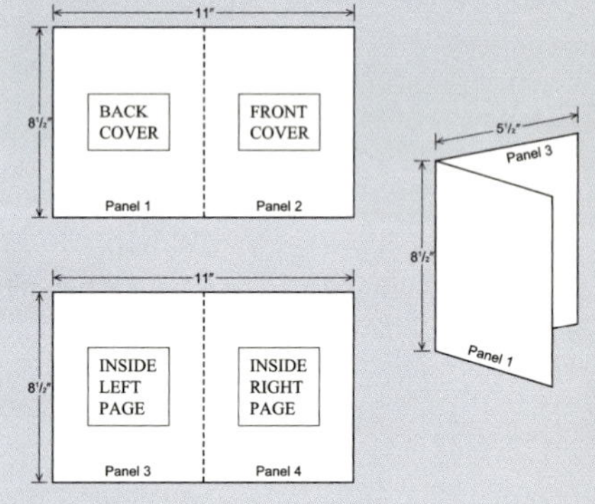

EXERCISE 10

Open a Document; Insert and Delete Text; Insert a Date Automatically; Undo/Redo an Action

Directions

1. Open **1.3net**, the file you created in Exercise 3, or open **d2.10net** from the Data CD. 
2. Save the file as **2.10net**.
3. Create the full-block letter shown on page 59.
4. Begin the date 2.5" from the top of the page.
5. Use the Date feature to insert today's date.
6. Make the indicated insertions and deletions.
7. Correct spelling.
8. Change the writer's name to Matthew R. Edwards.
9. Undo the action.
10. Redo the action.
11. Undo the action.
12. Preview the document.
13. Print one copy.
14. Close the file; save the changes.

CONCEPT BUILDERS

The Date and Time feature allows the user to insert the current date and/or time into the document. The user can choose to have the date and/or time update automatically each time the document is opened.

DID YOU KNOW?

- An enclosure notation is indicated in a letter when something in addition to the letter is included in the envelope. It is positioned at the left margin, two lines below the reference initials. It may be noted in several ways:
  - Enc.
  - Enclosure
  - enclosure

Use the Help Index

How do I...?	**Enter the keyword(s)**
Insert the date automatically	Date

Skills Review

EXERCISE 27

SCANS

Directions

In Exercise 25, you enhanced a report about computer viruses. Because you are going to submit the report to your teacher, you need to create a report cover.

1. Create a new document.
2. Design a cover for the Computer Viruses report you completed in Exercise 25. Include the following information on the cover:

   Computer Viruses
   How to Protect Your Computer from Getting Infected
   By: Your Name
   Technology Applications 101
   Today's Date

3. Include the following in your desktop design:
   - A watermark or other graphic
   - Reverse text
   - Layered shapes and colors
   - Page border
   - Letter spacing
4. Print one copy.
5. Save the file; name it **3.27reportcover**.
6. Close the document window.

Include this exercise in your portfolio.

Save frequently to prevent losing data.

Insert inside address and salutation

Today's date

4x

Ms. Shawn Demetri
30 Shadow Road
Bellevue, WA 98006

2x

Dear Ms. Demetri:

2x

More than a million companies ~~distribute~~ disseminate information on the Internet. Overall Traffic on the Internet continues to grow, increasing exponentially each year.

Because of this astounding growth in the number of users, via the Internet businesses are ~~rapidly~~ tapping into the speed and cost savings of online communications. Therefore, it is important ~~that~~ for you to have ~~some~~ basic knowledge about computers linked to the Internet.

~~Each computer linked to the Internet has its own address.~~ For example, To send a message to an Internet address, a special format must be used. You will learn the parts of An Internet address, which ~~may~~ looks something like this: msmith@sla.ohiostate.edu

Insert

The Internet and World Wide Web Conference is a one-day program that will give you all the information you need to use this invaluable tool.

¶ The conference is broken into tracks. Beginners will receive an overview of the Net and learn the basics, like getting online and addressing Internet mail.

¶ The enclosed brochure will give you detailed information.

2x

Cordially,

4x

Matt Edwards
Conference Director

2x

me/yo

2x

Enclosure

Directions *continued*

7. On the inside right page, do the following:
   a. Insert a picture of a remote control.
   b. Use a callout AutoShape to label the buttons on the remote control as shown.
   c. At approximately the middle of the page, enter the remaining text as shown.
8. Print one copy.
9. Save the file; name it **3.26manual**.
10. Close the file.

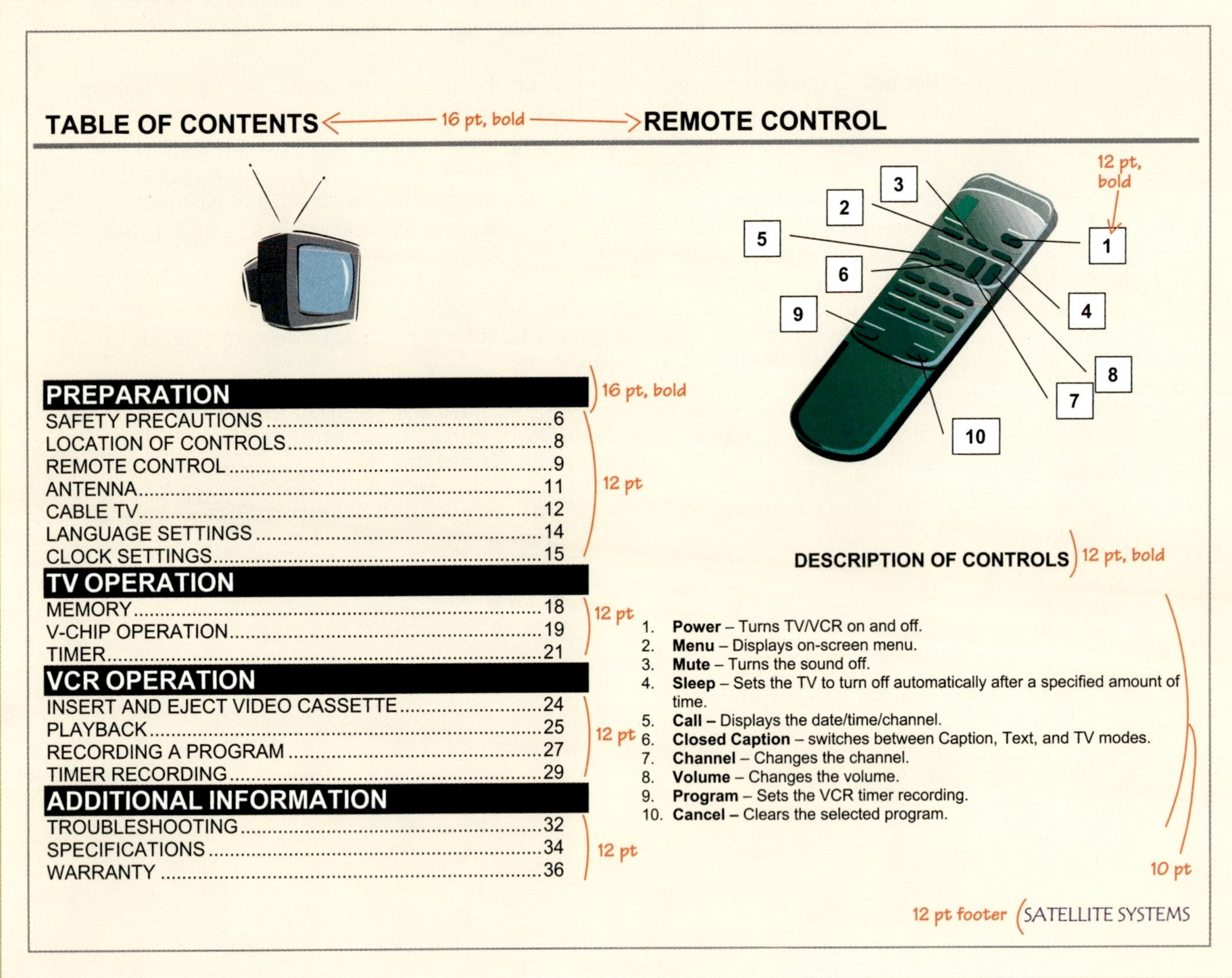

Inside page

Open a Document; Insert and Delete Text; Save As; Prepare an Envelope

EXERCISE 11

SCANS

Directions

1. Open **1.5hr**, the file you created in Exercise 5, or open **d2.11hr** from the Data CD. 
2. Save the file as **2.11hr**.
3. Make the insertions and deletions shown on page 61.
4. Correct spelling.
5. Preview the document.
6. Prepare an envelope; do not include a return address. Attach the envelope to the document.
7. Print one copy.
8. Close the file; save the changes.

Use the Help Index

How do I....?	Enter the keyword(s):
Prepare an envelope	Envelope

VOCABULARY

Delivery address
Return address

CONCEPT BUILDERS

- Use the Save As option when you want to save a document under a different file name or in a different location.
- The ***delivery address*** on an envelope is the same as the inside address in the letter.
- The ***return address*** on an envelope is the address of the sender.

HOT TIPS

You can make an envelope part of your document by clicking Add to Document from the Envelopes and Labels dialog box. This is helpful if you want to edit or print the envelope at a later time.

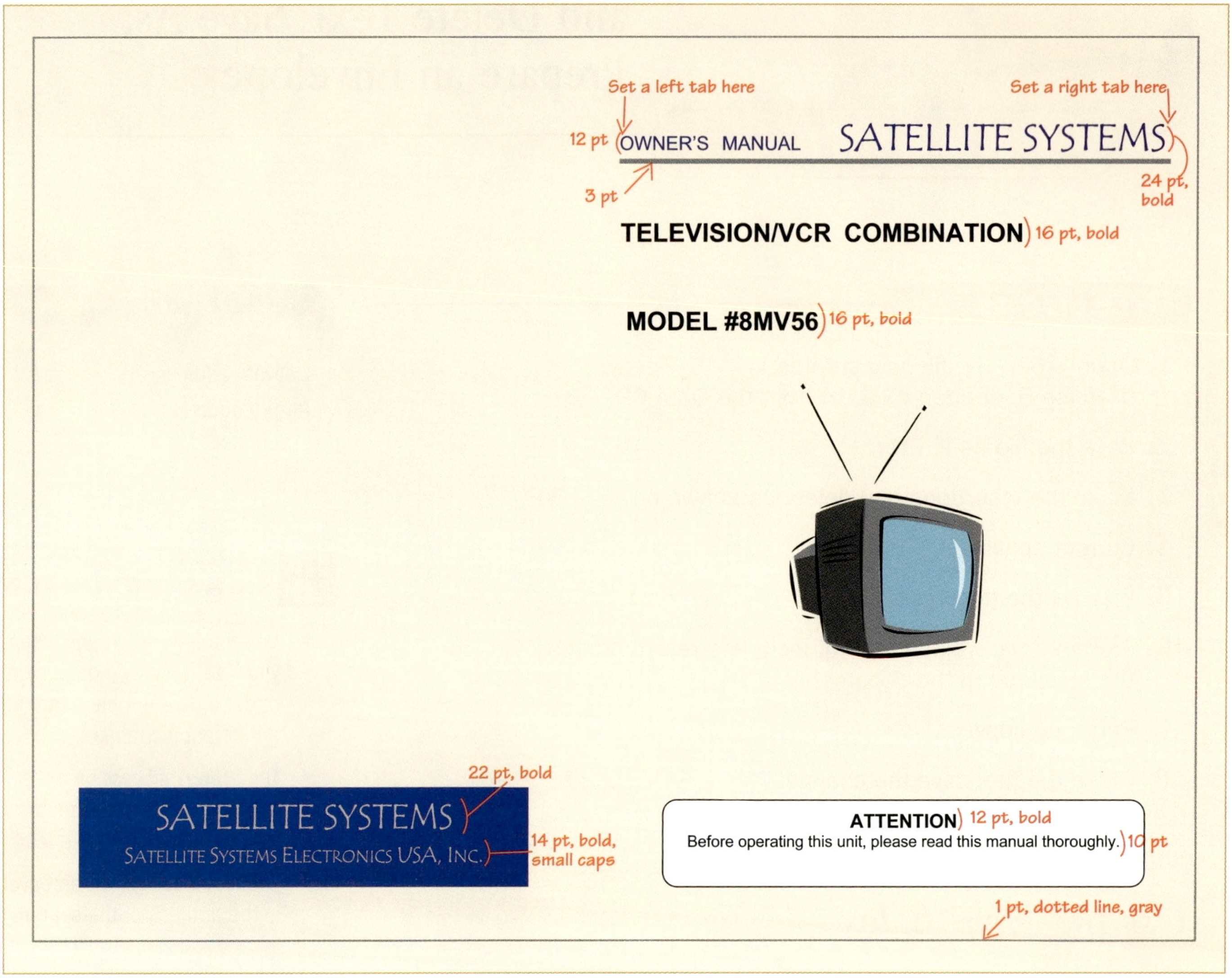

Set a left tab here

Set a right tab here

12 pt OWNER'S MANUAL SATELLITE SYSTEMS 24 pt, bold

3 pt

TELEVISION/VCR COMBINATION 16 pt, bold

MODEL #8MV56 16 pt, bold

22 pt, bold

SATELLITE SYSTEMS

SATELLITE SYSTEMS ELECTRONICS USA, INC. 14 pt, bold, small caps

ATTENTION 12 pt, bold

Before operating this unit, please read this manual thoroughly. 10 pt

1 pt, dotted line, gray

Back and front covers

6. On the inside left page, do the following:

a. Insert clip art of a TV as shown.

b. Begin the Table of Contents text approximately 3" from the top of the page.

i. Set a right-aligned tab at 4.5" and apply a dot leader.

ii. Insert the text as shown, using a sans serif font in the font sizes shown.

iii. Apply black paragraph shading as shown.

HOT TIPS

To plan a pamphlet, use blank pieces of paper, fold them as you would the printed final copy, and mark the pages. This way, you can visualize what information belongs on what page.

Today's date

Ms. Cathy Scruggs
67 Horatio Street
New York, NY 10003

Dear Ms. Scruggs:

As we discussed at the interview,

strives to improve the quality of life of our employees and

The Human Resources Department writes job descriptions and determines salary ranges for those positions. It is the responsibility of the HR Department to recruit the best applicants for open positions within the firm.

As manager, you e all

including health and fringe benefits,

HR staff is also responsible for disseminating information regarding employee benefits and investment plans to staff members, for training employees, and for providing opportunities for advancement within the company.

our 401k

You must be an individual who likes to interact with people if you want to work in the Human Resources Department.

¶It gives me great pleasure to offer you the position of Human Resources manager at Trilogy Broadcasting Company.

You will oversee four HR coordinators, whose work includes writing job descriptions, filing résumés, and building and maintaining employee and labor relations.

Your start date will be April 15. Please be sure to bring your social security card and driver's license (or other form of picture ID) for pre-employment processing on your first day.

Sincerely,

Janet Bass
Executive Vice President

jb/yo

Use Special Page Layouts

EXERCISE 26

SCANS

Directions

1. Start a new document using an 8½" by 11" page to create the brochure shown on pages 349 – 350.
2. Set up the pages as follows:
   a. Use landscape orientation.
   b. Set margins to 1" top, .75" bottom, and .5" left and right.
   c. Apply a 1 pt, dotted line page border. Color it gray.
3. Format the first page (the back and front covers).
   a. On the back cover, do the following:
      - Draw a text box on the bottom left of the page. Size it to .85" high by 4" wide. Enter the text as shown. Fill the text box blue and color the text gray.
   b. On the front cover, do the following:
      i. Set a left-aligned tab at 5.125" and a right-aligned tab at 10".
      ii. Enter the text as shown in the illustration using a sans serif font.
      iii. Draw a horizontal line approximately 5" long and position it as shown. Set the width to 3 pt. Color it gray.
      iv. Insert a relevant clip art object on the cover.
      v. Draw a rounded rectangle on the bottom right of the page. Size it to .75" high by 4.25" wide. Enter the text in the shape as shown.
4. Create a hard page break and then a continuous section break at the bottom of the first page.
5. Format the second page as follows:
   a. Set two columns.
   b. Draw a solid gray line approximately 10" long. Set the width to 3 pt.
   c. Insert a footer that says `Satellite Systems` as shown. Suppress the footer on the first page.

VOCABULARY

Brochure

CONCEPT BUILDERS

A ***brochure*** is a small pamphlet, booklet, or manual that provides information about a product or product line, a place, a service, an event, or a schedule. Some brochures are printed on 8½" by 11" paper using landscape orientation, and folded into thirds like a leaflet or in half like a booklet. In a two-fold brochure, the first page (Panels 1 and 2) is the outside page; the second page (Panels 3 and 4) is the inside page. These two pages will ultimately be printed back to back and folded in half.

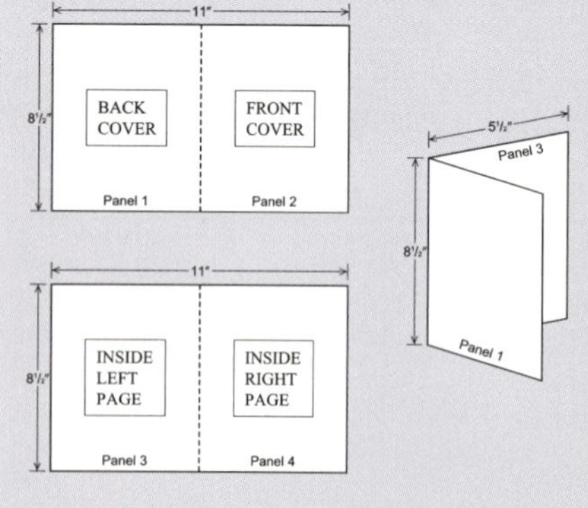

EXERCISE 12

Open a Document; Insert and Delete Text; Save As; Delete a Comment; Prepare an Envelope

Directions

1. Open **2.9bp**, the file you created in Exercise 9, or open **d2.12bp** from the Data CD.
2. Save the file as **2.12bp**.
3. Make the insertions and deletions shown on page 63.
4. Prepare an envelope; do not include a return address.
5. Delete the comment.
6. Correct spelling.
7. Preview the document.
8. Print one copy.
9. Close the file; save the changes.

Use the Help Index

How do I...?	**Enter the keyword(s)**
Delete a comment	Comment

removing it and keeping system damage to a minimum. Always keep a clean emergency bootable disk on hand that will allow you to reboot your computer from the floppy disk drive. This is necessary because *computer viruses* will load themselves into your computer's memory and infect even more programs. Most anti-virus software programs will allow you to create an emergency floppy disk. The table below details common viruses and the damage they can do. These are the current known viruses: an emergency floppy disk.

The table below details common viruses and the damage they can do. These are the current known viruses:

VIRUS NAME	DAMAGE
The Form	Clicking noise from computer speakers
Empire Money	Alters boot sector
AntiExe	Corrupts .exe files of a certain length
Natas	Infects program files and alters boot sector
Ripper	Randomly corrupts information saved to disk
Stealth Boot B	Confuses memory managers; may prevent Windows from loading

SCAN, SCAN, SCAN

Once you suspect your system has,been invaded and you have restarted your system from an emergency floppy disk, the next step is to scan your hard drive and all floppy disks. Your anti-virus program will provide you with instructions for detecting infected files and either repairing or destroying them. As an extra precaution, you may want to repeat the entire scanning process frequently during the next several weeks to make sure you are not being re-infected.

COMPUTER VIRUSES: *How to Protect Your Computer*

Illustration B Page 2

Today's date

Mr. Jeffrey Thompson
500 West Lafayette Boulevard
Detroit, MI 48226

Dear Mr. Thompson:

Insert

It was a pleasure meeting you last week at the Business Financing Conference in Las Vegas. I was very impressed with your Cyber Café idea. I would be very interested in meeting with you in Detroit to discuss the small business loan options that the Bank of Michigan has to offer. Our staff of small business advisors is available to consult with you about your venture.

Before we meet, however, you should provide us with a detailed business plan. A business plan is a descriptive report of the business you want to open. It describes the products or services you want to sell and what makes your business unique, including the location of the business

A good business plan also includes a marketing plan, a management plan, a financial plan, and financial projections. ~~The business plan plays a critical role when applying for a business loan.~~

If you need information about how to construct a business plan, ~~you can go to~~ visit the Small Business Administration's Web site.

Insert

After we meet and review your business plan, you will complete a loan application for us.

Insert

Please call my assistant, Paul Eichler, at (248) 555-5555 to schedule an appointment. We look forward to working with you.

Sincerely,

Tyrone Simmons
Financing Department

ts/yo

COMPUTER VIRUSES:
How to Protect Your Computer from Getting Infected

Viruses are actually much less common than most people are led to believe. Like biological viruses, *computer viruses* can only be spread by contact with the outside world. The most common way to contract a *computer virus* is by running programs from an infected floppy disk or by running infected software. Once a *computer virus* gets inside your system,

> *"Once a computer virus gets inside your system, it can attach itself to other programs and infect other floppy disks."*

it can attach itself to other programs and infect other floppy disks you may use.

The good news is that there are many things you can do to protect your home computer from viruses.

VIRUS PROTECTION SOFTWARE

Many *computer virus* detection programs are designed to keep running while you work on the computer. If the program detects any suspicious behavior, it alerts you immediately and allows you to scan for a *computer virus*.

STRANGE BEHAVIOR

As soon as you detect any kind of abnormal behavior, it is best to assume the worst. Immediately save any open files, quit all applications and turn off your computer. The sooner you can detect the *computer virus*, the better your chances are of

Illustration B Page 1

Skills Review

EXERCISE 13

In this exercise, you will create a full-block letter from edited text. You will have to provide an appropriate salutation and closing.

SCANS

Directions

1. Open **d2.13eq** from the Data CD.
2. Save the file as **2.13equity**.
3. Create a full-block letter from the text shown on page 65.
   - Use today's date.
   - Send this letter to:

     Ms. Unique Jenkins
     34 Eaton Avenue
     Rochester, NY 14692-6771
   - The letter is from Vicky Singh, Vice President.
4. Make the indicated insertions and deletions.
   NOTE: *The exercise is double-spaced so edits can be seen more clearly.*
5. Correct spelling and grammatical errors.
   NOTE: *Write out all contractions.*
6. **Word 2000 Users:** Skip this step.
   Add Unique Jenkins to your Contacts list.
7. Prepare an envelope; do not include a return address. Attach the envelope to the document.
8. Preview the document.
9. Print one copy.
10. Close the file; save the changes.

Directions *continued*

6. Insert a watermark behind the heading as shown, using any relevant graphic.

7. Using the drawing tools, create the "bug" graphic.
   a. Group all the parts.
   b. Size it to .3" high by .9" wide.
   c. Copy the bug seven times and position each as shown.

8. Create two columns from the text. Insert the additional text, as shown in the illustration.
   NOTE: *To have the virus table span two columns, apply a two-column format up to where you will insert the table. Then create a section break or change the column layout back to one column. After you insert the table, apply a two-column format to the remaining text.*

9. Insert the **d3.25virus** file from the Data CD where indicated on Page 2 of the illustration. 
   a. Delete the table title.
   b. Center the column headings.
   c. Adjust the column widths so the table appears centered within the document.
   d. Apply any table and line borders you prefer.
   e. Color the column-head row as you prefer.

10. Create a drop capital at the beginning of each paragraph. Drop each two lines below the paragraph.

11. Create a pull quote (text box) as shown.
    a. Size the box to 1.3" high by 2.35" wide.
    b. Remove the left and right text box border lines and apply 2¼ pt top and bottom lines.
    c. Center and set the quote to sans serif, 11 pt, and italic.

12. Insert a relevant clip art object on page 2, as shown in the illustration.

13. Create a WordArt object with the words `Good Luck`. Color it as you prefer.
    - Position the WordArt at the bottom of the last column on page 2.

14. Preview the document.

15. Print one copy.

16. Save the file; name it **3.25protect1**.

17. Close the document window.

Becase you are a valued CMB customer, you deserve an oppportunity to make the most of the equity in your home. That's why we want you to ~~know about~~ the CMB Home Equity Line of Credit—~~a line of credit~~ that puts the equity in your home to work for you. ~~We know that your morgage is low and~~ that you may have a substansial amount of home equity. Making the most of your home equity is smart ~~at this time,~~ since the prime rate is at its lowest level in years. ~~Among the other reasons to get a CMB Home Equity Line of Credit are the fact that~~ there are no up-front costs, interest is tax deductible, it is a smart way to consolidate bills, and you pay only for what you use. In adddition, ~~you get~~ a valuable ~~case~~ "reserve," and you protect ~~yourself~~ against rising interest rates. Our CMB Home Equity Advisors will give you informaation about the equity that you have available in your home and answer any questions you ~~may~~ have. Call us any day Monday through Friday, 8 a.m. to 10 p.m., Saturday, 8:30 a.m. to 5 p.m. ~~You can use it to meet your finansial goals and/or needs~~. ~~Please call us~~ at 1-800-CMB-5555 ~~today~~. ~~Please don't~~ miss the chance to take the equity you have in your home. ~~This offer expires on June 30, 2003.~~

Create Pull Quotes

EXERCISE 25

SCANS

Directions

1. Open **9.88protect**, which you created in Unit 2 and is shown below in Illustration A, or open **d3.25protect1** from the Data CD.
2. Save the file as **3.25protect1**.
3. Follow Steps 4 – 13 to create the publication shown in Illustration B on pages 346 – 347.
4. Apply a paragraph border to the main heading.
   a. Left-align and set the text to 20 pt, bold.
   b. Set the text color to yellow and fill the box with black (to create a reverse text effect).
5. Apply a paragraph border to the subheading.
   - Right-align the text.

COMPUTER VIRUSES:
How to Protect Your Computer from Getting Infected

Viruses are actually much less common than most people are led to believe. Like biological viruses, *computer viruses* can only be spread by contact with the outside world. The most common way to contract a *computer virus* is by running programs from an infected floppy disk or by running infected software. Once a *computer virus* gets inside your system, it can attach itself to other programs and infect other floppy disks you may use. The good news is that there are many things you can do to protect your home computer from viruses.

VIRUS PROTECTION SOFTWARE

Many *computer virus* detection programs are designed to keep running while you work on the computer. If the program detects any suspicious behavior, it alerts you immediately and allows you to scan for a *computer virus*.

STRANGE BEHAVIOR

As soon as you detect any kind of abnormal behavior, it is best to assume the worst. Immediately save any open files, quit all applications and turn off your computer. The sooner you can detect the *computer virus*, the better your chances are of removing it and keeping system damage to a minimum. Always keep a clean emergency bootable disk on hand that will allow you to reboot your computer from the floppy disk drive. This is necessary because *computer viruses* will load themselves into your computer's

Illustration A Page 1

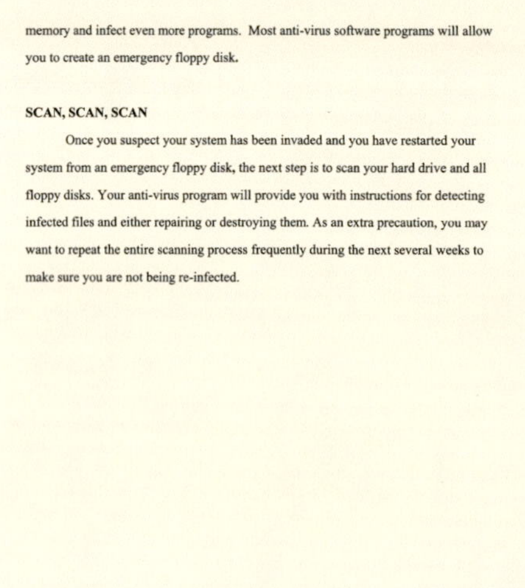

2

memory and infect even more programs. Most anti-virus software programs will allow you to create an emergency floppy disk.

SCAN, SCAN, SCAN

Once you suspect your system has been invaded and you have restarted your system from an emergency floppy disk, the next step is to scan your hard drive and all floppy disks. Your anti-virus program will provide you with instructions for detecting infected files and either repairing or destroying them. As an extra precaution, you may want to repeat the entire scanning process frequently during the next several weeks to make sure you are not being re-infected.

COMPUTER VIRUSES: *How to Protect Your Computer*

Illustration A Page 2

VOCABULARY

Pull quote

CONCEPT BUILDERS

- A ***pull quote*** is text set off in a box, generally larger than the surrounding type, and consists of important or interesting text from the body copy. Its purpose is to attract the reader's attention.
- Pull quotes are made by creating a text box and removing the left and right borders.
- By default, a document contains one section. You can break your document into multiple sections and format each one differently. To do so, you must create a section break. Click Insert, Break.
- There are several different types of section breaks—Next page, Continuous, Even page, and Odd page. Each break option creates a break in a different location in the document. The continuous section break creates a break at the insertion point location.

Skills Review

EXERCISE 14

In this exercise, you will create a full-block letter from edited text. You will have to provide an appropriate salutation and closing.

SCANS

Directions

1. Open **d2.14off** from the Data CD. 

2. Save the file as **2.14offer**.

3. Create a full-block letter from the text shown on page 67.
   a. Use today's date.
   b. Send this letter to:
      Mr. Lee Ebert
      11133 Big Bend Boulevard
      St. Louis, MO 63122-5799
   c. Include an appropriate closing.
   d. The letter is from Ben Schmidt, Manager of College Recruiting.

4. Make the indicated insertions and deletions.
NOTE: *The illustration is double-spaced so edits can be seen more clearly.*

5. Correct spelling and grammatical errors.

6. **Word 2000 Users:** Skip this step.
Add Lee Ebert to your Contacts list.

7. Change Mr. Schmidt's title to Manager.

8. Undo the change.

9. Delete the next-to-last paragraph (Please feel free . . .).

10. Undo the change.

11. Redo the change.

12. Prepare an envelope; do not include a return address. Attach the envelope to the document.

DID YOU KNOW?

- The proofreaders' mark to capitalize is: ≡
- The proofreaders' mark to indicate a spelling error is: (sp)

36 pt, italic;
4 pt letter spacing

Write ★ Direct ★ Shoot ★ Edit

LEARN FILM MAKING

Write, direct, shoot, and edit
your own films
during our eight-week
summer workshop
at:

9/12

THE NEW YORK FILM SCHOOL 11 pt

NO PREREQUISITES REQUIRED
●
IN OUR INTENSIVE
EIGHT-WEEK COURSE:
●
LEARN THE CONCEPTS OF
WRITING A SCREENPLAN
●
DIRECT YOUR OWN FILM
●
SHOOT WITH 16MM CAMERAS
●
WORK WITH LIGHTING AND SOUND
●
SUPPORTIVE ENVIRONMENT
●
TAUGHT BY NATIONALLY ACCLAIMED INSTRUCTORS

10 pt

TUITION: $3,500.00 Bold

THE NEW YORK FILM SCHOOL
270 LAFAYETTE STREET
NEW YORK, NY 10003
212-555-3874

10 pt;
6 pt letter
spacing

Directions *continued*

13. Preview the document.

14. Print one copy.

15. Close the file; save the changes.

at an annual salary of $38,000

We are pleased to confirm your acceptance of our offer to join CHASIN'S in our Buyer's Training Program. All offers are considered confidensial and we would appreciate the same consideration on your end. We will expect you to arrive on August 1 at 9:00 a.m. Enter the building through the 60th Street entrance, and come directly to the Placement Office on the third floor. To satisfy the immigration law, bring on your first day documentation to verify identity and eligibillity to work in the United States. We are enclsoing employment papers and benefit forms. Please bring them on your first day and we will review them during the Orientation. Please feel free to contact us if you have any questions. We assure you that will will do all that we can to assist and direct you in your career with CHASIN'S and look forward to your long association with us.

Create Reverse Text; Use Letter Spacing

EXERCISE 24

Directions

1. Create a new document.
2. Create the flyer shown on page 343.
3. Set 1" left and right margins and .5" top and bottom margins.
4. Create a watermark using any relevant graphic.
   - Size it to fill the page.
5. Enter the text shown.
   - Set the font, font size, leading, and letter spacing amounts as indicated in the illustration.
6. Apply text boxes where shown.
   a. Color each box black.
   b. Set the font color for "LEARN FILM MAKING" and "THE NEW YORK FILM SCHOOL" to yellow.
7. Preview the exercise.
8. Print one copy.
9. Save the file; name it **3.24makefilm**. Do not close the document window.
10. Save the file as a Web page; name it **3.24makefilmweb**. Change the Web page title to: `The New York Film School`
11. Close the document window.
12. Open your Web browser.
13. Open **3.24makefilmweb**.
14. Exit the Web browser. Close all files and save them.

LESSON 3

Text Alignments, Enhancements, and Effects

EXERCISE 15
Align Text; Center Text Vertically

EXERCISE 16
Align Text; Use Bold, Italic, and Underline

EXERCISE 17
Align Text; Use Bold, Italic, and Underline

EXERCISE 18
Change Fonts and Font Size

EXERCISE 19
Change Fonts and Font Size; Use Symbols

EXERCISE 20
Change Fonts, Font Size, and Font Color; Use Symbols; Copy Formatting

EXERCISE 21
Change Fonts, Font Size, and Font Color; Copy Formatting; Use Symbols, Bullets, and Numbering

EXERCISE 22
Change Fonts and Font Size; Use Symbols, Bullets, and Numbering; Format Bullets

EXERCISE 23
Change Fonts and Font Size; Use Symbols, Bullets, and Numbering

EXERCISE 24
Change Fonts and Font Size; Use Symbols

EXERCISE 25
Skills Review

EXERCISE 26
Skills Review

Directions *continued*

b. Change all press release text to sans serif.

c. Apply black paragraph shading to TWO NEW PRODUCTS FOR DESKTOP PUBLISHING!

- Expand the letter spacing to 2 pt.

d. Insert a hard return after each product name and delete the comma.

Begin each paragraph with a capital letter.

e. Create a drop capital at the beginning of each paragraph. Drop it two lines below the paragraph.

f. Change the line spacing to single for the product information.

g. Set the paragraph spacing before and after the product information to 6 pt.

h. Insert a decorative bullet before each product name.

i. Set the font color for each product name to blue.

j. Expand the letter spacing to 3 pt for the product names.

k. Draw a decorative 4½ pt line between product information.

l. Apply a 4½ pt blue-dotted page border.

8. Preview the document.

9. Print one copy.

10. Close the file; save the changes.

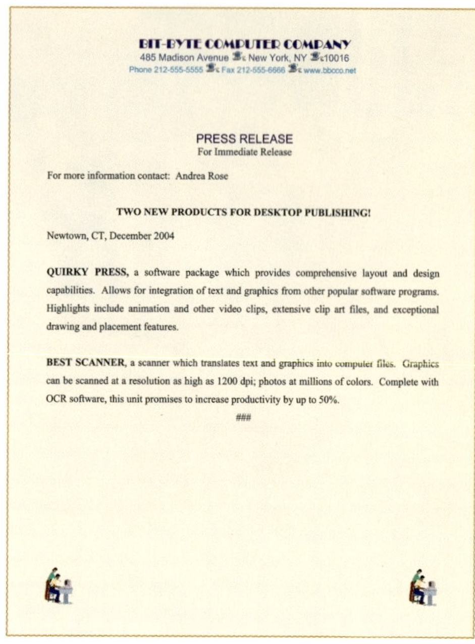

BIT-BYTE COMPUTER COMPANY
485 Madison Avenue New York, NY 10016
Phone 212-555-5555 Fax 212-555-6666 www.bbcco.net

PRESS RELEASE
For Immediate Release

For more information contact: Andrea Rose

TWO NEW PRODUCTS FOR DESKTOP PUBLISHING!

Newtown, CT, December 2004

QUIRKY PRESS, a software package which provides comprehensive layout and design capabilities. Allows for integration of text and graphics from other popular software programs. Highlights include animation and other video clips, extensive clip art files, and exceptional drawing and placement features.

BEST SCANNER, a scanner which translates text and graphics into computer files. Graphics can be scanned at a resolution as high as 1200 dpi; photos at millions of colors. Complete with OCR software, this unit promises to increase productivity by up to 50%.

###

Illustration A

Use the Help Index

How do I...?	**Enter the keyword(s):**
Adjust character spacing	Expanded spacing

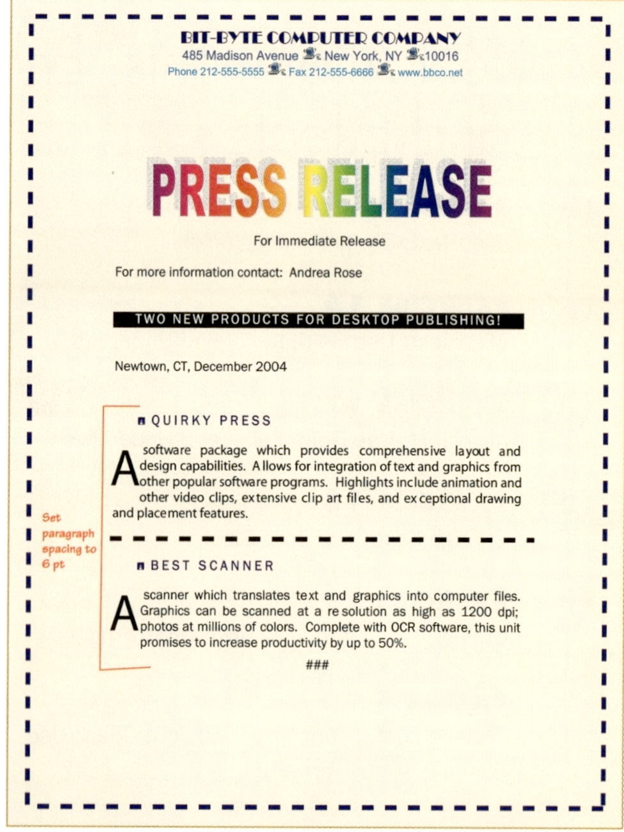

BIT-BYTE COMPUTER COMPANY
485 Madison Avenue New York, NY 10016
Phone 212-555-5555 Fax 212-555-6666 www.bbco.net

PRESS RELEASE
For Immediate Release

For more information contact: Andrea Rose

TWO NEW PRODUCTS FOR DESKTOP PUBLISHING!

Newtown, CT, December 2004

QUIRKY PRESS

A software package which provides comprehensive layout and design capabilities. Allows for integration of text and graphics from other popular software programs. Highlights include animation and other video clips, extensive clip art files, and exceptional drawing and placement features.

BEST SCANNER

A scanner which translates text and graphics into computer files. Graphics can be scanned at a resolution as high as 1200 dpi; photos at millions of colors. Complete with OCR software, this unit promises to increase productivity by up to 50%.

###

Illustration B

Align Text; Center Text Vertically

EXERCISE 15

Directions

1. Create a new document.
2. Begin the exercise at the top of your screen.
3. Use the default margins and fonts.
4. Key the paragraphs exactly as shown on page 70, using the proper text alignments.
5. Vertically center the exercise on the page.
6. Correct spelling.
7. Preview the document.
8. Print one copy.
9. Save the file; name it **3.15confer**.

Use the Help Index

How do I...?	**Enter the keyword(s)**
Center text	Center
Right-align text	Right-align
Justify text	Justify
Center text vertically	Vertical alignment

VOCABULARY

Aligned center
Aligned right
Aligned left
Justified

CONCEPT BUILDERS

- Text can be ***aligned left*** (the default), ***center, right,*** or ***justified.***
- Justified text displays lines that are even at the left and right margins (except for the last line).
- You can change alignments before or after entering text.
- You can center text vertically between the top and bottom edges of the page. To do so, click File, Page Setup, and select the option you want from the Layout tab.

DID YOU KNOW?

The proofreaders' mark for center align is:] [

Create Reverse Text; Use Letter Spacing

EXERCISE 23

Directions

1. Open **1.2bblet**, which you created in Lesson 1 of this unit, or open **d3.23bblet** from the Data CD.
2. Resave the file as **3.23pressrelease**.
3. Insert **9.93release**, which you created in Unit 2 (or use **d3.23release** from the Data CD) into the **3.23pressrelease** file, as shown in Illustration A on page 341.
4. Begin the press release at 2".
5. Set 1.5" left and right margins.
6. Delete the graphics in the lower-left and -right corners.
7. Redesign the press release, as shown in Illustration B on page 341, as follows:
   a. Replace the title with any WordArt object.
      - Apply a shadow effect.

VOCABULARY

Reverse text
Kerning

CONCEPT BUILDERS

- ***Reverse text*** is text that appears white against a dark background. If you create a text box and fill it black, or if you apply black shading to text or a paragraph, the text will automatically appear white.
- Word allows you to adjust the relative space between characters. You can expand or condense space evenly among all selected characters. Or, you can kern characters. ***Kerning*** slightly alters the space between pairs of letters. Letter spacing is measured either in points or by percentage.
- You can also scale letters, that is, you can set their width. The width of characters is measured by a percentage.
- To set character spacing, click Format, Font, and then click the Character Spacing tab to select appropriate options. Some examples of character spacing are shown below.

  This is practice text—**normal**

  This is practice text—**expanded 2 pt**

  This is practice text—**expanded 2 pt and scaled 150%**

  This is practice text—**expanded 2 pt and scaled 80%**

  This is practice text—**expanded 5 pt**

  This is practice text—**condensed .5 pt**

  This is practice text—**condensed 1 pt**

The Internet and World Wide Web
Information Conference

4x

Internet Sessions

3x

Justify

Our unique one-day conference provides many different training sessions on various levels of Internet learning. Our presenters are among the top experts in their field. They will provide you with cutting-edge facts about the Information Superhighway.

2x

Session One
Introduction to the Internet

2x

Justify

Who should attend: Anyone who has little or no experience on the Internet and is interested in understanding the basics of the Internet and World Wide Web.
Overview: What is the Information Superhighway? You will learn what the Internet is and how to use it to communicate.

2x

Session Two
Getting Connected

2x

Justify

Who should attend: Anyone interested in basic Internet access information. Recommended for beginners.
Overview: What equipment do I need? In this session, you will learn how the Internet was started, what it is, and the basics of accessing the Internet for business through online services.

2x

Session Three
World Wide Web Tour

2x

Justify

Who should attend: This session is a must for anyone interested in using the World Wide Web for business applications.
Overview: This session offers you the facts you need to effectively use this resource.

To enroll:
Call toll free
1-800-555-4444
Or:
E-mail us at
INTER@sem.com

Use the Help Index

How Do I...?	**Enter the keyword(s):**
Apply a paragraph border/shading	Paragraph border

Internet Sessions

Our unique one-day conference provides many different training sessions on different levels of Internet learning. Our presenters are among the top specialists in their field. They will provide you with cutting-edge information about the Information Superhighway.

Session One*

Introduction to the Internet

Those who should attend:
Anyone who has little or no experience on the Internet and is interested in understanding the fundamentals of the Internet and World Wide Web.
Summary:
What is the Information Superhighway? In this session, you will learn what the Internet is and how to use it to communicate.

Session Two

Getting Connected

Those who should attend:
Anyone interested in basic Internet access information. Recommended for beginners.
Summary:
What equipment do I need? In this session, you will learn how the Internet was started, what it is, and the basics of accessing the Internet for business through online services.

Session Three

World Wide Web Tour

Those who should attend:
This session is a must for anyone interested in using the World Wide Web for its business applications.
Summary:
In this session, you will discover the facts you need to use this resource effectively.

*This session will not be offered on Thursdays.

To enroll...

Illustration B

Align Text; Use Bold, Italic, and Underline

EXERCISE 16

SCANS

Directions

1. Create a new document.
2. Begin the exercise at the top of your screen.
3. Use the default margins and fonts.
4. Key the announcement provided using the text alignments and enhancements shown on page 72.
5. **Word 2000 Users:** Skip this step.
   Apply italic to the indicated text items simultaneously.
6. Vertically center the exercise.
7. Correct spelling.
8. Preview the document.
9. Print one copy.
10. Save the file; name it **3.16party**.

Use the Help Index

How do I ...?	**Enter the keyword(s)**
Underline	Underline
Bold text	Bold
Italicize text	Italic

VOCABULARY

Bold
Italic
Continuous underline
Non-continuous underline

HOT TIPS

To format multiple blocks of text simultaneously, select the first text item you want to format and then press the Ctrl key as you select additional text items. When all of your text is selected, make your formatting selections. This feature is not available to Word 2000 users.

DID YOU KNOW?

- The proofreaders' mark for bold is: ~~~~ or bf.
- The proofreaders' mark for underline is: ______ or u/s.
- The proofreaders' mark for italic is: ______ or ital.

CONCEPT BUILDERS

- ***Bold,*** underline, double underline, ***italic,*** and highlight are effects used to emphasize or enhance text.
- You can enhance text before or after you enter it.
- When you underline a sentence using a ***continuous underline*** style, you underline the words and the spaces between them. A ***non-continuous underline*** style, however, underlines only the words, not the spaces between them.

Create Watermarks; Use Paragraph Borders and Shading

EXERCISE 22

Directions

1. Open **5.50confer**, which you created in Unit 2 and is shown in Illustration A, or open **d3.22confer** from the Data CD. 
2. Save the file as **3.22conferdtp**.
3. Redesign the flyer, as shown in Illustration B on page 339:
   a. Set 1.5" left and right margins.
   b. Set the heading text as shown to sans serif, 30 pt, bold. Color the text as you prefer. Apply a shadow to it.
   c. Create two columns after the heading.
   d. Set all text within the columns to serif, 10 pt. Apply bold to session titles.
   e. Insert a relevant graphic as a watermark as shown.
      - Size it to 5" high by 5" wide.
   f. Create a drop capital for the first paragraph. Drop it three lines below the text.
   g. Apply a paragraph border around Session One, Session Two, and Session Three.
      - Color each box as you prefer.
      - Center and set the text within the box to sans serif, bold.
   h. Move "To enroll" below "This session will not be offered on Thursdays."
   i. Create a WordArt object for the "To enroll" information and position it as shown.
      - Size it to fill the space.
4. Preview the document.
5. Print one copy.
6. Close the file; save the changes.

CONCEPT BUILDERS

Paragraph borders are lines that appear around a paragraph to add emphasis to text. You can place single, double, thick, or dotted lines around text blocks. You also apply shading to paragraphs or text. To do so, click Format, Borders and Shading, and choose the appropriate options.

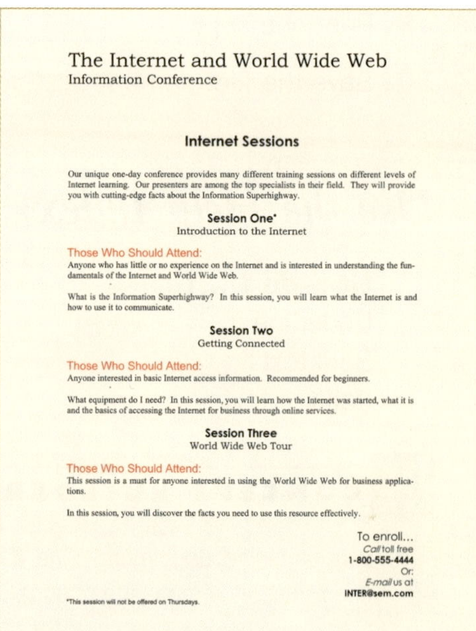

The Internet and World Wide Web
Information Conference

Internet Sessions

Our unique one-day conference provides many different training sessions on different levels of Internet learning. Our presenters are among the top specialists in their field. They will provide you with cutting-edge facts about the Information Superhighway.

Session One*
Introduction to the Internet

Those Who Should Attend:
Anyone who has little or no experience on the Internet and is interested in understanding the fundamentals of the Internet and World Wide Web.

What is the Information Superhighway? In this session, you will learn what the Internet is and how to use it to communicate.

Session Two
Getting Connected

Those Who Should Attend:
Anyone interested in basic Internet access information. Recommended for beginners.

What equipment do I need? In this session, you will learn how the Internet was started, what it is and the basics of accessing the Internet for business through online services.

Session Three
World Wide Web Tour

Those Who Should Attend:
This session is a must for anyone interested in using the World Wide Web for business applications.

In this session, you will discover the facts you need to use this resource effectively.

To enroll...
Call toll free
1-800-555-4444
Or:
E-mail us at
INTER@sem.com

*This session will not be offered on Thursdays.

Illustration A

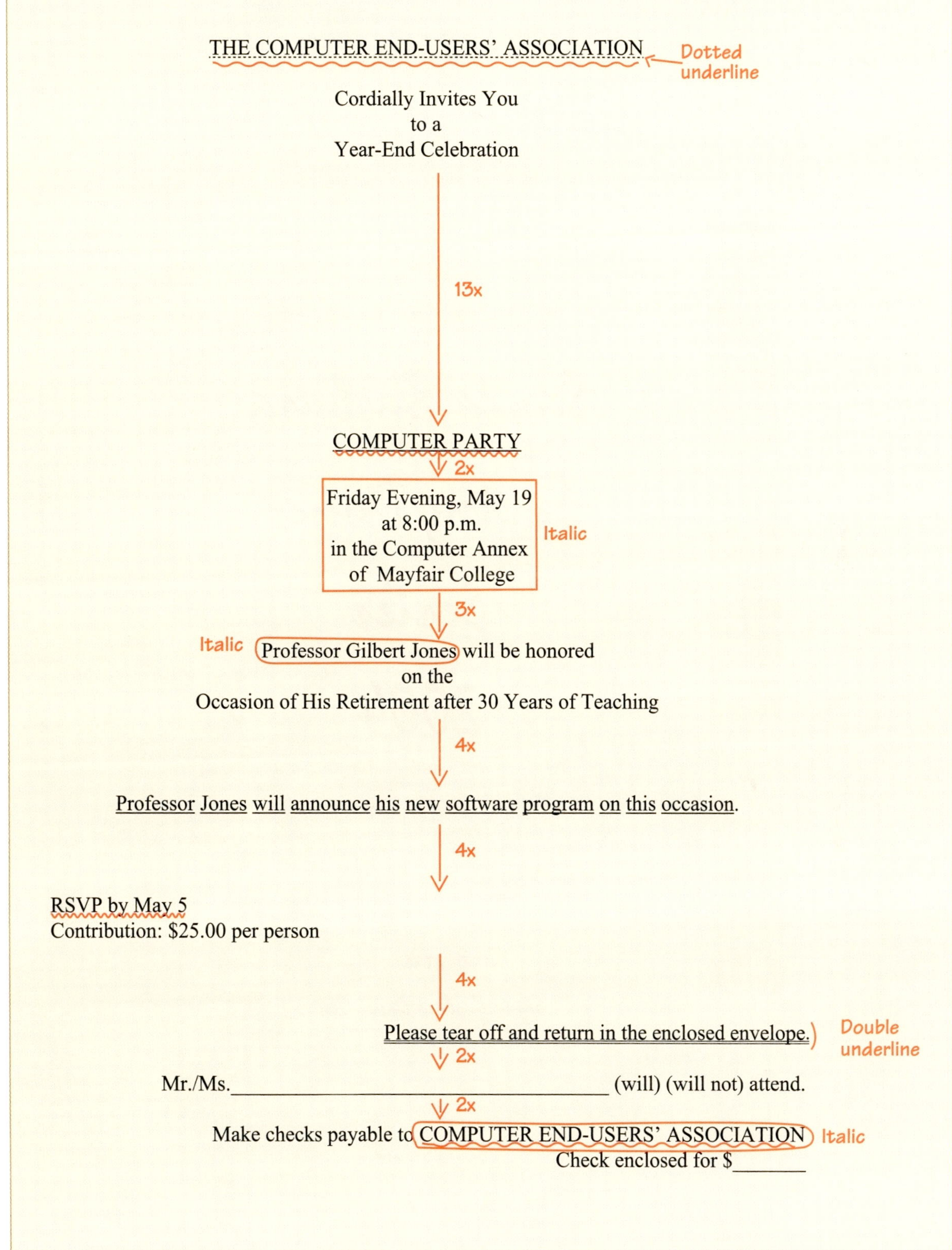

THE COMPUTER END-USERS' ASSOCIATION

Cordially Invites You
to a
Year-End Celebration

COMPUTER PARTY

Friday Evening, May 19
at 8:00 p.m.
in the Computer Annex
of Mayfair College

Professor Gilbert Jones will be honored
on the
Occasion of His Retirement after 30 Years of Teaching

Professor Jones will announce his new software program on this occasion.

RSVP by May 5
Contribution: $25.00 per person

Please tear off and return in the enclosed envelope.

Mr./Ms.__________________________________ (will) (will not) attend.

Make checks payable to COMPUTER END-USERS' ASSOCIATION
Check enclosed for $_______

Use the Help Index

How Do I...?	**Enter the keyword(s):**
Create a watermark	Watermark

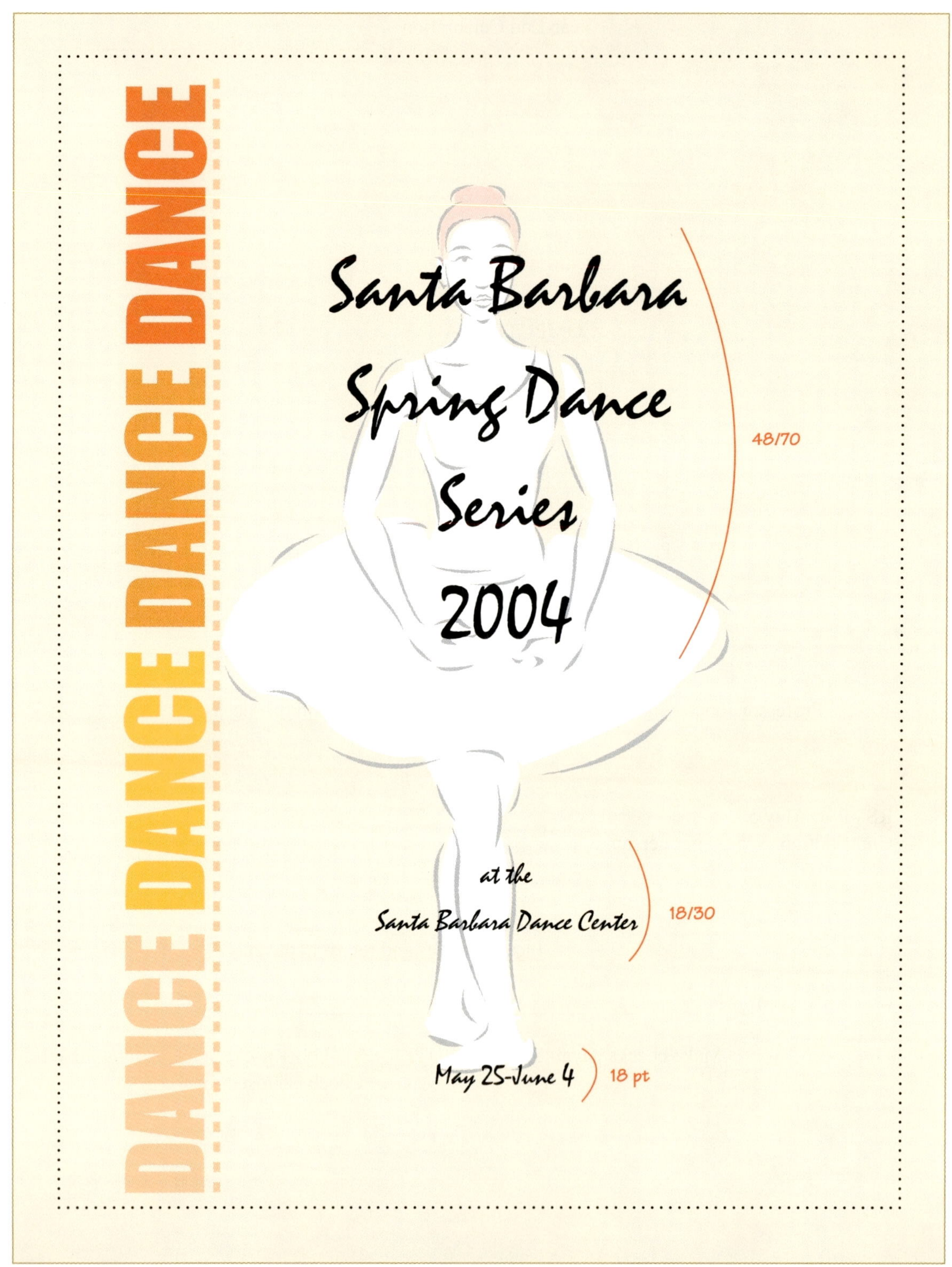

Align Text; Use Bold, Italic, and Underline

EXERCISE 17

SCANS

Directions

1. Create a new document.
2. Begin the exercise at the top of your screen.
3. Use the default margins and fonts.
4. Key the flyer provided, using the text alignments and enhancements shown on the right.
5. Vertically center the exercise.
6. Correct spelling.
7. Preview the document.
8. Print one copy.
9. Save the file; name it **3.17eat**.

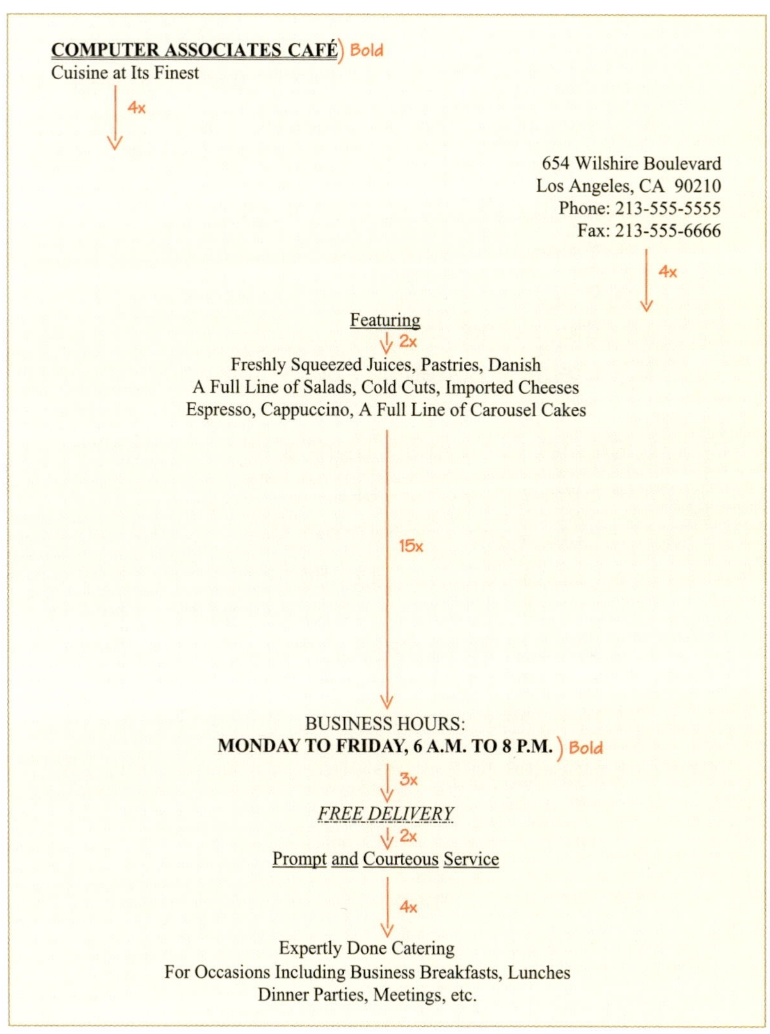

COMPUTER ASSOCIATES CAFÉ) Bold
Cuisine at Its Finest

4x

654 Wilshire Boulevard
Los Angeles, CA 90210
Phone: 213-555-5555
Fax: 213-555-6666

4x

Featuring

2x

Freshly Squeezed Juices, Pastries, Danish
A Full Line of Salads, Cold Cuts, Imported Cheeses
Espresso, Cappuccino, A Full Line of Carousel Cakes

15x

BUSINESS HOURS:
MONDAY TO FRIDAY, 6 A.M. TO 8 P.M.) Bold

3x

FREE DELIVERY

2x

Prompt and Courteous Service

4x

Expertly Done Catering
For Occasions Including Business Breakfasts, Lunches
Dinner Parties, Meetings, etc.

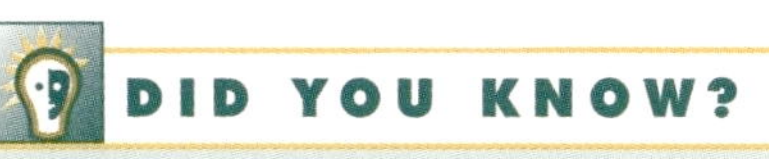

DID YOU KNOW?

Word automatically inserts the accent mark for words like café and protégé.

Create Watermarks

EXERCISE 21

Directions

SCANS

1. Create a new document.
2. Create the flyer shown in the illustration on page 337 as follows:
   a. Create a text box and insert the word DANCE four times.
      - Change the text direction.
      - Set the text to sans serif, 66 pt.
      - Color each word a different shade of orange.
      - Position the text box at the left side of the page. Remove the text box border.
      - Create a dotted line below the words in a complementary color.

   b. Create a watermark using a relevant graphic.
      - Size it to fill the page.

   c. Create a second text box.
      - Choose the No Fill option.

      NOTE: *By default, a text box is opaque—that is, it is filled with a white color. To make it clear (so the watermark is visible), you need to choose No Fill from the text box color options.*
      - Enter the text shown and center and set it to a script font.
      - Use the font sizes and leading amounts shown in the exercise.

   d. Apply a decorative page border.
3. Preview the document.
4. Print one copy.
5. Save the file; name it **3.21sanbar**.

VOCABULARY

Watermark

CONCEPT BUILDERS

- A ***watermark*** is any text or picture that appears behind regular text in a document.
- To create a watermark, click Format, Background. In the Printed Watermark dialog box that opens, choose to place a picture or text as your watermark. However, if you want to use an AutoShape or a clip art object as your watermark, you must insert it into the document through the Header and Footer feature. **Word 2000 Users:** All watermarks are created through the Header and Footer feature.

Change Fonts and Font Size

EXERCISE 18

Directions

1. Open **3.15confer**, the file you created in Exercise 15, or open **d3.18confer** from the Data CD. 
2. Save the file as **3.18confer**.
3. Make the revisions shown on page 75.
4. Change the fonts and font sizes, as indicated.
   a. Use a serif, 11 pt font for all body text.
   b. **Word 2000 Users:** Skip this step.
   Use the Reveal Formatting task pane to change the font, font style, and font size of the heading.
   NOTE: *Use the recommended serif font, if it is available to you. Otherwise, substitute another serif font.*
5. Correct spelling.
6. Preview the document.
7. Print one copy.
8. Save the changes and close the file.

VOCABULARY

Font
Font size
Point size
Font face
Serif
Sans serif
Script

DID YOU KNOW?

- For short documents, it is recommended that you do not use more than two font faces in a single document.
- A serif face is more readable and generally used for document text.
- Sans serif font faces are typically used for headlines; script faces are used for formal invitations and announcements.

CONCEPT BUILDERS

- A ***font*** is a complete set of characters in a specific face, style, and size. The default ***font size*** in most software is Times New Roman, 12 point.
- ***Point size*** measures the height of characters. A point is approximately 1/72 of an inch.
- A ***font face*** (often called a typeface or just font) is the design of a character.
- There are basically three types of font faces: serif, sans serif, and script. A ***serif*** face has lines, curves, or edges extending from the ends of the letter (P), a ***sans serif*** face is straight edged (P), and a ***script*** face looks like handwriting (𝒫).
- The Reveal Formatting task pane allows you to view the formatting that has been applied to selected text. You can also change the formatting of selected text in the Reveal Formatting task pane by clicking a blue underlined option and making your selections from the dialog box that opens. The task pane is not available to Word 2000 users.

Creating Effective Presentations

Creating Effective Presentations

One day, you might be likely to find yourself in this situation: your employer says, "We need to get a presentation together for the DataAir Project fast!" Because the deadline for such a "request" is usually immediate, you reach for your presentation graphics software program.

The following four pointers can help make noticeable improvements to your next presentation:

ANALYZE YOUR AUDIENCE. Take the time to determine who will be listening. Ask yourself, "Why are you giving this presentation?"

MAKE A PLAN. After you have determined your audience, decide what to say and how to say it. Create an outline after you have analyzed what items you must cover and how you want your audience to react.

KEEP IT SHORT. Resist creating a lengthy presentation. The longer the presentation, the greater the danger of losing your audience's attention.

KEEP THE NUMBER OF WORDS PER SLIDE TO A MINIMUM. The general rule is to limit the number of words per slide to eight. It is better to have more slides with less information than vice versa.

VARY YOUR VISUALS. Keep your presentation moving by blending different types of slides. Add graphics and photographs to create a variety of visual elements.

Presentation graphics programs make it easy to gather and update an engineering, scientific, or business presentation. You may not have time to create a spectacular multimedia show, but that does not mean that your presentation will not be engaging and effective. Just follow the five tips below. The rest is easy.

✓ANALYZE YOUR AUDIENCE
✓ MAKE A PLAN
✓ KEEP IT SHORT
✓ KEEP THE NUMBER OF WORDS PER SLIDE TO A MINIMUM
✓ VARY YOUR VISUALS

Illustration B

Use the Help Index

How do I...?	Enter the Keyword(s)
Change font	Font
Change font size	Font size
Apply small caps	Small caps
View text formatting	Reveal formatting

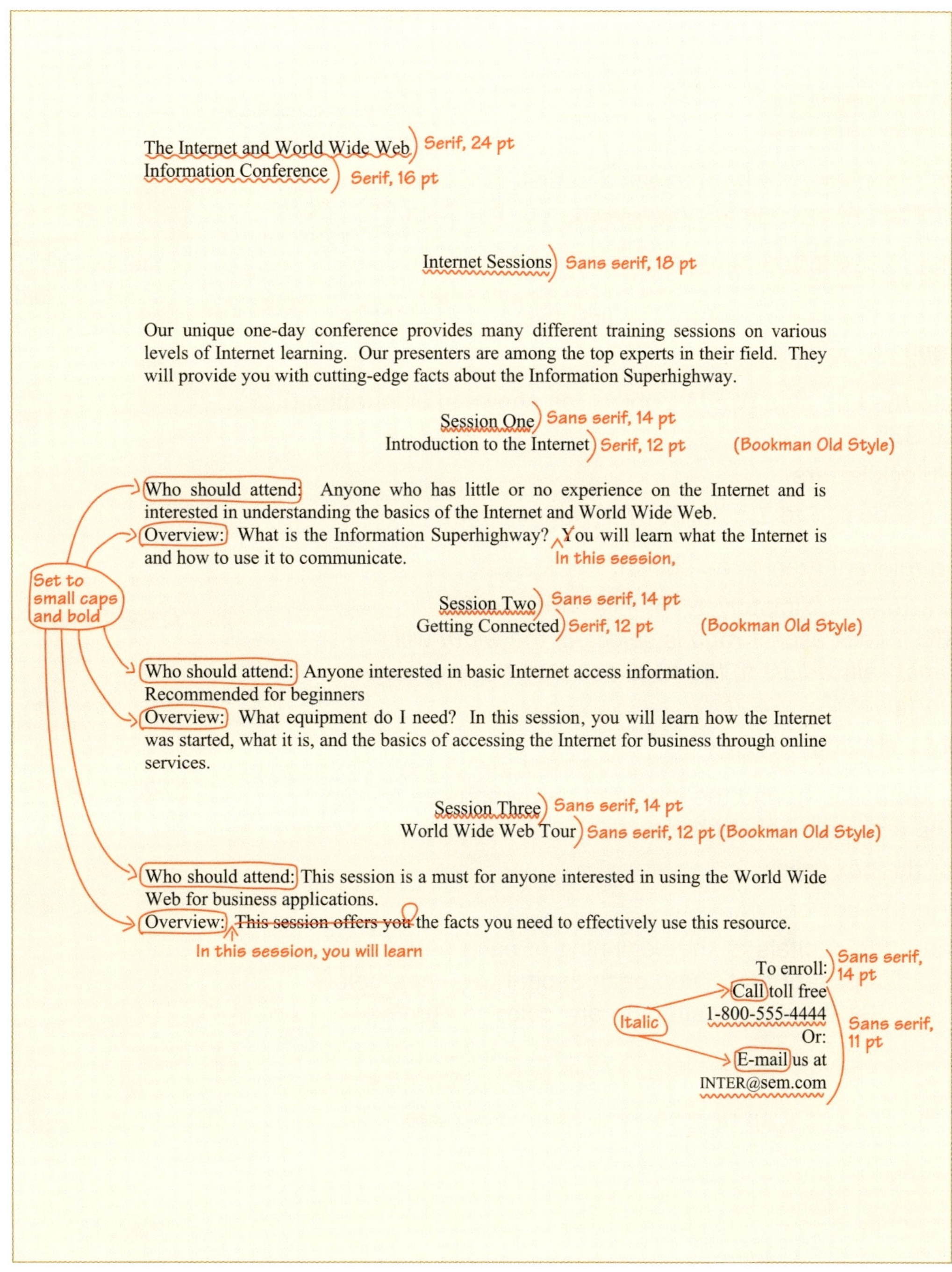

The Internet and World Wide Web
Information Conference

Internet Sessions

Our unique one-day conference provides many different training sessions on various levels of Internet learning. Our presenters are among the top experts in their field. They will provide you with cutting-edge facts about the Information Superhighway.

Session One
Introduction to the Internet

Who should attend: Anyone who has little or no experience on the Internet and is interested in understanding the basics of the Internet and World Wide Web.
Overview: What is the Information Superhighway? You will learn what the Internet is and how to use it to communicate.

Session Two
Getting Connected

Who should attend: Anyone interested in basic Internet access information. Recommended for beginners
Overview: What equipment do I need? In this session, you will learn how the Internet was started, what it is, and the basics of accessing the Internet for business through online services.

Session Three
World Wide Web Tour

Who should attend: This session is a must for anyone interested in using the World Wide Web for business applications.
Overview: This session offers you the facts you need to effectively use this resource.

To enroll:
Call toll free
1-800-555-4444
Or:
E-mail us at
INTER@sem.com

Apply Text Design

EXERCISE 20

Directions

1. Open **4.33present**, which you created in Unit 2 and is shown in Illustration A, or open **d3.20present** from the Data CD.
2. Save the file as **3.20present**.
3. Change the first-line indent for the first two and the last paragraphs to .5".
4. Recreate the title as a WordArt object, as shown in Illustration B on page 335.
   a. Use block letters.
   b. Size the design to 1.5" high by 4" wide.
5. Insert a relevant graphic as shown.
   a. Size it to approximately 1.75" high by 2" wide.
   NOTE: *If Lock aspect ratio is selected, the width will automatically adjust to the height so that the object remains proportionate.*
   b. Apply a shadow effect.
6. Draw a rectangle around the indented paragraphs as shown. Send the rectangle behind the text.
   a. Color the box yellow.
   b. Delete the box border.
   c. Create drop capitals at the beginning of each paragraph using a sans serif font. Drop each capital two lines below the text. Set the drop capitals to any color you prefer.
7. Apply a decorative page border.
8. Adjust the document as necessary to fit on one page.
9. Preview the document.
10. Print one copy.
11. Close the file; save the changes.

HOT TIPS

You can highlight a word and then select the WordArt option. This eliminates the need to reenter the text in the text design box.

Creating Effective Presentations

One day, you might be likely to find yourself in this situation: your employer says, "We need to get a presentation together for the DataAir Project fast!" Because the deadline for such a "request" is usually immediate, you reach for your presentation graphics software program.

The following four pointers can help make noticeable improvements to your next presentation:

ANALYZE YOUR AUDIENCE. Take the time to determine who will be listening. Ask yourself, "Why are you giving this presentation?"

MAKE A PLAN. After you have determined your audience, decide what to say and how to say it. Create an outline after you have analyzed what items you must cover and how you want your audience to react.

KEEP IT SHORT. Resist creating a lengthy presentation. The longer the presentation, the greater the danger of losing your audience's attention.

KEEP THE NUMBER OF WORDS PER SLIDE TO A MINIMUM. The general rule is to limit the number of words per slide to eight. It is better to have more slides with less information than vice versa.

VARY YOUR VISUALS. Keep your presentation moving by blending different types of slides. Add graphics and photographs to create a variety of visual elements.

Presentation graphics programs make it easy to gather and update an engineering, scientific, or business presentation. You may not have time to create a spectacular multimedia show, but that does not mean that your presentation will not be engaging and effective. Just follow the five tips below. The rest is easy.

✓ANALYZE YOUR AUDIENCE
✓ MAKE A PLAN
✓ KEEP IT SHORT
✓ KEEP THE NUMBER OF WORDS PER SLIDE TO A MINIMUM
✓ VARY YOUR VISUALS

Illustration A

Change Fonts and Font Size; Use Symbols

EXERCISE 19

SCANS

Directions

1. Open **3.17eat,** the file you created in Exercise 17, or open **d3.19eat** from the Data CD. 
2. Save the file as **3.19eat**.
3. Make the revisions shown on page 77.
4. Change the fonts and font sizes as indicated.
   NOTE: *Use the recommended fonts if they are available to you. Otherwise, substitute other serif and sans serif fonts.*
5. Insert a symbol of your choice, where indicated, unless one is specified.
   NOTE: *If necessary, delete space between paragraphs to keep the exercise on one page.*
6. Correct spelling.
7. Preview the document.
8. Print one copy.
9. Close the file; save the changes.

Use the Help Index

How do I...?	Enter the Keyword(s)
Insert a symbol	Symbol
Make text superscript	Superscript

VOCABULARY

Superscript
Subscript
Symbol

CONCEPT BUILDERS

- Symbols are ornamental fonts or special characters.
- "Wingdings" is an example of an ornamental font collection.
- A superscript is a character that prints above the writing line (x^2); a subscript is a character that prints below the writing line (H_2O).

DID YOU KNOW?

Symbols can be used to:

- Separate items on a page:

  Wingdings

  ✪✻❁❖

  Graphics

  or

- Emphasize items in a list

  ✂Food

  ✂Clothing

  ✂Shelter

Company News Briefs ♦ A Monthly Publication of CABLECOM, Inc. ♦ May, 2004

New Videophone Sales Off to Great Start

CableCom's new Videophone Supreme, just released in March, had a 22% increase in sales during the month of April.

The new Videophone Supreme enables home computer users to send voice and images over standard phone lines or Internet connections (56K modem, ISDN, DSL, cable modem, etc.).

The Videophone Supreme will be featured on CableCom's Web site beginning May 12.

Windows Lunch Hour Workshops

During the month of May, there will be ongoing lunch hour workshops available to all Windows users. Learn new features, keystrokes, and online options with the Microsoft® Network.

Workshops will be held in the Information Services Conference Room on the 15th floor on Mondays, Wednesdays, and Fridays from 12 noon to 1:00 p.m. There will be a weekly sign-up sheet posted in the 15th floor lobby announcing the focus of each workshop.

Seating is limited to 15 people per workshop, so please sign up early for desired sessions.

CableCom Annual Spring Fling Company Picnic

All CableCom employees and family members are invited to attend this year's Spring Fling Company Picnic.

Festivities will begin at 12 noon on Saturday, June 19 at the South Lawns in Washington Memorial Park. Food and soft drinks will be provided. Bring your gear for softball, Frisbee and volleyball.

Enjoy good food and good friends

Please RSVP to Karen Watson at extension 44 by Monday, May 17, and let her know how many family members will be attending.

CableCom Has An Updated Web Site!

Drop in online and see what's new at CableCom (http://www.cable-com.net).

Illustration B

Insert a symbol

Insert symbol

COMPUTER ASSOCIATES CAFÉ TM Arial, 22 pt, bold

Cuisine At Its Finest Times New Roman, 16 pt

Insert superscript

654 Wilshire Boulevard 1

Los Angeles, CA 90210

Phone: 213-555-5555

Fax: 213-555-6666

Arial, 12 pt

Italic

Featuring Times New Roman, 12 pt

Replace commas with symbols

Leave one space before and after symbol

Freshly Squeezed Juices, Pastries and Danish

A Full Line of Salads, Cold Cuts, Imported Cheeses

Espresso, Cappuccino, A Full Line of Carousel Cakes

A Full Line of Waters (H_2O) and Beverages

Arial, 13 pt

BUSINESS HOURS: Times New Roman, 12 pt

Arial, 14 pt **MONDAY** TO **FRIDAY 6 A. M.** TO **8 P. M.** 2 Insert superscript

Insert a symbol

FREE DELIVERY

Times New Roman, 14 pt, bold

Arial Narrow, 12 pt Prompt and Courteous Service

Arial Narrow, 12 pt

Expertly Done Catering

For Occasions Including Business Breakfasts, Lunches,

Dinner Parties, Meetings, etc.

2x

1 New location opening in December, 2003.

2 Open until 9:30 p.m. on Thursdays.

Times New Roman, 8 pt

Use WordArt; Create Drop Capitals

EXERCISE 19

Directions

1. Open **d3.19news** from the Data CD, which is shown in Illustration A. Save the file as **3.19news**.

2. Recreate the title as a WordArt object, as shown in Illustration B on page 333.
   - Size the design to .75" high by 6.0" wide.
   - Apply a gradient fill using any colors you want.
3. Create drop capitals at the beginning of each paragraph as shown. Drop each capital two lines below the text.
4. Preview the document.
5. Print one copy.
6. Close the file; save the changes.

Drop capital

A ***drop capital*** is an enlarged capital letter that drops below the first line of body text. It is usually the first letter of a paragraph.

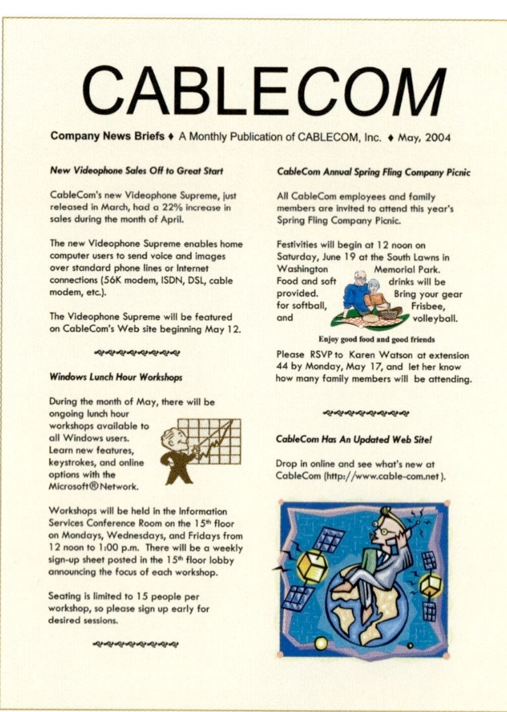

CABLECOM

Company News Briefs ♦ A Monthly Publication of CABLECOM, Inc. ♦ May, 2004

New Videophone Sales Off to Great Start

CableCom's new Videophone Supreme, just released in March, had a 22% increase in sales during the month of April.

The new Videophone Supreme enables home computer users to send voice and images over standard phone lines or Internet connections (56K modem, ISDN, DSL, cable modem, etc.).

The Videophone Supreme will be featured on CableCom's Web site beginning May 12.

Windows Lunch Hour Workshops

During the month of May, there will be ongoing lunch hour workshops available to all Windows users. Learn new features, keystrokes, and online options with the Microsoft® Network.

Workshops will be held in the Information Services Conference Room on the 15th floor on Mondays, Wednesdays, and Fridays from 12 noon to 1:00 p.m. There will be a weekly sign-up sheet posted in the 15th floor lobby announcing the focus of each workshop.

Seating is limited to 15 people per workshop, so please sign up early for desired sessions.

CableCom Annual Spring Fling Company Picnic

All CableCom employees and family members are invited to attend this year's Spring Fling Company Picnic.

Festivities will begin at 12 noon on Saturday, June 19 at the South Lawns in Washington Memorial Park. Food and soft drinks will be provided. Bring your gear for softball, Frisbee, and volleyball.

Enjoy good food and good friends

Please RSVP to Karen Watson at extension 44 by Monday, May 17, and let her know how many family members will be attending.

CableCom Has An Updated Web Site!

Drop in online and see what's new at CableCom (http://www.cable-com.net).

Illustration A

Use the Help Index

How Do I...?	**Enter the keyword(s):**
Create a drop capital	Drop cap

Change Fonts, Font Size, and Font Color; Use Symbols; Copy Formatting

EXERCISE 20

SCANS

Directions

1. Create a new document.
2. Begin the exercise at the top of your screen.
3. Use the default margins.
4. Key the advertisement provided on page 80 using the alignments shown, or open **d3.20montreal** from the Data CD. 
5. Save the file as **3.20montreal**.
6. Justify the first paragraph.
7. Right-align the title, MAJOR FESTIVALS AND EVENTS, as well as the listed festivals and events.
8. Change the fonts and font sizes as follows:
   a. Set "Festivals" to script, 72 pt. Set the font color to red.
   b. Set "in" to Arial, 14 pt, bold.
   c. Set "Montreal" in the subtitle to Arial, 20 pt, bold.
   d. Set "Montreal" in the first paragraph to Arial, 14 pt, bold, and italic. Copy the formatting to the other circled words in the paragraph and to MAJOR FESTIVALS AND EVENTS.
   e. Set the first event to Times New Roman, 12 pt, bold. Copy the formatting to the remaining events.
   f. Set the first date to Times New Roman, 10 pt, italic. Copy the formatting to the remaining dates.
9. Delete the "e" in each occurrence of "Montreal" and replace it with a multinational symbol that includes the accent mark (é).

VOCABULARY

Format Painter

NOTE

Fonts
If you do not have the fonts specified, explore the fonts you do have and use similar ones.

CONCEPT BUILDERS

- You can apply color to fonts.
- You must have a color printer to output color.
- The ***Format Painter*** feature allows you to copy formatting such as font face, style, and size from one block of text to another.

Use the Help Index

How Do I...?	**Enter the keyword(s):**
Create a text design	WordArt

Thank You Around the World

Practice text is used by desktop designers to experiment with placement of objects as well as typefaces,

typestyles, type sizes, and leading in a document. Practice text is also referred to as "dummy" text. Some desktop publishing software programs provide a *lorem ipsum* file. This file contains text that looks like Latin (but it's not). Practice text is used by desktop designers to experiment with placement of objects as well as typefaces, typestyles, type sizes, and leading in a document. Practice text is also referred to as "dummy" text. Some desktop publishing software programs provide a *lorem ipsum* file. This file contains text that looks like Latin (but it's not). Practice text is used by desktop designers to experiment with placement of objects as well as typefaces, typestyles, type sizes, and leading in a document.

Practice text is also referred to as "dummy"

Danke Schoen

text. Some desktop publishing software programs provide a *lorem ipsum* file. This file contains text that looks like Latin (but it's not).

Practice text is used by desktop designers to experiment with placement of objects as well as typefaces, typestyles, type sizes, and leading in a document.

Gracias

Practice text is also referred to as "dummy" text. Some desktop publishing software programs provide a *lorem ipsum* file. This file contains text that looks like Latin (but it's not). Practice text is used by desktop designers to experiment with placement of objects as well as typefaces, typestyles, type sizes, and leading in a document. Practice text is also referred to as "dummy" text. Some desktop publishing software programs provide a *lorem ipsum* file. This file contains text that looks like Latin (but it's not).

Grazie

Practice text is used by desktop designers to experiment with placement of objects as well as typefaces, typestyles, type sizes, and leading in a document. Practice text is also referred to as "dummy" text. Some desktop publishing software programs provide a *lorem ipsum* file. This file contains text that looks like Latin (but it's not).

Practice text is used by desktop designers to experiment with placement of objects as well as typefaces,

Directions *continued*

10. Replace the letters in the following words with a multinational symbol that includes the proper accent mark:
    - Napoléon . . . at Île Sainte-Hélène
    - Festival de Théâtre des Amériques
    - Les Fêtes Gourmandes
    - Insert the word Montreal two lines below the last date; insert any symbol instead of the "o." Apply bold to the word. Set the color of the symbol to red.
11. Correct spelling.
12. Preview the document.
13. Print one copy.
14. Close the file; save the changes.

Use the Help Index

How do I...?	**Enter the Keyword(s)**
Change font color	Color

Use WordArt

EXERCISE 18

SCANS

Directions

1. Open **d3.18practice** from the Data CD. Save the file as **3.18merci**. 
2. Delete the word TITLE.
3. Create the following title as a WordArt object: `Thank You Around the World`
   - Size the design to .72" high by 5.7" wide and position it in the center as the new title as shown in the illustration on page 331.
4. Create a different text design and font for each of the following words. Size and apply an effect for each as directed.
   a. `Merci`
      - Size it to 1" high by 1.5" wide.
      - Wrap text on the top and bottom of the object.

   b. `Grazie`
      - Size it to 1" high by 2" wide.
      - Wrap text around the object.

   c. `Danke Schoen`
      - Size it to .60" high by 2.17" wide.
      - Wrap text around the object.
      - Use a script font.

   d. `Gracias`
      - Size it to .5" high by 1.5" wide.
      - Wrap text around the object.
      - Rotate the object.
5. Delete any text that runs onto the second page.
6. Preview the document.
7. Print one copy.
8. Close the file; save the changes.

VOCABULARY

Text design
WordArt

CONCEPT BUILDERS

- ***Text design*** is the ability to create special effects with text. In Word, this is referred to as WordArt.
- The ***WordArt*** feature lets you create a graphic object using text. Using Word's predesigned WordArt styles, you can create interesting text effects.
- You can size, position, copy, or delete WordArt objects just as you can any other object. You can also apply text-wrap options to WordArt objects.

DID YOU KNOW?

Desktop publishers often use practice text for experimenting with the placement of objects in their documents.

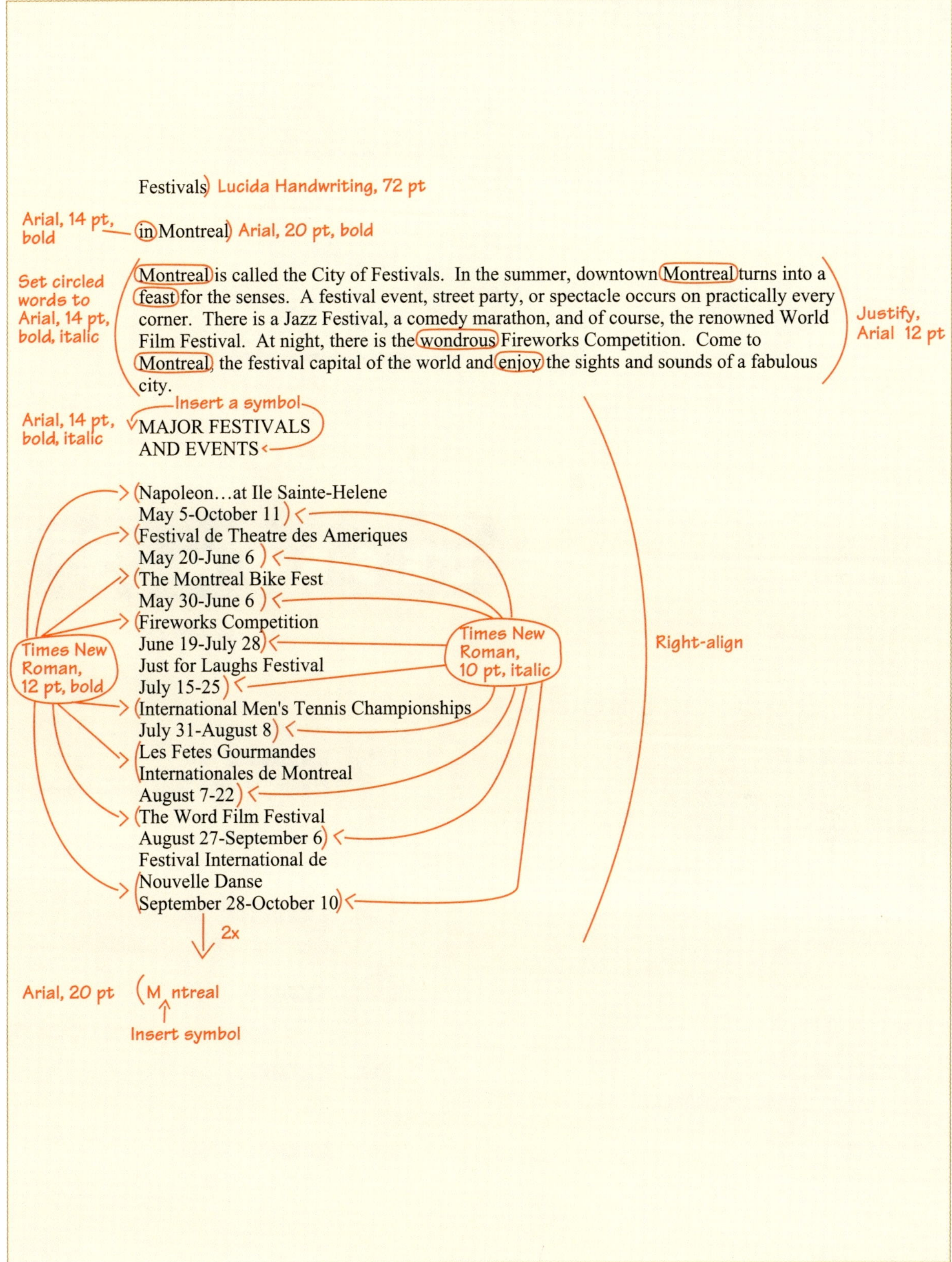

Festivals

in Montreal

Montreal is called the City of Festivals. In the summer, downtown Montreal turns into a feast for the senses. A festival event, street party, or spectacle occurs on practically every corner. There is a Jazz Festival, a comedy marathon, and of course, the renowned World Film Festival. At night, there is the wondrous Fireworks Competition. Come to Montreal, the festival capital of the world and enjoy the sights and sounds of a fabulous city.

MAJOR FESTIVALS
AND EVENTS

Napoleon…at Ile Sainte-Helene
May 5-October 11
Festival de Theatre des Ameriques
May 20-June 6
The Montreal Bike Fest
May 30-June 6
Fireworks Competition
June 19-July 28
Just for Laughs Festival
July 15-25
International Men's Tennis Championships
July 31-August 8
Les Fetes Gourmandes
Internationales de Montreal
August 7-22
The Word Film Festival
August 27-September 6
Festival International de
Nouvelle Danse
September 28-October 10

M ntreal

LESSON 3

Add Special Effects

EXERCISE 18
Use WordArt

EXERCISE 19
Use WordArt; Create Drop Capitals

EXERCISE 20
Apply Text Design

EXERCISE 21
Create Watermarks

EXERCISE 22
Create Watermarks; Use Paragraph Borders and Shading

EXERCISE 23
Create Reverse Text; Use Letter Spacing

EXERCISE 24
Create Reverse Text; Use Letter Spacing

EXERCISE 25
Create Pull Quotes

EXERCISE 26
Use Special Page Layouts

EXERCISE 27
Skills Review

EXERCISE 28
Skills Review

EXERCISE 29
Skills Review

Change Fonts, Font Size, and Font Color; Copy Formatting; Use Symbols, Bullets, and Numbering

EXERCISE 21

Directions

1. Create a new document.
2. Key the exercise shown on page 82.
3. Begin the letterhead at the top of your screen.
4. Use the default margins.
5. Set the letterhead text to the fonts and sizes indicated in the exercise. Copy the formatting for the address, city, and state to the phone number and Web site address.
6. Insert any symbol you want, where shown.
7. Add bullets and a numbered list, where shown.
8. Save the file as **3.21cclet**.
   NOTE: *The letterhead will remain saved as a separate file and will be used in subsequent exercises.*
9. Begin the letter 3" down from the top of the page.
10. Set the body text to a serif, 10 pt font.
11. Set the text "Riverside Bank Run for Children" in the first paragraph to a sans serif, 12 pt, bold font. Copy the formatting to the other occurrences in the remaining paragraphs.
12. Correct spelling.
13. Bold the enclosure notation.
14. Preview the document.
15. Undo the bolded enclosure notation.
16. Print one copy.
17. Save the exercise; name it **3.21run**.

VOCABULARY

Bullet

CONCEPT BUILDERS

- A ***bullet*** is a dot or symbol used to highlight points of information or to itemize a list.
- The Bullets and Numbering feature allows the user to insert bullets and/or numbers automatically to create bulleted or numbered lists. To access this feature, click Format, Bullets and Numbering.
- In a modified-block letter, the date, signature, and closing are aligned and placed at 3.5" or 4" from the left margin.

TIPS FOR CARING: PALMS
•
•
•
Feel like you're on vacation while sitting on your backyard!
TIPS FOR CARING: CACTI
•
•
•
BACKYARD NURSERIES

Use the Help Index

How do I...?	Enter the Keyword(s)
Apply bullets or numbering	Bullet

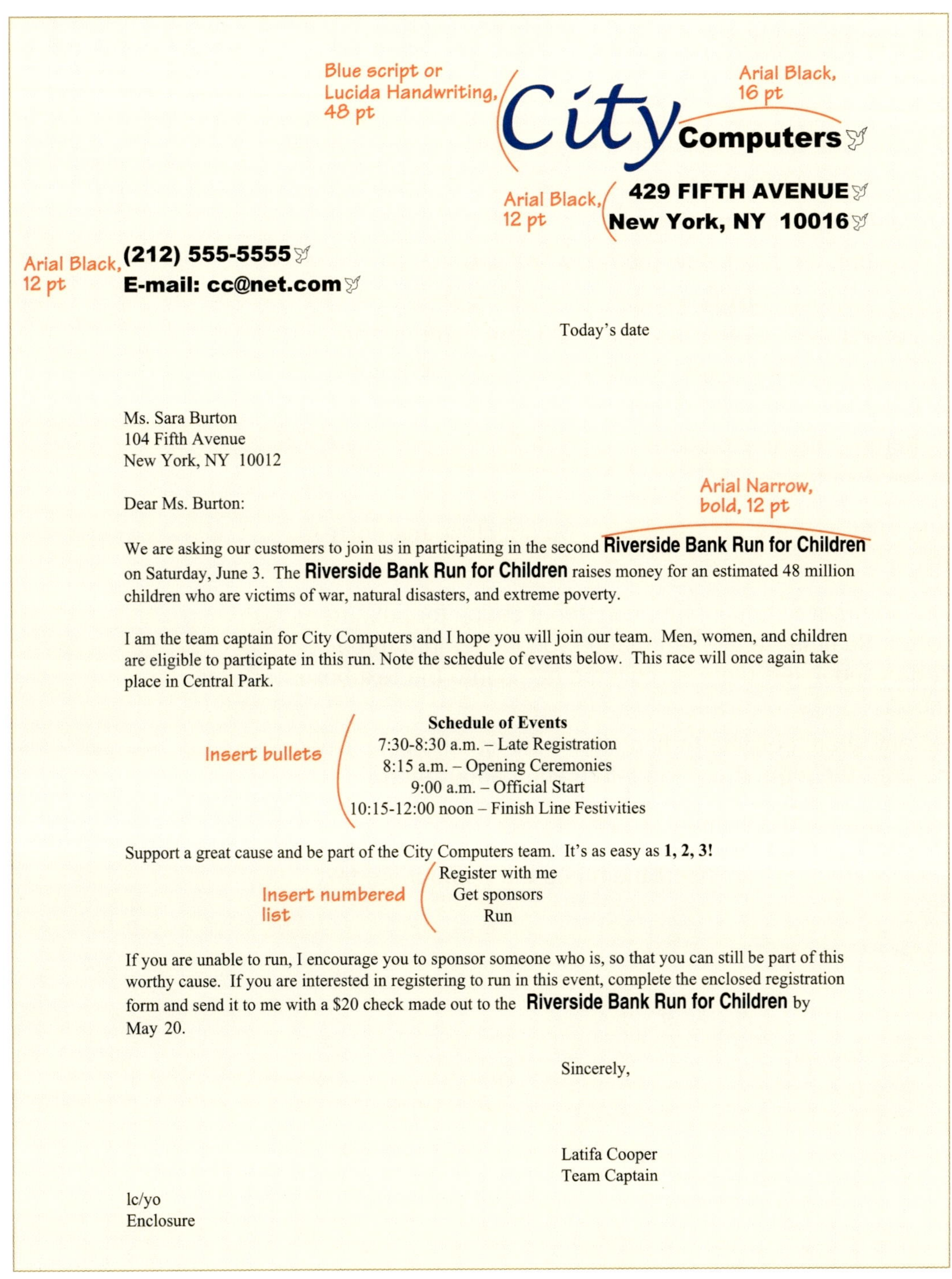

City Computers
429 FIFTH AVENUE
New York, NY 10016

(212) 555-5555
E-mail: cc@net.com

Today's date

Ms. Sara Burton
104 Fifth Avenue
New York, NY 10012

Dear Ms. Burton:

We are asking our customers to join us in participating in the second **Riverside Bank Run for Children** on Saturday, June 3. The **Riverside Bank Run for Children** raises money for an estimated 48 million children who are victims of war, natural disasters, and extreme poverty.

I am the team captain for City Computers and I hope you will join our team. Men, women, and children are eligible to participate in this run. Note the schedule of events below. This race will once again take place in Central Park.

Schedule of Events
7:30-8:30 a.m. – Late Registration
8:15 a.m. – Opening Ceremonies
9:00 a.m. – Official Start
10:15-12:00 noon – Finish Line Festivities

Support a great cause and be part of the City Computers team. It's as easy as **1, 2, 3!**
Register with me
Get sponsors
Run

If you are unable to run, I encourage you to sponsor someone who is, so that you can still be part of this worthy cause. If you are interested in registering to run in this event, complete the enclosed registration form and send it to me with a $20 check made out to the **Riverside Bank Run for Children** by May 20.

Sincerely,

Latifa Cooper
Team Captain

lc/yo
Enclosure

ii. Color it light green and apply a 1 pt black line border.

iii. Position it as shown.

iv. Layer the triangle so it is in front of the rectangle.

v. Group the shapes.

c. Create a text box.

i. Enter `BACKYARD NURSERIES` in a 10 pt, bold, sans serif font, and center-align the text. Color the text purple.

ii. Fill the box light green.

iii. Remove the line border.

iv. Position the box below the house as shown.

d. Create two more text boxes.

i. Enter `TIPS FOR CARING: PALMS` and `TIPS FOR CARING: CACTI` in a 10 pt sans serif font.

ii. Color each box light green.

iii. Remove the line borders.

iv. Position the text boxes as shown.

8. Save the file; name it **2.17backyard**. Do not close the document.

9. Use the Internet to find information about caring for palm trees and cacti. Summarize the information you gather into three short tips and insert them as bulleted items into the text boxes as shown.

- Use any search engine to find sites on cacti and palm trees, and print the sites that have information about them.

10. Switch to the Word document **2.17backyard**.

11. Summarize the tips and insert them into the appropriate text boxes.

12. Print one copy of the document.

13. Close the file; save the changes.

14. Close the browser.

Change Fonts and Font Size; Use Symbols, Bullets, and Numbering; Format Bullets

EXERCISE 22

Directions

1. Open **2.12bp,** the file you created in Exercise 12, or open **d3.22bp** from the Data CD.
2. Save the file as **3.22bp**.
3. At the top of your screen, create and center the letterhead shown on page 84.
   a. Set "Bank of Michigan" to a sans serif, 18 pt font. Set the font color to dark green.
   b. Set the remaining information to 10 pt.
   c. Insert any symbol you want between the information. Set the symbol color to dark green.
4. Adjust the dateline to begin approximately 2" down from the top of the page.
5. Change the font size for the letter to 10 pt.
6. Make the indicated insertions and deletions in the exercise shown on the next page.
7. Change the color of the bullets to green.
8. Correct spelling.
9. Preview the document.
10. Print one copy.
11. Close the file; save the changes.

HOT TIPS

You can select bullets independently of text, allowing you to format bullets without affecting the text. This feature is not available to Word 2000 users.

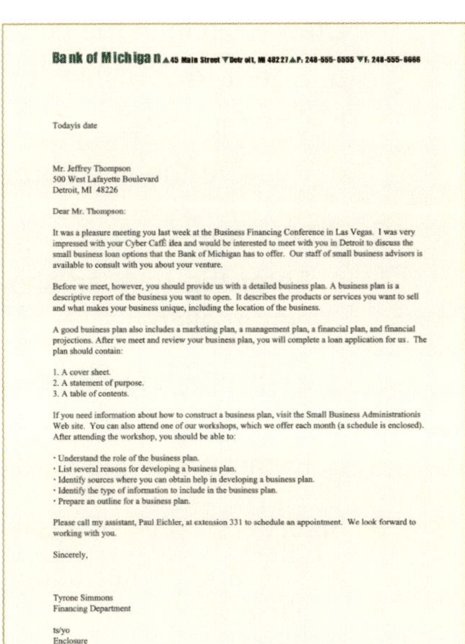

Bank of Michigan ▲45 Main Street ▼Detroit, MI 48227▲P: 248-555-5555 ▼F: 248-555-6666

Todayís date

Mr. Jeffrey Thompson
500 West Lafayette Boulevard
Detroit, MI 48226

Dear Mr. Thompson:

It was a pleasure meeting you last week at the Business Financing Conference in Las Vegas. I was very impressed with your Cyber CafÈ idea and would be interested to meet with you in Detroit to discuss the small business loan options that the Bank of Michigan has to offer. Our staff of small business advisors is available to consult with you about your venture.

Before we meet, however, you should provide us with a detailed business plan. A business plan is a descriptive report of the business you want to open. It describes the products or services you want to sell and what makes your business unique, including the location of the business.

A good business plan also includes a marketing plan, a management plan, a financial plan, and financial projections. After we meet and review your business plan, you will complete a loan application for us. The plan should contain:

1. A cover sheet.
2. A statement of purpose.
3. A table of contents.

If you need information about how to construct a business plan, visit the Small Business Administrationís Web site. You can also attend one of our workshops, which we offer each month (a schedule is enclosed). After attending the workshop, you should be able to:

- Understand the role of the business plan.
- List several reasons for developing a business plan.
- Identify sources where you can obtain help in developing a business plan.
- Identify the type of information to include in the business plan.
- Prepare an outline for a business plan.

Please call my assistant, Paul Eichler, at extension 331 to schedule an appointment. We look forward to working with you.

Sincerely,

Tyrone Simmons
Financing Department

ts/yo
Enclosure

Solution

Skills Review

EXERCISE 17

SCANS

Directions

1. Create a new document, as shown on page 328.
2. Set 1.25" left and right margins and 1" top and bottom margins.
3. Draw a square.
   a. Size it to 10" high by 7.8" wide.
   b. Color it light green.
   c. Apply a 1.5 pt black line border.
4. Draw a circle in the center of the square.
   a. Size it to 7.5" high by 7.5" wide.
   b. Color it white.
   c. Remove the line border.
5. Create a text box.
   a. Enter the text, as shown, using a 20 pt, bold, serif font, and center-align it.
   b. Color the text purple.
   c. Size the text box to approximately .4" high by 7.4" wide.
   d. Remove the line border.
6. Insert a graphic of a palm tree and a cactus plant.
   - Size and center each to fit the top and bottom halves of the circle as shown.
     NOTE: *If these graphics are not available, you can download them from the Internet at www.clip-art.com or http://dgl.microsoft.com.*
7. Create the logo as follows:
   a. Draw a triangle.
      - Size it to approximately .25" high by 1.5" wide.
      - Color it light green and apply a 1 pt black line border.
   b. Draw a rectangle.
      i. Size it to approximately .2" high by .075" wide.

Bank of Michigan • 45 Main Street • Detroit, MI 48227 • P: 248-555-5555 • F: 248-555-6666

Today's date

Mr. Jeffrey Thompson
500 West Lafayette Boulevard
Detroit, MI 48226

Dear Mr. Thompson:

It was a pleasure meeting you last week at the Business Financing and Conference in Las Vegas. I was very impressed with your Cyber Café idea. I would be very interested in meeting with you in Detroit to discuss the small business loan options that the Bank of Michigan has to offer. Our staff of small business advisors is available to consult with you about your venture.

Before we meet, however, you should provide us with a detailed business plan. A business plan is a descriptive report of the business you want to open. It describes the products or services you want to sell and what makes your business unique, including the location of the business.

A good business plan also includes a marketing plan, a management plan, a financial plan, and financial projections. After we meet and review your business plan, you will complete a loan application for us.

If you need information about how to construct a business plan, visit the Small Business Administration's Web site.

Insert

Please call my assistant, Paul Eichler, at extension 331 (248) 555-5555 to schedule an appointment. We look forward to working with you.

Sincerely,

Tyrone Simmons
Financing Department

ts/yo
Enclosure

The plan should contain:

1. A cover sheet.
2. A statement of purpose.
3. A table of contents.

You can also attend one of our workshops, which we offer each month (a schedule is enclosed). After attending the workshop, you should be able to:

• Understand the role of the business plan.
• List several reasons for developing a business plan.
• Identify sources where you can obtain help in developing a business plan.
• Identify the type of information to include in the business plan.
• Prepare an outline for a business plan.

Skills Review

EXERCISE 16

SCANS

Directions

1. Open **2.15eat**.
2. Review the flyer.
3. Create a new document.
4. Create a different logo for the Computer Associates Café.
5. Save the file; name it **2.16caflogo**. Do not close the file.
6. Switch to **2.15eat**.
7. Delete all logos.
8. Change the fonts, font sizes, alignments, and logo placement to create another flyer.
9. Include information about surfing the Internet while enjoying coffee. Remove the footnotes.
10. Copy the logo created in **2.16caflogo** and place it as you prefer in this document.
11. Preview the document.
12. Print one copy.
13. Save the file; name it **2.16neweat**.

Include this exercise in your portfolio.

Change Fonts and Font Size; Use Symbols, Bullets, and Numbering

EXERCISE 23

Directions

SCANS

1. Open **3.16party,** the file you created in Exercise 16, or open **d3.23party** from the Data CD.
2. Save the file as **3.23party**.
3. Make the revisions shown in the illustration on page 86.
4. Change the fonts and font sizes indicated in the exercise.
5. Copy the formatting from one line to the next, where appropriate.
6. Use any serif font except Times New Roman.
7. Insert a symbol of your choice, where indicated, unless one is specified.
   NOTE: *If necessary, delete space between paragraphs to keep the exercise on one page.*
8. Preview the document; a sample solution is shown on this page.
9. Print one copy.
10. Close the file; save the changes.

THE COMPUTER END-USERS' ASSOCIATION

Cordially Invites You
to a
Year-End Celebration

❋❋❋❋

❋❋❋❋ **COMPUTER PARTY** ❋❋❋❋

Friday Evening, May 19
at
8:00 p.m.
in the Computer Annex
of Mayfair College

Professor Gilbert Jones will be honored
on the
Occasion of His Retirement after 30 Years of Teaching

<u>Professor Jones will announce his new software program on this occasion</u>.

- **RSVP by May 5**
- Contribution $25.00 per person

Do the following:
1. Fill out the information below.
2. Make checks payable to ***COMPUTER END-USERS' ASSOCIATION.***
3. Tear off and return in the enclosed envelope.

Name________________________ ❒ will ❒ will not attend.

Name of Guest____________________Check enclosed for $_____

Solution

Directions *continued*

13. Close **2.15eat**; save the changes.
14. Close **2.15logo**.

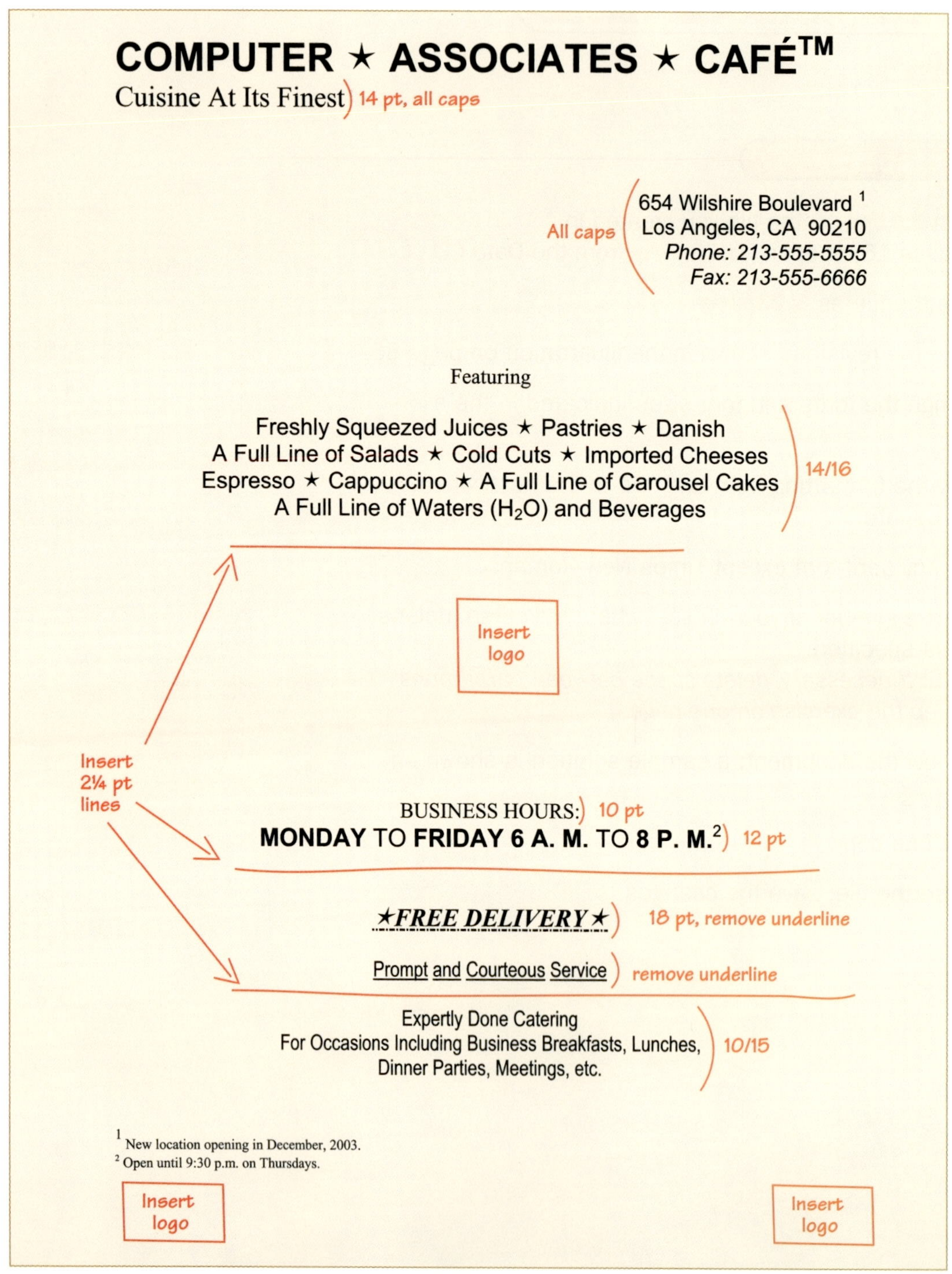

Illustration B

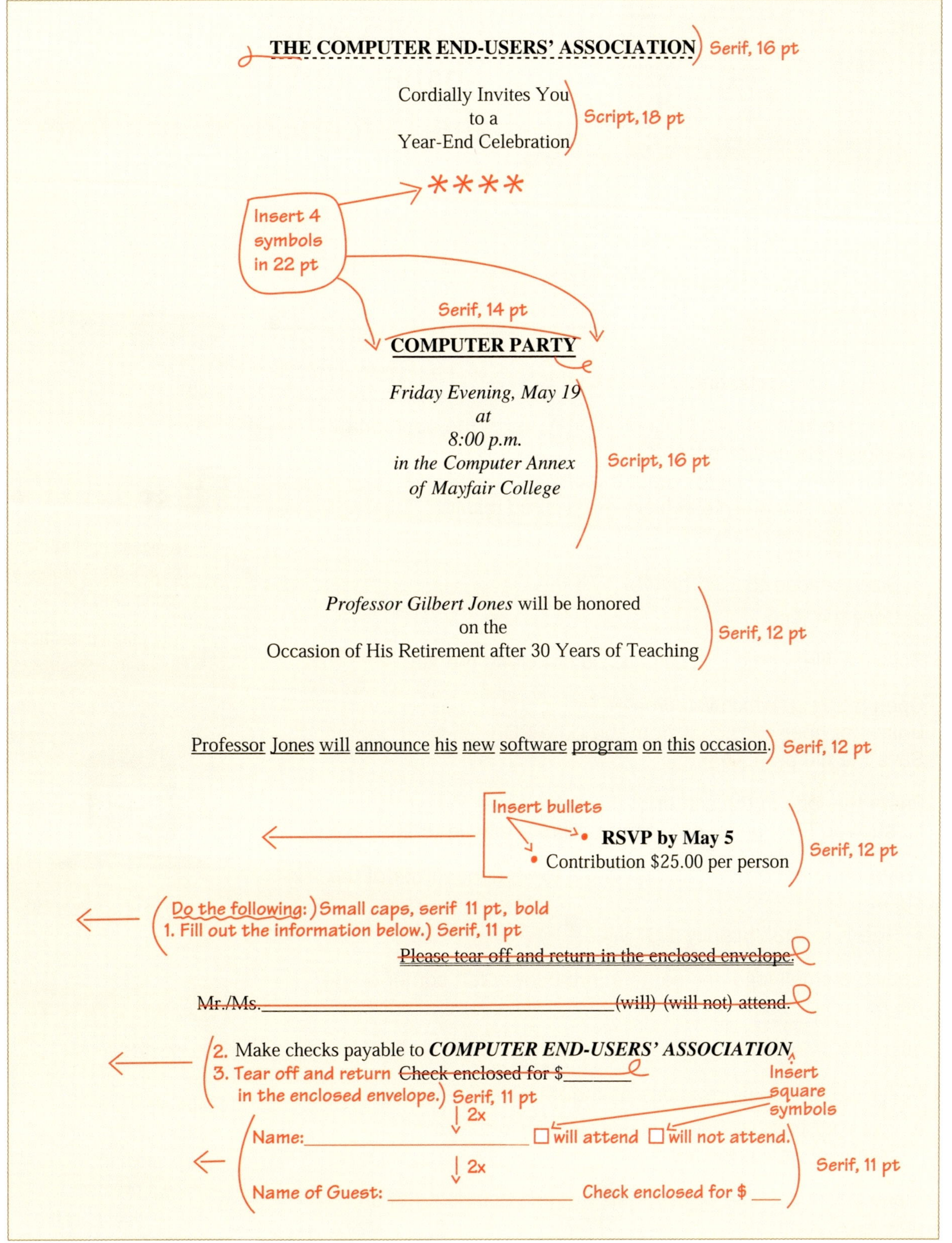

THE COMPUTER END-USERS' ASSOCIATION

Cordially Invites You
to a
Year-End Celebration

COMPUTER PARTY

Friday Evening, May 19
at
8:00 p.m.
in the Computer Annex
of Mayfair College

Professor Gilbert Jones will be honored
on the
Occasion of His Retirement after 30 Years of Teaching

Professor Jones will announce his new software program on this occasion.

- **RSVP by May 5**
- Contribution $25.00 per person

Please tear off and return in the enclosed envelope.

Mr./Ms.________________________(will) (will not) attend.

Make checks payable to ***COMPUTER END-USERS' ASSOCIATION***

Check enclosed for $______

Copy, Group, and Ungroup Shapes and Objects; Change the Direction of an Object

EXERCISE 15

SCANS

Directions

1. Create a new document.
2. Create the logo, shown in Illustration A, using the appropriate drawing tools and colors.
   NOTE: *The tools used to create the object are indicated. Layer the shapes appropriately to achieve the desired result.*
3. Group the logo.
   a. Size the logo to 1.6" high by 2" wide.
   b. Copy the logo.
4. Save the file; name it **2.15logo**. Do not close the file.
5. Open **3.19eat**, which you created in Unit 2, or open **d2.15eat** from the Data CD.  Save the file as **2.15eat**.
6. Paste the logo in the center of the exercise as indicated in Illustration B on page 324; center-align it relative to the page.
7. Paste another copy of the logo in the lower-right corner of the page.
   - Size it to .98" high by 1.3" wide.
8. Copy the small logo and paste it in the lower-left corner of the page.
9. Align the small logos in the middle, relative to each other.
10. Make the remaining revisions as indicated in Illustration B.
    - Use your creativity and apply any color to the text (or graphics) as you prefer.
11. Make any necessary adjustments so the document fits on one page.
12. Preview the document and print one copy.

VOCABULARY

Logo

CONCEPT BUILDERS

- A ***logo*** is a symbol, picture, or saying that creates an image of a company.
- You can flip or rotate objects, if these features are available.

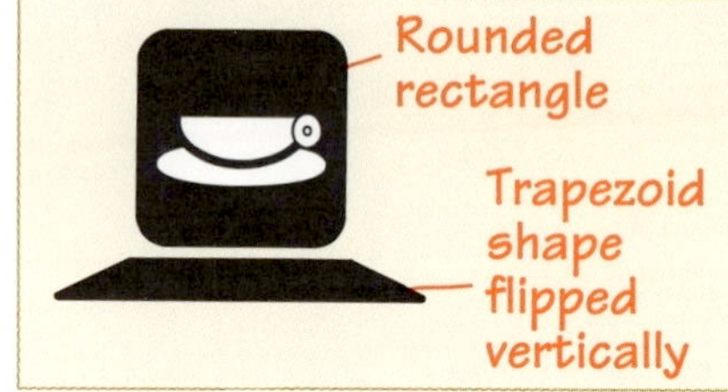

Illustration A

HOT TIPS

To create the saucer, draw an oval. To create the cup, draw another oval and place it over the saucer. Create a square and place it over the oval to create the top of the cup. Apply the borders and colors appropriately to complete the image.

Change Fonts and Font Size; Use Symbols

EXERCISE 24

SCANS

Directions

1. Create a new document.
2. Use the default margins.
3. Begin the letterhead at the top of your screen. Set the letterhead text to the fonts and sizes indicated in the illustration on page 88.
4. Insert any symbols you want, where shown, and color them as indicated.
5. Preview the document.
6. Print one copy.
7. Save the file; name it **3.24tennis**.

VOCABULARY

Personal business letter

CONCEPT BUILDERS

A ***personal business letter*** is written on behalf of the sender, not the entire company. Personal business letters are written on a personal letterhead and do not require the sender's title or reference initials.

Directions *continued*

16. Paste the small globe to the left of the footer text.
17. Copy the small globe and paste it to the right of the footer text.
18. Align the objects in the middle, relative to each other.
19. Preview the document.
20. Print one copy.
21. Save the file; name it **2.14gcc**.

Calisto MT
or serif, 14 pt, bold

Blue symbols, 14 pt

◊ **Lisa Howe** ◊

Arial Narrow,
10 pt

1029 Shore Road ◊ Brooklyn, NY 11209
(718) 555-8029 ◊ lhowe@abc.net

Blue symbols, 10 pt

Today's Date

Ms. Susan Barnes
249 State Street
New Haven, CT 06520

Dear Susan:

Congratulations on your win in the statewide Connecticut Tennis Tournament.

It is no surprise to me that you won since your performance against me on the tennis court last summer was outstanding. I look forward to playing with you again soon.

Let me know if you hear of any upcoming tournaments, as I would enjoy participating.

Once more, my congratulations to you!

Sincerely,

Lisa Howe

Copy, Group, Ungroup, and Regroup Shapes and Objects; Align and Distribute Objects

EXERCISE 14

SCANS

Directions

1. Open **2.12layer**, the file you created in Exercise 12.
2. Copy the globe.
3. Close the document.
4. Create a new document.
5. Paste the globe in the center of the new document.
6. Ungroup the globe.
7. Change the line width to 12 pt.
8. Regroup the globe.
9. Size the globe to 1.5" high x 1.5" wide.
10. Set 1" left and right margins.
11. Create the letterhead text shown on page 322.
    a. Set the company name to a decorative 16 pt font.
    b. Set the address and phone information to a 10 pt sans serif font.
12. Position the globe to the left of the letterhead text and apply a text-wrap option to flow the text around the graphic.
13. Copy the globe graphic once and paste it in the center of the page.
14. Ungroup the object.
    a. Change the line width to 4 pt.
    b. Group the object again.
    c. Size it to .5" high by .5" wide.
    d. Cut the globe (to the Clipboard).
15. Insert the bottom text as a footer.

VOCABULARY

Ungroup
Regroup

CONCEPT BUILDERS

- To edit a grouped object, you must ***ungroup*** it, or break the whole into individual parts.
- The ***Regroup*** command allows you to group objects that were separated using the Ungroup command.
- The Align and Distribute option on the Draw menu allows you to align or distribute objects in relation to each other, or to distribute them evenly on the page.

Skills Review

EXERCISE 25

In this exercise, you will create your own letterhead to use to write a personal letter of complaint.

You ordered new computer equipment from City Computers that included:

- Kell Computer P6400 GX
- 64 MB RAM
- 14-32X CD-ROM
- 17" Monitor
- 13 GB Hard Drive
- 3-year on-site Warranty

However, your order, which arrived today, was incorrect. You received a 15" monitor and you were charged $1,600, $100 more than the agreed-upon price of $1,500. Your confirmation number is 9000021.

Directions

SCANS

1. Create a new document.
2. Use the default margins.
3. Create your own letterhead using any fonts, font sizes, and font colors.
4. Include your name, address, and phone number in the letterhead.
5. Begin the letterhead at the top of your screen.
6. Save the file as **3.25mylet**. Do not close the file.
7. Write a full-block letter to:
   Mr. Robert Manes, Manager
   City Computers
   429 Fifth Avenue
   New York, NY 10016
   - Tell Mr. Manes your problem and how you would like to see it resolved.
8. Correct spelling.

PORTFOLIO

Include this exercise in your portfolio.

DID YOU KNOW?

A personal letter does not require that you include a title (after your name) or reference initials.

Illustration A

Illustration B

Directions *continued*

9. Print one copy.
10. Save the file as **3.25problem**.
11. Open **3.25mylet**.
    NOTE: *Your personalized letterhead should be intact because you saved it under its own file name.*
12. Close **3.25mylet**.

Copy and Group Shapes and Objects

EXERCISE 13

SCANS

Directions

1. Create a new document.
2. Using the appropriate drawing tools and AutoShapes, create the designs shown in Illustration A on page 320.
   a. Copy any shape that is used more than once and paste it as shown.
   b. Use the line widths indicated.
   c. Color the shapes as shown.
   d. Group each design.
3. Size each design as follows:
   - Musical note: 2" high by 1.58" wide
   - Flower: 2" high by 2" wide
   - Owl: 2" high by 2" wide
   - Film strip: 3" high by 1" wide
   - Tree: 2.5" high by 2" wide
4. Move each design on the page, as shown in Illustration B on page 320.
5. Copy the tree and position it in the center of the page.
6. Preview the document.
7. Print one copy.
8. Save the file; name it **2.13objects**.

HOT TIPS

- To create the flower, draw a series of solid circles and place them close to each other. Then group the circles.
- Use the Freeform option to create the tree.

Skills Review

EXERCISE 26

In this exercise, you have been asked to create two flyers for the Willow Canyon High School Computer Club. Each flyer should contain the same information, but you should design them differently.

Use any text alignments, fonts, font sizes, font colors, and/or symbols you prefer to make your flyers attractive. Remember, a flyer should attract the reader's immediate attention.

Directions

SCANS

1. Include the following points of information in your flyer:
   a. The Willow Canyon High School Computer Club needs new members to help plan and design the 2003 issue of WILLOW, the school's literary magazine.
   b. Learn how to put together a literary magazine!
   c. Meetings are held every Thursday at 2:30 p.m. in Room A234.
   d. Spring meetings will be held April 1, 8, 15, 22, and 29, and May 5, 12, and 19.
   e. Club members will also become involved with:
      - Choosing software.
      - Gathering information for database reporting.
      - Creating designs with desktop publishing software.
      - Creating presentations.
      - Using spreadsheet software for grade averages.
      - Preparing résumés.
   f. Interested students should see Steve Yodice, senior class president, in the Senior Office, Room A111.
2. Correct spelling.
3. Print one copy of each flyer.
4. Save the file; name it **3.26schoolad**.

Include this exercise in your portfolio.

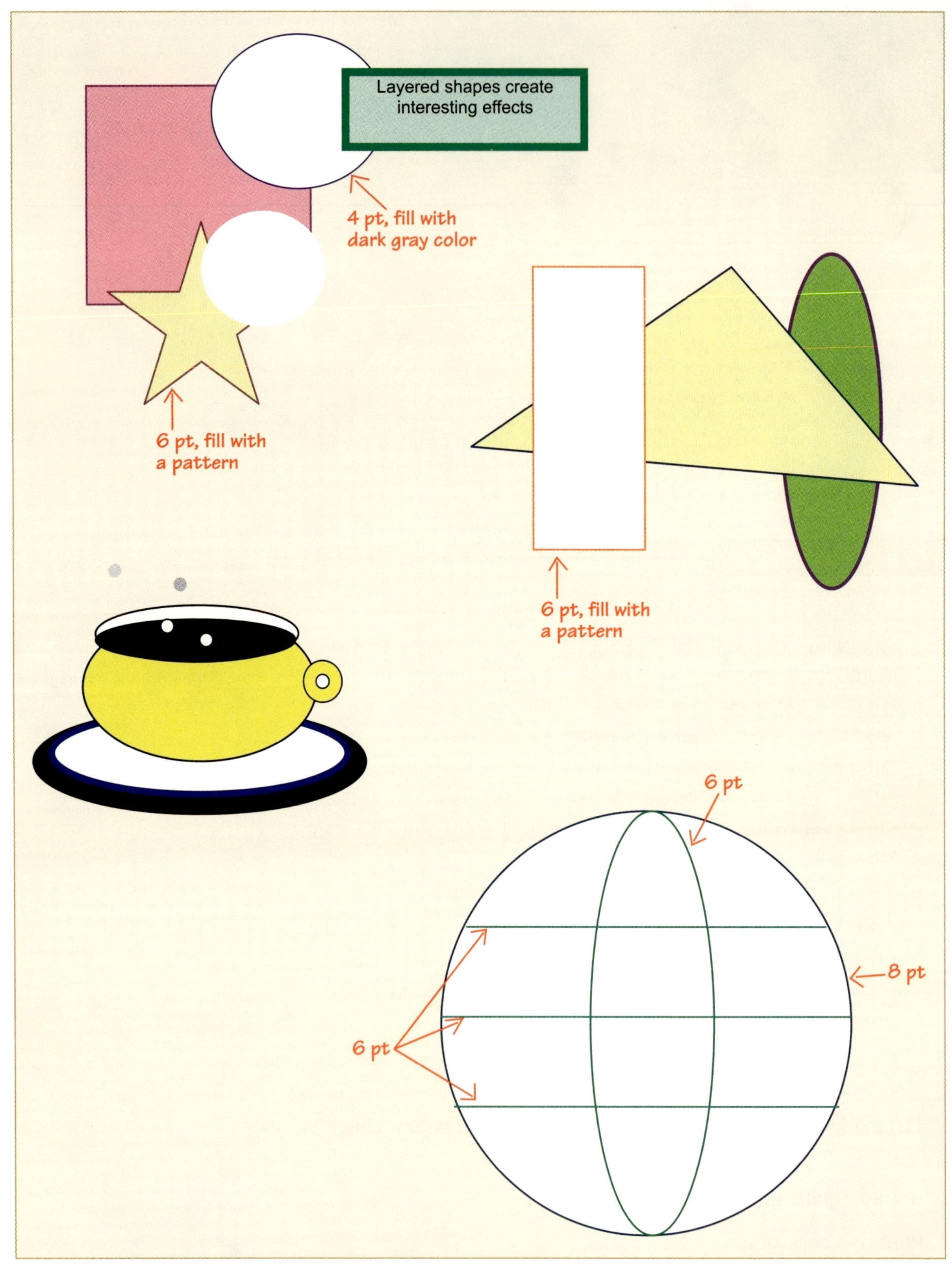
Layered shapes create interesting effects
4 pt, fill with dark gray color
6 pt, fill with a pattern
6 pt, fill with a pattern
6 pt
8 pt
6 pt

LESSON 4

Basic Document Formatting and Editing

EXERCISE 27
Indent Text; Change Line Spacing

EXERCISE 28
Indent Text; Change Line Spacing

EXERCISE 29
Indent Text; Change Line Spacing; Change Paragraph Spacing; Set Margins

EXERCISE 30
Indent Text; Change Paragraph Spacing; Set Margins

EXERCISE 31
Move Text (Cut and Paste); Set Margins; Change Case

EXERCISE 32
Move Text (Drag and Drop); Change Case

EXERCISE 33
Move and Copy Text; Change Case

EXERCISE 34
Move and Copy Text; Set Tab Stops

EXERCISE 35
Copy Text; Set Tabs with Leaders

EXERCISE 36
Skills Review

EXERCISE 37
Skills Review

Group and Layer Objects

EXERCISE 12

SCANS

Directions

1. Create a new document.
2. Using the appropriate drawing tools, create and layer the shapes as shown in the illustration on page 318.
   a. Use any sizes you want for your shapes.
   b. Change the line widths and line colors as indicated.
   c. Rearrange the stacking order of the first group of shapes.
   d. Group each cluster of shapes.
3. Preview the document.
4. Print one copy.
5. Save the file; name it **2.12layer**.

VOCABULARY

Send to Back
Bring to Front
Group

Use the Help Index

How Do I...?	**Enter the keyword(s):**
Group shapes	Group
Layer objects	Layer

CONCEPT BUILDERS

- When you layer or stack shapes on top of each other, you create shadowing and other effects.
- To rearrange the order of layered shapes or objects, first select the shape or object you want to reorder. Then click Draw on the Drawing toolbar, click Order, and choose the layering option you want. You can use the Send to Back and Bring to Front commands. ***Send to Back*** moves an item to the bottom of all the other items in the stack; ***Bring to Front*** moves an item to the top of all other items in the stack.
- When you ***group*** objects, you create one object out of individual parts. Grouped objects behave like a single object.
- To group objects, hold down the Shift key as you select the individual objects, or drag the pointer tool around all the objects (to select them all at once). Then click Draw on the Drawing toolbar and click Group.

Indent Text; Change Line Spacing

EXERCISE 27

Directions

1. Create a new document.
2. Begin the exercise 2" down from the top of the page.
3. Use the default margins.
4. Center and set the report title to serif, 14 pt, bold; set the body text to serif, 11 pt.
5. Key the paragraphs provided, as shown on page 94.
6. Set line spacing to double for the first three paragraphs.
7. Set a 1" first-line indent for the first three paragraphs.
8. Return the first-line indent to zero (0).
9. Indent the remaining paragraphs .5" from the left and right margins.
10. Correct spelling.
11. Preview the document.
12. Print one copy.
13. Save the file; name it **4.27present**.

VOCABULARY

Left indent
Right indent
First-line indent

CONCEPT BUILDERS

- The ***Left*** and ***Right Indent*** feature on most software sets a temporary left and/or right margin for paragraph text.
- You can also create a first-line indent using this feature. A ***first-line indent*** lets you specify the amount of space each new paragraph is indented. When you press the Enter key, the insertion point automatically moves to the indented setting.
- Use line spacing to specify the distance between lines of text. The default line spacing is set to single.

DID YOU KNOW?

- The proofreaders' mark for left indent is: [. The mark for right indent is:].
- Reports are generally double-spaced. Press the Enter key four times (or twice if you are set for double spacing) after the title of a report.

Use the Help Index

How Do I...?	Enter the keyword(s):
Indent paragraphs	Indent
Change line spacing	Line spacing

Use the Help Index

How Do I...?	Enter the keyword(s):
Draw a shape	Draw

Illustration B

HOT TIPS

- To display the Drawing toolbar, click View, select Toolbars, and click Drawing.
- To draw a perfect circle or a perfect square, hold down the Shift key as you drag the insertion point.
- To draw a freeform shape, click the AutoShapes list arrow on the Drawing toolbar, select Lines, and click the Freeform option.

DID YOU KNOW?

It is not necessary to create your drawing within the drawing canvas. You can delete the canvas by pressing the Delete key before you begin drawing. You can also draw the object outside the canvas (which automatically deletes the canvas) and then position the object as you prefer.

CREATING EFFECTIVE PRESENTATIONS

One day, you are likely to find yourself in this situation: your employer walks up to you and says, "We need to get a presentation together for the DataAir Project fast!" Because the deadline for such a "request" is usually immediate, you reach for your presentation graphics program.

Presentation graphics programs make it easy to gather and update an engineering, scientific, or business presentation. You may not have time to create a wondrous multimedia show, but that does not mean that your presentation will not be engaging and effective.

The following four pointers can help make noticeable improvements to your next presentation:

.5" .5"

Make a Plan. After you have determined your audience, decide what to say and how to say it. Create an outline after you have analyzed what items you must cover and how you want your audience to react.

Analyze Your Audience. Take the time to determine who will be listening. Ask yourself, "Why are you giving this presentation?"

Keep the Number of Words per Slide to a Minimum. The general rule is to limit the number of words per slide to eight. It is better to have more slides with less information than vice versa.

Keep it Short. Resist creating a lengthy presentation. The longer the presentation, the greater the danger of losing your audience's attention.

Create, Position, and Size a Shape; Apply a Border and Fill

EXERCISE 11

SCANS

Directions

1. Create a new document.
2. Using the appropriate drawing tools and AutoShapes, draw the shapes shown in Illustration A.
   NOTE: *Do not draw the shapes inside the drawing canvas (if this feature is available to you).*
   a. Position each shape at the left side of the page.
   b. Size each shape to 1" high by 1" wide.
   c. Fill each shape with a different color and/or pattern, and apply any border line style and color you prefer. Vary your selections.
3. Save the file; name it **2.11shapes**.
4. Resize each shape to 2" high by 2" wide and move each shape to a new location on the page, as shown in Illustration B on page 316.
5. Create a hexagon in the center of the page.
   a. Size it to 2" wide by 2" high.
   b. Fill it with any gradient color and apply any border line style and color you prefer.
6. Apply a 3-D effect to the circle and a shadow effect to the square. Change the fill of the starburst and heart, and the line style of the square, as shown in Illustration B.
7. Preview the document.
8. Print one copy.
9. Close the file; save the changes.

Illustration A

VOCABULARY

Drawing canvas

CONCEPT BUILDERS

- Word contains drawing tools that enable you to draw shapes and designs, which you can insert into your publication. These tools are found on the Drawing toolbar.
- Shapes are considered objects. Like other objects, you can move, copy, size, rotate, and delete shapes.
- You can fill a shape with a solid or gradient color and/or a pattern. You can also change the shape's border line style and color.
- You can only fill a closed shape with a color or pattern.
- In addition to shapes you can draw, Word also contains AutoShapes, which are predesigned shapes (lines, connectors, block arrows, stars and banners, flowchart elements, callouts, and basic shapes).
- When you draw a shape, a drawing canvas appears. A ***drawing canvas*** is a non-printing border with space for drawing. The canvas makes it easier to create complex drawings within a Word document. The drawing canvas is not available to Word 2000 users.

Indent Text; Change Line Spacing

EXERCISE 28

Directions

1. Create a new document.
2. Use the default margins.
3. Key the exercise provided, as shown on page 96; start the letterhead at the top of your screen.
4. Create the letterhead in a sans serif font using the following font sizes:
   - 24 pt for "Software"
   - 48 pt for "&"
   - 16 pt for "Company"
   - 12 pt for the address and phone information
5. Begin the dateline 2.5" down from the top of the page.
6. Set the body text to serif, 10 pt.
7. Set a 1" left indent for the middle paragraphs, as shown; set the line spacing to 1.5 lines.
8. Bold the first occurrence of GRAPHIC SOLUTIONS.
   - Copy this formatting to the remaining occurrences.
9. Justify body text.
10. Check spelling.
11. Preview the document.
12. Print one copy.
13. Save the file; name it **4.28ad**.
14. Close the document window.

LESSON 2

Work with Drawing Tools

EXERCISE 11
Create, Position, and Size a Shape; Apply a Border and Fill

EXERCISE 12
Group and Layer Objects

EXERCISE 13
Copy and Group Shapes and Objects

EXERCISE 14
Copy, Group, Ungroup, and Regroup Shapes and Objects; Align and Distribute Objects

EXERCISE 15
Copy, Group, and Ungroup Shapes and Objects; Change the Direction of an Object

EXERCISE 16
Skills Review

EXERCISE 17
Skills Review

888 Franklin Boulevard
Fairfield, New Jersey 07004
(201) 555-5555

Today's date

Mr. Stan Smith, Creative Director
Sari & Sari Advertising
575 Madison Avenue
New York, NY 10016

Dear Mr. Smith:

I know your agency is considering purchasing a new page layout software program. You told me that you wanted a layout program that could display outstanding text and graphics and, at the same time, integrate other software you have in your office. Let me list some of the outstanding features of **GRAPHIC SOLUTIONS.**

GRAPHIC SOLUTIONS is a complete graphic arts workshop, with powerful composition and graphics-handling capability.

GRAPHIC SOLUTIONS gives you sophisticated composition capabilities, enabling you to handle virtually any job.

GRAPHIC SOLUTIONS supports Windows XP, giving you an even wider range of page layout, graphics, and integration alternatives.

As you know, I am the east-coast representative for the **GRAPHIC SOLUTIONS** software program. Please phone me so that I may set up an appointment with you to demonstrate this outstanding piece of software. I know that it will meet all your needs.

Sincerely,

Fred Nelson
Product Manager

fn/yo

Directions *continued*

9. Print one copy.
10. Close the file; save the changes.

Restaurant San Domenico

Specials for Today, [Insert today's date]
Stuffed artichoke
Osso bucco
Broccoli rabe

APPETIZERS/?
Shrimp cocktail with lemon/Lattuga sminuzzata con limone - $8.00
Tomato and mozzarella cheese salad with basil/Insalata di pomodoro, mozzarella e basilico - $6.00

PASTA AND RICE/PASTA E RISO
Spaghetti Bolognaise/Spaghetti alla Bolognese o alla Napoletana - $12.50
Risotto with Parmesan cheese/Risotto al Parmigiano - $11.20
Ravioli with Parmesan cheese/Ravioli alla monegasca gratinati al Parmigiano -$13.00

FISH/
Charcoaled fresh salmon, baked potato/Salmone fresco all griglia, patata al cartoccio - $15.00
Boiled sea-bass fillet with sautéed carrots/Filetto di branzino al naturale con carote Vichy - $18.50
Roasted lobster, an assortment of seasonal vegetables with tarragon/Astice arrosto, giardiniera di verdure al dragoncello - $20.00

MEAT/?
Tartar steak, green salad, and french fries/Bistecca alla tartara con insalata e patate fritte - $14.00
Grilled and sliced filet of beef with garlic and basil/Fettina di filetto di manzo alla griglia con aglio e basilico - $15.50
Grilled lamb chops in a traditional style, potato and green beans/Costolette d'agnello grigliate all'antica, duo di patate e fagiolini - $18.00

DESSERTS/DOLCI
Pastry of the day/Pasticceria del giorno - $4.00
Home-made ice cream or sherbet/Gelati e sorbetti della casa - $3.00
Cream caramel - Crème caramel - $3.50

Dinner served from 6:30 p.m. (18:30) to 10:15 p.m. (22.15)
Prix fixes menu served from 5:30 p.m. - 7:00 p.m. $30/€?/£?
Tasting menu $38.50/€?/£?

Indent Text; Change Line Spacing; Change Paragraph Spacing; Set Margins

EXERCISE 29

Directions

1. Create a new document.
2. Begin the exercise at the top of your screen.
3. Set 1" left and right margins and a .5" bottom margin.
4. Set line spacing to 15 pt for the first two paragraphs.
5. Center and set the report title to serif, 14 pt, bold; set the body text to serif, 11 pt.
6. Set paragraph spacing to 6 pt *after* each paragraph.
7. Key the paragraphs provided, as shown on page 98.
   NOTE: *Because you have set line and paragraph spacing, you need only press the Enter key once after each paragraph.*
8. Indent the paragraphs .5" from the left and right margins.
9. Set "Book" to sans serif, 11 pt, bold.
   - Copy the formatting from "Book" to the remaining side headings.
10. Correct spelling.
11. Preview the document.
12. Print one copy.
13. Save the file; name it **4.29citation**.
14. Close the document window.

Use the Help Index

How Do I...?	**Enter the keyword(s):**
Set paragraph spacing	Paragraph space
Set margins	Margin

VOCABULARY

Paragraph spacing
Leading
Margins

CONCEPT BUILDERS

- The ***Paragraph Spacing*** feature allows you to insert additional space between paragraphs, headings, or subheadings as you type the document.
- Line spacing can be measured in lines or in points.
- Line spacing measured in points (a more precise measurement) is referred to as ***leading*** (pronounced "ledding").
- ***Margins*** are the blank areas at each edge of a page. In Word, the default left and right margins are 1.25"; the default top and bottom margins are 1".

DID YOU KNOW?

- 12 pt leading is equivalent to single spacing.
- Reducing the leading amount reduces the readability of text; increasing the leading amount increases the readability of the text.
- The names of publications are entered in all capital letters or italicized.

Skills Review

EXERCISE 10

Your friend is the owner of an Italian restaurant in New York City that is frequented by tourists. You have been asked to design a new menu that includes menu items in English and Italian, as well as prices in U.S. dollars, euros, and British pounds for the prix fixes and tasting menus. Because the currency values change daily, you will need to update the menu each day to reflect these changes (as well as to list your daily specials). To make this task easier, insert a hyperlink to the conversion site.

SCANS

Directions

1. Open **d1.10intmenu** from the Data CD. 
   Save the file as **1.10intmenu**.
2. Set any margins to make the text fit attractively.
3. Design your menu using the desktop elements you have learned thus far. Include graphics, symbols, lines, text boxes, and special effects as you prefer.
4. Prices for the prix fixes and tasting menus will be shown in U.S. dollars, euros, and British pounds. Use the Internet to convert the dollar amounts to the euro and pound currencies, and insert them where indicated by a question mark.
   - Use any search engine to find a currency conversion site and convert the dollar amounts indicated in the exercise.
5. Menu categories will be shown in English and Italian. Use the Internet to look up the translation of menu categories and insert them where you see a question mark (?).
   - Use any search engine to find a translation site and translate the indicated words.
6. Switch to the Word document shown on page 313.
7. Insert a hyperlink on the pound symbol to the conversion Web site.
8. Preview the document.

PORTFOLIO

Include this exercise in your portfolio.

DID YOU KNOW?

The symbol for a British pound is £ and the symbol for a euro is €.

CITATIONS

Citations are references made by a writer to indicate whether he/she has paraphrased or quoted material from another source (a book, newspaper, magazine, encyclopedia, the Internet, etc.). It is necessary to cite someone else's ideas, words, statistics, artwork, or lab results. Failing to do so is called plagiarism, which can have serious legal repercussions.

Citations that appear at the bottom of a page are called footnotes, those located at the end of a document are called endnotes, and those that immediately follow the quoted or paraphrased sentence or paragraph are known as internal citations. When a footnote or endnote cites the same source as the citation that immediately precedes it, the abbreviation ibid., meaning "in the same place," is used rather than rewriting the entry. Below are examples of how to write footnotes and endnotes cited from various sources.

Book

Author's Name, *Title*, (City where published: Publishing Company, Year Published), page number.

James Steuben, *The End of an Era*, (New York: One, Two, Three Publishing, Inc., 2001), p. 23.

Newspaper

Author's Name, "Title of Article," *Name of Newspaper*, Date, section, page number.

Jesse Winters, "Brooklyn Schools Get Facelift," *New York Times*, June 3, 2003, sec. A, p. 23.

Magazine Article

Author's Name, "Title of Article," *Name of Magazine*, Date of Magazine Issue, page number.

Laura Cummings, "Replacing Body Fat with Muscle Mass," *Exercise Weekly*, June 12, 2003, p. 23.

World Wide Web Address

Author's Name, "Title of Article/Web Site," <web address>, date posted on Internet (if available).

Dennis Peanon, "The End of Vietnam," <http://www.ufla.edu/history/vietnam/2.html>, April 10, 2003.

E-Mail Message

Author's Name, <e-mail address of sender>, "Subject of E-mail," to whom message was sent, date message was sent.

Marie D'Angelo, <mdangelo@ecosystem.com>, "Warning: Depletion of the Ozone Layer," E-mail to Mark Binda, September 5, 2003.

SPRINGFIELD
NEWS BRIEFS
A Quarterly Publication of Springfield Community College March 2004

SCC Summer Registration Day—May 31
Registration Day for summer classes will be held in Glisan Hall from 8:00 a.m. to 4:00 p.m., Monday, May 31. All students who have not registered in advance can still do so on Registration Day.

For limited enrollment classes, students must complete all forms, pay all necessary fees, and sign course lists. For open enrollment classes, students may simply attend the first meeting of the class.

Summer Session Calendar

May 31	Last day to arrange for payment of summer courses, sign class lists
June 3	**Classes begin**
June 17	Last day to declare or drop credit/no credit option
June 28	Last day to add units
July 1	Last day to drop units
July 4-5	Holiday, no classes
July 26-30	Eight-week term exams
July 30	**Eight-week term ends**

Senior Art Show Exhibit
A reception for senior art students will be held at the Turn Gallery on Monday, May 24 at 7:00 p.m. The exhibit features various works by graduating students, including sculpture, oil painting, photography, and installation. Refreshments will be served.

5K Fun Run to Benefit Local Scholarship Fund
SCC is hosting its annual 5K Fun Run, Saturday, June 5. Runners and walkers are welcome to come to the Westside Hills Park south side entrance at 8:30 a.m. and sign up to enter. No pre-registration is necessary. Cost: $12. All proceeds go directly to the Local Scholarship Fund, benefiting college-bound Springfield High School students.

Four-Week Intensive Chinese Language Study in Beijing
The SCC summer travel program is hosting a rigorous four-week seminar at Beijing University in Beijing, China. Note the location of the university in relation to the city of Beijing. [insert map]

[Insert a paragraph that describes brief facts about the capitol city Beijing]

Interested students should see Costa Mendez in the Study Abroad Office.

Indent Text; Change Paragraph Spacing; Set Margins

EXERCISE 30

Directions

1. Create a new document.
2. Key the exercise provided 2" down from the top of the page, as shown below.
3. Set 1.5" left and right margins.
4. Center and set the title to serif, 14 pt, bold; set the body text to serif, 12 pt.
5. Set line spacing to single.
6. Set paragraph spacing to 10 pt *after* each entry.
7. Create .5" hanging indents for each paragraph, as shown. Key the remaining paragraphs, as shown.
   NOTE: *Because you have set paragraph spacing, you need only press the Enter key once after each paragraph.*
8. Vertically center the exercise.
9. Correct spelling.
10. Preview the document.
11. Print one copy.
12. Save the file; name it **4.30biblio**.
13. Close the document window.

VOCABULARY

Hanging indent   Bibliography

CONCEPT BUILDERS

- A ***hanging indent*** is created when all lines in a paragraph are indented except the first line. Hanging indents are created using the Indent features.
- A ***bibliography*** identifies sources used, quoted, or paraphrased within a document.

BIBLIOGRAPY

Atkins, Neil P. "What Exactly Do They Want?" *Educational Leadership*, February, 2001.

Colson, Diane E. *Using Words Effectively*. New York: Collins, McMann and Guilford, Inc., 2002.

Klaus, Harry J., and Bill Samson. *The Effects of War*. New York: West and West, 2001.

Parker, Roger. "Adding Effective Visuals," *Looking Good in Print*, September, 2003.

Peanon, Dennis. "The End of Vietnam," http://www.ufla.edu/vietnam/2.html, April 10, 2001.

Watson, Goodwin. "Resistance to Change." *The Planning of Change*, New York: Horte and Winton, Inc., 2002.

Directions *continued*

g. Enter this URL: `www.encarta.msn.com`

h. Click in the **Search MSN Learning & Research** box, enter `Beijing, China`, and click **Go.**

i. Click **Beijing.**

j. Print the page.

k. Close the browser.

9. Using the information from the printed Web page, write one paragraph that gives concise facts about this capital city. Insert the paragraph where indicated.

10. Insert the map where indicated. Size and position it as you prefer to fit your layout. Use any text-wrap option.

11. Preview the document.

12. Print one copy.

13. Close the file; save the changes.

14. Close the document window.

Move Text (Cut and Paste); Set Margins; Change Case

EXERCISE 31

Directions

1. Open **4.28ad**, the file you created in Exercise 28, or open **d4.31ad** from the Data CD. 
2. Save the file as **4.31ad**.
3. Make the indicated revisions in the exercise, as shown on page 101.
4. Set .75" left and right margins.
5. Indent the middle paragraphs 1" from the right margin and set line spacing to single.
6. Change the case of each occurrence of the words GRAPHIC SOLUTIONS to title case (initial capital for each word).
7. Make the indicated revisions.
8. Use the "cut and paste" procedure to move the text, as shown.
9. Correct spelling.
10. Preview the document.
11. Print one copy.
12. Save the changes; close the file.

Use the Help Index

How Do I...?	**Enter the keyword(s):**
Change case	Uppercase
Move text	Move

VOCABULARY

Cut and paste   Clipboard

CONCEPT BUILDERS

- ***Cut and paste*** is a procedure that moves a block of text, a sentence, paragraph, page, or column to another location in the same document or another document.
- The ***Clipboard*** is temporary memory within the computer. Text "cut" from the screen is placed temporarily on the Clipboard. The Paste procedure retrieves the text from the Clipboard and places it in a specified location in the document.

DID YOU KNOW?

- The Clipboard can hold up to 24 items, which you can display by viewing the Clipboard task pane. The task pane allows you to paste multiple selections in a different order than that in which you cut or copied them. **Word 2000 Users:** The Clipboard can hold up to 12 items. To paste items from the Clipboard, view the Clipboard toolbar and click the items to paste.
- You can convert text you enter in one case (uppercase, lowercase, or initial capitals) to another case.
- The proofreaders' mark to move text is:

Skills Review

EXERCISE 9

You work on the Springfield Community College school newsletter and have been asked to redesign this month's issue. The articles and information for the newsletter have been written and appear on page 311. However, the last article, which announces a Study Abroad Program at Beijing University in Beijing, China, should include some concise facts about this capital city and show a map of where the capital is located in relation to the university. You will use the Internet to get this information.

SCANS

PORTFOLIO

Include this exercise in your portfolio.

Directions

1. Open **d1.9sccbrief** from the Data CD.  Save the file as **1.9sccbrief**.
2. Set any margins you want to make the text fit attractively.
3. Use two or three columns as you prefer.
4. Use any fonts and font sizes.
5. Insert a relevant graphic.
6. Modify the border around "Summer Session Calendar" and add shading.
7. Use lines as appropriate.
8. Use the Internet to find a map of China showing Beijing and to research information about the city of Beijing as follows:
   a. Open your browser. Enter this URL: `www.expedia.com`
   b. Click the **maps** tab.
   c. Click **Find a Map.**
   d. Click in the **Search for a place** radio button.
      - Click the **Region** list arrow and select **World** (topographic maps).
      - Click in the **Place name** box and enter: `Beijing, China`
   e. Click **Find a map.**
   f. Save the map; name it **1.9chinamap**.

888 Franklin Boulevard
Fairfield, New Jersey 07004
(201) 555-5555

Today's date

Mr. Stan Smith, Creative Director
Sari & Sari Advertising
575 Madison Avenue
New York, NY 10016

Dear Mr. Smith:

Ital — When we last spoke,

I know your agency is considering purchasing a new page layout software program. You told me that you wanted a layout program that could display outstanding text and graphics and, at the same time, integrate other software you have in your office. ~~Let me~~ list some of the outstanding features of **GRAPHIC SOLUTIONS.**

ed below are

GRAPHIC SOLUTIONS is a complete graphic arts workshop, with powerful composition and graphics-handling capability.

GRAPHIC SOLUTIONS gives you sophisticated composition capabilities, enabling you to handle virtually any job.

Move

GRAPHIC SOLUTIONS supports Windows XP, giving you an even wider range of page layout, graphics, and integration alternatives.

As you know, I am the east-coast representative for the **GRAPHIC SOLUTIONS** software program. Please phone me so that I may set up an appointment with you to demonstrate this outstanding piece of software. I ~~know~~ that ~~it~~ will meet all your needs.

am certain — Graphic Solutions

¶ I am enclosing a brochure detailing the features of Graphic Solutions.

Sincerely,

Fred Nelson
Product Manager

fn/yo
Enclosure

4
Star
Travel
Service,
Inc.
Cruise Itineraries
Honeymoon Destinations
Car Rentals
Safari Packages
The Complete Travel Agency
Stop in at either of our two locations. Our friendly, knowledgeable
staff is ready to serve your every travel need.
East Side
100 East End Avenue
New York, NY 10024
P: 212-555-5555
F: 212-555-6666
E-mail: trav@mind.com
West Side
50 West End Avenue
New York, NY 10023
P: 212-555-7777
F: 212-555-8888
E-mail: travone@mind.com

Move Text (Drag and Drop); Change Case

EXERCISE 32

Directions

1. Open **4.29citation**, the file you created in Exercise 29, or open **d4.32citation** from the Data CD. 
2. Save the file as **4.32citation**.
3. Change the title to title case (initial capital for each word).
   - Set the title to script, 22 pt.
4. Justify text for the first two paragraphs.
5. Make the indicated revisions in the exercise, as shown on page 103.
6. Use drag and drop to move the citation types into alphabetical order.
7. Change the side headings to uppercase.
8. Correct spelling.
9. Preview the document.
10. Print one copy.
11. Save the changes; close the file.

VOCABULARY

Drag and drop

CONCEPT BUILDERS

Drag and drop is a method of moving text with your mouse. Once you select the text, click anywhere on the selected text and drag it to its new location.

HOT TIPS

If text does not move properly, click Undo to reverse the move.

DID YOU KNOW?

The proofreaders' mark to capitalize text is: ≡

8. Center the bottom text and set it to sans serif, 14/26.

9. Create two text boxes.
   a. Size them to approximately 1.5" high by 2.20" wide.
   b. Enter the text as shown.
      - Center the headings (East Side, West Side) and set them to serif, 14 pt, bold in any color you prefer.
      - Center the remaining text and set it to sans serif, 10 pt. Insert any symbol you want between the text as shown.
   c. Position the boxes at the left and right margins, as shown, and apply a text-wrap option to flow text around the graphic.
   d. Color each box as you prefer. Apply a box border in any width and/or color you want.

10. Apply any page border you want.
    NOTE: *Be sure the text box and line colors complement the page border color.*

11. Preview the document.

12. Print one copy.

13. Save the file; name it **1.8travelad**.

14. Close the document window.

Use the Help Index

How Do I...?	**Enter the keyword(s):**
Apply a page border	Border

CITATIONS

Citations are references made by a writer to indicate whether he/she has paraphrased or quoted material from another source (a book, newspaper, magazine, encyclopedia, the Internet, etc.). It is necessary to cite someone else's ideas, words, statistics, artwork, or lab results. Failing to do so is called plagiarism, which can have serious legal repercussions.

Citations that appear at the bottom of a page are called footnotes, those located at the end of a document are called endnotes, and those that immediately follow the quoted or paraphrased sentence or paragraph are known as internal citations. When a footnote or endnote cites the same source as the citation that immediately precedes it, the abbreviation ibid., meaning "in the same place," is used rather than rewriting the entry. Below are examples of how to write footnotes and endnotes cited from various sources.

Book

Author's Name, *Title*, (City where published: Publishing Company, Year Published), page number.

James Steuben, *The End of an Era*, (New York: One, Two, Three Publishing, Inc., 2001), p. 23.

Newspaper

Author's Name, "Title of Article," *Name of Newspaper*, Date, section, page number.

Jesse Winters, "Brooklyn Schools Get Facelift," *New York Times*, June 3, 2003, sec. A, p. 23.

Magazine Article

Author's Name, "Title of Article," *Name of Magazine*, Date of Magazine Issue, page number.

Laura Cummings, "Replacing Body Fat with Muscle Mass," *Exercise Weekly*, June 12, 2003, p. 23.

World Wide Web Address

Author's Name, "Title of Article/Web Site," <web address>, date posted on Internet (if available).

Dennis Peanon, "The End of Vietnam," <http://www.ufla.edu/history/vietnam/2.html>, April 10, 2003.

E-Mail Message

Author's Name, <e-mail address of sender>, "Subject of E-mail," to whom message was sent, date message was sent.

Marie D'Angelo, <mdangelo@ecosystem.com>, "Warning: Depletion of the Ozone Layer," E-mail to Mark Binda, September 5, 2003.

Use Text Boxes, Text Box Borders, Shading, and Special Effects; Use Page Borders

EXERCISE 8

Directions

1. Create a new document.
2. Begin the flyer, shown on page 308, at the top of the page.
3. Enter `Star Travel Service, Inc.` at the left margin; set the text to Arial Black, 20/26.
4. Create a text box and insert the number `4`.
   a. Size the box to 1.48" high by .88" wide.
   b. Set the number "4" to Arial, bold, 90 pt.
   c. Color the text box any color you prefer.
   d. Position the box at the left margin and apply a text-wrap option that allows the text to wrap around the graphic.
   e. Create a 3-D effect.
5. Display gridlines; set the horizontal and vertical spacing to .125".
6. Create four text boxes.
   a. Size each to .5" high by 5" wide.
   b. Position each box below the other, 1/8" apart. Align the boxes at the left side of the page.
   NOTE: *Remember, each box on the grid is equal to 1/8".*
   c. Center and set the text within each box to sans serif, 18 pt.
   d. Color each box as you prefer.
7. Create a text box.
   a. Size it to 3" high by .5" wide.
   b. Position the box to the right of the four other text boxes.
   c. Center and set `The Complete Travel Agency` to sans serif, 14 pt, bold, and italic.
   d. Change the text direction so that the text is facing the four text boxes.
   e. Color the box as you prefer.

CONCEPT BUILDERS

- You can apply a border around an entire page.
- Changing the line style can change the border effect. Word provides border graphics, which can create interesting results.

Move and Copy Text; Change Case

EXERCISE 33

Directions

1. Open **4.27present**, the file you created in Exercise 27, or open **d4.33present** from the Data CD. 
2. Save the file as **4.33present**.
3. Change the title to title case (initial capital for each word) and set the font to script, 36 pt, bold.
4. Set 1" left and right margins; set .5" top and bottom margins. Begin the title at 1" from the top of the page.
5. Set a 1" first-line indent for the first three paragraphs.
6. Justify all document text.
7. Make the indicated revisions in the exercise provided.
8. Use drag and drop to move the text, as shown on page 105.
9. Copy and paste each pointer two lines below the last paragraph and format each as follows:
   - Single-space
   - Center-align
   - Bullet each using a check mark (if available)

   NOTE: *Word allows you to collect and paste multiple items. Use the Clipboard task pane to complete this step.*
   Word 2000 Users: *Use the Clipboard toolbar to do so.*
10. Correct spelling.
11. Preview the document.
12. Print one copy.
13. Save the changes and close the file.

VOCABULARY

Copy and paste

DID YOU KNOW?

- ***Copy and paste*** is a procedure that leaves text in its original location while placing a duplicate in a different location in the same document or another document.
- When you copy text, it remains on the screen while a copy of it is placed on the Clipboard. Text remains on the Clipboard until you copy another selection (or until you exit Windows). Thus, you can paste the same selection into many different locations. Generally, each time you cut or copy text, you replace the previous cut or copied text on the Clipboard. However, Office applications allow you to collect and paste multiple items.

Discover Wildlife at the Zoo

The zoological parks throughout the United States are one of the most popular cultural and recreational attractions in those cities that have them. Visit http://dir.yahoo.com/Science/Biology/Zoology/Zoos for a complete listing of the zoos in the United States and in the world. Below is a highlight of two of the country's most popular zoos, one on the east coast and one on the west coast.

The Bronx Zoo

Location: Bronx, New York.
Directions:
Hours: 9 a.m-5 p.m. daily. Check holiday schedules.
Telephone:
Fax:
E-mail:
Web:
Admission: $7.95 for adults; $4.95 for children 4 and under and senior citizens.

The Bronx Zoo is home to more than 4,000 animals and some of the world's endangered species. The zoo sits on 265 wooded acres. The Children's Zoo allows young visitors to pet and feed domestic animals. The Bronx Zoo is the largest metropolitan wildlife conservation park in the United States.

Now, if you can't visit New York, but want to get acquainted with this zoo, visit the Bronx Zoo Web site at: www.bronxzoo.com

The San Diego Zoo boasts the largest wild animal park and zoo in the country, with over 1,800 acres. The huge enclosures allow animals to roam in their natural environment. Visitors can walk among the colorful Australian parrots in the aviary or head into the backcountry and see elephants, rhinos and pandas. The nighttime zoo begins in June and continues until September. Visitors can see their favorite animals move through moonlight and shadows.

While you won't get the sights and smells of the real thing, the San Diego Zoo's Web site will give you a sampling of this world-famous west coast attraction. Visit: www.sandiegozoo.org

San Diego Zoo

Location: San Diego, California
Directions:
Hours: 9 a.m.-5 p.m. daily. Check holiday schedules.
Telephone:
Fax:
E-mail:
Web:
Admission: $7.95 for adults; $4.95 for children 4 and under and senior citizens.

Use the Help Index

How Do I...?	Enter the keyword(s):
Copy and paste	Copy

CREATING EFFECTIVE PRESENTATIONS

One day, you ~~are~~ might be likely to find yourself in this situation: your employer ~~walks up to you and~~ says, "We need to get a presentation together for the DataAir Project fast!" Because the deadline for such a "request" is usually immediate, you reach for your presentation graphics software program.

Presentation graphics programs make it easy to gather and update an engineering, scientific, or business presentation. You may not have time to create a ~~wondrous~~ spectacular multimedia show, but that does not mean that your presentation will not be engaging and effective. Just follow the five tips below. The rest is easy.

The following ~~four~~ five pointers can help make noticeable improvements to your next presentation:

Make a Plan. After you have ~~determined~~ identified your audience, decide what to say and how to say it. Create an outline after you have analyzed what items you must cover and how you want your audience to react.

Analyze Your Audience. Take the time to determine who will be listening. Ask yourself, "Why are you giving this presentation?"

Keep the Number of Words per Slide to a Minimum. ~~The general rule is to~~ limit the number of words per slide to eight. It is better to have more slides with less information than vice versa.

Keep it Short. Resist creating a lengthy presentation. The longer the presentation, the greater the danger of losing your audience's attention.

Vary your visuals. Keep your presentation moving by blending different types of slides. Add graphics and photographs to create a variety of visual elements.

Move / Copy / Move / Move / 2x / Paste

c. Insert the text for the Bronx Zoo, as shown in the illustration on page 305, using a sans serif, 10 pt font.

d. Position the text box as shown.

e. Apply a shadow effect.

NOTE: *Experiment with text box placement to avoid awkward line breaks.*

7. Create a second text box.

a. Size it to 2.90" high by 1.75" wide.

b. Color the text box a light shade of blue; color the text box border and the heading within the box dark blue.

c. Insert the text for the San Diego Zoo, as shown, using a sans serif, 10 pt font.

d. Position the text box as shown.

e. Apply a shadow effect.

8. Insert two graphics of animals.

a. Size them proportionally to fit within the text as shown. Use a text-wrap option that allows text to flow around the graphics.

b. Apply a shadow effect to each graphic.

9. Preview the document.

10. Print one copy.

11. Close the file; save the changes.

12. Close the document window.

To size a text box by a specific amount, click Format, Text Box, click the Size tab, and enter the amount you need in the Height and Width boxes.

Use the Help Index

How Do I...?	**Enter the keyword(s):**
Create a text box	Text box

Move and Copy Text; Set Tab Stops

EXERCISE 34

Directions

1. Create a new document. Key the exercise provided or open **d4.34db** from the Data CD. 
2. Save the file as **4.34dbase**.
3. Begin the exercise at the top of the screen, as shown on page 108.
4. Center and set the title to sans serif, 16 pt, bold.
5. Apply bullets to the paragraphs, as shown in the illustration.
6. Set the body text to sans serif, 12 pt.
7. Set left and right margins to .75" for the first and last paragraphs; set top and bottom margins to .5"; set left and right margins to 1.5" for the bulleted paragraphs.
8. Set line spacing to 1.5 lines for the first and last paragraphs.
9. Set left tab stops at 1.5" and 4" from the left margin for the tabular column text.
   - Key the text in single space, as shown in the illustration.
10. Justify all text.
11. Change the case to uppercase for the words *Item, Class, Manufacturer, Model, Serial Number, Cost, Purchase Date, Warranty,* and *Location* as indicated in the illustration.
12. Move the last paragraph and the tabular column text to become the first paragraph.

VOCABULARY

Custom tabs
Tabular column

CONCEPT BUILDERS

- ***Custom tabs*** are tab settings that you make, which affect the way text aligns once you begin to enter it. When you set a custom tab, default tabs to the left of it are deleted.
- A ***tabular column*** is created when text is entered at a tab stop and forms a column of data.

Use Text Boxes, Text Box Borders, Shading, and Special Effects

EXERCISE 7

Directions

1. Open **8.73zoo**, which you created in Unit 2, or open **d1.7zoo** from the Data CD.
2. Save the file as **1.7zoo**.
3. Adjust the exercise to begin at the top of the page.
4. Change the line spacing between paragraphs to single.
5. Change the document font size to 11 pt.
6. Create a text box.
   a. Size it to approximately 2.90" high by 1.75" wide.
   b. Color the text box a light shade of yellow; color the text box border and the heading within the box orange.

VOCABULARY

Text box

CONCEPT BUILDERS

- A ***text box*** allows you to set off text in a box, which you can then position anywhere on a page. Text that you enter inside a text box becomes part of the box and moves as you move the box. As with other objects, you can resize, reposition, copy, or delete a text box using the same techniques learned earlier.
  Note: *When you insert a text box, a drawing canvas appears. The drawing canvas provides a workspace in which you can control the layout of text and diagrams. It prevents a graphic or text box from breaking apart across a page. You can choose to draw a text box outside the drawing canvas.* **Word 2000 Users:** The drawing canvas is not available to you.
- You can rotate text in a text box using the same procedure you used to rotate text in a table cell.
- With most software, it is possible to change the text box border and/or its shading.
- You can apply shadow and 3-D effects to text boxes, graphics, or lines.

Text box with fill and border color

Text box with 3-D effect

Text box with shadow effect

Directions *continued*

13. Move the bulleted paragraphs into the following order:
    - Organize your information . . .
    - Add, update, and delete . . .
    - Search information . . .
    - Sort information . . .
    - Generate lists . . .
14. Copy the text, as shown, and paste it two lines below the last paragraph in the order indicated in Step 13.
    - Set the copied text to 10 pt.
15. Correct spelling.
16. Preview the document.
17. Print one copy.
18. Save the changes and close the file.

Use the Help Index

How Do I...?	**Enter the keyword(s):**
Set a tab stop	Tab

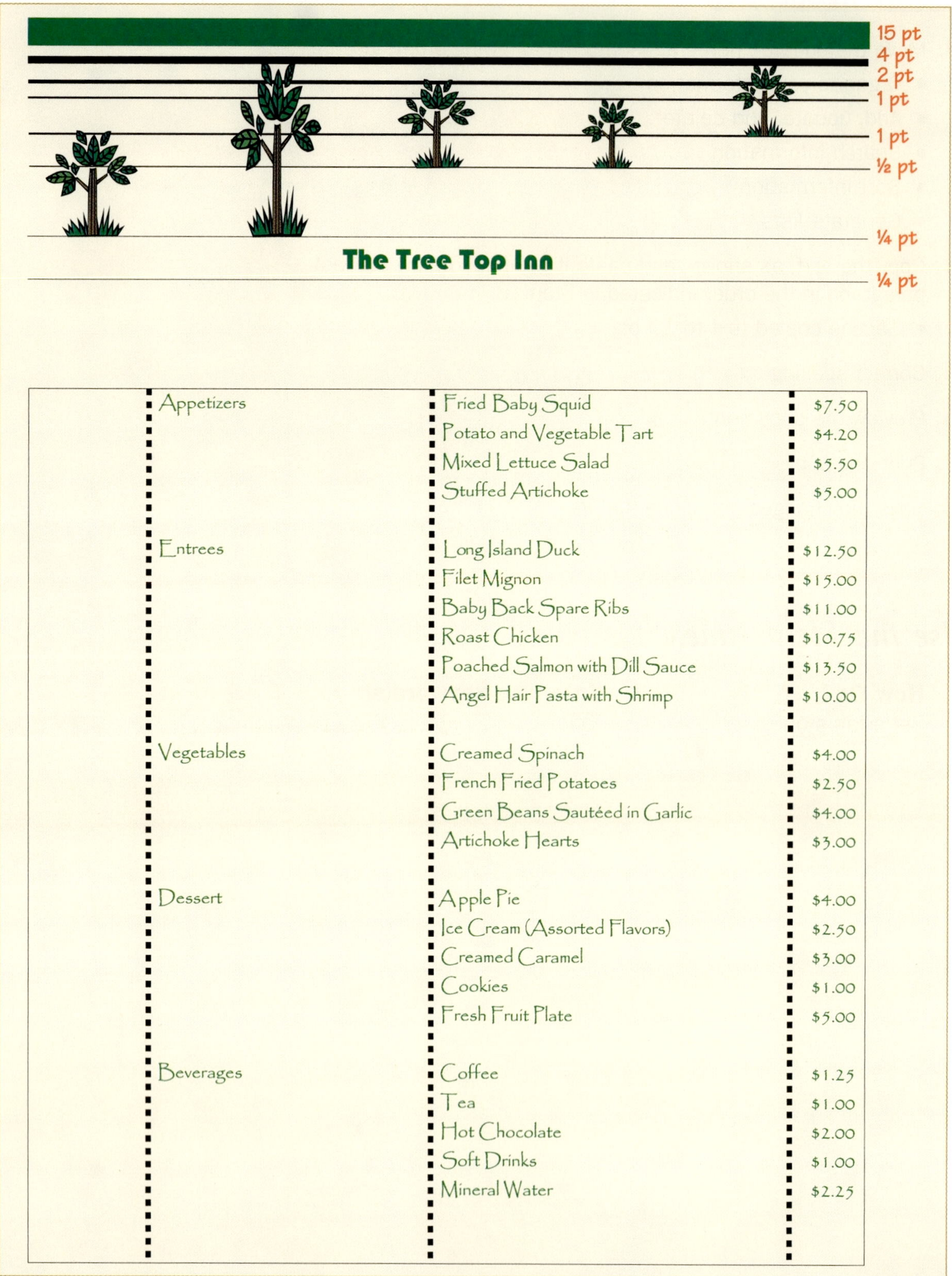

The Tree Top Inn

Appetizers	Fried Baby Squid	$7.50
	Potato and Vegetable Tart	$4.20
	Mixed Lettuce Salad	$5.50
	Stuffed Artichoke	$5.00
Entrees	Long Island Duck	$12.50
	Filet Mignon	$15.00
	Baby Back Spare Ribs	$11.00
	Roast Chicken	$10.75
	Poached Salmon with Dill Sauce	$13.50
	Angel Hair Pasta with Shrimp	$10.00
Vegetables	Creamed Spinach	$4.00
	French Fried Potatoes	$2.50
	Green Beans Sautéed in Garlic	$4.00
	Artichoke Hearts	$3.00
Dessert	Apple Pie	$4.00
	Ice Cream (Assorted Flavors)	$2.50
	Creamed Caramel	$3.00
	Cookies	$1.00
	Fresh Fruit Plate	$5.00
Beverages	Coffee	$1.25
	Tea	$1.00
	Hot Chocolate	$2.00
	Soft Drinks	$1.00
	Mineral Water	$2.25

WHAT IS A DATABASE AND HOW DOES A DATABASE SYSTEM WORK?

A database system offers you great flexibility in managing your data. To dramatize this point, let us refer to an inventory example similar to the one you may want to set up for your business, school, club, or home. Inventory is a good example of a database because it involves the tracking of many separate categories of information. The inventory database has features that will allow you to:

- Add, update, and delete information. Your information usually grows and often changes. You will always be adding items to inventory, changing locations, and removing obsolete or damaged items.
- Generate lists and reports. You can create a report of all items, broken down by location, which you can check periodically to track losses.
- Organize your information into logical categories. You can break down your inventory, for example, into Item, Class (class of information), Manufacturer, Model, Serial Number, Cost, Purchase Date, Warranty, Location, etc.
- Search information by any category under a variety of conditions.
- Sort information by any category. You can rearrange your data by any of the categories.

A database is a collection of information organized so that the database software in use can select specified pieces of data. Think of a database as an electronic filing system. Some examples of database use include:

Set tab at 1.5" | Set tab at 4"

Computerized library systems	Automated teller machines
Flight reservation systems	Internal Revenue Service
Inventory systems	Phone directories

Copy

Move

¶ Basically then, a database can:

2x

Set to 10 pt

Directions *continued*

f. Copy the bottom line twice and paste one copy ½" below the previous line; paste the other copy ¼" below the previous line. Size both lines to ¼ pt.

g. Insert a tree graphic.

   i. Copy the graphic four times.

   ii. Position and size the graphics as shown.

   iii. Choose a text-wrap option that places the graphic in front of text (to enable the graphic to sit on top of the lines).

h. Insert and center the restaurant name between the lines, as shown, in a decorative, 16 pt font. Color the text green.

7. Preview the document.

8. Print one copy.

9. Save the file; name it **1.6food**.

10. Close the document window.

Use the Help Index

How do I...?	**Enter the Keyword(s):**
Change gridline spacing	Gridline spacing

Copy Text; Set Tabs with Leaders

EXERCISE 35

SCANS

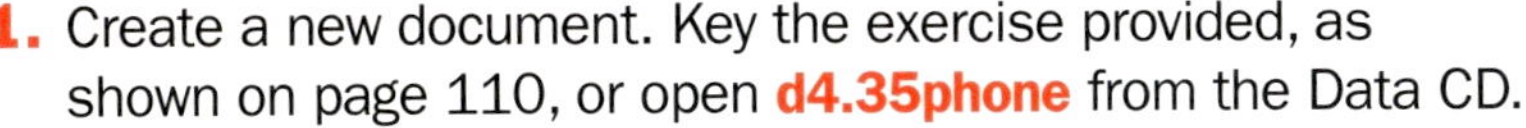

Directions

1. Create a new document. Key the exercise provided, as shown on page 110, or open **d4.35phone** from the Data CD. 
2. Save the file as **4.35phonecharges**.
3. Set 1" left and right margins for the letterhead.
4. Begin the letterhead at the top of the page.
   a. Use a sans serif font.
   b. Set "Telecom" to 28 pt, bold.
   c. Set "Telephone" to 18 pt, bold.
   d. Set "Company" to 14 pt.
   e. Insert an appropriate symbol, as shown.
   f. Set the remaining address and phone information to 12 pt.
5. Use the default margins for the letter.
6. Set the font for the letter to serif, 12 pt.
7. Set the following tabs from the left margin:
   - Left tab at 1"
   - Left tab at 2.5"
   - Right tab at 4"
   - Decimal tab with leader at 5"
8. Insert the first line of tabular information, as shown.
9. Copy the information twice. Edit the time and charges for the second line.
10. Move "We are sorry for this error." in the second paragraph to become the last sentence in the last paragraph.
11. Check spelling.
12. Preview the document; print one copy.
13. Save the changes and close the file.

VOCABULARY

Right tab
Decimal tab
Leader

CONCEPT BUILDERS

- A ***right tab*** moves text to the left from the tab setting as you enter text.
- A ***decimal tab*** moves text before the decimal point to the left of the tab setting. Text entered after the decimal point moves to the right of the tab. The decimal points stay aligned.
- A ***leader*** can be a dot or any other symbol that leads the reader's eye from one location on a page to another.

Use Lines, Line Styles, and Line Colors

EXERCISE 6

SCANS

Directions

1. Create a new document.
2. Set 1" left and right margins and .5" top and bottom margins.
3. Create a four-column table that begins 3" down from the top of the page.
   a. Size the first column to 1", the second column to 2", the third column to 3", and the fourth column to .5".
   b. Adjust the vertical line of the first and last columns so they begin and end at the side margins.
4. Insert the text as shown in the illustration on page 302.
   a. Set the text to sans serif, 10 pt. Color the text green.
   b. Right-align the last column of text.
5. Create a ¼ pt solid line border around the table and create column lines using a 3 pt dotted line as shown. Remove all other table lines.
6. Create the design at the top of the page as follows:
   a. Display gridlines; set the vertical and horizontal spacing to .125" (⅛").
      NOTE: *Gridlines are generally set ⅛" apart.*
   b. Draw a 15 pt line from the left to the right margin at the top margin. Color it green.
   c. Draw a 4 pt line from the left to the right margin ⅛" below the 15 pt line.
   d. Copy the bottom line and paste two copies ⅛" below the previous one. Size the first line to 2 pt and the second line to 1 pt.
   e. Copy the bottom line and paste two copies ¼" below the previous one. Size the first line to 1 pt; size the second line to ½ pt.
      NOTE: *¼" is equal to two boxes on the grid.*

Directions *continued*

Use the Help Index

How Do I...?	**Enter the keyword(s):**
Set a leader	Leader

Telecom☎Telephone Company
777 Big Ben Boulevard
St. Louis, MO 63122-5709

Phone: 314-555-5555
Fax: 314-555-6666
E-Mail: ttc@tel.com

Today's date

Mr. Ted Brown
9988 Main Street
St. Louis, MO 63122-5798

Dear Mr. Brown:

Because of a computer error, the following phone calls that you made on April 19 did not appear on your April statement. These charges will be applied to your May phone bill.

The information below shows the destination and number you called, the time you were on the line, and the charge. We are sorry for this error.

Washington DC	202-555-5555	15..................$3.83
Washington DC	202-555-5555	10..................$2.28
Washington DC	202-555-5555	15..................$3.83

If you have any questions, please call our customer service representative in your area, Ms. Jane Winston.

Cordially,

Francis Szukics
Sales Representative

fs/yo

Use the Help Index

How Do I...?	Enter the keyword(s):
Draw a line	Line
Change line style	Line or line style
Change line color	Line or line color
Add an arrowhead	Arrow

THE
COMPUTER END-USERS'
ASSOCIATION
16/17

Cordially Invites You
to a
Year-End Celebration
14/14

☆ ☆ ☆ ☆

COMPUTER
☆ PARTY ☆
48/40

Friday Evening,
May 19
at 8:00 p.m.
in the Computer Annex
of Mayfair College
14/16

☆ *Professor Gilbert Jones* ☆ 16 pt, italic

will be honored
on the
Occasion of His Retirement
after 30 Years of Teaching
Professor Jones will announce
his new software program
on this occasion.
14/16

RSVP by May 5.
Contribution $25.00 per person
14/16

Please tear off and return in the enclosed envelope

Your Name________________ Guest Name________________

Make checks payable to
COMPUTER END-USERS' ASSOCIATION
Check enclosed for $_______.

Illustration B

CONCEPT BUILDERS

- In Word, you can draw a variety of lines:

  Straight

  Curved

  Freeform

  Scribble

- A line is considered an object because you can size, move, and position it. You can also rotate lines.
- Like a graphic, you must select a line to move, size, or position it.
- Word also allows you to draw arrows.
- You can change the style, width, and color of lines and arrows.
- When you select the line tool, the mouse pointer changes to a ***crosshair*** (+).

Skills Review

EXERCISE 36

You work for Travel Tours and Itineraries, a travel agency that organizes tours and travel schedules. In this exercise, you have been asked to prepare a flyer that announces two tours to Spain.

SCANS

Directions

1. Create a new document. Key the exercise provided or open **d4.36travel** from the Data CD. 
2. Save the file as **4.36travel**.
3. Set 1" left and right margins and .5" top and bottom margins.
4. Use the alignments and indents shown on page 112 to format the document.
5. Use any sans serif font for the document in the font sizes indicated in the exercise.
6. Create appropriate tab stops and insert the tabular column text, as shown.
7. Change each occurrence of DAY(S) to initial capitals (title case).
8. Change the font size for "Highlights include:" and the bulleted information below it to 10 pt.
9. Move "Highlights include:" and the bulleted information so that it appears after Day 8.
10. Copy "Highlights include:" and the bulleted information and paste it after Day 15.
11. Add the following two bullets to the Highlights for Southern Spain:
    - Services of a professional tour director throughout.
    - Four dinners (Seville-1, Cordoba-1, Granada-2) included.
12. Correct spelling.

Use Lines, Line Styles, and Line Colors

EXERCISE 5

Directions

1. Open **3.23party**, which you created in Unit 2 and is shown in Illustration A, or open **d1.5party** from the Data CD.
2. Save the file as **1.5party**.
3. Make the following revisions to create the invitation shown in Illustration B, shown on page 299:
   a. Set .5" top and bottom margins.
   b. Change the font, font size, and leading as shown.
   c. Change the font colors as shown.
   d. Remove all underlining.
   e. Change the symbol to a star; add or delete symbols as shown.
   f. Insert 1 pt lines below "PARTY" and "Professor Gilbert Jones."
   g. Insert a dotted line across the page to create a tear-off.
   h. Edit the tear-off information as shown.
   i. Insert arrows as shown; color them green.
   j. Insert an appropriate graphic.
      - Size the graphic to approximately .85" high by 1.25" wide.
      - Copy the graphic twice and position each next to the other as shown.
4. Preview the document.
5. Print one copy.
6. Close the file; save the changes.

Crosshair

In desktop publishing, lines are often referred to as "rules."

THE COMPUTER END-USERS' ASSOCIATION

Cordially Invites You
to a
Year-End Celebration

✻ ✻ ✻ ✻

✻ ✻ ✻ ✻ COMPUTER PARTY ✻ ✻ ✻ ✻

Friday Evening, May 19
at 8:00 p.m.
in the Computer Annex
of Mayfair College

Professor Gilbert Jones will be honored
on the
Occasion of His Retirement after 30 Years of Teaching

Professor Jones will announce his new software program on this occasion.

- **RSVP by May 5**
- Contribution $25.00 per person

DO THE FOLLOWING:
1. Fill out the information below.
2. Make checks payable to *COMPUTER END-USERS' ASSOCIATION.*
3. Tear off and return in the enclosed envelope.

Name______________________ ❒ will ❒ will not attend.

Name o f Guest______________________ Check enclosed for $_____

Illustration A

Directions *continued*

13. Preview the document.

14. Print one copy.

15. Save the changes and close the file.

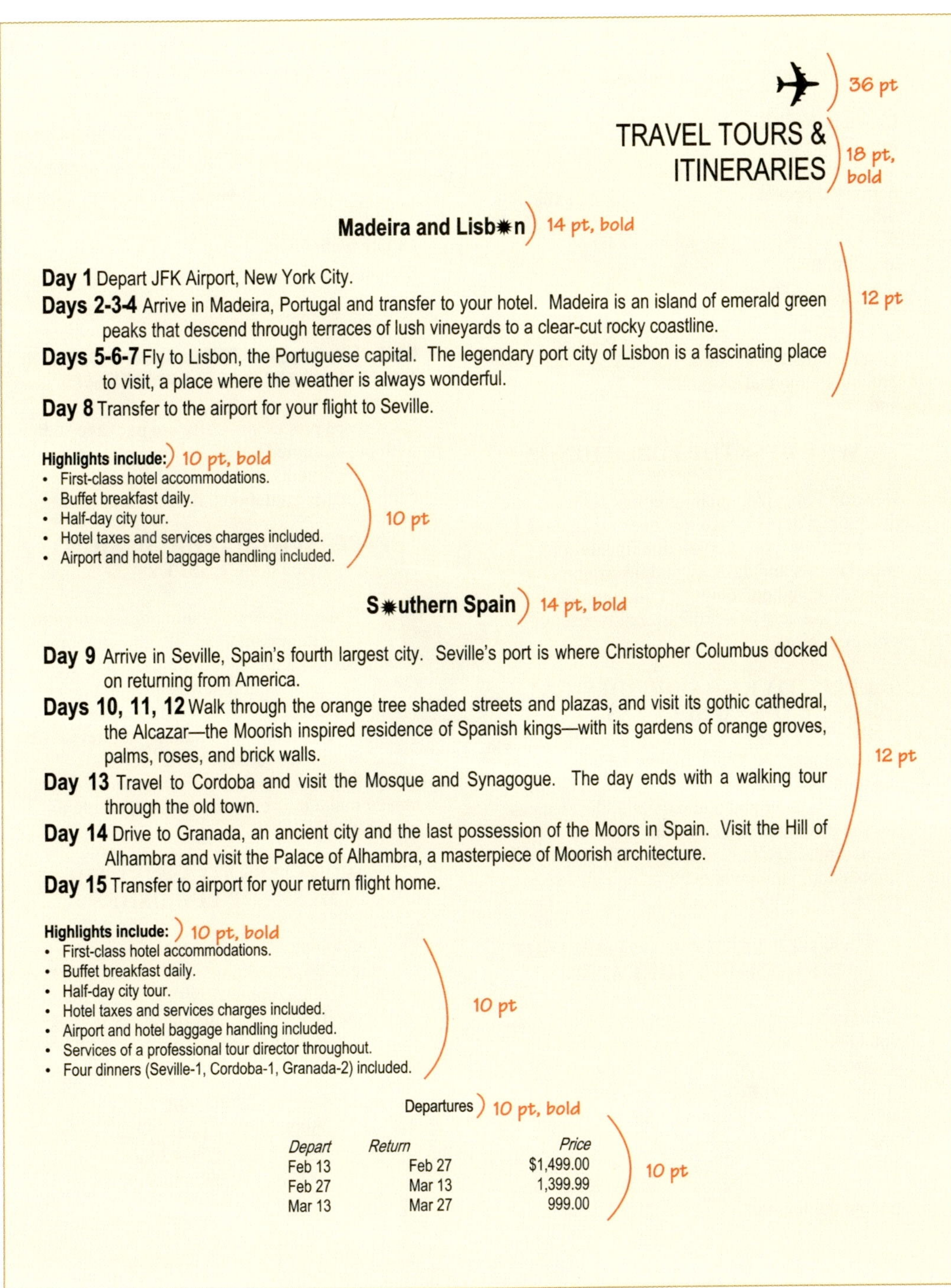

TRAVEL TOURS &
ITINERARIES

Madeira and Lisbon

Day 1 Depart JFK Airport, New York City.

Days 2-3-4 Arrive in Madeira, Portugal and transfer to your hotel. Madeira is an island of emerald green peaks that descend through terraces of lush vineyards to a clear-cut rocky coastline.

Days 5-6-7 Fly to Lisbon, the Portuguese capital. The legendary port city of Lisbon is a fascinating place to visit, a place where the weather is always wonderful.

Day 8 Transfer to the airport for your flight to Seville.

Highlights include:
- First-class hotel accommodations.
- Buffet breakfast daily.
- Half-day city tour.
- Hotel taxes and services charges included.
- Airport and hotel baggage handling included.

Southern Spain

Day 9 Arrive in Seville, Spain's fourth largest city. Seville's port is where Christopher Columbus docked on returning from America.

Days 10, 11, 12 Walk through the orange tree shaded streets and plazas, and visit its gothic cathedral, the Alcazar—the Moorish inspired residence of Spanish kings—with its gardens of orange groves, palms, roses, and brick walls.

Day 13 Travel to Cordoba and visit the Mosque and Synagogue. The day ends with a walking tour through the old town.

Day 14 Drive to Granada, an ancient city and the last possession of the Moors in Spain. Visit the Hill of Alhambra and visit the Palace of Alhambra, a masterpiece of Moorish architecture.

Day 15 Transfer to airport for your return flight home.

Highlights include:
- First-class hotel accommodations.
- Buffet breakfast daily.
- Half-day city tour.
- Hotel taxes and services charges included.
- Airport and hotel baggage handling included.
- Services of a professional tour director throughout.
- Four dinners (Seville-1, Cordoba-1, Granada-2) included.

Departures

Depart	*Return*	*Price*
Feb 13	Feb 27	$1,499.00
Feb 27	Mar 13	1,399.99
Mar 13	Mar 27	999.00

Desktop Publishing

Until recently, graphic design was done by art directors and design professionals whose livelihoods depended on creating effective graphic designs.

Desktop Publishing has changed all that.

Desktop Publishing has brought graphic design into the office and home. It has permitted people other than art directors to create attractive, effective printed materials, such as newsletters, advertisements, brochures, manuals and other documents.

No More Pen and Ink

WHY DESKTOP PUBLISHING?

Desktop Publishing enables computer users to design and develop publications at their desks. They can set type, prepare line illustrations, page layouts and designs, and insert graphics (already saved on computer) into their designs without the help of a professional typesetter or art director.

EFFECTIVE GRAPHIC DESIGN LEADS TO SUCCESS

Effective graphic design makes it easier for readers to understand the message. If the message is clear and eye-catching, the chances are the customer will buy your product. If your printed message fails to create a favorable first impression, you never get a second chance to make a first impression.

CAN DTP BE DONE WITH WORD PROCESSING SOFTWARE?

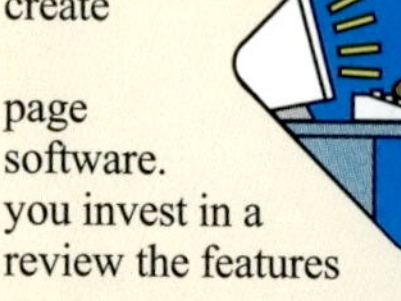

Word processing software packages let you create many of the same documents that you can create using sophisticated page layout software. However, before you invest in a software package, review the features of page layout software vs. word processing software with desktop capabilities. Be sure the software you choose can handle your design needs. Shown below are a few examples of letterheads created at the desktop using word processing software.

City Computers
429 FIFTH AVENUE
New York, NY 10016

(212) 555-5555
E-mail: cc@net.com

Bank of Michigan ▲ 45 Main Street ▲ Detroit, MI 48227 ▲ P: 248-555-5555 ▲ F: 248-555-6666

Most word processing software packages come with pre-designed templates for creating a variety of documents such as brochures, business cards, forms, invitations, reports, and résumés.

EFFECTIVE GRAPHIC DESIGN IS A NECESSITY

Today, effective graphic design is more important than ever. People are bombarded with print communications. Magazines and newspapers are more crowded with ads. Mailboxes are swollen with catalogs and newsletters. Your message has a lot of competition. Therefore, it is even more important to make it as effective and appealing as possible.

WEB SITES TO ASSIST THE DESKTOP PUBLISHER

The desktop designer can access Web sites that offer free designs, clip art, and fonts. The Web can also provide the user with information about various software programs for the desktop publisher. Visit the following sites to get FREE clip art:

Clipart.com
Absolutely Free Clip Art
clipartconnexion.com
Clip Art Warehouse

Illustration B

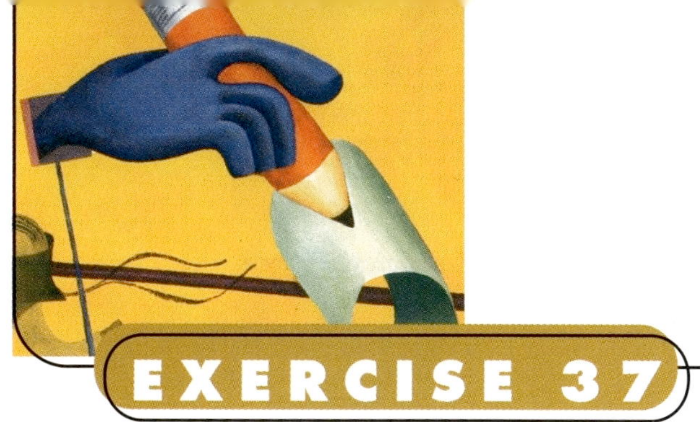

Skills Review

EXERCISE 37

In this exercise, you will revise a document you created earlier. To make the Schedule of Events information easier to read, reformat it to include dot leaders.

Directions

SCANS

1. Open **3.21run**, the file you created in Exercise 21, or open **d4.37run** from the Data CD. 
2. Save the file as **4.37run**.
3. Change each occurrence of Riverside Bank Run for Children to uppercase.
4. Set left and right margins to 1" for the letterhead; set the bottom margin to .5".
   NOTE: *If you are prompted to fix the margins so they are not set outside the printable area of the page, click Fix.*
5. Left-align the Schedule of Events information and remove the bullets.
6. Set a left tab at 1.5" and a left tab with dot leader at 3.5" from the left edge of the page.
7. Tab the event time to 1.5"; tab the event to 3.5".
8. Make the indicated revisions, as shown on page 114.
9. Move the text, as shown.
10. Correct spelling.
11. Preview the document.
12. Print one copy.
13. Close the file; save the changes.

HOT TIPS

When setting tab stops for existing text, select the text first. Then set the tab stops.

Directions *continued*

4. Create a caption below the first graphic in sans serif, 9 pt as shown.
5. Preview the document.
6. Print one copy.
7. Close the file; save the changes.

DESKTOP PUBLISHING

Until recently, graphic design was done by art directors and design professionals whose livelihoods depended on creating effective graphic designs.

Desktop Publishing has changed all that.

Desktop Publishing has brought graphic design into the office and home. It has permitted people other than art directors to create attractive, effective printed materials, such as newsletters, advertisements, brochures, manuals, and other documents.

WHY DESKTOP PUBLISHING?

Desktop Publishing enables computer users to design and develop publications at their desks. They can set type, prepare line illustrations, page layouts and designs, and insert graphics (already saved on computer) into their designs without the help of a professional typesetter or art director.

EFFECTIVE GRAPHIC DESIGN LEADS TO SUCCESS

Effective graphic design makes it easier for readers to understand the message. If the message is clear and eye-catching, the chances are the customer will buy your product. If your printed message fails to create a favorable first impression, you never get a second chance to make a first impression.

Desktop Publishing

CAN DTP BE DONE WITH WORD PROCESSING SOFTWARE?

Word processing software packages let you create many of the same documents that you can create using sophisticated page layout software. However, before you invest in a software package, review the features of page layout software vs. word processing software with desktop capabilities. Be sure the software you choose can handle your design needs. Shown below are a few exam ples of letterheads created at the desktop using word processing software.

City **Computers**
429 FIFTH AVENUE
New York, NY 10016
(212) 555-5555
E-mail: cc@net.com

Bank of Michigan 45 Main Street Detroit, MI 48227 P: 248-555-5555 F: 248-555-6666

Most word processing software packages come with pre-designed templates for creating a variety of documents such as brochures, business cards, forms, invitations, reports, and résumés.

EFFECTIVE GRAPHIC DESIGN IS A NECESSITY

Today, effective graphic design is more important than ever. People are bombarded with print communications. Magazines and newspapers are more crowded with

A Report by Your Name 2

Desktop Publishing

ads. Mailboxes are swollen with catalogs and newsletters. Your message has a lot of competition. Therefore, it is even more important to make it as effective and appealing as possible.

WEB SITES TO ASSIST THE DESKTOP PUBLISHER

The desktop designer can access Web sites that offer free designs, clip art, and fonts. The Web can also provide the user with information about various software programs for the desktop publisher. Visit the following sites to get FREE clip art:

Clip-Art.com
Absolutely Free Clip Art
clipartconnexion.com
Clip Art Warehouse

A Report by Your Name 3

Illustration A

Computers

429 FIFTH AVENUE
New York, NY 10016

(212) 555-5555
E-mail: cc@net.com

Today's date

Ms. Sara Burton
104 Fifth Avenue
New York, NY 10012

Dear Ms. Burton:

is a 5k run that

We are asking our customers to join us in participating in the second **Riverside Bank Run for Children** on Saturday, June 3. The **Riverside Bank Run for Children** raises money for an estimated 48 million children who are victims of war, natural disasters, and extreme poverty.

I am the team captain for City Computers, and I hope you will join our team. Men, women, and children are eligible to participate in this run. Note the schedule of events below. This race will once again take place in Central Park.

Schedule of Events
7:30-8:30 a.m. – Late Registration
8:15 a.m. – Opening Ceremonies
9:00 a.m. – Official Start
10:15-12:00 noon – Finish Line Festivities

Support a great cause and be part of the City Computers team. It's as easy as **1, 2, 3!**

1. Register with me
2. Get sponsors
3. Run

If you are unable to run, I encourage you to sponsor someone who is, so that you can still be part of this worthy cause. If you are interested in registering to run in this event, complete the enclosed registration form and send it to me with a $20 check made out to the **Riverside Bank Run for Children** by May 20.

¶ If you have any questions, please call me at extension 4888.

Sincerely,

Latifa Cooper
Team Captain

lc/yo
Enclosure

Use Text-Wrap; Insert a Caption

EXERCISE 4

Directions

1. Open **7.68dtp**, which you created in Unit 2 and is shown in Illustration A on page 296, or open **d1.4dtp** from the Data CD.
2. Save the file as **1.4dtp**.
3. Make the following revisions to create Illustration B, shown on page 297:
   a. Set .5" top and bottom margins.
   b. Begin the exercise at the top of the page.
   c. Set the heading to script, 36 pt. Change the case to initial capitals (title case).
   d. Create two newspaper-style columns.
   e. Change the font size and leading for the first and second paragraphs to 10/12, italic. Apply bold to the second paragraph.
   f. Change the font size and leading for the remaining document text to 11/12.
   g. Set paragraph spacing for the document to 6 pt before and after each paragraph (but not for the illustrations of the letterheads). Single-space the text.
   h. Center and set headline text to serif, 12 pt.
   i. Delete the tabs at the start of each paragraph and left-align paragraph text.
   j. Reduce the font sizes for the illustrations of the letterheads as shown.
   k. Insert relevant graphics where shown.
      - Size each graphic to approximately 1.25" high by 1.25" wide. **NOTE:** *If Lock aspect ratio is selected, Word will automatically resize the object so that it remains proportional. Deselect this option so that you can size the object as instructed.*
      - Wrap text on the left side of the first graphic and around the second and third graphics as shown. Use a Square wrap option for the first graphic; use a Tight wrap option for the remaining graphics.

CONCEPT BUILDERS

Word contains a text-wrap option that allows you to place a graphic behind text.

LESSON 5

Additional Document Formatting and Editing

EXERCISE 38
Apply a Style; Edit a Style

EXERCISE 39
Create a New Style

EXERCISE 40
Use a Template

EXERCISE 41
Use a Template

EXERCISE 42
Outline Text

EXERCISE 43
Outline Text

EXERCISE 44
Edit an Outline

EXERCISE 45
Hyphenate Text; Use the Thesaurus

EXERCISE 46
Hyphenate Text; Use the Thesaurus

EXERCISE 47
Find and Replace Text

EXERCISE 48
Find and Replace Text

EXERCISE 49
Skills Review

EXERCISE 50
Skills Review

Directions *continued*

4. Preview the document.
5. Print one copy.
6. Close the file; save the changes.
7. Close the document window.

Adjust the object after inserting it to avoid awkward line breaks within the text.

Use the Help Index

How Do I...?	**Enter the keyword(s):**
Wrap text around an object	Wrap text
Set leading	Leading
Create a caption	Caption

CABLE*COM* **Company News Briefs**
A Monthly Publication of CABLECOM, Inc.

May, 2004

New Videophone Sales Off to Great Start

CableCom's new Videophone Supreme, just released in March, had a 22% increase in sales during the month of April.

The new Videophone Supreme enables home computer users to send voice and images over standard phone lines or Internet connections (56K modem, ISDN, DSL, cable modem, etc.).

The Videophone Supreme will be featured on CableCom's Web Site beginning May 12.

Windows Lunch Hour Workshops

During the month of May, there will be ongoing lunch hour workshops available to all Windows users. Learn new features, keystrokes, and online options with the Microsoft® Network.

Workshops will be held in the Information Services Conference Room on the 15th floor on Mondays, Wednesdays, and Fridays from 12 noon to 1:00 p.m. There will be a weekly sign-up sheet posted in the 15th floor lobby announcing the focus of each workshop.

Seating is limited to 15 people per workshop, so please sign up early for desired sessions.

CableCom Annual Spring Fling Company Picnic

All CableCom employees and family members are invited to attend this year's Spring Fling Company Picnic.

Festivities will begin at 12 noon on Saturday, June 19 at the South Lawns in Washington Memorial Park. Food and soft drinks will be provided. Bring your gear for softball, Frisbee, and volleyball.

Please RSVP to Karen Watson at extension 44 by Monday, May 17, and let her know how many family members will be attending.

Illustration A

CABLE*COM*

Company News Briefs ♦ A Monthly Publication of CABLECOM, Inc. ♦ May, 2004

New Videophone Sales Off to Great Start

CableCom's new Videophone Supreme, just released in March, had a 22% increase in sales during the month of April.

The new Videophone Supreme enables home computer users to send voice and images over standard phone lines or Internet connections (56K modem, ISDN, DSL, cable modem, etc.).

The Videophone Supreme will be featured on CableCom's Web Site beginning May 12.

Windows Lunch Hour Workshops

During the month of May, there will be ongoing lunch hour workshops available to all Windows users. Learn new features, keystrokes, and online options with the Microsoft® Network.

Workshops will be held in the Information Services Conference Room on the 15th floor on Mondays, Wednesdays, and Fridays from 12 noon to 1:00 p.m. There will be a weekly sign-up sheet posted in the 15th floor lobby announcing the focus of each workshop.

Seating is limited to 15 people per workshop, so please sign up early for desired sessions.

CableCom Annual Spring Fling Company Picnic

All CableCom employees and family members are invited to attend this year's Spring Fling Company Picnic.

Festivities will begin at 12 noon on Saturday, June 19 at the South Lawns in Washington Memorial Park. Food and soft drinks will be provided. Bring your gear for softball, Frisbee, and volleyball.

Enjoy good food and good friends

Please RSVP to Karen Watson at extension 44 by Monday, May 17, and let her know how many family members will be attending.

CableCom Has An Updated Web Site!

Drop in online and see what's new at CableCom (http://www.cable-com.net).

Illustration B

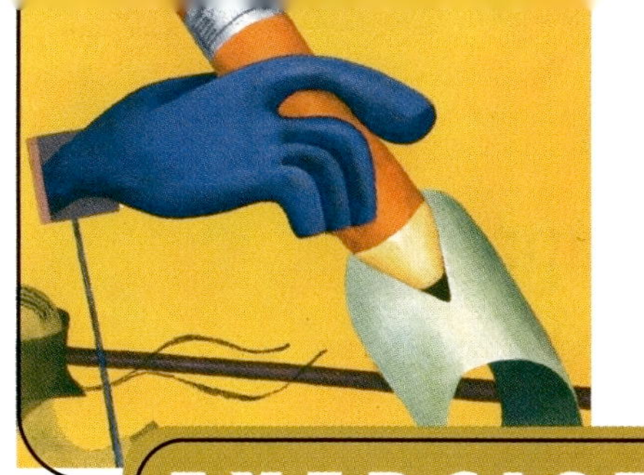

Apply a Style; Edit a Style

EXERCISE 38

SCANS

Directions

1. Open **d5.38voicetech** from the Data CD.
   a. Save the file as **5.38voicetech**.
   b. Make the revisions shown on page 117.
2. Set the left and right margins to 1"; set the top and bottom margins to .5".
   NOTE: *If you are prompted to fix the margins because one of them is outside the printable area of the page, click Fix.*
3. Apply a predesigned style that uses a sans serif, 16 pt, bold font to the title, "Technology Forum." Re-center the title, if necessary (marked as style "C" in the illustration).
4. Apply a predesigned style to the headings shown (marked as style "A" in the illustration). Select a style that uses a sans serif, 14 pt, bold, and italic font.
5. Apply a predesigned style that uses a sans serif, 13 pt font to the subheadings (marked as style "B" in the illustration).
6. Change the "A" headings to a 12 pt font.
7. Change the "B" headings to an 11 pt font.
8. Change the font color of the date, time, and location to the color of the room where the seminar/lecture will take place.
9. Indent the names of the speaker/panelists .5" from the left margin; apply italic to the text.
10. Set "Seminars" and "Lectures" to a decorative, 14 pt, bold font.
11. Center and set the last line to 10 pt, bold.
12. Preview the document.
13. Print one copy.
14. Close the file; save the changes.

VOCABULARY

Style

CONCEPT BUILDERS

- A ***style*** is a collection of formats (font, font size, alignment) that you can apply to selected text. Instead of applying each characteristic separately, you can apply all the characteristics in one step.
- Using styles ensures consistency of formatting. If you change one characteristic in the style, all text formatted with that style is updated automatically to reflect the new formatting.
- Word contains predesigned styles. Review the styles that are available and notice the styles available when you create a new document.
- You can access styles in the Styles and Formatting task pane. **Word 2000 Users:** You can access styles in the Style list on the Formatting toolbar or by selecting Styles on the Format menu.

HOT TIPS

To display the Styles and Formatting task pane, you can either click the Styles and Formatting button on the Formatting toolbar or select Styles and Formatting on the Format menu.

Use Text-Wrap; Insert a Caption

EXERCISE 3

Directions

1. Open **8.72news**, which you created in Unit 2 and is shown in Illustration A on page 294, or open **d1.3news** from the Data CD. 

2. Save the file as **1.3news**.

3. Make the following revisions to create Illustration B, shown on page 294:

a. Set the top and bottom margins for the whole document to .5" and the left and right margins to 1".
NOTE: *If you are prompted to fix the margins because they are outside the printable area, click Fix.*

b. Set the newsletter to begin at the top of the page.

c. Center and set the font for the newsletter name to sans serif, 72 pt.

d. Center and set the nameplate text to sans serif, 12 pt. Apply bold to "Company News Briefs." Insert a symbol between the nameplate text as shown.

e. Set the font face, font size, and leading for the body text of the document to sans serif, 12/13.

f. Left-align and apply bold and italic to all headlines.

g. Insert relevant graphics where shown.

i. Size the first two graphics to 1" high by 1.25" wide; size the third graphic to fill the space at the bottom of the newsletter.
NOTE: *If Lock aspect ratio is selected, Word will automatically resize the object so that it remains proportional. Deselect this option so that you can size the object as instructed.*

ii. Wrap text on the left side of first graphic and on both sides of the second graphic.

h. Create a caption below the second graphic as shown.

- Click **New Label**, enter the caption text, and click **OK** twice.
- Delete the number "1" that automatically appears after the caption.
Select the caption text and set the font for the caption to sans serif, 9 pt, bold.

i. Add the last news item as shown.

VOCABULARY

Caption

DID YOU KNOW?

In desktop publishing, text set to a 10 pt font size with 12 pt leading is referred to as "10 on 12" and indicated as 10/12.

CONCEPT BUILDERS

- A ***caption*** is explanatory text accompanying a graphic or chart.
- To insert a caption, click Insert, select Reference, and click Caption. Make your selections and click OK.
- When you insert a caption in Word, it appears above or below the image to which you have added it. It also appears with a label or number (Figure 1, Table 2, Equation 3). You can edit a caption as you would text.

Use the Help Index

How Do I...?
Apply a style

Enter the keyword(s):
Style

- In Word, once you apply formats to text, you create a style that will appear in the styles list for that document.
- If you position the insertion point over a style name in the Styles and Formatting task pane, a ScreenTip displays its characteristics. **Word 2000 Users:** The style name will appear in the style list.

C ← Technology Forum
3rd Annual Summer Convention
July 12-14, 2004
Embassy Hotel, Detroit, MI

The Technology Forum will reconvene this summer in Detroit to discuss and share new insights in the ever-changing field of technology. This year, the focus of the convention will be voice technology and its integration into present and future applications. We hope you will join us as the industry's top professionals come out to participate in this three-day event.

Seminars
A → Speech Technology and Internet Businesses
B → How will voice technology affect how business is conducted over the Internet?
July 12, 3 p.m. The Green Room
Panelists:
Joan Bayer, Empire Communications
Marion Laurel, Regent Communications
Daria Winters, Wilmington Development
A → Perfecting and Customizing Voice Recognition
B → How to tailor voice recognition vocabularies to the needs of your business.
July 13, 1 p.m. The Red Room
Panelists:
Denis Ryu, Penison Technologies
Marion Laurel, Regent Communications
Daria Winters, Wilmington Development
A → Translating Speech into Text
B → Come explore the progress that has been made in this technology. How will it change the face of personal computing?
July 14, 2 p.m. The Blue Room
Panelists:
Joy Baker, Baker Institute of Technology
Randy Kelp, Rogers and Taft Communications
Chris Friedman, Simpson Computing Corporation of America

Lectures
A → Where Are We Now? The Advancement in Voice Technology
July 12, 10 a.m. The Turquoise Auditorium
Speaker:
Lawrence Pehn, CEO, Washington Speech Systems
B → The Impact of Voice Technology in the Workplace
July 14, 10 a.m. The Turquoise Auditorium
Speaker:
Barbara Simoneli, Liberty Technology Group

For registration information, call 1-800-555-TALK

Directions *continued*

11. Delete the graphics at the top right and left margins.

12. Preview the document.

13. Print one copy.

14. Save the file; name it **1.2bblet**.

15. Close the document window.

Create a New Style

EXERCISE 39

SCANS

Directions

1. Open **d5.39dance** from the Data CD. 
   a. Save the file as **5.39dance**.
   b. Make the revisions shown on page 119.
2. Set top and bottom margins to .5".
3. Create the following style; name it DANCETYPE.
   - Set the font to red, sans serif, 16 pt, bold, and italic.
4. Create the following style; name it DANCE.
   - Set the font to script, 14 pt.
5. Create the following style; name it DATES.
   a. Indent text .5" from the left margin.
   b. Set the font to sans serif, 10 pt, bold, and italic.
6. Create the following style; name it BY.
   a. Indent text .5" from the left margin.
   b. Set the font to sans serif, 10 pt.
7. Create the following style; name it DETAILS.
   a. Set the font to sans serif, 10 pt, bold, and italic.
   b. Right-align the text.
8. Apply the styles to the exercise as follows:
   a. DANCETYPE style to text indicated as "A."
   b. DANCE style to text indicated as "B."
   c. DATES style to text indicated as "C."
   d. BY style to text indicated as "D."
   e. DETAILS style to text indicated as "E."
9. Format the subtitles below "Santa Barbara Spring Dance Series," as shown in the illustration.

CONCEPT BUILDERS

You can create styles based on existing text that you have already formatted, or you can create a new style before you enter text.

Insert, Position, Size, Copy, and Delete an Object; Use Text-Wrap

EXERCISE 2

Directions

1. Create a new document.
2. Set .75" left and right margins and .5" top and bottom margins.
3. Center and set the letterhead text using a sans serif font as shown in the illustration on page 292. Set the font size and font color as follows:
   - Company name: Broadway, 16 pt, dark blue
   - Address: 12 pt, light blue
   - Phone, fax, and Web information: 10 pt, turquoise blue
4. Display gridlines. Set the horizontal and vertical spacing to .5".
5. Insert a relevant graphic at the top left margin. Apply the "In front of text" wrap option.
   - Size it to .5" high by .5" wide.
     NOTE: *If Lock aspect ratio is selected, Word will automatically resize the object so that it remains proportional. Deselect this option so that you can size the object as instructed.*
6. Copy the graphic once.
   - Paste and position it at the top-right margin.
7. Copy the graphic again.
   - Paste and position it at the bottom-left margin.
8. Copy the graphic again.
   - Paste and position it at the bottom-right margin.
9. Insert another appropriate graphic. Apply the "In line with text" wrap option, if necessary.
   a. Size it to .15" high by .15" wide.
   b. Position it between the address and zip code as shown.
10. Copy the graphic three times and place each image between the remaining letterhead text as shown.

VOCABULARY

Inline graphics

CONCEPT BUILDERS

- You can copy, delete, and align objects using the same procedures you have used with text. To copy, delete, or align an object, you must first select it to display its sizing handles.
- Word allows you to position a graphic within text as an inline graphic. ***Inline graphics*** move along with the text to which they are anchored when that text is repositioned.
- Gridlines are a series of boxes that you can display on screen, allowing you to place objects more precisely. To display gridlines, display the Drawing toolbar. Then click Draw, Grid, and select the Display gridlines on-screen option.

10. Preview the document.
11. Print one copy.
12. Close the file; save the changes.

San serif, 10 pt, bold, italic

A — Santa Barbara Spring Dance Series
at the
Santa Barbara Dance Center
May 25-June 4
(San serif, 12 pt, bold, italic)

A — Ballet
B — El Primavera del Sol
C — May 25, June 1
D — Music by Francis Herreros
Choreography by Michael Knotter

B — Van der Bek
C — May 26, May 31
D — Music by Rolf Wittink
Choreography by Cynthia Manning

B — Levity
C — May 27, June 3
D — Music by Loren Piercy
Choreography by Alexis Regent

A — Jazz
B — El Rio
C — May 28, June 2
D — Music by Jorge Vasquez
Choreography by Sandra Lee and Adam

B — Sundance
C — May 29, June 4
D — Music by Roger Levin
Choreography by Vanessa Powers

A — Tap
B — Sound Factory
C — May 30, June 3
D — Music by Laura Belle
Choreography by Mark Cage

B — Lightning
C — May 25, June 1
D — Music by Latrell Melling
Choreography by Dameon Sanders and Jennifer Green

E — Event Prices
Price per event: $20, $30, $40
Entire Program: $100, $150

E — How To Order
By Phone: 310.555.9838
The Internet: www.sbdance.net

Use the Help Index

How Do I...?	Enter the keyword(s):
Insert a graphic	Insert clip art
Change text wrapping styles	Wrap text

CONCEPT BUILDERS

- To size an object, click the object to display its ***sizing handles;*** then drag on a handle or set the size in the appropriate dialog box. Drag a corner handle to size an object proportionally or a middle handle to change only the height or width.

- To rotate an image, click and drag the green ***rotate handle*** left or right to the appropriate angle. As you drag the handle, a dotted box indicates the placement.
- When you insert an image into a document, it is set to lay out in line with the text on the page. This can affect the layout of the page and the way you want to position the image. To change the text-wrapping style, click the Text Wrapping button on the Picture toolbar and select the style you want.
- To position an object, drag it to a location on the page or set its horizontal and/or vertical position in the appropriate dialog box.
- You can save images in different formats that carry a file name extension identifying the image type. For example, you might see .bmp as a file name extension, which indicates that the image is a Windows bitmap, a format that almost all Windows applications recognize and use for photographs and illustrations. Other common image formats include .gif, .jpg, .wpm, and .tif.

Festivals

in Montréal

Montréal is called the City of Festivals. In the summer, downtown ***Montréal*** turns into a ***feast*** for the senses. A festival event, street party, or spectacle occurs on practically every corner. There is a Jazz Festival, a comedy marathon, and of course, the renowned World Film Festival. At night, there is the ***wondrous*** Fireworks Competition. Come to ***Montréal,*** the festival capital of the world, and ***enjoy*** the sights and sounds of a fabulous city.

MAJOR FESTIVALS AND EVENTS

Napoléon...at Île Sainte-Hélène
May 5-October 11

Festival de Théâtre des Amériques
May 20-June 6

The Montréal Bike Fest
May 30-June 6

Fireworks Competition
June 19-July 28

Just for Laughs Festival
July 15-25

International Men's Tennis Championships
July 31-August 8

Internationales de Montréal
August 7-22

The Word Film Festival
August 27-September 6

Festival International de Nouvelle Danse
September 28-October 10

M✱ntréal

Use a Template

EXERCISE 40

SCANS

Directions

1. Click **File, New.** Preview the available memo templates and then select one.
2. Key the exercise provided, as shown on page 121.
   NOTE: *If the template has a place for the company name, insert and center it. Format it as follows:*
   a. Set the first line of the company name to a decorative, 20 pt font.
   b. Set "Computer Stores" to a sans serif, 18 pt, bold font.
   c. Set the branch information to a sans serif, 14 pt, italic font.
3. Review the styles used in the template.
4. Set left and right margins to 1.5".
5. Create the memo text as shown.
6. Correct spelling.
7. Move the last three sentences in the first paragraph ("I would suggest . . .") to become the last three sentences in the second paragraph.
8. Preview the document.
9. Print one copy.
10. Save the file; name it **5.40memo**.
11. Close the document window.

VOCABULARY

Memorandum
Re:
Template

CONCEPT BUILDERS

- A ***memorandum*** is a written communication within a company.
- ***Re:*** in the memorandum heading means in reference to or subject.
- CC in the memo heading refers to courtesy copy or copies.
- A ***template*** is a document that contains formatting, pictures, or text that may be reused to create new documents.
- Word comes with numerous templates that you can use to create a variety of different documents.
- Word contains a Wizard option within the template group. A wizard guides you through the steps for creating the document template.

Using the Help Index

How Do I...?	**Enter the keyword(s):**
Access a template	Template

Copy a Picture from a Web Site; Insert, Position, Size, and Rotate an Object; Use Text-Wrap

EXERCISE 1

SCANS

Directions

1. Open **3.20montreal**, which you created in Unit 2, or open **d1.1montreal** from the Data CD.  Save the file as **1.1montreal**.
2. Insert and position seven relevant graphics as shown in the illustration on page 290. Copy one of the pictures from the Web as follows:
   a. Open your browser.
      - Enter this URL: `http://www.montreal.com/tourism/index2.html`
   b. Copy the graphic of the Montreal skyline and paste it into the document.
   c. Apply the "In front of text" wrap option.
3. Size and rotate the graphics proportionally to fit within the space.
4. Preview the document.
5. Print one copy.
6. Close the file; save the changes.

VOCABULARY

Object
Clip art
Text-wrap
Sizing handles
Rotate handle

INTERNET CONCEPT BUILDERS

To copy a picture from a Web page, right-click the picture and choose Save Picture As from the menu. Use the Insert command to import the picture. Once the picture is inserted, apply a text-wrap option so you can manipulate the image.

CONCEPT BUILDERS

- An ***object*** is an item that you can select and manipulate. An object includes clip art, photographs, charts, shapes, drawn lines, and sound and video clips—items that will contribute to the visual impact of a document.
- ***Clip art*** is a collection of ready-made illustrations that are available when you install Word. You can also copy images from the Internet or purchase them on a CD or disk.
- Photographs may include downloaded images from a digital camera or scanned images.
- Word provides several ***text-wrap*** options, which control how text wraps around a graphic or other object. To change the way text wraps, select the object and choose a text-wrap option in the Layout tab of the Format Picture dialog box or click the button on the Picture toolbar.

DID YOU KNOW?

- Click File, New to access templates. You can also access templates by clicking the appropriate link in the New Document task pane. **Word 2000 Users:** The New Document task pane is not available to you.
- Templates contain placeholders, which are boxes that identify the placement and location of text and contain preset text formats.

Memo

To: Chris Del Gatto, Corporate Financial Manager

From: Monica Giles

CC: Dineen Price

Date: Today's

Re: Two-Year Sales Comparison

As requested, I have compiled the sales figures for the last two years of all software items we stock. As you can see, the Business/Suite Software is still our strong seller. I would suggest that we eliminate Fax Software and Charts, Forms, and Graphs. There has been a significant decrease on these products this year. This is largely a result of the fact that these products are now part of Suite Software.

I know you are eager to assemble the sales results from all the Bit-Byte branches to aid you in the long-term planning of our organization. We talked about discontinuing several products to reduce our line.

mg

LESSON 1

Work with Objects, Lines, and Text Boxes

EXERCISE 1
Copy a Picture from a Web Site; Insert, Position, Size, and Rotate an Object; Use Text-Wrap

EXERCISE 2
Insert, Position, Size, Copy, and Delete an Object; Use Text-Wrap

EXERCISE 3
Use Text-Wrap; Insert a Caption

EXERCISE 4
Use Text-Wrap; Insert a Caption

EXERCISE 5
Use Lines, Line Styles, and Line Colors

EXERCISE 6
Use Lines, Line Styles, and Line Colors

EXERCISE 7
Use Text Boxes, Text Box Borders, Shading, and Special Effects

EXERCISE 8
Use Text Boxes, Text Box Borders, Shading, and Special Effects; Use Page Borders

EXERCISE 9
Skills Review

EXERCISE 10
Skills Review

Use a Template

EXERCISE 41

SCANS

Directions

1. Click **File, New.** Preview the available résumé templates and then select one.
2. Key the exercise provided, as shown on page 123.
3. Create the résumé, as shown. Make any necessary changes to the template side headings to include the information illustrated.
4. Correct spelling.
5. Preview the document.
6. Print one copy.
7. Save the file; name it **5.41resume**.
8. Close the document window.

VOCABULARY

Résumé

DID YOU KNOW?

- A ***résumé*** is a document that lists your personal experience, skills, and abilities, and it is used to gain employment.
- Résumés should not exceed one page.

LESSON 1
Work with Objects, Lines, and Text Boxes

LESSON 2
Work with Drawing Tools

LESSON 3
Add Special Effects

JENNIFER MCCAREN

OBJECTIVE

To apply my creativity and marketing skills to a marketing managerial position at a cosmetics or fragrance company.

EXPERIENCE

May 2001-Present Waring and Waring Advertising New York, NY

Assistant Account Executive

- Liaison between agency and client for Turner Apparel, Aspen Cosmetics, and On-Time Watches.
- Managed two account coordinators on the Aspen Cosmetics account.

May 1998-May 2001 Paxton Apparel New York, NY

Administrative Assistant

- Assistant to president, Eastern Sales
- Responsibilities included originating correspondence, preparing and executing documents and reports, coordinating travel schedules, filing, and phone.
- This part-time job helped pay for my college education.

Summer 1997 Clothes Horse Brooklyn, NY

Salesperson

- Responsibilities included coordinating and creating work schedules.
- Highest sales for month of July.

EDUCATION

August 1997-May 2001 Marymount Manhattan College New York, NY

- Bachelor of Arts, Psychology.
- Dean's list, Spring 1998, Fall 1999, and Spring 2000.

SKILLS

Excellent working knowledge of Office XP (including Word, Excel, PowerPoint, Access, and FrontPage). Keyboarding: 55 words per minute. Excellent written and verbal skills. Fluent in Spanish.

REFERENCES

Available upon request.

444 WEST END AVENUE • NEW YORK, NY 10021 • PHONE (212) 555-5590
FAX (212) 555-4444 • E-MAIL MCCAREN@ING.COM

SCANS

PROJECT 3

You are planning to purchase a computer for your home. You have decided to use the Internet to research configurations and prices of various computer models. You will then create a table showing this comparison.

Compare a low-priced model to a medium-priced model from one manufacturer. Then compare a low-priced model to a medium-priced model from another manufacturer. When reviewing your research, indicate whether the price includes a monitor and/or a printer by shading the Yes/No cells in the table. Note what each manufacturer is offering you for the price of each computer.

Title of Table							
			Computer Name	Computer Name		Computer Name	Computer Name
Specifications		MANUFACTURER			MANUFACTURER		
	Processor						
	Memory						
	Monitor		Yes / No	Yes / No		Yes / No	Yes / No
	Hard Drive						
	CD-ROM/DVD						
	Printer		Yes / No	Yes / No		Yes / No	Yes / No
	Price						

- Create a table like the one illustrated (provide your own title). Use any table formatting features you prefer to make the table attractive. Save the table as **computermanuf**.
- Use the Internet to find the information you need to complete the table.

Outline Text

EXERCISE 42

Directions

1. Create a new document.
2. Use the default margins.
3. Begin the exercise at the top of your screen.
4. Create the numbered outline, as shown on page 125. (Use the Outline options in the Outline Numbered tab in the Bullets and Numbering dialog box.)
5. Correct spelling.
6. Preview the document.
7. Print one copy.
8. Save the file; name it **5.42intro**.

VOCABULARY

Outline

CONCEPT BUILDERS

- An ***outline*** is used to organize information in a hierarchical structure before writing a report or delivering a speech.
- An outline is composed of levels and sublevels.
- Using an outline numbered list, you can create a traditional outline that contains numbered and lettered items.

Use the Help Index

How Do I...?	**Enter the keyword(s):**
Outline Text	Outline

HOT TIPS

Hot Tips
Use the Tab key or the Increase Indent button on the Formatting toolbar to advance text to the next-lower level. Use the Decrease Indent button to return to a higher level.

PROJECT 2

SCANS

In Exercise 86, the Nature of Work, you searched the Internet about various careers and created a table summarizing the Job Outlook and the Average Starting Salary in that career.

Of the careers listed in that table, choose one that interests you. Then use a proper report format (see Exercise 62) to write a report about that career and include the sections shown below. The report should be a minimum of two pages in length and should include a header and page numbers on the second and subsequent pages. You may position the header and page numbers as you prefer. Save the report as **careerreport**.

Introduction
(Introduce the career you chose and explain why this career interests you.)

Career Description
(Describe the duties, working conditions, and benefits of entering this career choice.)

Training and Other Qualifications
(Explain the amount of time required to train for the career and other qualifications that might be necessary.)

Employment Projections
(Explain the future outlook for employment in this career. Indicate if you will need to relocate in order to obtain employment in this career.)

Salary
(Describe the salary projections for this career.)

Career Advancement
(What opportunities are there for advancement? Does advancement require higher education?)

Summary
(End the report by summarizing your career topic.)

- Insert the file **8.86careers** (completed in Exercise 86), or insert **dproj2careers** from the Data CD.  Then tell readers that this table summarizes other career options. Explain that reviewing these options might interest them in researching another career in depth.
- Use the Internet to assist you in writing this report. If you have a live connection, you can visit the following sites and/or conduct your own search for the needed information:
  www.bls.gov
  http://content.monster.com/jobprofiles
- Include a bibliography (see Exercise 30 for a proper format). Save the bibliography as **careerbiblio**.
- Include a title page that indicates the name of your career, your name, and today's date. You may use any font, font sizes, alignments, text boxes, and paragraph or page borders you prefer. Do not include graphics. Save the title page as **careertitle**.

NOTE

It is recommended that you complete a self-assessment from one of the following Web sites to see if the career you chose fits your personality. You can only accomplish this part of the project if you have a live connection.

http://www.mpc.edu/cl/climain.htm
www.careerkey.org
http://www.review.com/career/careerquizhome.cfm?careers=6

1) Introduction to COMPUVEST, Inc.
2) COMPUVEST'S Strategy
3) Our Evolution
    a) Large corporations
    b) End users
        i) International
        ii) National
    c) Small businesses
4) Our Client Franchise Is Large, Global, and Well Diversified
5) How Are We Organized to Serve Our Clients?
6) Our Goals for the Next Century
7) Our Client Needs and Market Opportunities Require Product Development
    a) Product innovation
    b) Sales in leading markets and growth industries
    c) To serve our clients with complex computer needs
    d) To provide innovative, responsive, integrated services that our clients value
    e) To earn a growing share of the computer services industry
8) Conclusion

Word Processing

END-OF-UNIT PROJECTS

PROJECT 1

SCANS

You work for a local radio station, WKFM-On-The-Air, located at 99 Main Street in Newark, New Jersey 92249. The company's e-mail address is WKFM@spring.com and its Web site is www.WKFMradio.com.

WKFM-On-The-Air is planning to develop its own live radio Web site. The station is not sure whether people know that live radio sites exist, or what they think of this concept.

- Create a letterhead for the company (do not use graphics). Save the letterhead as **wkfmlethd**.
- Write a letter to the individuals listed. In your letter, ask the recipients to listen to the existing radio Web sites listed here. Then ask them to fill out the enclosed questionnaire (we assume a questionnaire has been prepared) or e-mail you whether or not they liked the sites and why. Explain that when they return the questionnaire or respond by e-mail, WKFM will send them two tickets to attend the National Ballet. This is WKFM's way of saying "thank you" for taking the time to give them feedback. Use the Merge feature to create the form letter and data file. Merge the document and print one copy. Save the data source as **wkfmdata**. Save the form letter as **wkfmformlet**. Save the merged letter as **wkfmfinal**.

  Ms. Irene Brill
  10 Elm Street
  Oakridge, TN 37830
  E-mail: ib@canm.com

  Mr. John Brown
  303 Walnut Avenue
  Newark, NJ 90234

  Ms. Michelle Pieper
  456 Midway Drive
  Davenport, IA 52807
  E-mail: shelly@canm.com

  Mr. Gil Conte
  50 Grovehill Court
  Marquette, MI 49855

  Mr. Brent MacNamera
  50 Pacific Avenue
  San Francisco, CA 94115

  http://radio.broadcast.com
  www.live365.com
  www.live-radio.net/info.shtml
  www.ontheair.com
  http://espnradio.espn.go.com/espnradio/index

- E-mail a copy of the letter to those who have an e-mail address and print a copy of the message. (Those recipients will then be able to launch the Web sites directly from the letter, if they wish.)
- Create a label for each person in the data file. Save the labels as **wkfmlabels**.

Outline Text

EXERCISE 43

Directions

1. Create a new document.
2. Switch to outline view.
3. Set the left and right margins to 1".
4. Begin the exercise at the top of your screen.
5. Key the exercise provided, as shown on page 127.
6. Correct spelling.
7. Preview the document.
8. Modify the style for the first heading level as follows:
   a. Set the font color to red.
   b. Set the font style to italic.
9. Apply the new style to each first heading level.
10. Print one copy.
11. Save the file; name it **5.43altech**.
12. Close the document window.

CONCEPT BUILDERS

- When you enter text in outline view, styles are applied to each level to distinguish them from one another. The level is indicated on the Outlining toolbar and the style is indicated on the Formatting toolbar and in the Styles and Formatting task pane. **Word 2000 Users:** This task pane is not available to you.
- Each level is preceded by a heading symbol. A plus sign (+) indicates that subtext follows the heading; a minus sign (-) indicates that no subtext follows the heading. Heading symbols do not print.

HOT TIPS

- The Outlining toolbar contains buttons to make working with outlines easier.
- Use the Tab key or click the Demote button on the Outlining toolbar to advance to the next-lower level. Click the Promote button to convert text to a higher level heading.

ESSAY

1. Distinguish between an AutoText entry and a macro.

2. Explain how to resize an object.

3. Explain the difference between a data source document and a main document, the documents used in the mail merge process.

4. Explain how you would use styles in a document.

5. 5. Go to www.google.com. Research and explain three emerging technologies.

- **Historical Hires**
- **Full-time Hires by Gender**
- **Summer Intern Historical Hires**
- **Summer Interns by Gender**
- **New Initiatives**
    - ***Women's Panels***
    - ***Career Counselors' Conferences***
    - ***"Round Robin" Interview Format***
    - ***Upgrading Interviewing Skills***
        - **Workshops**
        - **Role Playing**
    - ***Internet Home Page***
    - ***Video Seminars***
- **Short-Term Assignment Undergraduate Training Program**
    - ***18-Month Program***
    - ***Formal Classroom Training***
        - **Rotations**
        - **Simulations**
    - ***Broad Exposure and Experience Before Placement***
    - ***Expanding Program Internationally***
- **Introducing...The Recruiters**
- **Welcome Aboard!**

TRUE / FALSE

Circle the T if the statement is true or F if the statement is false.

T F 1. Reducing the leading amount increases the readability of text.

T F 2. Internal citations are another way of citing quoted material.

T F 3. A footer and a footnote are the same.

T F 4. You can insert headers, footers, and page numbers after you type a document.

T F 5. When text is "cut," it is placed temporarily in the computer's memory and disappears from the screen.

T F 6. You can copy text that you find on the Web and insert it into a document.

T F 7. A Web browser allows you to view Web documents in a readable format.

T F 8. A Web address is the same as a URL (Uniform Resource Locator).

T F 9. Once you create a hyperlink to a site, you cannot change it.

T F 10. You create a macro to record repetitive tasks.

T F 11. It is not possible to attach a file to an e-mail message.

T F 12. If you wanted to send the same e-mail to five people, you would have to send each message separately.

T F 13. Setting a page to print in landscape orientation prints the page horizontally.

T F 14. You can align data within a table cell in various ways during the table-creation process or afterward.

T F 15. Inserting a nonbreaking space between words prevents them from breaking during word-wrap.

Edit an Outline

EXERCISE 44

Directions

VOCABULARY

Collapse
Expand

1. Open **5.42intro**, the file you created in Exercise 42, or open **d5.44intro** from the Data CD.
2. Save the file as **5.44intro**.
3. Make the indicated revisions shown below.

1) Introduction to COMPUVEST, Inc.
2) COMPUVEST'S Strategy
3) Our Evolution
   a) Large corporations
   b) End users
      i) International
      ii) National
   c) Small businesses
4) Our Client Franchise Is Large, Global, and Well Diversified
5) How Are We Organized to Serve Our Clients?
6) Our Goals for the Next Century
7) Our Client Needs and Market Opportunities Require Product Development
   a) Product innovation
   b) Sales in leading markets and growth industries
   c) To serve our clients with complex computer needs
   d) To provide innovative, responsive, integrated services that our clients value
   e) To earn a growing share of the computer services industry
8) Conclusion

Move to become 5

4. Preview the document.
5. Print one copy.
6. Close the file; save the changes.
7. Open **5.43altech** or open **d5.44altech** from the Data CD.

26. If you wanted to find the synonym for a particular word, you would use this feature:

A. Grammar check.
B. Spell check.
C. Thesaurus.
D. Comments.

27. An endnote appears at the end of a document but contains the same information as a(n):

A. Footnote.
B. Bibliography.
C. Endnote.
D. Ibid.

28. If you wanted to send the same document to 50 different people, you would use the following feature:

A. Find and Replace.
B. Merge.
C. Macro.
D. Footnote.

29. If you wanted to alphabetize a list of names, you would use the following feature(s):

A. Merge.
B. Find and Replace.
C. Column.
D. Table and Sort.

30. When a file is saved in HTML format, it is likely that the file will be used as:

A. An itinerary.
B. A DOS file.
C. A Web page.
D. A bitmapped image.

31. An example of a domain name is:

A. .com
B. .edu
C. .mil
D. .org
E. All of the above

32. If you wanted to record a Web site that you visited frequently, you would create:

A. A browser.
B. An e-mail address.
C. A bookmark or Favorites folder.
D. A history list.

33. To have text fill one column and then fill the next column, you would set the column style as:

A. Parallel.
B. Newspaper.
C. Gutter.
D. None of the above

34. A software program that "crawls" the Web and automatically catalogs the home pages is called:

A. A Web browser.
B. A search engine.
C. Word processing.
D. Windows.

35. If you wanted to use a document that contained page and paragraph formatting that you could customize, you would use:

A. A style.
B. A template.
C. A table.
D. A theme.

Directions *continued*

8. Save the file as **5.44altech**.
9. Make the indicated revisions shown below.
10. Collapse the Level 3 headings.
11. Preview the document.
12. Expand all the headings.
13. Print one copy.
14. Close the file; save the changes.

You can ***collapse*** an outline to hide body text and subheadings under the headings. This allows you to rearrange the order of the outline more easily. You can ***expand*** an outline to display all levels of text.

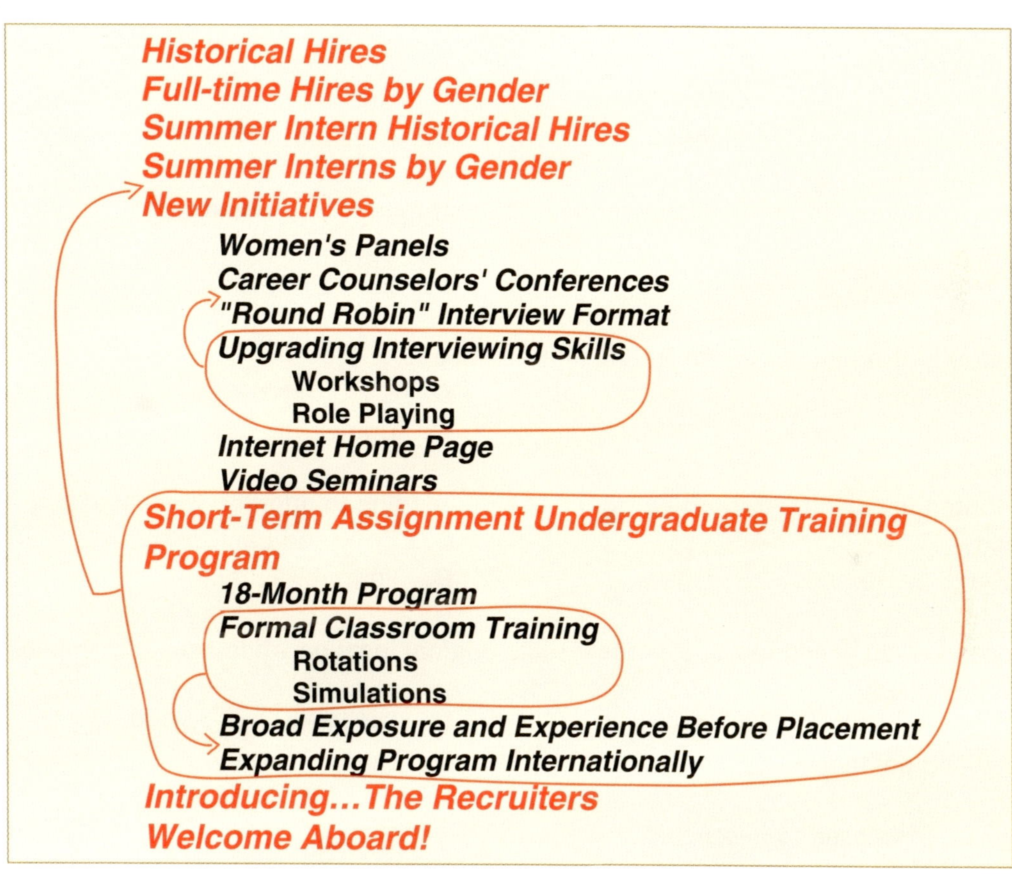

Use the Help Index

How Do I...?	**Enter the keyword(s):**
Collapse a heading	Collapse
Expand a heading	Expand

16. **Text that you have justified appears:**

A. Evenly at the left and right margins.
B. With a ragged right margin.
C. With an even left margin.
D. With an even left margin and a jagged right margin.

17. **Use the following font style(s) to emphasize or enhance text:**

A. Bold.
B. Underline.
C. Italic.
D. All of the above

18. **Font sizes are measured in:**

A. Inches.
B. Centimeters.
C. Points.
D. None of the above

19. **A serif font face is:**

A. More readable.
B. Generally used for headlines.
C. Straight-edged.
D. Available in the most varieties.

20. **If you were creating a formal announcement, the font face to use would be:**

A. Serif.
B. Sans serif.
C. Script.
D. Baskerville.

21. **A character that prints above the writing line is called a:**

A. Superscript.
B. Subscript.
C. Superfont.
D. Uppercase.

22. **If you wanted to copy the formatting from one side heading to another, you would use:**

A. Zoom.
B. Cut and paste.
C. Copy and paste.
D. Format Painter.

23. **The procedure you would use to leave text in its original location while placing a duplicate in a different location is:**

A. Cut and paste.
B. Copy and paste.
C. Header and footer.
D. Find and replace.

24. **Leading is a term used to describe:**

A. Paragraph formatting.
B. Line spacing as measured in points.
C. Line spacing as measured in inches.
D. Character spacing.

25. **The document listing your personal experience, skills, and abilities, and used to gain employment is:**

A. A letter of introduction.
B. A memorandum.
C. An itinerary.
D. A résumé.

Hyphenate Text; Use the Thesaurus

EXERCISE 45

Directions

1. Create a new document. Key the exercise shown below or open **d5.45newtips** from the Data CD.
2. Save the file as **5.45newtips**.
3. Begin the exercise at the top of your screen.
4. Set left and right margins to 1.25".
5. Use a serif, 12 pt font for the text.
6. Justify the paragraphs.
7. Use the Thesaurus feature to replace the highlighted words shown in the illustration.
8. Hyphenate the document.
9. Change the bold words to uppercase.
10. Correct spelling.
11. Preview the document.
12. Print one copy.
13. Close the file; save the changes.

Use a Minimum of Colors. Just because your computer allows you to use millions of colors on a slide does not mean you must use all of them. Work with a few colors. Stay away from dark characters on a light background. The less contrast between typed characters and background colors, the less strain on the eyes.

Avoid Too Many Special Effects. Many presentation packages now include attractive animation and sound transitions. These effects should enhance your message, not compete with it. Bouncing logos may be effective for an opening and closing, but use them sparingly. If viewers get caught up in the special effects, they will miss your communication.

VOCABULARY

Thesaurus
Hyphenate
Hyphenation zone

CONCEPT BUILDERS

- The ***Thesaurus*** feature lists the synonyms, sometimes the antonyms, and the part of speech of the looked-up word.
- You can ***hyphenate*** a document to break up words (by syllable) at the end of a line to produce a tighter right margin.
- A ***hyphenation zone*** is the area at the end of a line of text in which the automatic hyphenation feature divides words.

Use the Help Index

How Do I...?	Enter the keyword(s):
Access the Thesaurus feature	Thesaurus
Hyphenate	Hyphenation
Change hyphenation zone	Hyphenation

7. **The inside address of a letter is:**
   - **A.** The name and address of the person to whom you are sending the letter.
   - **B.** The name and address of the person writing the letter.
   - **C.** The name and title of the person who signs the letter.
   - **D.** None of the above

8. **The proofreaders' mark ^ indicates:**
   - **A.** Insertion.
   - **B.** Deletion.
   - **C.** Close up space.
   - **D.** New paragraph.

9. **The proofreaders' mark ¶ indicates:**
   - **A.** Insertion.
   - **B.** Deletion.
   - **C.** Close up space.
   - **D.** New paragraph.

10. **The Comments feature allows the user to:**
    - **A.** Insert a password.
    - **B.** Hide notes when printed.
    - **C.** Insert hidden notes that can be read on the screen.
    - **D.** B and C

11. **As you create a document, codes are inserted. These codes:**
    - **A.** Appear when you print the document.
    - **B.** Do not appear when you print the document.
    - **C.** Appear when you turn on the codes.
    - **D.** B and C
    - **E.** None of the above

12. **Use the _________ command to reverse an action.**
    - **A.** Backspace
    - **B.** Delete
    - **C.** Undo
    - **D.** Escape

13. **The proofreaders' mark ℓ indicates:**
    - **A.** Insertion.
    - **B.** New paragraph.
    - **C.** Move text.
    - **D.** Deletion.

14. **The proofreaders' mark … or stet indicates:**
    - **A.** Move text.
    - **B.** Underline.
    - **C.** Type in all caps.
    - **D.** Let the original stand.

15. **The Save As option is used to:**
    - **A.** Save a document for the first time.
    - **B.** Save a document under a different file name, as a different file type, or in a different location.
    - **C.** Resave a document.
    - **D.** A and B

Hyphenate Text; Use the Thesaurus

EXERCISE 46

Directions

1. Create a new document. Key the exercise shown on page 132 or open **d5.46organize** from the Data CD. 
2. Save the file as **5.46organize**.
3. Begin the exercise 2" down from the top of your screen.
4. Set left and right margins to 1".
5. Format the title and subtitle as follows:
   a. Center and set the title to sans serif, 16 pt.
   b. Center and set the subtitle to sans serif, 12 pt.
6. Use a 12 pt, sans serif font for the remaining text.
7. Set line spacing to 1.5 lines.
8. Apply a style to the side headings that uses a sans serif, bold, and italic format.
   NOTE: *If this style is not available, create a new style using these characteristics.*
9. Center and set the last three lines to italic.
10. Justify the paragraphs.
11. Use the Thesaurus feature to replace highlighted words. Make any grammatical changes necessary after replacing these words.
12. Hyphenate the document.
13. Correct spelling.
14. Preview the document.
15. Print one copy.
16. Close the file; save the changes.

Word Processing

END-OF-UNIT ASSESSMENT

MULTIPLE CHOICE

Make the selection that best responds to the following statements:

1. Word-wrap:

A. Automatically hyphenates words.
B. Automatically advances the insertion point to the next line as text is typed.
C. Requires use of the Enter key at the end of each line.
D. None of the above

2. Use the _________ key(s) to begin a new paragraph.

A. Backspace
B. Right arrow
C. Enter
D. Ctrl + Enter

3. To move to the beginning of a document, press:

A. Ctrl + Home.
B. Home.
C. Page Up.
D. End.

4. Selecting the Zoom option from the View menu allows you to:

A. Set the magnification of data on the screen to a specific percentage.
B. Maximize the window.
C. Restore the window.
D. Minimize the window.

5. When you press the Tab key, the insertion point advances:

A. 1.5 inches.
B. .25 inches.
C. 1 inch.
D. .5 inches.

6. The part of a letter that includes the writer's name and title is called the:

A. Body.
B. Closing.
C. Salutation.
D. Footer.

ORGANIZE +....

The Answer to all Your Database Needs

Do you work with Data frequently?

Organize+ provides you with comprehensive control over how you manage your Data. Even as a beginner, you will find organizing your Data much easier...even without the use of Help screens.

Do you share Data with other people?

Organize+ lets you share Data with other people. You can let them just view or edit some parts of the Data, or you can permit them to have total access. When information changes, all Data is updated at once.

Do you need to get answers quickly about your Data?

Organize+ makes it easy to work with related Data and get answers quickly. For example, you might want answers to questions such as: Which customers are more than 90 days late in paying their bills? Or, which customers have not yet placed an order?

Do you have the same Data saved in more than one place?

With Organize+, you can save information in one place and enable its use in many places.

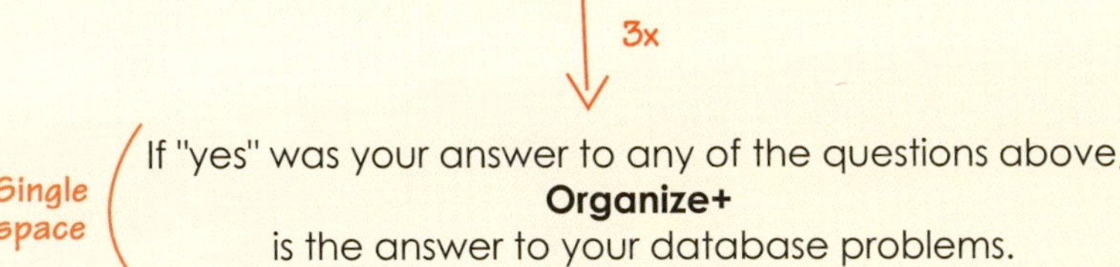

If "yes" was your answer to any of the questions above,
Organize+
is the answer to your database problems.

Create Letterhead

Today's date

«Title» «First» «Last»
«Company»
«Address»
«City», «St» «Zip»

Dear «Title» «Last»:

Thank you for your contribution to the Riverbank Run for Children in the amount of $«Amount».

Because you are a long-time supporter of our organization, we are enclosing «Total» tickets to the American Ballet Theater as our way of saying thank you. You will be attending the performance on «Date», which will feature «Name».

If you cannot attend this performance, please call Shirley Yuen at 1-800-555-5555. Once again, thank you for your generous contribution.

Sincerely,

Mark Marche
Fund Coordinator

mm/yo

enclosure

Illustration B

Find and Replace Text

EXERCISE 47

Directions

1. Open **4.31ad**, the file you created in Exercise 31, or open **d5.47ad** from the Data CD.
2. Save the file as **5.47ad**.
3. Make the revisions shown in the exercise on page 134.
4. Hyphenate the document.
5. Use the Thesaurus feature to replace the highlighted words shown in the exercise.
6. Find each occurrence of Graphic Solutions and replace it with: `GRAPHIC ARTS SOLUTIONS`
7. Correct spelling and grammar, if necessary.
8. Preview the document.
9. Print one copy.
10. Close the file; save the changes.

VOCABULARY

Find and Replace

CONCEPT BUILDERS

The ***Find and Replace*** feature scans your document and searches for occurrences of specified text, symbols, or formatting and replaces them with other specified text.

Use the Help Index

How Do I...?	**Enter the keyword(s):**
Find and replace text	Find and replace

Title	First	Last	Company	Address	City	St	Zip	Amount	Total	Date	Name
Mr.	Chris	Apostol	Pierre, Ltd.	50 East 60 Street	New York	NY	10022	250	3	June 5	Sleeping Beauty
Ms.	Martha	Blue		600 Fifth Avenue	New York	NY	10003	500	3	June 5	Sleeping Beauty
Ms.	Donna	Brown	Larson, Inc.	400 Pearman Road	Anderson	SC	29622	750	--	--	--
Mr.	Ted	Brown		87 Queens Blvd.	Queens	NY	11367	10,000	4	June 8	Swan Lake
Ms.	Diane	Elberg		33 Big Bend Street	St. Louis	MO	63122	400	--	--	--
Ms.	Anne	Frosch		18 Avenue M	Brooklyn	NY	11210	50	--	--	--
Mr.	Van	Giles		45 Icon Road	Kearney	NE	68847	850	--	--	--
Ms.	Kamisha	Jones		890 Summerhill Lane	Medford	NJ	08055	1,000	--	--	--
Ms.	Laurie	McLaughlin		33 Brier Lane	Huntington	NY	11556	50	--	--	--
Ms.	Judy	Olson		10 Hempstead Avenue	Rockville Center	NY	11510	5,700	4	June 8	Swan Lake
Mr.	Nathan	Pilgrim		63 Kirk Blvd.	Cedar Rapids	IA	52406	6,100	--	--	--
Mr.	Raymond	Rodriguez		351 Hudson Avenue	Costa Mesa	CA	91109	1,000	--	--	--
Mr.	Lee	Sarkov		3550 Anderson Street	Madison	WI	53704	2,100	--	--	--
Mr.	Frank	Szukics		100 Lumber Street	Bloomington	IL	61723	15,000	--	--	--
Mr.	Bruce	Webster		898 Willow Lane	New York	NY	10021	36,000	10	June 8	Swan Lake
Mr.	Pat	Yanez		77 Jay Street	Bronx	NY	11456	100	--	--	--
Mr.	Richard	Hickox	West Industries	1015 Grand Street	Glendale	CA	91200	100	--	--	--
Ms.	Chris	Rowe		77 East Main Street	Bay Shore	NY		500	**4**	**June 5**	**Sleeping Beauty**
Ms.	Jane	Brown	Beverly Industries	23 Popham Road	Scarsdale	NY		400	**4**	**June 8**	**Swan Lake**
Mr.	Darin	Harris		765 Bryant Avenue	Merrick	NY	11555	600	**6**	**June 8**	**Swan Lake**
Ms.		Murphy	KCMP Productions	121 West 21 Street	New York	NY	10025	50	**--**	**--**	**--**
Ms.	Sarah	Miles	ABC Manufacturing	330 Canterbury Lane	Wyckoff	NJ		185	**--**	**--**	**--**

Add records

Illustration A

Software & Company

888 Franklin Boulevard
Fairfield, New Jersey 07004
(201) 555-5555

Today's date

Mr. Stan Smith, Creative Director
Sari & Sari Advertising
575 Madison Avenue
New York, NY 10016

Dear Mr. Smith:

As you know, I am the east-coast representative for the **Graphic Solutions** software program. I know your agency is considering purchasing a new page layout software program. When we last spoke, you told me that you wanted a layout program that could display outstanding text and graphics *and*, at the same time, integrate other software you have in your office. I am certain that **Graphic Solutions** will meet all your needs. ¶ Listed below are some of the outstanding features of **Graphic Solutions.**

Graphic Solutions supports Windows XP, giving you an even wider range of page layout, graphics, and integration alternatives.

Graphic Solutions gives you sophisticated composition capabilities, enabling you to handle virtually any job.

giving you

Graphic Solutions is a complete graphic arts workshop, ~~with~~ powerful composition and graphics-handling capability.

Please phone me so that I may set up an appointment with you to demonstrate this outstanding piece of software.

outlining

I am enclosing a brochure ~~detailing~~ the features of **Graphic Solutions.**

Sincerely,

As a matter of fact, Jerry Forbes of the Loeb Agency purchased this software several months ago. You might want to talk to him about the software's merits.

Fred Nelson
Product Manager

fn/yo
Enclosure

Directions *continued*

7. Design the letterhead for the Riverbank Run for Children using the following information:

```
Riverbank Run for Children
888 Madison Avenue
New York, NY 10032
Phone: (212) 555-5555
Fax: (212) 555-6666
E-mail: rr@wind.com
Web: www.rrfchildren.org
```

7. Correct spelling.
8. Merge the form and data source documents using the conditions indicated in the exercise scenario.
9. Print one copy of the merged letters.
10. Save the merged letters; name them **10.108fundfin**.
11. Create and save a new document to create labels; name it **10.108fundlabel**.
12. Merge the label document with the selected records in the data source document.
13. Close all files.
14. Close the browser.

Find and Replace Text

EXERCISE 48

Directions

1. Open **5.46organize**, the file you created in Exercise 46, or open **d5.48organize** from the Data CD. 
2. Save the file as **5.48organize**.
3. Make the revisions shown on page 136.
4. Find each occurrence of Organize+ (including the title) and replace it with `Organize Plus`, with bold applied.
5. Find each occurrence of Data and replace it with: `data`
6. Edit the style that was used for the side headings: change the font to script and remove the bold and italic; change the font color to blue.
7. Apply the edited style to the side headings.
8. Correct spelling.
9. Preview the document.
10. Print one copy.
11. Close the file; save the changes.

Skills Review

EXERCISE 108

The Riverbank Run for Children is a nonprofit charity organization. Mark Marche, its fund coordinator, has asked you to send a letter to people who have contributed more than $200 to the organization and who live in New York. Before you can start on this project, you will need to update the existing data file with the names and addresses of new donors and missing zip codes. You can use the Internet to find the missing zip codes.

Mr. Marche thinks the letterhead could have more appeal and would like you to redesign it.

Directions

SCANS

1. Open **d10.108funddata** from the Data CD. Save the file as **10.108funddata**. 
2. Add the new records, as shown in Illustration A on page 276.
3. Resave the file. Do not close it.
4. Use the Internet to find the missing zip codes. Once you find a zip code, copy it into the data file.
   a. Open your browser. Enter this URL: `www.usps.gov`
   b. Click **Find ZIP Codes.**
   c. Enter the delivery address, city, and state for Chris Rowe. Click **Process.**
   d. Enter the delivery address, city, and state for Jane Brown. Click **Process.**
   e. Enter the delivery address, city, and state for Sarah Miles. Click **Process.**
5. Resave the **10.108funddata** file.
6. Create the form letter as shown in Illustration B on page 277.

ORGANIZE +....

The Answer to all Your Database Needs) Change to 14 pt

Do you work with Data frequently?

1" Organize+ provides you with extensive control over how you arrange your Data. Even as a novice, you will find organizing your Data much easier...even without the ~~use~~ assistance of Help screens.

Do you share Data with other people?

1" Organize+ lets you share Data with other people. You can allow them just to view or edit some parts of the Data, or you can permit them to have total access. When information changes, all Data is updated at once for everyone using it.

Move

Do you need to get answers quickly about your Data?

1" Organize+ makes it very easy to work with related Data and get answers fast. For example, you might need answers to questions such as: Which customers are more than 90 days late in paying their bills? Or, which customers have not yet placed an order?

Move

Do you have the same Data saved in more than one place?

1" With Organize+, you can save information in one place and enable its use in numerous places.

If yes was your answer to any of the questions above,

Organize+

is the answer to All your database ~~problems~~ Needs.

WHAT IS A DATABASE AND HOW DOES A DATABASE SYSTEM WORK?

A database is a collection of information organized so that the database software in use can select specified pieces of data. Think of a database as an electronic filing system. Some examples of database use include:

Computerized library systems	Automated teller machines
Flight reservation systems	Internal Revenue Service
Inventory systems	Phone directories

A database system offers you great flexibility in managing your data. To dramatize this point, let us refer to an inventory example similar to the one you may want to set up for your business, school, club, or home. Inventory is a good example of a database because it involves the tracking of many separate categories of information. The inventory database has features that will allow you to:

- Organize your information into logical categories. You can break down your inventory, for example, into ITEM, CLASS (class of information), MANUFACTURER, MODEL, SERIAL NUMBER, COST, PURCHASE DATE, WARRANTY, LOCATION, etc.
- Add, update, and delete information. Your information usually grows, and often changes. You will always be adding items to inventory, changing locations, and removing obsolete or damaged items.
- Search information by any category under a variety of conditions.
- Sort information by any category. You can rearrange your data by any of the categories.
- Generate lists and reports. You can create a report of all items, broken down by location, which you can check periodically to track losses.

Basically then, a database can:

[Insert database]

Organize your information into logical categories
Add, update, and delete information
Search information by any category
Sort information by any category
Generate lists and reports

The following is an example of a database query. Note that the data is sorted in descending order by COST and by ITEM. If you wanted to display only those items that cost more than $1,000, you could do so. If you wanted to display records of only those computers that cost less than $1,500, you could do that too.

Skills Review

EXERCISE 49

SCANS

In this exercise, you will create a résumé for yourself using one of the templates in your software.

Directions

1. Create a new document.
2. Click **File, New.** Access a résumé template that is different from the one used in Exercise 41.
3. Set 1" left and right margins.
4. Create your own résumé, using Exercise 41 as a guide.
   NOTE: *You can edit the styles used, if you want, to create a unique résumé.*
5. Correct spelling.
6. Preview the document.
7. Print one copy.
8. Save the file; name it **5.49myown**.
9. Close the document window.

PORTFOLIO

Include this exercise in your portfolio.

Export a Database to a Word Document

EXERCISE 107

Directions

SCANS

In this exercise, you will insert a database into a Word document.

1. Open the Word document **d10.107dbase** from the Data CD. 
2. Save the document as **10.107dbase**.
   a. Insert the paragraph shown in the illustration on page 273. Set the line spacing for this paragraph to 1.5 lines.
   b. Set the top margin to 2".
   c. Do not close the file.
3. Open the **equipinv** database from the Data CD. 
4. Export the **4-19eqprice** query as a Rich Text file; name it **4.23eqprice**.
5. Switch to **10.107dbase**.
6. Insert the file **10.107eqprice** where indicated in the illustration. Center it between the margins.
7. Insert a left-aligned footer that reads, `How Does a Database System Work?` Set the font to script, 12 pt.
8. Insert a right-aligned page number at the bottom right of all pages in the document.
9. Save the file.
10. Print one copy.
11. Close all files and programs.

DID YOU KNOW?

To export database data to a Word document, click the name of the table or query you want to export and then click File, Export. The Export Table dialog box will open. Click the Save as type list arrow and select Rich Text Format. Then enter a new file name and click Export. The database will become a Word file. To insert this Word file into a document, open the document to receive the database table or query. Then use the Insert, File commands in Word.

Skills Review

EXERCISE 50

In an effort to enhance the announcement for the Internet and World Wide Web Conference, your boss would like to try different ways of presenting the side headings. Because you now know how to create and apply styles, you have been asked to edit the announcement you created earlier by changing the side headings and applying different styles to them.

Directions

SCANS

1. Open **3.18confer**, the file you created in Exercise 18, or open **d5.50confer** from the Data CD. 
2. Save the file as **5.50confer**.
3. Make the revisions shown on page 139.
4. Set top and bottom margins to .5".
5. Find each occurrence of WHO SHOULD ATTEND and replace it with: `Those Who Should Attend`
6. Find each occurrence of OVERVIEW and replace it with: `Summary`
7. Using the Thesaurus feature, replace the highlighted words shown in the illustration.
8. Hyphenate the document. Change the hyphenation zone to .15.
9. Create a style for "Those Who Should Attend" using the following characteristics; name it: `WSA`
   - Use a red, sans serif, 14 pt font.
10. Create a style for "Summary" using the following characteristics; name it: `SU`
    - Use a green, sans serif, 12 pt, italic font.
11. Apply the WSA style to each occurrence of "Those Who Should Attend."
12. Apply the SU style to each occurrence of "Summary."
13. Preview the document.

15. Preview the Word document. Make any necessary changes to the document (including changing the chart size) to make the document fit on two pages.
16. Print one copy.
17. Close the file; save the changes.

Use the Help Index

How Do I...?	**Enter the keyword(s):**
Insert a worksheet as a linked object	Linked object

888 Franklin Boulevard
Fairfield, New Jersey 07004
(201) 555-5555

Today's date

Mr. Stan Smith, Creative Director
Sari & Sari Advertising
575 Madison Avenue
New York, NY 10016

Dear Mr. Smith:

As you know, I am the east-coast representative for the **GRAPHIC ARTS SOLUTIONS** software program. I know your agency is considering purchasing a new page layout software program. When we last spoke, you told me that you desired a layout program that could display outstanding text and graphics *and*, at the same time, combine other software you have in your office. I am certain that **GRAPHIC ARTS SOLUTIONS** will meet all your needs. Jerry Forbes of the Loeb Agency purchased this software several months ago. You might want to talk to him about the software's merits.

Listed below are some of the excellent features of **GRAPHIC ARTS SOLUTIONS.**

> **GRAPHIC ARTS SOLUTIONS** supports Windows XP, giving you an even wider range of page layout, graphics, and integration alternatives.
>
> **GRAPHIC ARTS SOLUTIONS** gives you sophisticated composition capabilities, enabling you to handle practically any job.
>
> **GRAPHIC ARTS SOLUTIONS** is a complete graphic arts workshop, giving you strong composition and graphics-handling capability.

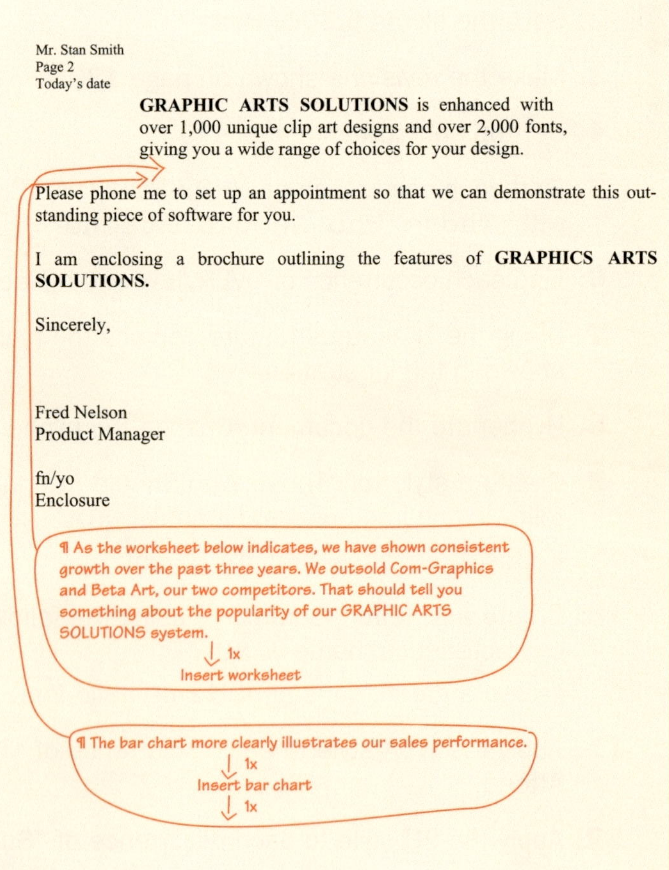

Mr. Stan Smith
Page 2
Today's date

> **GRAPHIC ARTS SOLUTIONS** is enhanced with over 1,000 unique clip art designs and over 2,000 fonts, giving you a wide range of choices for your design.

Please phone me to set up an appointment so that we can demonstrate this outstanding piece of software for you.

I am enclosing a brochure outlining the features of **GRAPHICS ARTS SOLUTIONS.**

Sincerely,

Fred Nelson
Product Manager

fn/yo
Enclosure

14. Print one copy.
15. Close the file; save the changes.

The Internet and World Wide Web

Information Conference

Internet Sessions

Our unique one-day conference provides many different training sessions on various levels of Internet learning. Our presenters are among the top experts in their field. They will provide you with cutting-edge facts about the Information Superhighway.

Session One

* ← Add superscript asterisk

Introduction to the Internet

WHO SHOULD ATTEND: Anyone who has little or no experience on the Internet and is interested in understanding the basics of the Internet and World Wide Web.

OVERVIEW: What is the Information Superhighway? In this session, you will learn what the Internet is and how to use it to communicate.

Session Two

Getting Connected

WHO SHOULD ATTEND: Anyone interested in basic Internet access information. Recommended for beginners.

OVERVIEW: What equipment do I need? In this session, you will learn how the Internet was started, what it is, and the basics of accessing the Internet for business through online services.

Session Three

World Wide Web Tour

WHO SHOULD ATTEND: This session is a must for anyone interested in using the World Wide Web for business applications.

OVERVIEW: In this session, you will learn the facts you need to effectively use this resource.

* This session will not be offered on Thursdays.) Set to sans serif, 8 pt

To enroll:
Call toll free
1-800-555-4444
Or:
E-mail us at
INTER@sem.com

Insert a Worksheet and Chart as Linked Objects into a Word Document

EXERCISE 106

SCANS

Directions

1. Open the file **7.61ad** that you completed in Exercise 61. Or, open **d10.106ad** from the Data CD. The two-page letter is shown in the illustration on page 271.

2. Save the file as **10.106adgrow**.
3. Open the workbook file **d10.106grow** from the Data CD.

4. Save the file as **10.106grow**.
5. Switch to the Word file.
6. Make the revisions in the Word document as shown in the illustration.
7. Switch to the workbook file and click the **GA SOLUTIONS** tab.
8. Copy the range A4:D7 from the worksheet and paste it into the Word document as a linked file where shown.
   - Center the worksheet between the margins.
   - Leave one blank line before and after the worksheet.
9. Switch to the workbook file and click the **3 YEARS** tab.
10. Copy the bar chart and paste it into the Word document as a linked file where shown.
    - Leave one blank line before and after the chart.
11. Switch to the workbook file and click the **GA SOLUTIONS** tab.
12. Change the YEAR 3 sales amount for BETA ARTS to: `$500,000`
13. Close the workbook; save the changes.
14. Switch to the Word document. Notice that the changes made to the worksheet are reflected in the inserted worksheet and chart.

VOCABULARY

Link File

CONCEPT BUILDERS

- Use the ***Link File*** option when you want information in the Word document (destination file) to update when the data in the worksheet or the chart (source file) is modified.
- To link a file, select the data (or chart) in the source file to copy and then paste it in the destination file using the Paste Special option on the Edit menu. Then select the Paste Link option in the Paste Special dialog box and select Microsoft Excel Worksheet Object or Microsoft Excel Chart Object.
- Any change you make to the worksheet in the source or destination file appears in both places.

DID YOU KNOW?

Linked objects will update each time you open the file. However, you can manually update links by clicking Edit, Links, and then clicking Update Now.

LESSON 6

Work with the Internet

JUMPBALL,

INC.

OCTOBER SALES ANALYSIS

We have seen record high sales at Jumpball, Inc. this month. Since the launch of Jumpball.com, Internet sales have increased significantly and have become our most profitable sales source. Catalog sales have gone down, which we attribute to the increase in Internet sales.

Below is a chart that shows the breakdown of sales from each sales source.

Due to the high volume of Internet traffic, we plan to begin a marketing campaign next month to draw our catalog users to the Internet to browse and make their purchases. If we can do this, we will eliminate the expense of putting out a monthly catalog without losing those sales.

We plan to continue retail expansion on an as-needed basis. Three months ago, we opened our second retail store in Los Angeles, CA. Since then, store sales have increased, but not dramatically. We are currently putting together a report to determine where the majority of our sales are made. We will then consider the cost and potential profit of establishing a retail store there.

Insert chart

Illustration A

	A	B	C	D	E	F
1	JUMPBALL,					
2	INC.					
3	OCTOBER SALES					
4						
5	**SALES SOURCE**	**SNEAKERS**	**BASKETBALLS**	**WATCHES**	**TOTAL**	
6	STORE	19,658.45	9,076.83	14,680.30	$43,415.58	
7	CATALOG	17,443.76	7,531.63	6,331.87	$31,307.26	
8	INTERNET	30,629.03	11,321.13	10,181.46	$52,131.62	
9						
10	**GRAND TOTAL**				$126,854.46	

Illustration B

Launch and Navigate the Web Browser; Switch Between Applications; Exit the Browser

EXERCISE 51

SCANS

Directions

1. Start Word.
2. Create a new document.
3. Display the Web toolbar.
4. Using the mouse, point to each button on the Web toolbar and notice the description that appears.
5. Click the **Search the Web** button.
   NOTE: *The browser window will replace the Word window. The MSN Search page will appear, as shown in Figure 6.1 on page 142.*
6. Click a hyperlink that appears on the MSN Search page.
7. Switch to Word.
8. Switch to the browser window. Click three more hyperlinks to view three more pages. Click the **Back** button to return to the previous page.

VOCABULARY

Internet
World Wide Web (WWW)
Web browser
Web page
Home page
Hyperlinks

NOTE

The exercises in this chapter are illustrated using Internet Explorer. However, you can complete the exercises using another browser.

INTERNET CONCEPT BUILDERS

- The ***Internet*** is a worldwide network of linked computers. The ***World Wide Web (WWW)*** is a service of the Internet in which pages, created by companies, individuals, schools, and government agencies around the world, are linked to each other.
- A ***Web browser*** is a software program that displays the information you retrieve from the Internet in a readable format. Internet Explorer is the Web browser that comes with the Office suite. Netscape Navigator is another popular browser.
- A ***Web page*** is a visual presentation of an idea using text, graphics, sound, and video that is viewed over the Internet. A Web site is a collection of linked Web pages.
- The ***home page*** is the first page of a Web site and contains general information as well as links to other related pages.
- ***Hyperlinks*** appear as underlined or colored text or graphics. When clicked, a hyperlink takes you to a new page with related information.

Insert a Chart as an Embedded Object into a Word Document

EXERCISE 105

SCANS

Directions

1. Open the Word file **d10.105jbanalysis** from the Data CD. The report is shown in Illustration A on page 269. 
2. Save the file as **10.105jbanalysis**.
3. Open the workbook file **10.105jboctsales** from the Data CD. 
   NOTE: *Click Update, if prompted, to update all linked information.*
4. Save the file as **10.105jboctsales**.
5. Click the **JBPIE** chart.
6. Copy the JBPIE chart and paste it as an embedded object in the Word document where shown in Illustration A.
7. Double-click the chart to open the worksheet software.
8. Click the **JBSTCOLSO** tab.
9. Close the Excel window.
   NOTE: *The stacked column chart should now appear in the document.*
10. Size and center the chart horizontally to fit between the margins and keep the document on one page.
11. Print one copy of the document.
12. Close the document file; save the changes.

CONCEPT BUILDERS

- In this exercise, you will copy a chart and paste it as an embedded object into a Word document.
- To insert a chart as an embedded object, copy the chart from the workbook file and then paste it into the Word document using the Paste Special command on the Edit menu. You will paste the chart as a Microsoft Excel Chart Object.
- As with an embedded worksheet, you can edit, size, move, copy, or delete an embedded chart.
- To edit a chart embedded in a document, double-click the chart to launch Excel and make any necessary changes to the chart data. Click outside the borders of the chart to return to the Word document.

Directions *continued*

9. Click the **Forward** button to return to the next page.
10. Click the **Home** button to return to your home page.
11. Close the browser.
12. Close Word.

Use the Help Index

How Do I...?	**Enter the keyword(s):**
Display the Web toolbar	Web toolbar
Launch the browser	Launch browser

Figure 6.1 Web browser

Memo

To: Jack Smith, President

From: Deborah Wilson, Sales Manager

CC: -

Date: 12/3/04

Re: Weekly Sales by Salesperson for December

The December sales promotion was extremely profitable for the company and rewarded outstanding members of the sales staff as well. Total sales for the month were $39,236.48.

Two of the salespeople exceeded $9,000.00, qualifying them for the higher 3% bonus. Hugh Olson had the highest sales, followed closely by Larry Ryan. John Pierce did well also.

¶ Sales for each of the five salespersons are shown in the following worksheet:

Events like this motivate the staff to be more effective and to reach sales levels they were unaware they could attain. It is a pleasure to compensate these exceptional employees with this special bonus.

Insert spreadsheet here. Leave one blank line before and after insertion.

Illustration A

WEEKLY SALES BY SALESPERSON
DECEMBER

WEEK ENDING	*ALTMAN*	*DIAZ*	*OLSON*	*PIERCE*	*RYAN*	***WEEKLY TOTALS***	***HIGHEST WEEKLY***	***LOWEST WEEKLY***
3-Dec-2003	$1,540.00	$1,854.00	$3,222.00	$2,876.00	$2,000.00	$2,000.00	$2,000.00	$2,000.00
10-Dec-2003	1,100.00	856.23	1,976.00	654.56	1,846.00	1,846.00	1,846.00	1,846.00
17-Dec-2003	567.20	777.77	1,287.00	2,569.50	1,234.87	1,234.87	1,234.87	1,234.87
24-Dec-2003	987.35	1,345.54	876.50	1,900.00	3,180.00	3,180.00	3,180.00	3,180.00
31-Dec-2003	1,675.00	1,234.00	2,121.21	712.00	843.75	843.75	843.75	843.75
TOTALS	$5,869.55	$6,067.54	$9,482.71	$8,712.06	$9,104.62	$ 9,104.62		
HIGHEST	$1,675.00	$1,854.00	$3,222.00	$2,876.00	$3,180.00	$ 3,180.00		
LOWEST	$ 567.20	$ 777.77	$ 876.50	$ 654.56	$ 843.75	$ 843.75		
BONUS	**$58.70**	**$60.68**	**$284.48**	**$87.12**	**$273.14**			

Illustration B December

Access a Web Site Using a Web Address (URL); Print Web Pages

EXERCISE 52

SCANS

Directions

1. Open your Web browser.
2. As shown in Figure 6.2, enter the following Web address (URL) on the Address line; then press the **Enter** key:
   `www.job-interview.net`
   NOTE: *Depending on your browser, the Address line may be referred to as "location" or "net site."*

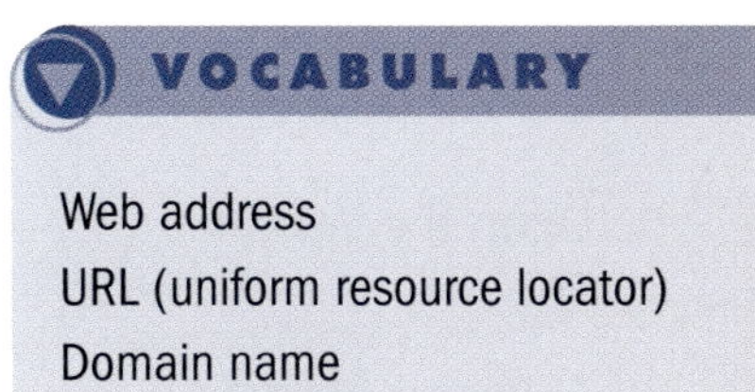

VOCABULARY

Web address
URL (uniform resource locator)
Domain name

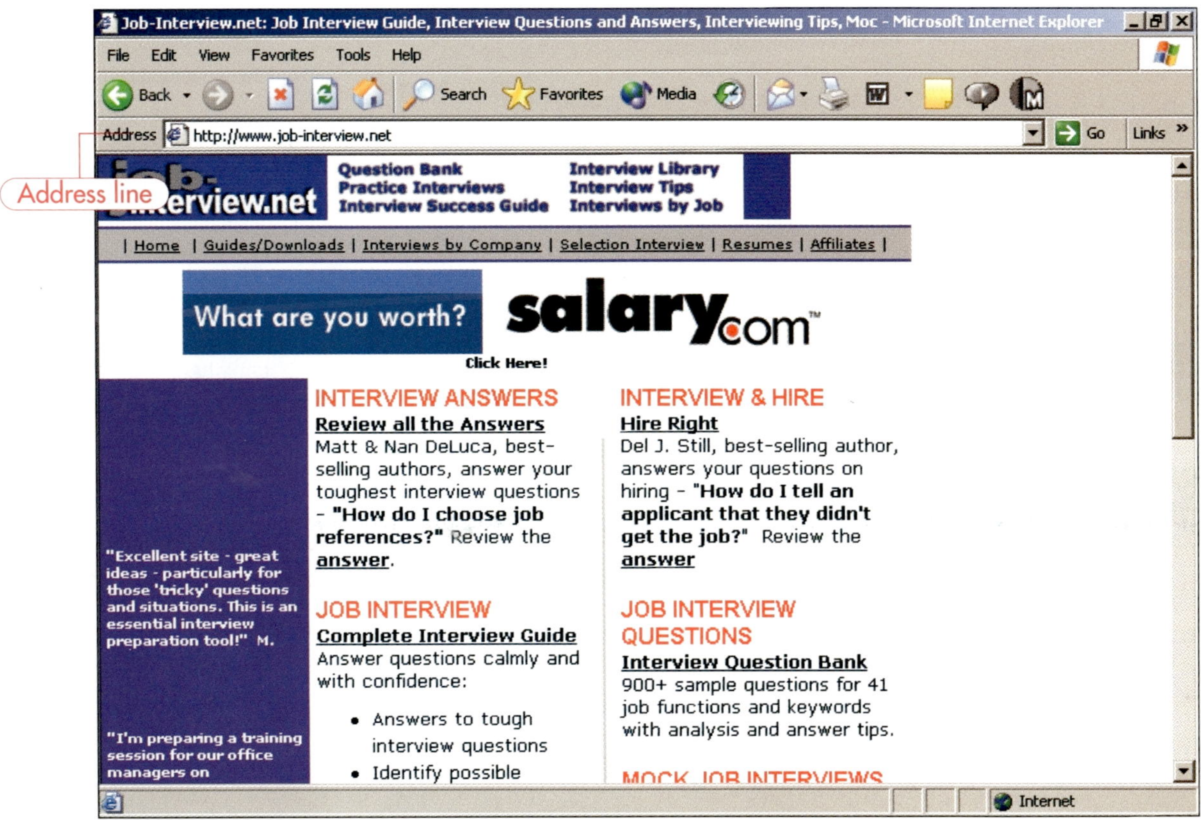

Figure 6.2 Web browser

Insert a Worksheet as an Embedded Object into a Word Document

EXERCISE 104

SCANS

Directions

1. Open the Word file **d10.104jacksmith** from the Data CD. The memo is shown in Illustration A on page 267. 
2. Save the file as **10.104jacksmith**.
3. Insert the text shown in Illustration A.
4. Open the workbook file **d10.104bonus** from the Data CD. 
5. Save the file as **10.104bonus**.
6. Click the **DECEMBER** tab on the workbook. The worksheet is shown in Illustration B on page 267.
7. Copy the range A4:G12 and paste it into the memo as an embedded object where shown.
8. Size and center the table horizontally to fit between the margins.
9. Double-click the worksheet to open Excel.
10. Apply bold to the names of the salespeople. Close the Excel window.
11. Print one copy of the document.
12. Close the document file; save the changes.
13. Close the workbook file.

Use the Help Index

How Do I...?	**Enter the keyword(s):**
Insert a worksheet as an embedded object	Embed worksheet

VOCABULARY

Embedded object

CONCEPT BUILDERS

- In this exercise, you will copy data from a worksheet (source file) and paste it as an embedded object into a Word document (destination file). An ***embedded object*** is an object placed in a destination file that becomes part of that file, which you can edit in its source application.
- To insert data as an embedded object, copy the data from the worksheet and then paste it into the Word document using the Paste Special command on the Edit menu. You will paste the worksheet as a Microsoft Excel Worksheet object.
- As with other objects, you can size, move, copy, or delete an embedded object. To edit worksheet data that you have embedded in a document, double-click the object to launch Excel and make any necessary changes to the data. Click outside the borders of Excel to return to the Word document.

Directions *continued*

3. Scroll down and click **Interviewer's Question Bank.**
   a. Scroll down and click **CAREER/JOB INDEX.**
   b. Scroll down and click **Teacher.**
4. Click the **Back** button to return to the previous page.
5. Click the **Forward** button to return to the interview questions.
6. Print one copy of the questions.
7. Enter the following Web address (URL) on the Address line; then press the **Enter** key:
   `www.dell.com`
   a. Click **About Dell.**
   b. Click **Direct Access.**
   c. Click **Executive Biographies** and scroll down.
   d. Click **Michael S. Dell.**
8. Print one copy of the page(s).
9. Click the **Back** button to return to the previous page.
10. Click **Home** to return to the home page.
11. Enter the following Web address (URL) on the Address line; then press the **Enter** key:
    `www.microsoft.com/windows/ie/ie5/tour/`
    a. Click **The basics.**
    b. Click **Basics of the Internet.**
12. Print one copy of the page(s). Read the information and keep the printed copy as a reference.
13. Exit your browser.

CONCEPT BUILDERS

- Every Web site has a unique location or ***Web address,*** which is referred to as a ***URL (uniform resource locator).***
- The URL suffix is called a domain name. A ***domain name*** identifies the Web site as a commercial (.com), noncommercial (.org), government (.gov), educational (.edu), U.S. military (.mil), or network (.net) organization.
- One way to access a Web site is to enter its correct address into the address line of the browser.

Memo

To: Chris Del Gatto, Corporate Financial Manager

From: Monica Giles

CC: Dineen Price

Date: Today's

Re: Two-Year Sales Comparison

As requested, I have compiled the sales figures for the last two years of all software items we stock. As you can see, the Business/Suite Software is still our strong seller.

I know you are eager to assemble the sales results from all the Bit-Byte branches to aid you in long-term planning of our organization. We talked about discontinuing several products to reduce our line. I would suggest that we eliminate Fax Software and Charts, Forms, and Graphs. There has been a significant decrease on these products this year. This is largely a result of the fact that these products are now part of Suite Software.

mg

Insert worksheet here. Leave one blank line before and after insertion.

Illustration A

BIT-BYTE COMPUTER STORES

SALES INCOME COMPARISON - 2 YEARS

CATALOG NUMBER	ITEM NO	ITEM	YEAR 1	YEAR 2	% OF TOTAL YEAR 2 SALES	NET CHANGE
334	5001	BUSINESS SUITE	44,109.88	145,999.99	43.79%	101,890.11
335	5002	FAX	6,500.00	2,222.12	0.67%	(4,277.88)
336	5003	CHARTS, FORMS, GRAPHS	8,111.10	1,988.98	0.60%	(6,122.12)
337	5004	WEB	33,899.77	77,999.29	23.39%	44,099.52
338	5005	VOICE RECOGNITION	18,420.00	29,654.00	8.89%	11,234.00
339	5006	GRAPHIC	44,222.00	42,000.00	12.60%	(2,222.00)
340	5007	OPERATING SYSTEM	20,222.12	18,994.32	5.70%	(1,227.80)
341	5008	GAMES	10,233.00	14,555.30	4.37%	4,322.30
	TOTAL		**$185,717.87**	**$333,414.00**	100.00%	**$147,696.13**
		Highest Sales	44,222.00	145,999.99		101,890.11
		Lowest Sales	6,500.00	1,988.98		(6,122.12)
		Average Sales	23,214.73	41,676.75		18,462.02
		Number of Products	8			

Illustration B Software

Use Placeholders; Create and Organize Placeholder File Folders; Open a Web Site from a Placeholder

EXERCISE 53

SCANS

Directions

1. Open Internet Explorer or another browser.
2. Create a new Favorites (or Bookmark) folder as follows:
   a. Click the **Favorites** (or **Bookmark**) button on the menu.
   b. Click **Organize Favorites** (or **Edit Bookmarks**).
   c. Click **Create Folder** (or **File/New Folder**).
   d. Enter `CEOs` as the folder name and press the **Enter** key.
      NOTE: *The initials CEO stand for chief executive officer.*
   e. Click **Close** to close the dialog box, if necessary.
3. Enter the following Web address on the Address line; then press the **Enter** key:
   `www.apple.com/pr/bios/jobs.html`
4. Add this site to the CEOs Favorites (or Bookmark) folder.
5. Create a new Favorites (or Bookmark) folder; name it: `Careers`
6. For each of the following sites, enter the Web address on the Address line and press the **Enter** key. Read the content of the site; then add it to either the CEOs or Careers Favorites (or Bookmark) folder, as appropriate.
   `www.dell.com/us/en/gen/corporate/biography/biography_generic_michael_dell.htm`
   `www.careercity.com`
   `http://stats.bls.gov`
   `www.microsoft.com/billgates/bio.asp`

Use the Help Index

How Do I...?	**Enter the keyword(s):**
Create a Favorites folder	Favorites folder

VOCABULARY

Placeholder
Bookmarking
Favorites folder
History list

INTERNET CONCEPT BUILDERS

- A ***placeholder*** allows you to record a site that you would like to revisit. Adding a placeholder is often referred to as adding a ***bookmark*** to a site (in Netscape Navigator) or adding a site to a ***Favorites folder*** (in Internet Explorer). The terminology depends on the browser you are using.
- When you want to revisit a site that you saved in a Favorites folder, click the Favorites button on the toolbar and click the site that you want to open in the Favorites pane.
- Most browsers record a ***history list*** of the sites you have visited and allow you to jump back to a recently visited site. To view a history list, click the list arrow to the right of the Address line. You can also click the History button on the toolbar.

DID YOU KNOW?

You can create folders to organize Web sites, just as you did to organize your Word files.

Insert a Worksheet into a Word Document

EXERCISE 103

SCANS

Directions

1. Open the Word file **5.40memo** that you created in Exercise 40. The memo is shown in Illustration A on page 265. Or, open **d10.103memo** from the Data CD. 
2. Save the file as **10.103memo**.
3. Open the workbook file **d10.103sales** from the Data CD. 
4. Save the file as **10.103sales**.
5. Click the SOFTWARE tab on the workbook. The worksheet is shown in Illustration B on page 265.
6. Copy the ITEM, YEAR 1, and YEAR 2 columns of the worksheet (as indicated by the highlighted data), and paste them into the memo where shown in Illustration A.
7. Center the table horizontally within the document.
8. Apply line borders to the table, if they do not automatically appear.
9. Save the file as **10.103memosales**.
10. Print one copy of the document. Close all files.

VOCABULARY

Integrate
Source file
Destination file

CONCEPT BUILDERS

- Office XP allows you to ***integrate,*** or share, data between Office applications. Data is shared between the ***source file*** (the file where the data originates) and the ***destination file*** (the file that receives the data).
- You can easily insert a worksheet into a Word document by copying the columns and rows from the worksheet and then pasting them into the Word document. To copy and paste data between applications, the source and destination files should both be open.
- The pasted worksheet behaves like a table. You can edit the data and apply formatting, but you cannot edit the formulas. The inserted worksheet has no connection to the original workbook file.

Copy Text from a Web Site; Save a Web Page

EXERCISE 54

SCANS

Directions

1. Start Word.
2. Open **d6.54memohr** from the Data CD.  Save the file as **6.54memohr**.
3. Open your browser.
4. Enter the following Web address on the Address line; then press the **Enter** key:
   `http://www.osha.gov`
   - Click **Newsroom.**
   - Click **Fact Sheets.**
   - Click **Program Highlights by Subject.**
   - Scroll down and click **OSHA: Employee Workplace Rights and Responsibilities–[95-35]**
5. Mark this site (add it to your Favorites or Bookmark folder).
6. Save the Web page; name it **6.54rights**.
7. Copy the text beginning with the sentence, "The OSHA Act gives employees many rights and responsibilities. They have the right to:" and ending with the last item marked with an asterisk.
   a. Switch to the Word document.
   b. Paste the text into the memo where indicated in the illustration on page 147.
8. Format the memo as follows:
   a. Apply the same font to the copied text that was used in the paragraph above it.
   b. Replace the asterisks with bullets.
   c. Adjust short lines so they extend to the margins.

INTERNET CONCEPT BUILDERS

- You can copy text that you find on the Web into a document. **IMPORTANT:** *Be sure to cite the source of Internet material that you use in a document.*
- Web sites change constantly. Therefore, if you want to keep a Web page for later reference, you can save it. The process of saving a Web page is the same as saving a file.

HOT TIPS

To copy text from a Web site to a document, do the following:

1. Select (highlight) the text you want to copy from the Web site.
2. Click Copy or press the Ctrl + C keys.
3. Switch to the document where the text will be inserted.
4. Click Paste or press the Ctrl + V keys.

Merge E-mail with a Data Source Document

EXERCISE 102

Directions

1. Create a new Word document.
2. Use the default margins.
3. Begin the exercise at the top of your screen.
4. Enter the e-mail message, as shown in the illustration below.
5. Insert the proper merge code for each variable indicated. Use the data source **d10.102joydata**, which is located on the Data CD.  (This data source has been updated and now includes each person's e-mail address.)
6. Insert an e-mail signature into the document.
7. Enter your name and apply a 12 pt, script font.
8. Enter the following title below your name in 10 pt, Times New Roman:
   `Administrative Assistant`
   `Office of the Dean of Students`
9. Merge the main and data source documents to e-mail.
10. In the Merge to E-mail dialog box, select the E-mail field as your recipient.
11. Enter the following in the Subject line: `Congratulations`
12. E-mail all of the records.
13. Save the merged e-mail message; name it **10.102joyemail**.

> As a reminder, «First», the awards ceremony will be held on «Date» at 7:30 in Room «Rm». We look forward to seeing you and your parents there.
>
> Again, congratulations to you on being awarded the «Dept» Department Award for highest honors in «Subject».

VOCABULARY

E-mail signature

CONCEPT BUILDERS

- Word allows you to merge an e-mail with a data source. In this case, the e-mail message is the main document and the data source can be a list of e-mail contacts from your Outlook address book or another database with e-mail addresses in it.
- An ***e-mail signature*** is text and/or pictures that you can automatically insert into an outgoing e-mail message. To customize an e-mail signature, click Tools, Options. In the General tab, click the E-mail Options button and make your selections.

Directions *continued*

9. Print one copy.
10. Close the file; save the changes.
11. Close the browser.

BIT-BYTE
COMPUTER STORES
Ocean View Branch

Memo

To: Human Resource Personnel

From: Peter Gregorian, Director

CC: Wendina McMillin, Asst. Director

Date: Today's

Re: Employee Workplace Rights and Responsibilities

Please be sure that all Welcome kits contain the Employee Workplace Rights and Responsibilities as outlined in the Occupational Safety and Health Act of 1970. This act created the Occupational Safety and Health Administration (OSHA) within the Department of Labor. We are all familiar with the regulations; however, we must be sure that all of our printed materials include this information from the Act of 1970:

[Insert text from Web site here]

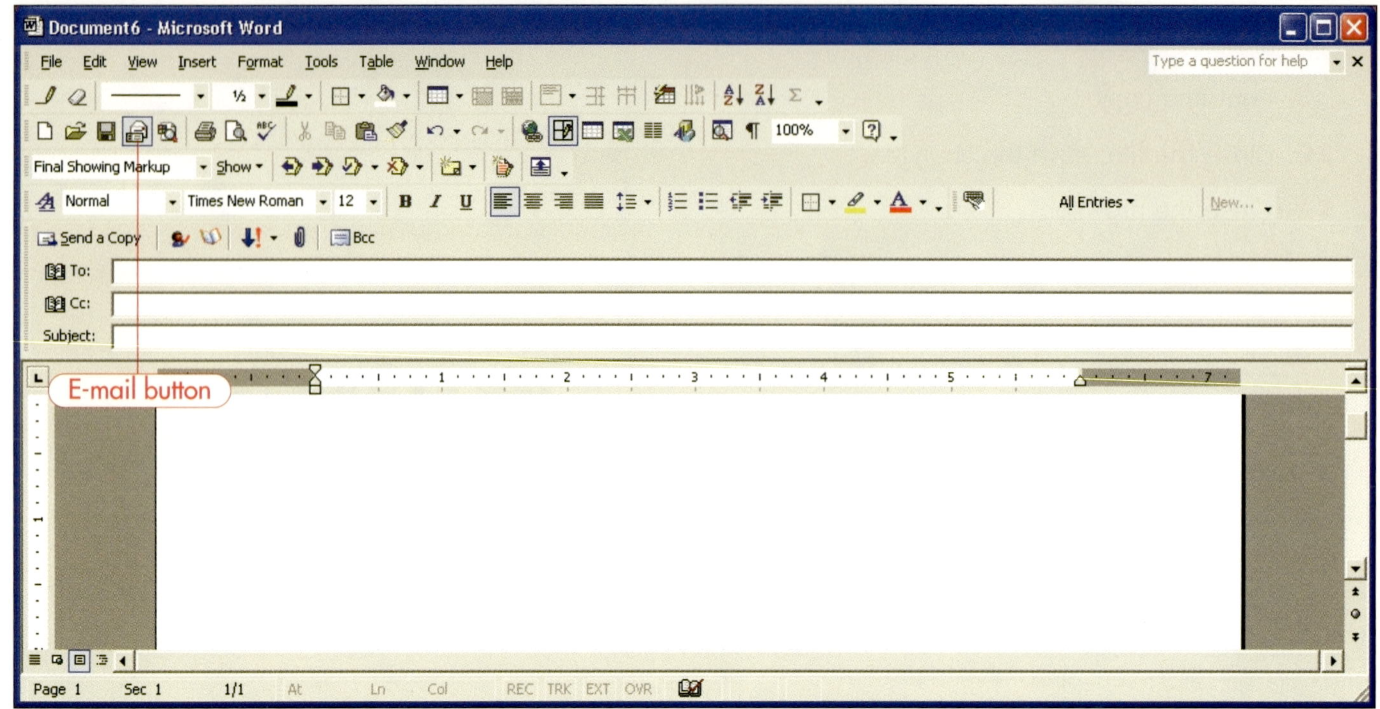

Figure 9.1 Word 2002 e-mail screen

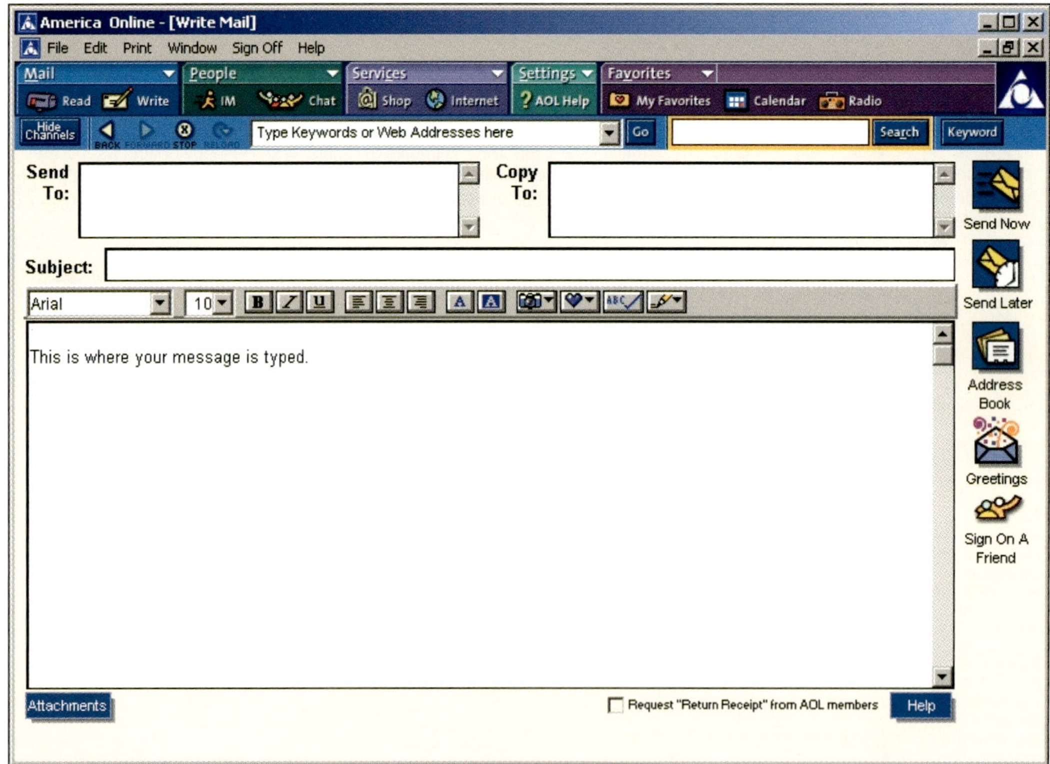

Figure 9.2 AOL e-mail screen

Copy Text from a Web Site; Save a Web Page; Insert a Bookmark; Create and Edit a Hyperlink

EXERCISE 55

Directions

SCANS

1. Start Word.
2. Open **d.55dctourlet** from the Data CD. 
   Save the file as **6.55tour1**.
3. Set .75" left and right margins and .5" top and bottom margins.
4. Create the letter as shown on page 150.
   - Set the font for the document to serif, 10 pt.
5. Open your browser.
6. Enter the following Web address on the address line; then press the **Enter** key:
   `www.whitehouse.gov`
   - Click **History and Tours.**
   - Click **White House Tours.**
7. Mark this site.
8. Save the Web page; name it **6.55whtourinfo**.
9. Copy the paragraphs "White House Tours" and "White House Visitor Center."
   a. Switch to Word.
   b. Paste the information into the letter where indicated in the illustration on page 150.
10. Format the text as follows:
    a. Apply the same font to the copied text that was used in the letter.
    b. Bold the side headings and color them purple.
    c. Adjust short lines so they extend to the margins, if necessary.

INTERNET CONCEPT BUILDERS

- You can insert a hyperlink into a document that will link to a Web site. When you click the link, you will go to that site. This is only useful when the document is onscreen and you are connected to the Internet.
- You can also insert hyperlinks in a document that will link to a location within the same document, to another document created in the same application, or to a document in another application.
- A bookmark allows you to mark a location in a document and return to it at a later time. You can identify the bookmark location by giving it a name.
- You can insert a hyperlink in a document that allows you to jump to the named bookmark location in the same document or in another document.

Directions *continued*

8. Send your message.
   NOTE: *If you have a live Internet connection, the message will be sent. If you do not have a live connection, you will get a message that you need to connect to your service provider. If this happens, click the Close button on each dialog box until you return to the start screen.*
9. Open the copy of the message you sent to yourself.
10. Download the attached file.
11. Open the file.
12. Switch to the open e-mail message.
13. Click the hyperlink to the Web site (if you have a live connection only; otherwise, skip this step). Print a copy of the Web pages. Then close the browser.
14. Close the e-mail program.
15. Create a new Word document.
16. Enter the following at the top of your screen:
    `Netiquette refers to using proper manners on the Internet. There are many Web sites that outline "netiquette," including: http://www.albion.com/netiquette and http://usyd.edu.au/su/netting/email/extras/netiquette.html.`
17. Click the E-mail button on the Standard toolbar.
18. Enter the e-mail address of your teacher or a classmate in the To box.
19. Send yourself a copy.
20. Enter the following in the Subject box: `E-Mail Etiquette`
21. Send your message.
    NOTE: *If you do not have a live connection, your message will not be sent.*
22. Close the file; do not save the changes.

CONCEPT BUILDERS

- ***E-mail,*** which is an abbreviation for "electronic mail," refers to the transmission of messages over communication networks. You can send a message or a document to a single person via e-mail or to an entire group simultaneously.
- Every e-mail user has a unique e-mail address.
- You can send the same message to several users at once. This is called ***broadcasting*** or creating a ***list-serve.***
- You can send a saved Word document as a ***file attachment*** to an e-mail message or you can create and send a new e-mail message from within a Word document.
- Notice the Word 2002 e-mail screen shown in Figure 9.1 on page 262. The screen was accessed by clicking the E-mail button, which appears on the Standard toolbar.
- Compare the Word 2002 e-mail screen to the AOL e-mail screen shown in Figure 9.2 on page 262. Notice the similarities and differences.

Directions *continued*

11. Select the text "Smithsonian."
    - Create a hyperlink to: `http://www.si.edu/`
12. Select the text "The Pentagon."
    - Create a hyperlink to: `http://www.defenselink.mil/pubs/pentagon/`
13. Select the text "National Gallery of Art."
    - Create a hyperlink to: `http://www.nga.gov/`
14. Select the text "Library of Congress."
    - Create a hyperlink to: `www.loc.com/`
15. Select the text "Please call me."
    - Link to the phone number which has been bookmarked.
16. Print one copy of the letter.
17. Edit the hyperlink, www.loc.com, to be: `www.loc.gov`
18. Click each hyperlink to see if it works properly.
19. Return to the letter.
20. Remove the link to the Pentagon.
21. Close the file; save the changes.
22. Close the browser.

Use the Help Index

How Do I...?	**Enter the keyword(s):**
Insert hyperlinks	Hyperlink

Send E-mail; Attach a File to an E-mail

EXERCISE 101

Directions

SCANS

1. Open the e-mail program available to you. Open a new e-mail message.
2. Enter the e-mail address of your teacher or a classmate in "Send to," "To," or "Recipient" text box.
   NOTE: *The box name varies, depending on the e-mail software you are using.*
3. Send yourself a copy.
4. Enter the following in the Subject text box:

   ```
   E-mail Etiquette and Accuracy Check of
   Data on the Attached
   ```

5. Enter the following in the message text box:

   ```
   Found two interesting sites on "net
   etiquette" (called netiquette) as it
   applies to e-mail. Visit them at:
   www.albion.com/netiquette and
   www.usyd.edu.au/su/netting/email/extras/
   netiquette.html. Share them with the staff.

   On another topic—please double-check the
   attached list for accuracy and let me know
   if I can proceed with the mailings.
   ```

6. Attach **d10.101joydata** from the Data CD. 
7. Print one copy of your e-mail message.

VOCABULARY

E-mail
Broadcasting
List-serve
File attachment

CONCEPT BUILDERS

- Netiquette refers to using proper manners on the Internet.
- Visit:
  http://www.albion.com/netiquette
  and
  http://usyd.edu.au/su/netting/email/extras/netiquette.html
  These sites outline "netiquette" as it applies to e-mail.

D.C. Tours

114 PENNSYLVANIA AVENUE ◻ WASHINGTON, D.C. 20045
(202) 555-TOUR

Insert a bookmark

April 5, 2004

Ms. Deborah Sprewell
4546 Western Road
Savannah, GA 31405

Dear Ms. Sprewell:

I am glad that you have chosen D.C. Tours to help plan your family's trip to Washington, D.C. As you probably know, the spring is an ideal time to visit the nation's capital.

As per your request, below please find information on White House tours, which I found on the official White House Web site, www.whitehouse.gov.

[Insert text from Web site here]

In addition to The White House, I highly recommend that you and your family visit the following museums, monuments, and buildings.

Jefferson Memorial	Library of Congress	Lincoln Memorial
National Gallery of Art	Vietnam Veterans Memorial Wall	The Pentagon
Smithsonian	Tomb of the Unknown Soldier	Washington Monument

If there is any additional information that you might need, please call me. I look forward to working with you again soon.

Sincerely,

Beth Friedman
Travel Consultant

bf/yo

Title	First	Last	Address	City	St	Zip	S or D	Dept	Subject	Date	Rm
Mr.	Robert	Kline	765 Beverly Drive	Beverly Hills	CA	90211	son	English	Literature	June 14	D22 2
Ms.	Wilma	Jones	767 Burton Way	Beverly Hills	CA	90219	daughter	English	Journalism	June 14	D22 2
Ms.	Monica	Peters	20 Columbia Court	Los Angeles	CA	90012	daughter	History	American History	June 17	A234
Mr.	Bill	Giles	33-99 South Beverly Drive	Beverly Hills	CA	90219	son	Math	Calculus	June 18	C298
Ms.	Sally	Ubell	76 Pico Drive	Los Angeles	CA	90002	daughter	History	European History	June 17	A234
Mr.	**Herman**	**Miller**	**66 Wilshire Boulevard**	**Los Angeles**	**CA**	**90102**	**son**	**History**	**Latin American Studies**	**June 17**	**A234**
Ms.	**Wilma**	**Hall**	**77 Sunset Boulevard**	**Los Angeles**	**CA**	**90110**	**daughter**	**English**	**Communications**	**June 14**	**D222**
Ms.	**Nancy**	**Ray**	**87-10 Iris Drive**	**Irvine**	**CA**	**92715**	**daughter**	**English**	**Comparative Literature**	**June 14**	**D222**
Mr.	**Tom**	**Burns**	**91 Via Colinas**	**West Lake Village**	**CA**	**91368**	**son**	**Math**	**Logic**	**June 18**	**C298**

Search the Internet

EXERCISE 56

Directions

SCANS

1. Open your browser.
2. Enter the following address of a search engine site on the Address line; then press the **Enter** key:
   `www.altavista.com`
3. Add this site to your Favorites folder (or bookmark the site).
4. Enter the text string `Los Angeles` in the Search box and press the **Enter** key.
   - Notice the results and the number of Web pages (sites) this search has yielded.
5. Print one copy of the displayed search results.
6. Enter the following address of a directory on the Address line; then press the **Enter** key:
   `www.yahoo.com`
7. Add this site to your Favorites folder (or bookmark the site).

VOCABULARY

Search engine
Directory
Text string

HOT TIPS

- Seek out multiple sites when you are researching a topic. Directories and search engines vary in their database contents and accuracy.
- Use a directory when you have a broad topic to research.
- Use a search engine when you have a narrow topic to research.

INTERNET CONCEPT BUILDERS

- A ***search engine*** is a software program that searches the Web and automatically indexes home pages. Popular search engines include HotBot, AltaVista, and Lycos.
- The term "search engine" is often used to describe both true search engines and directories. They are not the same.
- A ***directory*** depends on people to create its listings. You submit a short description to the directory for your entire site, or editors write one for sites they review. A search engine looks for matches only in the descriptions submitted. A directory displays information by major topic headings, which are broken down into smaller topics that are then broken down further. Yahoo and Google are examples of popular directories.
- A ***text string*** may be a word, words, or phrase you want to use in your search. The more specific the text string, the narrower the search.

Edit the Data Source; Merge with Conditions; Create and Merge Envelope and Label Main Documents

EXERCISE 100

Directions

SCANS

1. Open **10.97joydata**, the file you created in Exercise 97, or open **d10.100joydata** from the Data CD. 
2. Save the file as **10.100joydata**.
3. Add the data records to the file, as shown in the illustration on page 259.
4. Resave the file.
5. Merge the **10.97joyform** and **10.100joydata** documents only for those receiving English or History Department awards.
6. Correct spelling.
7. Print one copy of the merged letters.
8. Save the merged letters; name them **10.100joyfin2**.
9. Create and save an envelope main document; name it **10.100joyenv**.
10. Merge the envelope main document with the selected records in the data source document **10.100joydata**.
11. Use size 10, 4 ⅛" x 9 ½" envelopes.
12. Print an envelope for each person receiving an award in the English or History Departments. Include the return address of the college used in the **10.97joyform** document. (Enter `To the parents of` into the envelope file as the first line.)
13. Close all files.

8. Enter the text string `Los Angeles` in the Search box and press the **Enter** key.
   - Notice the results and the number of Web pages (sites) this search has yielded.
9. Print one copy of the displayed search results.
10. Compare the printouts and notice the difference between the results of a search engine and those of a directory.
11. Open your Favorites folder (or bookmarked sites) and return to the www.altavista.com site.
12. Enter the text string `Los Angeles restaurants` in the Search box and press the **Enter** key.
    - Notice the results and the number of Web pages (sites) this search has yielded. (Fewer sites should result.)
13. Print one copy of the displayed search results.
14. Open your Favorites folder (or bookmarked sites) and return to the www.yahoo.com site.
15. Enter the text string `Los Angeles restaurants` in the Search box.
    - Notice the results and the number of Web pages (sites) this search has yielded.
16. Print one copy of the displayed search results.
17. Compare the printouts and notice the difference between the results of a search engine and a directory when the search has been narrowed.
18. Close the browser.

DID YOU KNOW?

Search engines are often called "Web crawlers" or "spiders" because they crawl the Web.

Word provides a list of product numbers for Avery labels. If you are using a different brand, find an equivalent product number or experiment to find product equivalents.

Title	FirstName	LastName	Company	Address1	City	State	PostalCode	Date	Item	Newdate
Mr.	Daniel	Kenna		54 Beekman Place	Palo Alto	CA	94356	June 10	one dozen zip disks	July 1
Mr.	Jack	Lewis		59 Jasper Court	Chattanooga	TN	37406-0623	June 15	two 17" monitors	July 12
Ms.	Virginia	Martinez	CompuToll, Inc.	76 Riverbend Street	Los Angeles	CA	90210	June 25	two CD-ROM drives	August 1
Ms.	Helen	McCall	Regal Products	880 Halpin Road	Bellevue	WA	98006	June 18	five sound cards	July 22
Mr.	Michael	Jasper	MarketWorks	322 Columbia Place	Seattle	WA	98001	June 8	two Plaza 400 notebooks	July 2
Ms.	Shirley	Linn		55 Water Street	Santa Ana	CA	92701	June 12	three sound cards	July 12
Mr.	Manny	Ali	Carrier, Inc.	87 Highland Place	Reston	VA	22191	June 12	one set of speakers	July 12

Use the Help Index

How Do I...?	**Enter the keyword(s):**
Filter records	Mail merge select
Create envelopes while merging	Envelope merge
Create labels while merging	Label merge

Search the Internet

EXERCISE 57

SCANS

Directions

1. Open your browser.
2. Open your Favorites folder (or bookmarked sites) and return to the www.altavista.com site. (If you did not mark this site, access it from the Internet.)
3. Enter the text string `New York AND City` in the Search box and press the **Enter** key.
   a. Notice the results and the number of Web pages (sites) this search has yielded.
   b. Print one copy.
   c. Click the **Back** button, if necessary.
4. Enter the text string `Clinton OR Foreign Policy` in the Search box and press the **Enter** key.
   a. Notice the results and the number of Web pages (sites) this search has yielded.
   b. Print one copy.
   c. Click the **Back** button, if necessary.

VOCABULARY

Boolean operator
AND
OR
NOT

INTERNET CONCEPT BUILDERS

- A ***Boolean operator*** is a word or symbol that narrows a search so it is more specific. Although operators do help to filter sites, they are not perfect. The most common Boolean operators are the words AND, OR, NOT, and NEAR.
- Use ***AND*** when you want your results to include all the words in your text string. (Clinton AND Foreign Policy will find sites that contain all three words in the search results.)
- Use ***OR*** when you want your results to include one of the words in the text string. (Clinton OR Foreign Policy will find sites that contain either the word "Clinton" or the words "Foreign Policy.")
- Use ***NOT*** when you want your results to include only the words preceding the NOT operator. (New York NOT City will find sites that contain New York, but will not include sites that contain the words New York City.)

Edit the Data Source; Merge with Conditions; Create and Merge Envelope and Label Main Documents

EXERCISE 99

SCANS

Directions

1. Open **10.96sordata**, the file you created in Exercise 96, or open **d10.99sordata** from the Data CD. 
2. Add the data records to the file, as shown in the illustration on page 257.
3. Save and close the file; name it **10.99sordata**.
4. Merge the **10.96sorform** (also created in Exercise 96) and **10.99sordata** documents only for those who live in Washington.
5. Correct spelling.
6. Print one copy of the merged letters.
7. Save the merged letters; name them **10.99sorfin2**.
8. Create and save an envelope main document; name it **10.99sorenv**. Use size 10, 4 1/8" x 9 ½" envelopes. Do not include a return address.
9. Merge the envelope main document with the data source document **10.99sordata**.
10. Create and save a mailing label main document; name it **10.99sorlabel**.
11. Use Avery–5160 Address labels (1" x 2.63").
12. Merge the mailing label main document with the data source document **10.99sordata**.
13. Print one copy of the labels. (Use plain paper to see how labels print on a page.)
14. Close all files.

Filter records

CONCEPT BUILDERS

- You can merge selected records rather than all the records contained in the data file.
- You can ***filter records*** by setting one or multiple conditions that the data records must meet in order to be included in the merge. For example, you might want to merge only those records within a specific zip code or state.
- You can use mail merge to create a set of labels or to prepare envelopes for mailing your new document. The label or envelope file is the main document.

DID YOU KNOW?

To prepare envelopes and labels, you can use the same data source document you used with the main document.

Directions *continued*

5. Enter the text string `New York NOT City` in the Search box and press the **Enter** key.
   a. Notice the results and the number of Web pages (sites) this search has yielded.
   b. Print one copy.
   c. Click the **Back** button, if necessary.
6. Open your Favorites folder (or bookmarked sites) and return to the www.yahoo.com site. (If you did not mark this site, access it from the Internet.)
7. Enter the text string `New York AND City` in the Search box and press the **Enter** key.
   a. Notice the results and the number of Web pages (sites) this search has yielded.
   b. Print one copy.
   c. Click the **Back** button, if necessary.
8. Enter the text string `New York NOT City` in the Search box and press the **Enter** key.
   a. Notice the results and the number of Web pages (sites) this search has yielded.
   b. Print one copy.
   c. Click the **Back** button, if necessary.
9. Enter the text string `Clinton OR Foreign Policy` in the Search box and press the **Enter** key.
   - Notice the results and the number of Web pages (sites) this search has yielded.
10. Print one copy.
11. Click the **Home** button.
12. Compare the printouts and notice the difference between the results of a search engine and a directory when the search is narrowed using Boolean operators.
13. Close the browser.

Use the Help Index

How Do I...?	**Enter the keyword(s):**
Create a mail merge	Merge

To create envelopes and labels using the merge process, click Tools, select Letters and Mailings, and click Mail Merge Wizard to display the Mail Merge task pane. Then select Envelopes or Labels, depending on the type of document you want to create. You will use the database query as your recipient list.

Today's Date

«FIRST» «LAST»
«ADDRESS»
«CITY», NY «ZIP»

Dear «FIRST»,

The New York Chapter of the Web Computer Association will offer a weekend workshop and seminar to accountants on the use of accounting and financial software.

The workshop will take place on Saturday and Sunday, November 14 and 15, at the offices of R&R Dock Accounting Services, 125 Broadway, New York. The workshop will begin at 9:00 a.m. on each day and will conclude at 4:00 p.m. Refreshments will be served throughout the day.

Please confirm your attendance by October 31. I look forward to seeing you, «FIRST», at the workshop.

Cordially,

Harley Jones
President
New York Chapter

hj/

Skills Review

EXERCISE 58

Your boss, Michael Robbins, is traveling to New York City for a business trip next week and will be staying in Manhattan through the weekend. He has asked you to search the Web for five top tourist attractions to visit while he is there. Write a memo to your boss that includes links to the sites, as well as short descriptions of each site.

Directions

SCANS

1. Start your browser.
2. Enter the URL `www.google.com` and search for tourist attractions in New York City.
3. For each tourist attraction you find:
   a. Write down its name on a piece of paper.
   b. Add its Web site to your Favorites folder (or bookmark it).
4. Start Word.
5. Use a memo template to write a memo to your boss telling him about the tourist attractions that you found.
6. Enter the names of the tourist attractions in your memo.
   a. Link the name of the tourist attraction to its related Web site (which is either in your Favorites folder or bookmarked).
   b. Copy and paste one or two sentences describing each tourist attraction from the Web site into the memo.
7. Check the spelling.
8. Print a copy of the memo.
9. Save the file; name it **6.58nymemo**.

Include this exercise in your portfolio.

Merge a Database Table with a Word Document

EXERCISE 98

Directions

SCANS

In this exercise, you will merge the data from a database with a letter you create.

1. Launch the Mail Merge Wizard. You will use the **webcomputerassn** database file, found on the Data CD,  as the data source for this merge.
2. When prompted, use the query **10-98accountant**, in the **webcomputerassn** database, as the recipient list during the merge process.
3. Create the form letter and insert the relevant merge fields as shown on page 255.
   NOTE: *Because all the members in this database are from New York, in the form letter you will enter NY as the state (as shown)—not as a field code.*
4. Merge the form letter with the database query as a new document.
5. Save the file; name it **10.98seminaracct**.
6. Print one copy.
7. Prepare a label merge file using Avery 5160 address labels.
8. Merge the database query **10-98accountant** with the label file.
   NOTE: *Delete multiple occurrences of NY if they appear as labels.*
9. Save the label file; name it **10.98acctlabels**.
10. Print one copy of the labels.
11. Close all files and programs.

CONCEPT BUILDERS

A database table or query can serve as the data document in the merge process. To use a database table or query as the recipient list, choose the database file, which will display the tables and queries in that file. When prompted during the merge process, select a table or query as the recipient list to merge. The Mail Merge Wizard is not available to Word 2000 users.

Skills Review

EXERCISE 59

Most colleges require that you write a personal statement as part of the application process. It is wise to begin drafting your personal statement so that this task will be easy to accomplish once the real college admission process begins for you. In this exercise, you will visit a Web site that contains information about how to write a personal statement. After reading the information, you will draft a one-page personal statement of your own.

Directions

SCANS

1. Open your browser.
2. Use the Internet to learn about writing personal statements. Enter the URL: `http://uga.berkeley.edu/apa/personalstatement`
3. Click each of the links and print one copy of the pages that you would like to keep as a reference.
4. Mark this site.
5. Switch to Word.
6. Create a new document.
7. Set 1" left and right margins.
8. Set the font for the document to serif, 11 pt.
9. Set line spacing to double.
10. Using the guidelines outlined in the Web site, write a one-page personal statement.
11. Print one copy.
12. Save the file; name it **6.59mystatement**.
13. Close the file.
14. Close the browser.

Include this exercise in your portfolio.

Draft documents are prepared double-spaced.

Title	First	Last	Address	City	St	Zip	SorD	Dept	Subject	Date	Rm
Mr.	Robert	Kline	765 Beverly Drive	Beverly Hills	CA	90211	son	English	Literature	June 14	D222
Ms.	Wilma	Jones	767 Burton Way	Beverly Hills	CA	90219	daughter	English	Journalism	June 14	D222
Ms.	Monica	Peters	20 Columbia Court	Los Angeles	CA	90012	daughter	History	American History	June 17	A234
Mr.	Bill	Giles	33-99 South Beverly Drive	Beverly Hills	CA	90219	son	Math	Calculus	June 18	C298
Ms.	Sally	Ubell	76 Pico Drive	Los Angeles	CA	90002	daughter	History	European History	June 17	A234

Illustration A Joydata

Western Community College
Beverly Hills, CA 90210

Blue, serif, 12 pt, italic

Blue, script, 24 pt

Blue, serif, 10 pt, italic

Phone: 213-555-4444
Fax: 213-555-5555
E-mail: mailus@wecom.edu

Today's date

To the parents of
«Title» «First» «Last»
«Address»
«City», «St» «Zip»

Dear Parents:

Congratulations! Your «SorD», «First», has been selected to receive the «Dept» Department Award for highest honors in «Subject».

All «Dept» Department award winners will receive their awards at a special ceremony to be held at the college on «Date» at 7:30 p.m. in Room «Rm». Refreshments will be served.

We look forward to seeing you and your child at our awards ceremony. Once again, congratulations to you and «First» for this outstanding achievement.

Sincerely,

Patricia Miles
Dean of Students

pm/yo

Illustration B Joyform

LESSON 7

Work with Multiple-Page Documents and Multiple Documents

EXERCISE 60
Format a Two-Page Letter; Use Headers/Footers

EXERCISE 61
Format a Two-Page Letter; Use Headers/Footers; Track Changes

EXERCISE 62
Format a Multiple-Page Report; Use Headers/Footers; Insert Page Numbers; Track Changes

EXERCISE 63
Use Footnotes; Insert Page Numbers; Prevent Widow/Orphan Lines

EXERCISE 64
Use Footnotes, Headers, and Page Numbers; Prevent Widow/Orphan Lines

EXERCISE 65
Use Footnotes and Endnotes; Edit Headers and Footers; Insert Page Numbers; Prevent Widow/Orphan Lines

EXERCISE 66
Compare and Merge Documents

EXERCISE 67
Compare and Merge Documents; Edit Footnotes

EXERCISE 68
Display Multiple Documents; Switch Between Open Documents; Copy from One Document to Another

EXERCISE 69
Display Multiple Documents; Switch Between Open Documents; Copy from One Document to Another

EXERCISE 70
Skills Review

EXERCISE 71
Skills Review

Create and Merge Main and Data Source Documents

EXERCISE 97

Directions

SCANS

1. Create a data source document from records in the table shown on page 253 in Illustration A using a serif, 12 pt font.
2. Correct spelling.
3. Preview the document.
4. Print one copy.
5. Save and close the file; name it **10.97joydata**.
6. Create a new document.
7. Set 1.25" left and right margins.
8. Create the letterhead 1" down from the top of the page as shown on page 253 in Illustration B. Set the font and font sizes as indicated.
9. Begin the exercise 2.5" down from the top of the page.
10. Create the form letter shown in Illustration B using a serif, 12 pt font.
11. Insert the merge code for each variable shown.
12. Correct spelling.
13. Print one copy.
14. Save the file; name it **10.97joyform**.
15. Merge the main and data source documents into a new document.
16. Print one copy of the merged letters.
17. Save the merged letters; name them **10.97joyfin**.

Format a Two-Page Letter; Use Headers/Footers

EXERCISE 60

SCANS

Directions

1. Open **3.21cclet**, the file you created in Exercise 21, or open **d7.60cclet** from the Data CD.
2. Save the file as **7.60ocr.**
3. Set 1.25" left and right margins.
4. Begin the dateline 3.5" from the top of the page.
5. Key the letter shown on pages 159 – 160, using a serif, 12 pt font size.
6. Create a header that includes the name of the addressee, the page number, and today's date.
   a. Set the font for the header to 10 pt.
   b. Suppress the header on the first page.
7. Justify document text.
8. Hyphenate the document. Limit consecutive hyphens to two.
9. Correct spelling.
10. Preview the document.
11. Print one copy.
12. Close the file; save the changes.

Use the Help Index

How Do I...?	**Enter the keyword(s):**
Create a new page	Page break
Insert a header or footer	Header; footer

VOCABULARY

Soft page break — Header
Hard page break — Footer

DID YOU KNOW?

Headers, footers, and page numbers generally do not appear on the first page of a document.

CONCEPT BUILDERS

- When text is entered beyond the last line of a page, the software automatically ends one page and starts another. This is referred to as a ***soft page break.***
- Pressing the Ctrl + Enter keys before the end of the page creates a ***hard page break.*** Hard page breaks may be deleted.
- Once the insertion point is below the break line of the first page of a document, the page indicator on the status bar displays Page 2.
- A ***header*** is the same text appearing at the top of every page or specified pages; a ***footer*** is the same text appearing at the bottom of every page or specified pages.

Title	FirstName	LastName	Company	Address1	City	State	PostalCode	Date	Item	Newdate
Mr.	Daniel	Kenna		54 Beekman Place	Palo Alto	CA	94356	June 10	one dozen zip disks	July 1
Mr.	Jack	Lewis		59 Jasper Court	Chattanooga	TN	37406-0623	June 15	two 17" monitors	July 12
Ms.	Virginia	Martinez	CompuToll, Inc.	76 Riverbend Street	Los Angeles	CA	90210	June 25	two CD-ROM drives	August 1
Ms.	Helen	McCall	Regal Products	880 Halpin Road	Bellevue	WA	98006	June 18	five sound cards	July 22

Illustration A Sordata

888 Burton Way
Philadelphia, PA 19104
Phone: (215) 555-5555
Fax: (215) 555-9999
bbcs@mind.com

BIT-BYTE COMPUTER STORES

Today's date

«Title» «FirstName» «LastName»
«Company»
«Address1»
«City», «State» «PostalCode»

Dear «Title» «LastName»:

We regret the long delay in shipping your order of «Date» for «Item». Conditions beyond our control have made shipments out of our Philadelphia plant impossible.

Your order is now scheduled to ship on «Newdate».

We hope that this delay has not caused you any loss in business.

Cordially,

Joseph McBride
Shipping Manager

jm/yo

Illustration B Sorform

429 FIFTH AVENUE
New York, NY 10016

(212) 555-5555
E-mail: cc@net.com

Today's date

Mr. Leonard Ghurka, President
Legal Services, Inc.
56 Wall Street
New York, NY 10001

Dear Mr. Ghurka:

SUBJECT: OPTICAL CHARACTER RECOGNITION

Our store is now carrying a line of Optical Character Recognition systems (scanners and software). We thought we might acquaint you with these useful tools. If you see a need for it in your business, our staff will be more than happy to demonstrate the various products available.

You are probably familiar with Optical Character Recognition systems in their role at the supermarket checkout stand. A laser beam "reads" the bar code that is imprinted on an item and delivers the information—item, price, etc.—to the cash register. In an office, Optical Character Recognition works in a similar way. Many firms have hundreds of documents that have to be entered into their computers. Keying in all these documents would take up valuable time.

An Optical Character Recognition system provides a much faster alternative. An outstanding typist can type on the average of three characters per second. In comparison, an Optical Character Recognition system can achieve speeds of up to 250 characters a second. An Optical Character Recognition system "reads" a document and deciphers the letters and numbers. It then converts this information into digital form and transmits it to a computer.

Create and Merge Main and Data Source Documents

EXERCISE 96

SCANS

Directions

1. Create a data source document from records shown on page 251 in Illustration A.
2. Correct spelling.
3. Preview the document.
4. Print one copy.
5. Save and close the file; name it **10.96sordata**.
6. Create a new document.
7. Preview the available full-block letter templates and then select one.
8. Use the template's default margins.
   a. Insert the company name, address, and phone information, as shown.
   b. Set the company name to the same decorative font used in **5.40memo**, which you created in Exercise 40. Use the template's default font size.
   c. Set COMPUTER STORES to the same sans serif font used in **5.40memo**. Set the font size as you prefer.
9. Begin the exercise 2.5" from the top of the page.
10. Create the form letter, shown on page 251 in Illustration B, using the default template's font and font size.
11. Insert the proper merge code for each variable shown.
12. Correct spelling.
13. Print one copy.
14. Save the file; name it **10.96sorform**.
15. Merge the main and data source documents into a new document.
16. Print one copy of the merged letters.
17. Save the merged letters; name them **10.96sorfin**.

HOT TIPS

- In most letter templates, paragraph spacing has been set to leave a specified amount of space between paragraphs. Therefore, it is only necessary to press the Enter key once between paragraphs.
- Make any adjustments necessary to the spacing between letter parts in a template to conform to the spacing you have learned for letters.

Mr. Leonard Ghurka
Page 2
Today's date

OCR systems include an optical scanner for reading text and software for analyzing images. Most OCR systems use a combination of hardware and software to recognize characters, although some inexpensive systems do it entirely through software. Advanced OCR systems can read text in a large variety of fonts.

While Optical Character Recognition systems do have their problems, the advantages outweigh the problems.

If you feel that the OCR (as it is commonly referred to) can be advantageous to your business, please call me or anyone on our staff between 9:00 a.m. and 5:00 p.m. We will be delighted to give you or your company representative a full demonstration of the merits of these systems. Check the following Web sites, which offer OCR products. We carry all the products you will see.

www.irisusa.com
www.primerecognition.com

You might be interested to know that some scanners can read handwritten material.

Sincerely,

Rhoda Boylan
Product Manager

rb/yo

Title	FirstName	LastName	Company	Address1	City	State	PostalCode
Ms.	Jane	Addams	ABC Computer Sources	90 Pine Street	New York	NY	10011
Mr.	Brad	Phillips	Computoll Group, Inc.	485 Madison Avenue	New York	NY	10016
Ms.	Lorraine	Elra	Eastern Microwave	345 Ninth Avenue	New York	NY	10034

Illustration A Jobdata

Your Letterhead Here

Today's date

«Title» «FirstName» «LastName»
«Company»
«Address1»
«City», «State» «PostalCode»

Dear «Title» «LastName»:

Please consider me an applicant for the position of Web page designer that was advertised in the Sunday edition of the *New York Times.*

The enclosed résumé details my work experience and courses I have taken to prepare me for this position.

I look forward to meeting with you to discuss employment opportunities with your company. I can be reached at the phone number shown on this letter if you wish to schedule an interview.

Yours truly,

Peter Harris

Enclosure

Illustration B Jobform

CONCEPT BUILDERS

- After the merge commands are applied, the two documents are combined to form a new third document. You can merge the new third document to appear on the screen or send it directly to the printer.
- When creating the main document, insert space between merge codes just as you would if actual information were there.

DID YOU KNOW?

- Names of publications are typed in all capitals or italicized.
- It is recommended that you create the data source document first.

HOT TIPS

- Merge the documents on the screen before sending them to the printer. If the documents do not merge properly, check for merge code placement errors and then remerge the main and data source documents.
- Word provides a Mail Merge Wizard to help with the merge process. Click Tools, select Letters and Mailings, and click Mail Merge Wizard to display the Mail Merge task pane. The task pane steps you through the mail merge process. The Mail Merge Wizard is not available to Word 2000 users.

Format a Two-Page Letter; Use Headers/Footers; Track Changes

EXERCISE 61

SCANS

Directions

1. Open **5.47ad**, the file you created in Exercise 47, or open **d7.61ad** from the Data CD. 
2. Save the file as **7.61ad**.
3. Turn on the Track Changes feature.
4. Make the indicated revisions, as shown in the illustration on page 162.
5. Begin the dateline at 2.5" from the top of the page.
6. Set 1.25" left and right margins.
7. Change the document font to serif, 13 pt.
8. Create a header that includes the name of the addressee, the page number, and today's date.
   a. Set the font for the header to 10 pt.
   b. Suppress the header on the first page.
9. Correct spelling.
10. Accept all changes, except for the insertion in the last paragraph.
11. Preview the document.
12. Print one copy.
13. Close the file; save the changes.

Use the Help Index

How Do I...?	**Enter the keyword(s):**
Track changes	Track changes/review

CONCEPT BUILDERS

- Word allows you to keep track of the changes made to a document and who made the changes. The reader can accept or reject any revisions made.
- Strikethrough text indicates a deletion. Underlined and/or colored text indicates an insertion.
- If more than one person revises the document, each person's changes can be identified in a unique color.
- When you point to a revision on screen, the name of the person who made the edit will be displayed.

DID YOU KNOW?

You can change the way tracked changes appear in a document. You can use balloons in print and Web layout views to show tracked changes in the margins of a document. Click Tools, Options, and click the Track Changes tab to select this option.

HOT TIPS

- When the Track Changes feature is turned on, TRK appears on the status bar.
- The Reviewing toolbar contains buttons to make working with tracked changes easier.

Create and Merge Main and Data Source Documents

EXERCISE 95

SCANS

Directions

1. Create a data source document from the records in the table shown on the page 249 in Illustration A using a serif, 12 pt font.
2. Correct spelling.
3. Preview the document.
4. Print one copy.
5. Save and close the file; name it **10.95jobdata**.
6. Open **3.25mylet** (the letterhead you created for yourself in Exercise 25); or, using the default margins, create your own letterhead using any fonts, font sizes, and font colors you prefer. Include your name, address, and phone number in the letterhead.
7. Save the file as **10.95jobform**.
8. Set 1.25" left and right margins.
9. Begin the exercise 2.5" from the top of the page.
10. Create the form letter shown on page 249 in illustration B using a serif, 12 pt font. Insert the proper merge code for each variable indicated.
11. Correct spelling.
12. Print one copy.
13. Save the changes.
14. Merge the main and data source documents into a new document.
15. Print one copy of the merged letters.
16. Save the merged letters; name them **10.95jobfin**.

Use the Help Index

How Do I...?	**Enter the keyword(s):**
Merge documents	Merge or mail merge

VOCABULARY

Mail merge	Merge code
Merge	Data source
Main document	Record

CONCEPT BUILDERS

- The ***Mail Merge*** feature allows you to mass-produce letters, envelopes, mailing labels, and other documents so they appear personalized.
- The ***merge*** process combines two documents: a main document and a data source document.
- The ***main document*** contains information that does not change as well as merge codes where variable information will be inserted. A ***merge code*** acts as a placeholder for the variable information. All formatting, graphics, and paper size information should be included in the main document.
- The ***data source*** document contains variable information—that is, information that does change. The data source document contains many records. A ***record*** is a collection of related information about one person or one thing.

Continued on next page

888 Franklin Boulevard
Fairfield, New Jersey 07004
(201) 555-5555

Today's date

Mr. Stan Smith, Creative Director
Sari & Sari Advertising
575 Madison Avenue
New York, NY 10016

Dear Mr. Smith:

As you know, I am the east-coast representative for the **GRAPHIC ARTS SOLUTIONS** software program. I know your agency is considering purchasing a new page layout software program. When we last spoke, you told me that you desired a layout program that could display outstanding text and graphics *and*, at the same time, combine other software you have in your office. I am certain that **GRAPHIC ARTS SOLUTIONS** will meet all your needs. ~~As a matter of fact,~~ Jerry Forbes of the Loeb Agency purchased this software several months ago. You might want to talk to him about the software's merits.

Listed below are some of the excellent features of **GRAPHIC ARTS SOLUTIONS.**

> **GRAPHIC ARTS SOLUTIONS** supports Windows XP, giving you an even wider range of page layout, graphics, and integration alternatives.
>
> **GRAPHIC ARTS SOLUTIONS** gives you sophisticated composition capabilities, enabling you to handle practically any job.
>
> **GRAPHIC ARTS SOLUTIONS** is a complete graphic arts workshop, giving you strong composition and graphics-handling capability.

to | so that we can | for you

Please phone me ~~so that I may~~ set up an appointment ~~with you to~~ demonstrate this outstanding piece of software.

I am enclosing a brochure outlining the features of **GRAPHIC ARTS SOLUTIONS.**

Sincerely,

Fred Nelson
Product Manager

fn/yo
Enclosure

GRAPHIC ARTS SOLUTIONS is enhanced with over 1,000 unique clip art designs and over 2000 fonts, giving you a wide range of choices for your design.

Once you become familiar with **GRAPHIC ARTS SOLUTIONS,** you will find that it has an amazing array of tools designed to streamline your work.

LESSON 10

Integration

EXERCISE 95
Create and Merge Main and Data Source Documents

EXERCISE 96
Create and Merge Main and Data Source Documents

EXERCISE 97
Create and Merge Main and Data Source Documents

EXERCISE 98
Merge a Database Table with a Word Document

EXERCISE 99
Edit the Data Source; Merge with Conditions; Create and Merge Envelope and Label Main Documents

EXERCISE 100
Edit the Data Source; Merge with Conditions; Create and Merge Envelope and Label Main Documents

EXERCISE 101
Send E-mail; Attach a File to an E-mail

EXERCISE 102
Merge E-mail with a Data Source Document

EXERCISE 103
Insert a Worksheet into a Word Document

EXERCISE 104
Insert a Worksheet as an Embedded Object into a Word Document

EXERCISE 105
Insert a Chart as an Embedded Object into a Word Document

EXERCISE 106
Insert a Worksheet and Chart as Linked Objects into a Word Document

EXERCISE 107
Export a Database to a Word Document

EXERCISE 108
Skills Review

EXERCISE 62

Format a Multiple-Page Report; Use Headers/Footers; Insert Page Numbers; Track Changes

Directions

SCANS

1. Create a new document.
2. Set 2" left and right margins.
3. Set the document font to serif, 13 pt.
4. Key the exercise shown on page 165. Begin 1.5" down from the top of the page.
5. Set document spacing to triple (or exactly 36 pt).
6. Hyphenate the document; limit consecutive hyphens to two.
7. Include a right-aligned header that reads:
   `DESKTOP PUBLISHING`
   a. Set the font for the header to sans serif, 12 pt, bold.
   b. Suppress the header on the first page.
8. Include a left-aligned footer that reads `A Report by . . .` (insert your own name).
   a. Insert a right-aligned page number as part of the footer text.
   b. Set the font for the footer to serif, 10 pt, italic.
9. Correct spelling.
10. Preview the document.
11. Save the file; name it **7.62dtp**.

CONCEPT BUILDERS

You can insert page numbers as part of header or footer text, or you can insert them separately.

BULL & BEAR INVESTMENTS

60 Wall Street
New York, NY 10001
P: 212-555-5555
F: 212-555-7777
Email: bbinvest@net.com

Illustration A

Bull & Bear Investment Company
announces
a change in status for

Mark Mutual Funds

to a
Business Trust
organized under the laws
of the
Commonwealth of Massachusetts
Effective August 1, 2004

Illustration B

Directions *continued*

12. Turn the Track Changes feature on and insert the following text as the last two paragraphs.

> **CAN DTP BE DONE WITH WORD PROCESSING SOFTWARE?**
> Those word processing software packages that have DTP features let you create many of the same documents that you can create using sophisticated DTP page layout software. However, before you invest in a software package, review the features of page layout software vs. word processing software with desktop capabilities. Be sure it can perform the tasks you need to accomplish.
>
> **WEB SITES TO ASSIST THE DESKTOP PUBLISHER**
> The desktop designer can access Web sites that offer free designs, clip art, and fonts. The Web can also provide the user with information about various software programs for the desktop publisher. Visit the following sites to get FREE clip art:

13. Turn the Track Changes feature off.
14. Open your Web browser.
15. Enter the following URL: `www.clip-art.com`
16. Scroll down and copy the free clip art sites that appear below "Free Clip-Art," as shown in Figure 7.1.
    NOTE: *Because of the dynamic nature of Web sites, the Web site on your screen may not appear exactly as it does in Figure 7.1.*
    a. Paste the sites below the last paragraph you inserted.
    b. Set the font for the site text to 13 pt.
    c. Center the site text.
17. Close the browser.
18. Delete the second paragraph, "Desktop publishing has changed all that."
19. Accept the last two inserted paragraphs; reject the deleted paragraph.
20. Print one copy of the document.
21. Save the changes and close the file.

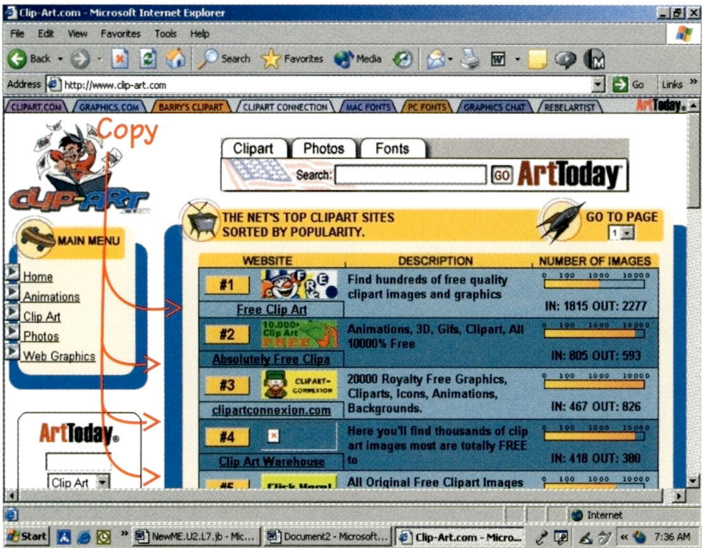

Figure 7.1

Directions *continued*

11. Save the file.

12. Close the document window.

Today's date
Mr. Peter Steedham
60 Sutton Place South
New York, NY 10020
Dear Investor: ¶Effective August 1, 2004, [**mm**] was reorganized and became a subsidiary of [**vs**], a business trust organized under the laws of the Commonwealth of Massachusetts.¶Prior to the reorganization, [**mm**] had been a series of [**vs**], which was also a Massachusetts business trust. ¶Except for the fact that [**mm**] is now a subsidiary of [**vs**], shares of [**mm**] represent the same interest in the Fund's assets, are the same class, and are subject to the same terms and conditions, fees and expenses, and confer the same rights as when [**mm**] was a series of [**vs**]. ¶The following ad will run in the New York Times one week prior to the effective change.¶[**Insert d9.94investad**]¶If you need further clarification on this issue, please phone me at 1-800-555-5555.¶Sincerely,
Robert Ludlam
Vice President
rl
[**Run CLOSING macro**]

DESKTOP PUBLISHING

Until recently, graphic design was done by art directors and design professionals whose livelihoods depended on creating effective graphic designs.

Desktop publishing has changed all that.

Desktop publishing has brought graphic design into the office and home. It has enabled people other than art directors to create attractive, effective printed materials, such as newsletters, advertisements, brochures, manuals, and other documents.

EFFECTIVE GRAPHIC DESIGN LEADS TO SUCCESS

Effective graphic design makes it easier for readers to understand the message. If the message is clear and attractive, the chances are the customer will buy your product. If your printed message fails to create a favorable first impression, you never get a second chance to make a first impression.

EFFECTIVE GRAPHIC DESIGN IS A NECESSITY

Today, effective graphic design is more important than ever. People are bombarded with print communications. Magazines and newspapers are more crowded with ads. Mailboxes are stuffed with catalogs and newsletters. Your message has a lot of competition. Therefore, it is even more important to make it as effective and appealing as possible.

WHY DESKTOP PUBLISHING?

Desktop publishing enables computer users to design and develop publications at their desks. They can set type, prepare line illustrations, page layouts and designs, and they can insert graphics (already saved on computer) into their designs without the aid of a professional typesetter or art director.

Skills Review

EXERCISE 94

You work for Bull and Bear Investments, a financial services company that manages investments for companies as well as individuals. You have been asked to prepare the following letter to investors, announcing a change in the organization of Mark Mutual Funds. Since "Mark Mutual Funds" and "Vector Special Investment Trust" are two names used frequently throughout the document, you will create AutoText entries for them and then play them where appropriate as you create the letter. You will also insert a file where noted.

Directions

SCANS

1. Create a new document.
2. Create the following AutoText in a sans serif, 12 pt, italic font; name it **mm.**
   `Mark Mutual Funds`
3. Create the following AutoText in a sans serif, 12 pt, bold font; name it **vs.**
   `Vector Special Investment Trust`
4. Create a macro to spell check and print; name it **CLOSING** and use **Alt + C** as the shortcut keys.
5. Close the document window.
6. Open **d9.94investment** found on the Data CD and shown in Illustration A on page 246; save the file as **9.94investor**.
7. Set 1" left and right margins and .5" top and bottom margins.
8. Set the font size for the document to 11 pt.
9. Create a full-block letter from the text shown below. As you type, play the macros and make the AutoText entries indicated.
10. Insert the file **d9.94investad**, found on the Data CD and shown in Illustration B, where noted. 

Use Footnotes; Insert Page Numbers; Prevent Widow/Orphan Lines

EXERCISE 63

SCANS

Directions

1. Create a new document.
2. Set 1" left and right margins.
3. Set line spacing to double.
4. Set the document font to serif, 12 pt.
5. Begin the exercise 2" down from the top of the page.
6. Center and set the title to 14 pt, bold.
7. Create the report shown on pages 167 – 169, inserting the indicated reference numbers and footnotes.
8. Using the Page Numbering feature, insert a page number in the bottom right of the page.
   - Suppress the number on the first page.
9. Insert a left-aligned header that reads:
   `A Brief History of Computers`
   a. Set the font for the header to serif, 10 pt, bold, and italic.
   b. Suppress the header on the first page.
10. Use widow/orphan control.
11. Correct spelling.
12. Preview the document.
13. Print one copy.
14. Save the file; name it **7.63history**.

Use the Help Index

How Do I...?	**Enter the keyword(s):**
Insert a footnote	Footnote
Insert a page number	Page number
Prevent widow/orphan lines	Orphan

VOCABULARY

Citation
Footnote
Widow/orphan lines

CONCEPT BUILDERS

- A ***citation*** is a reference, usually made in the form of a footnote or endnote, which gives credit to the source of any borrowed material used in a document, presentation, or report.
- A ***footnote*** appears at the bottom a page and gives the reader information about the source of quoted material. After you insert the first footnote, additional footnotes are numbered automatically.
- When a footnote or endnote cites the same source as the one that immediately precedes it, the abbreviation ibid., meaning "in the same place," is used rather than rewriting the entry.
- et al. (as shown in the footnote on page 167) is a Latin term that means "and others."
- A ***widow line*** is created when the last line of a paragraph remains by itself on top of the page.
- An ***orphan line*** is created when the first line of a paragraph appears as the last line of the page.

- A news or press release is a document prepared by a company or organization and sent to various newspapers and magazines to announce a new product, development, or item of special interest.

When you record a macro that changes font size and/or style, be sure to return to the original settings before turning off the Macro feature.

PRESS RELEASE) Bold

For Immediate Release

↓ 2x

Run → FSMARGIN macro → For more information contact: Andrea Rose

↓ 3x

Bold → **TWO NEW PRODUCTS FOR DESKTOP PUBLISHING!**

↓ 2x

Newtown, CT, December 2004

↓ 3x

Run → LINE macro

QUIRKY PRESS, a software package which provides comprehensive layout and design capabilities. Allows for integration of text and graphics from other popular software programs. Highlights include animation and other video clips, extensive clip art files, and exceptional drawing and placement features.

Bold

BEST SCANNER, a scanner which translates text and graphics into computer files. Graphics can be scanned at a resolution as high as 1200 dpi; photos at millions of colors. Complete with OCR software, this unit promises to increase productivity by up to 50%.

###

A footnote cited from a Web site is written as follows: Author's Name, Title of Article/Web Site, <web address>, date posted on Internet (if available).

A BRIEF HISTORY OF COMPUTERS

Computers are a part of so many aspects of our society today that it is hard to imagine life without them. To understand and appreciate fully the impact that computers have had on our lives, it is important to understand their evolution. What follows is a brief history of the development of computer technology. There are five generations of modern computer history, the first of which was considered to have occurred between 1944 and 1956. Long before the first generation of computers evolved (which was considered to have occurred between 1944 and 1956), computer development was well on its way.

Joseph Jacquard developed a loom for weaving cloth whose operation was controlled by means of cards with holes punched in them. This card laid the foundation for computer development. "In 1886, Herman Hollerith improved on Jacquard's punched card by developing a card that could be used with electrical rather than mechanical equipment. The Hollerith (or IBM) card is still very much in use."[1]

The first generation of computers was developed in the mid-1940s during the Second World War. They were needed to create ballistic charts for the U.S. Navy.
"In 1944, engineers from IBM and Howard Aiken of Harvard University developed a machine called the Mark I. This 50-foot long and 8-foot high machine was able to add, subtract, multiply, divide, and refer to data tables using punched cards."[2]

---

[1] Christina McClung et al., *Personal Computers for Executives* (New York: John Wiley & Sons, 1994), p. 2
[2] Ibid., p. 3.

Record a Macro; Run/Play a Macro

EXERCISE 93

SCANS

Directions

1. Create a new document.
2. Create a macro to change the font and font size to serif, 13 pt, and the left and right margins to 1.5"; name it: `FSMARGIN`
3. Create a macro to change the line spacing to 1.5 lines; name it: `LINE`
4. Close the document window.
5. Create a new document.
6. Begin the press release, shown in the illustration on page 243, at the top of the page.
   - Center and set the title, "PRESS RELEASE," to sans serif, 15 pt, bold.
   - Run the FSMARGIN macro where indicated.
   - Run the LINE macro for the paragraphs shown.
6. Center the page vertically.
8. Correct spelling.
9. Hyphenate and justify paragraph text.
10. Preview the document.
11. Print one copy.
12. Save the file; name it **9.93release**.

Use the Help Index

How Do I...?	Enter the keyword(s):
Record a macro	Macro
Run/play a macro	Macro

VOCABULARY

Macro

CONCEPT BUILDERS

- A ***macro*** is a saved series of commands and keystrokes that you can play with a single keystroke or mouse click. You can create a macro, for example, to change margins or line spacing.
- To record a macro, click Tools, Macro, Record New Macro. Then follow the instructions in the Record Macro dialog box.
- Once you have recorded and saved a macro, you can run (or play) it in your document when you need it.

DID YOU KNOW?

- Word provides an AutoText feature in addition to the Macro feature. However, you should use the Macro feature to save repetitive tasks, not text.

Another computer whose advancements were spurred by the war was the ENIAC computer, developed by a partnership between the U.S. government and the University of Pennsylvania. "The first all-electronic computer, based on vacuum tubes, was developed in 1946 by J. Presper Eckert and John W. Mauchley of the University of Pennsylvania. This computer could make calculations a thousand times faster than earlier devices."[3]

In 1947, John von Neuman joined the University of Pennsylvania team and developed a method for storing programs electronically. This invention of storing programs led the way for the development of today's computers.

The second generation of computers was developed between 1952 and 1963. The invention of the transistor changed the way computers were being developed. "The transistor replaced the large, cumbersome tube in televisions, radios, and computers. As a result, the size of electronic machinery has been shrinking ever since. The transistor was at work in the computer by 1956."[4] By the mid 1960s, business, universities, and the government used computers. The second generation of computers began to contain many of the things we find in computers today: printers, tape storage, disk storage, and memory.

The third generation of computers was developed between 1964 and 1971. These computers were characterized by the semiconductor chip which was developed in the early 1960s. Another third-generation development included the use of an operating system that allowed machines to run many different programs at once with a central program that monitored and coordinated the computer's memory.

---

[3] McClung, p. 8.
[4] Christopher LaMorte, et al, "Computers: History and Development," http://www.digitalcentury.com/encyclo/update/comp.hd.htm, May 1999.

429 FIFTH AVENUE
NEW YORK, NY 10016

(212) 555-5555
E-mail: cc@net.com

Today's date

Ms. Mary Vargas
98 Andrea Lane
Vienna, VA 22182

Dear Ms. Vargas:

Ms. Janis has referred your letter to me. As the owner of a new PC, it is important to protect your computer against *computer viruses.* Ms. Janis informed me that you do not have an anti-virus program loaded on your system. As you know, we are the distributors for ***Computer Virus Doctor***, an anti-virus detection program.

Computer Virus Doctor will scan your hard drive and floppy disks to determine if your files are infected. If they are, ***Computer Virus Doctor*** will prompt you to repair your drive or destroy the virus. A word of caution: repairing files is not a fail-safe technique, as residual virus codes may remain attached to the file even after it has been repaired.

¶ The table below describes known viruses and the damage they can do.

[*Insert the d9.92VIRUS file*]

Once you purchase ***Computer Virus Doctor***, we will upgrade the program every six months to detect any new known viruses. ***Computer Virus Doctor*** is easy to install. However, if you experience installation difficulties ~~any difficulty installing it~~, our customer support representatives will be available weekdays from 9:00 a.m. to 5:00 p.m. to assist you.

The enclosed literature will tell you more about ***Computer Virus Doctor***. Protect your system today from the damage of *computer viruses.*

Yours truly,

Linda Corin
Sales Manager

lc/yo
enclosure

The fourth generation of computers was characterized by the ongoing improvement of the silicon chip. "The Intel 4004 chip, developed in 1971, included all the components of a computer (central processing unit, memory, and input and output controls) on a minuscule chip. Not only was the silicon chip used for computers, but everyday household items such as microwave ovens, television sets, and automobiles with electronic fuel injection incorporated these microprocessors."[5] Computers were becoming cheaper, smaller, and faster. In 1981, IBM introduced its personal computer (PC) and began marketing it to the general public for use in the home, office, and school. "The number of personal computers in use more than doubled from 2 million in 1981 to 5.5 million in 1982. Then years later, 65 million PCs were being used."[6]

Many advances in the science of computer design and technology are taking place to form the fifth generation of computers. Computers that can interpret the spoken word and imitate human reasoning are evolving. It is difficult to imagine now how the computer will affect your life in the next twenty years. If only those inventors who led the way to modern computing could witness the speed of today's computers and our society's total dependence on them. How do you think they would react to the automatic teller machines (ATM) which let us conduct banking transactions from virtually anywhere in the world; or to computerized telephone switching centers that keep lines of communication untangled; or to supermarket scanners that calculate our grocery bills while keeping store inventory? It is difficult to imagine.

---

[5] Ibid.
[6] Ibid.

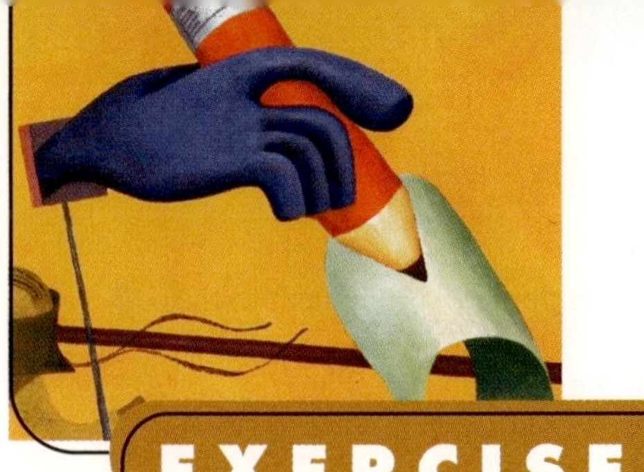

Insert a File

EXERCISE 92

Directions

1. Open **9.89doctor** or open **d9.92doctor** from the Data CD. 
2. Save the file as **9.92doctor**.
3. Change the top and bottom margins to 1".
4. Make the revisions shown in the illustration on page 241.
5. Insert the file **8.75virus**, created in Exercise 75, where indicated. Space twice before and after the insertion; or, insert **d9.92virus** from the Data CD (if you did not create the earlier exercise). 
6. Edit the table as follows:
   a. Delete the title.
   b. Center the column headings.
   c. Adjust the column widths so the table appears centered within the document.
   d. Apply a 1½ pt double-line table border and a 1½ pt border to Row 1.
   e. Apply dashed lines between cells.
   f. Apply a 5% shade to Row 1.
7. Create an appropriate page 2 header.
8. Preview the document.
9. Print one copy.
10. Close the file; save the changes.

Use Footnotes, Headers, and Page Numbers; Prevent Widow/Orphan Lines

EXERCISE 64

Directions

SCANS

1. Create a new document.
2. Set 1.25" left and right margins.
3. Set the document font size to serif, 13 pt.
4. Begin the exercise 2" down from the top of the page.
5. Center and set the title to 14 pt, bold.
6. Create the report shown in the illustration on page 171 in double space, inserting the footnotes indicated.
7. Include a right-aligned header that reads: `The World Wide Web`
   a. Set the header to a script, 16 pt, and bold font.
   b. Suppress the header on page 1.
8. Insert a page number on the bottom right of the page.
   - Suppress the number on page 1.
9. Use widow/orphan control.
10. Hyphenate the document. Limit consecutive hyphens to two.
11. Correct spelling.
12. Preview the document.
13. Print one copy.
14. Save the file; name it **7.64www**.

HOT TIPS

You can find the registered trademark (®) and trademark (™) symbols shown in the footnote among the symbols and/or special character fonts.

Copy to the new document

Creating Effective Presentations

One day, you might be likely to find yourself in this situation: your employer says, "We need to get a presentation together for the DataAir Project fast!" Because the deadline for such a "request" is usually immediate, you reach for your presentation graphics software program.

The following five pointers can help make noticeable improvements to your next presentation:

Copy to the new document

ANALYZE YOUR AUDIENCE. Take the time to determine who will be listening. Ask yourself, "Why are you giving this presentation?"

MAKE A PLAN. After you have determined your audience, decide what to say and how to say it. Create an outline after you have analyzed what items you must cover and how you want your audience to react.

KEEP IT SHORT. Resist creating a lengthy presentation. The longer the presentation, the greater the danger of losing your audience's attention.

KEEP THE NUMBER OF WORDS PER SLIDE TO A MINIMUM. The general rule is to limit the number of words per slide to eight. It is better to have more slides with less information than vice versa.

VARY YOUR VISUALS. Keep your presentation moving by blending different types of slides. Add graphics and photographs to create a variety of visual elements.

Presentation graphics programs make it easy to gather and update an engineering, scientific, or business presentation. You may not have time to create a spectacular multimedia show, but that does not mean that your presentation will not be engaging and effective. Just follow the five tips below. The rest is easy.

✓ **ANALYZE YOUR AUDIENCE**
✓ **MAKE A PLAN**
✓ **KEEP IT SHORT**
✓ **KEEP THE NUMBER OF WORDS PER SLIDE TO A MINIMUM**
✓ **VARY YOUR VISUALS**

THE WORLD WIDE WEB

The World Wide Web, commonly known as WWW, W^3, or The Web, was first developed to assist a group of European physicists exchange data and research materials rapidly. Technicians at the CERN research laboratory in Geneva, Switzerland developed the concept of hypertext, a powerful system that links related documents on different computers.

Hypertext documents differ from regular documents by built-in links that allow readers to jump to related topics by clicking a word or picture in the document. These links may connect to other documents as well as graphics, video files, audio files, and a number of other types of files that may be transmitted or stored on the Internet.[1] As a result, readers may browse information from many different servers without needing to know the location of the server. The Hypertext Transfer Protocol (HTTP), a system that exchanges information on the World Wide Web, holds hypertext together. HTTP is a network protocol, which is an agreed upon system for use with networks.[2]

Web servers are now located in countries around the world, providing Internet browsers with information in virtually any topic imaginable. Much of the information on the Web is published and made available by the academic and research community, and stored on computers in research centers, hospitals, universities, and other such institutions. The increasing use of the Web as a commercial forum prompted the W3 Organization, headed by CERN and MIT's Laboratory for Computer Science. The goal of CERN and MIT is to provide "an international initiative for a universal framework for the information Web and to insure the standardization and development of the Web for commerce, research, and future applications."[3] Now anyone can become a Web publisher and create hypertext documents with the use of an http or ftp server.

---

[1] Nancy Stevenson, Michael O'Mara, Bill Kirkner, et. al., *Special Edition Using CompuServe®*, (Indianapolis: Que® Corporation, 1999), p. 722.

[2] Daniel A. Tauber and Brenda Kienan, *Mosaic Access to the Internet*™ (San Francisco: SYBEX, Inc., 1995), p. 18.

[3] Tauber, pp. 20-21.

Insert a File

EXERCISE 91

Directions

1. Create a new document.
2. Open **4.33present** or open **d9.91present** from the Data CD. 
3. Save the file as **9.91present**.
4. Copy the main title in **9.91present** to the new document, as shown in the illustration on page 239.
   a. Edit the title to read: `Seven Tips to Create Effective Presentations`
   b. Press the Enter key twice.
5. Copy the information in **9.91present** to the new document, as shown in the illustration.
6. Close **9.91present**.
7. Insert the file **5.45newtips** (created in Exercise 45) two lines below the last paragraph; or, insert **d9.91newtips** from the Data CD (if you did not create the earlier exercise). 
8. Set the font size and alignments of the newly inserted file to match those in the document.
9. Use the Number feature to number each tip.
10. Center the new document vertically.
11. Preview the document.
12. Print one copy.
13. Save the new file; name it **9.91pretips**.
14. Close all files.

CONCEPT BUILDERS

- A file that you insert into a document becomes part of that document.
- The source file that you inserted will remain unchanged and you can insert it into another document when needed.
- To insert a file, position the insertion point at the location in the document where you want the insert to appear, click Insert, File, choose the file to insert, and click Insert.

Use the Help Index

How Do I...?	**Enter the keyword(s):**
Insert a file	Insert file

Use Footnotes and Endnotes; Edit Headers and Footers; Insert Page Numbers; Prevent Widow/Orphan Lines

EXERCISE 65

SCANS

Directions

1. Open **d7.65animate** from the Data CD. 
2. Save the file as **7.65animate**.
3. Set 1.25" left and right margins.
4. Begin the exercise provided 2" from the top of the page.
5. Center and set the title to serif, 16 pt, bold.
6. Create the report shown on page 173 –174, inserting the footnotes indicated.
7. Set the document font to serif, 13 pt.
8. Indent the quote 1" from the left and right margins. Set the remainder of the document text to double space.
9. Set side headings to sans serif, 14 pt, bold, and italic.
10. Include a centered header, which reads:
    `Animation Principles`
    a. Set the font for the header to sans serif, 14 pt, italic.
    b. Suppress the header on the first page.
11. Insert a page number on the bottom center of the page.
    - Suppress the number on the first page.
12. Use widow/orphan control.
13. Edit the header to read: `Principles of Animation`
14. Justify and hyphenate the document. Limit the consecutive hyphens to two.
15. Correct spelling.
16. Preview the document.
17. Print one copy.

DID YOU KNOW?

- An endnote appears at the end of a document but contains the same information as a footnote.
- When a quotation is longer than two lines, it is indented from the left and/or right margins and single-spaced.
- An indirect quotation, also known as paraphrased text, is a restatement of original material and does not require quotation marks. It does, however, require that you give credit to the author in the form of a footnote or endnote.

Last Will and Testament
of
John Richard Adams

4x

Insert w AutoText Entry here

3x

FIRST: I direct that all my just debts, the expenses of my last illness and funeral, as well as the expenses of administering my estate, be paid as soon as convenient.

SECOND: I give all my articles of personal, household, or domestic use or adornment, including automobile and boats, to my wife, Mary Adams or, if she does not survive me, to my children, Thomas Adams and Betsy Adams, as shall survive me, in shares substantially equal as to value.

THIRD: I give and devise all my residential real property, and all my interest in any policies of insurance thereon, to my wife, Mary Adams, if she survives me or, if she does not survive me, to my surviving children, to be held by them jointly.

3x

Insert w1 AutoText Entry here

18. Change the footnotes to endnotes. Change the number format for the endnotes to i, ii, iii.

19. Print one copy.

20. Close the file; save the changes.

PRINCIPLES OF ANIMATION

> "The first duty of the cartoon is not to picture or duplicate real action or things as they actually happen—but to give a caricature of line and action…."
>
> **Walt Disney**

One of the many reasons Walt Disney became successful was that he was able to give life to his cartoon characters. Once the character has a personality, the audience can identify with it and believe it. Walt believed the "true interpretation of caricature is the exaggeration of an illusion of the actual, possible, or probable."[1] This belief developed into several fundamental principles for Disney animators, which include squash and stretch, staging, secondary action, exaggeration, anticipation, and follow-through and overlapping action.[2]

1. SQUASH AND STRETCH

One of the most important innovations in animation is the concept of "squash and stretch." This technique involves creating several drawings for one action to show flexibility and pliability. The squashed position depicts the form either squeezed up and bunched together or flattened out by great pressure. The stretched position then depicts the same form lengthened to a very extended condition. Arms and legs, for example, swell and they bend and extend into long and flexible limbs. A character chewing food has ballooned cheeks, a jaw with extended stretching motions, and a mouth that moves from well below the nose to up beyond the nose.

2. STAGING

Staging is a general but essential principle in animation. It is the presentation of an idea, a mood, or an expression so that it is clearly recognizable and understood. Staging a spooky scene means including appropriate imagery: a full moon, a threatening sky, looming shadows, and an old house. Staging an action means the focus is on that action.

3. ANTICIPATION

Perhaps one of the oldest theater devices, anticipation, is what keeps the audience interested and prepared for upcoming scenes. If an action or a scene is not set up properly, the audience can miss the humor. Anticipatory moves, such as crouching before running or winding up before pitching, show the audience what the character will be doing next.

---

[1] Bob Thomas, *Walt Disney: An American Original*, (New York: Hyperion, 1994), p. 125.

[2] Frank Thomas and Ollie Johnson, *Disney Animation: The Illusion of Life*, (New York: Abbeville Press, 1984), p. 15.

Directions *continued*

8. Use the default margins.
9. Create the Last Will and Testament, as shown in the illustration on page 237, or open **d9.90will** from the Data CD.
10. Save the file; name it **9.90willfinal**.
11. Begin the document at the top of the page.
12. Use a script font for the heading in 16 pt, bold, and center it.
13. Set the body text to serif, 12 pt. Apply bold to the words, "FIRST," "SECOND," and "THIRD."
14. Set a first line indent of 1" for the first, second, and third paragraphs.
15. Insert the AutoText entries where indicated.
16. Using the Find feature, locate each asterisk and replace each with the following information where appropriate:
    a. John Richard Adams
    b. 105 Oakland Lane, Goshen, New York
    c. third
    d. John Richard Adams
    e. January
17. Save and then preview your work.
18. Print one copy.
19. Close all files.

4. SECONDARY ACTION

Secondary actions emphasize the primary actions and provide greater richness and dimension to the character or the action in the scene. If the primary action is a flustered character jumping up and down, his arm movements and hand gestures, following a different pattern from his moving body, can accentuate the character's confusion. If the primary focus is a mood or expression, such as a character crying, the secondary action might be a hand wiping a tear away.

5. EXAGGERATION

The purpose of exaggeration is not to distort, but to present a scene or character in an unreal way to make it seem more real. Lightning would not be convincing if it were drawn as it appears in a photograph. By exaggerating the bolts and adding flashes of light, animated lightning can seem more dramatic than the real thing.[3]

6. FOLLOW THROUGH AND OVERLAPPING ACTION

Once many of these elements are combined, the best way to bring life and magic to the scene is to make the action look natural by using "follow through" or "overlapping action." If a moving figure stops, for example, appendages continue to move, such as hair, ears, fleshy cheeks, hats, or clothes. The final result is animation with more vitality, realism, and life.

---

[3] Bob Thomas, *Disney's Art of Animation: From Mickey Mouse to Beauty and the Beast*, (New York: Hyperion, 1991), p. 74.

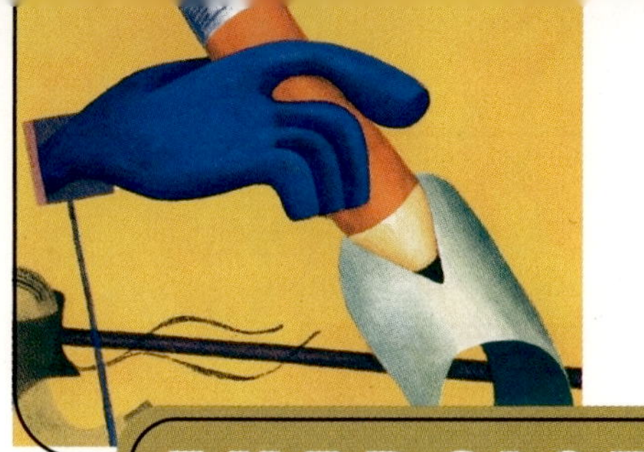

Insert AutoText; Find and Replace

EXERCISE 90

SCANS

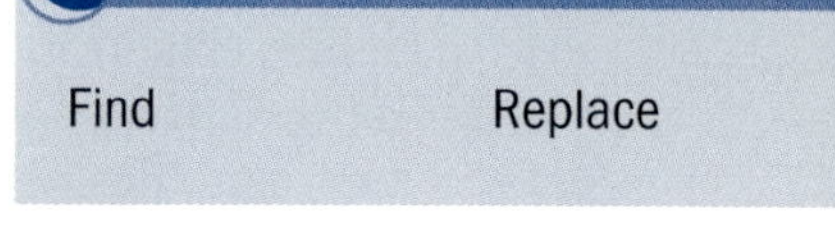

Find
Replace

The ***Find*** feature scans a document and searches for occurrences of specified text, symbols, or formatting. The ***Replace*** feature allows you to locate all occurrences of certain text and replace them with different text, special characters, or symbols.

Directions

1. Open a new document.
2. Use the default margins.
3. Create an AutoText entry for the paragraph shown below (include the asterisks [*] in the text as indicated); name the entry: `w`
4. Spell check the document.

> I, *, of *, do make, publish, and declare this to be my Last Will and Testament, hereby revoking all wills and codicils heretofore made by me.

5. Create an AutoText entry for the paragraphs shown below (you can type the paragraphs, then select them, and create the AutoText entry); name the entry: `w1`

> IN TESTIMONY WHEREOF, I have to this, my Last Will and Testament, subscribed by name and affixed by seal, this, * day of *, 2004.
>
> ______________________________________
> *
>
> Signed, sealed, published, and declared by the above-named testator, as and for his Last Will and Testament, in our presence, and we, at his request, in his presence and in the attesting witnesses', all on this * day of *, 2004.
>
> ________________________________residing at ________________________
>
> ________________________________residing at ________________________
>
> ________________________________residing at ________________________

6. Close the file without saving it.
7. Open a new document.

Compare and Merge Documents

EXERCISE 66

SCANS

Directions

1. Open **7.60ocr**, the file you created in Exercise 60, or open **d7.66ocr** from the Data CD. 
2. Save the file as **7.66ocr**.
3. Make the indicated revisions shown on pages 177 – 178.
4. Begin the title 2" from the top of the page.
5. Set 1.5" left and right margins.
6. Set line spacing to triple (or exactly 36 pt).
7. Insert the footnotes, as shown in the illustration.
8. Change the current header to read: `OPTICAL CHARACTER RECOGNITION`
   - Set the font for the header to serif, 14 pt, bold.
9. Include a footer that has your name at the left, a centered page number, and a right-aligned current date.
   a. Set the footer text to serif, 10 pt, italic.
   b. Suppress the header and footer on the first page.
10. Find each occurrence of Optical Character Recognition and replace it with OCR only where the occurrence is marked with an asterisk (*).
11. Find each occurrence of the word “systems” and replace with “units.”
12. Use widow/orphan control.
13. Edit the header to read: `OPTICAL CHARACTER RECOGITION AT WORK`
14. Correct spelling.

CONCEPT BUILDERS

- You can compare edits and revisions to a document to earlier versions of the document using the Compare and Merge Documents feature.
- You can merge the files you are comparing into the original document, the currently opened document, or a new document.
- **Word 2000 Users:** Use the Compare Documents feature to compare documents. When you do so, the files are merged into the open document. To merge the files into a new document, you must first compare them and then save them as a new file.
- Word uses the same revision marks that were used during the Track Changes procedure: strikethrough text indicates a deletion; underlined text indicates an insertion.

429 FIFTH AVENUE
NEW YORK, NY 10016

(212) 555-5555
E-mail: cc@net.com

Today's date

Ms. Mary Vargas
98 Andrea Lane
Vienna, VA 22182

Dear Ms. Vargas:

Ms. Janis has referred your letter to me. As the owner of a new PC, it is important to protect your computer against **[V]**es. Ms. Janis informed me that you do not have an anti-virus program loaded on your system. As you know, we are the distributors for **[D]**, an anti-virus detection program.

[D] will scan your hard drive and floppy disks to determine if your files are infected. If they are, **[D]** will prompt you to repair your drive or destroy the virus. A word of caution: repairing files is not a fail-safe technique, as residual virus codes may remain attached to the file even after it has been repaired.

Once you purchase **[D]**, we will upgrade the program every six months to detect any new known viruses. **[D]** is easy to install. However, if you experience any difficulty installing it, our customer support representatives will be available weekdays from 9 a.m. to 5 p.m. to assist you.

The enclosed literature will tell you more about **[D]**. Protect your system today from the damage of a **[V].**

[C]

enclosure

Directions *continued*

15. Print one copy.

16. Save the changes.

17. Compare **7.66ocr** to **7.60ocr** and merge them into a new document.
    NOTE: *If you are prompted that there are conflicting formatting changes, choose the current document (**7.66ocr**), and continue with the merge.*
    Word 2000 Users: Compare **7.66ocr** to **7.60ocr**.

18. Save the merged document as **7.66ocrmerged**.

19. Print one copy of **7.66ocrmerged**, showing all edits.
    - Compare the printout with the textbook exercise to be sure all insertions and deletions were made.

20. Close all files; save the changes.

Using the Help Index

How Do I...?	**Enter the keyword(s):**
Compare and merge documents	Compare documents

Insert AutoText

EXERCISE 89

SCANS

Directions

1. Open **d9.89cclet**. Save the file as **9.89doctor**.
2. Set 1" left and right margins and .5" top and bottom margins.
3. Create the letter shown in the illustration on page 234. Begin the dateline 2.5" from the top of the page.
4. Set the document font to serif, 12 pt.
5. Insert the V, C, and D AutoText entries that you saved in the previous exercise wherever they appear in the document.
6. Correct spelling.
7. Preview the document.
8. Print one copy.
9. Close the file; save the changes.

429 FIFTH AVENUE
New York, NY 10016

(212) 555-5555
E-mail: cc@net.com

Today's date

Mr. Leonard Ghurka, President
Legal Services, Inc.
56 Wall Street
New York, NY 10001

Dear Mr. Ghurka:

SUBJECT: OPTICAL CHARACTER RECOGNITION   Center and set to 14 pt, bold

Our store is now carrying a line of Optical Character Recognition systems (scanners and software). We thought we might acquaint you with these useful tools. If you see a need for it in your business, our staff will be more than happy to demonstrate the various products available.

(commonly referred to as OCR)

You are probably familiar with Optical Character Recognition systems in their role at the supermarket checkout stand. A laser beam "reads" the bar code that is imprinted on an item and delivers the information—item, price, etc.—to the cash register. ¶ In an office, *Optical Character Recognition works in a similar way. Many firms have hundreds of documents that have to be entered into their computers. Keying in all these documents would take up valuable time.

An *Optical Character Recognition system provides a much faster alternative. An outstanding typist can type on the average of three characters per second. In comparison, an *Optical Character Recognition system can achieve speeds of up to 250 characters a second.[1] An *Optical Character Recognition system "reads" a document and deciphers the letters and numbers. It then converts this information into digital form and transmits it to a computer.

Italic   May

[1]Sam Travers, "The Benefits of OCR," Internet Magazine (New York: 2002), p. 52

SCAN, SCAN, SCAN

Once you suspect your system has been invaded and you have restarted your system from an emergency **[F]**, the next step is to scan your hard drive and all **[F]**s. Your anti-virus program will provide you with instructions for detecting infected files and either repairing or destroying them. As an extra precaution, you may want to repeat the entire scanning process frequently during the next several weeks to make sure you are not being re-infected.

Mr. Leonard Ghurka
Page 2
Today's date

OCR systems include an optical scanner for reading text and software for analyzing images. Most OCR systems use a combination of hardware and software to recognize characters, although some inexpensive systems do it entirely through software. Advanced OCR systems can read text in a large variety of fonts. 2

While *Optical Character Recognition systems do have their problems, the advantages outweigh the problems.

Spell out system

If you feel that the OCR (as it is commonly referred to) can be advantageous to your business, please call me or anyone on our staff between 9:00 a.m. and 5:00 p.m. We will be delighted to give you or your company representative a full demonstration of the merits of these systems. Check the following Web sites, which offer OCR products. We carry all the products you will see.

by saving time and money.

illustrate and

www.irisusa.com
www.primerecognition.com

Center

You might be interested to know that some scanners can read handwritten material.

Sincerely,

Rhoda Boylan
Product Manager

rb/yo

2Ibid., p. 53

COMPUTER VIRUSES:
How to Protect Your Computer From Getting Infected

Viruses are actually much less common than most people are led to believe. Like biological viruses, **[V]**es can only be spread by contact with the outside world. The most common way to contract a **[V]** is by running programs from an infected **[F]** or by running infected software. Once a **[V]** gets inside your system, it can attach itself to other programs and infect other **[F]**s you may use. The good news is that there are many things you can do to protect your home computer from viruses.

VIRUS PROTECTION SOFTWARE

Many **[V]** detection programs are designed to keep running while you work on the computer. If the program detects any suspicious behavior, it alerts you immediately and allows you to scan for a **[V]**.

STRANGE BEHAVIOR

As soon as you detect any kind of abnormal behavior, it is best to assume the worst. Immediately save any open files, quit all applications and turn off your computer. The sooner you can detect the **[V]**, the better your chances are of removing it and keeping system damage to a minimum. Always keep a clean emergency bootable disk on hand that will allow you to reboot your computer from the **[F]** drive. This is necessary because **[V]**es will load themselves into your computer's memory and infect even more programs. Most anti-virus software programs will allow you to create an emergency **[F].**

Compare and Merge Documents; Edit Footnotes

EXERCISE 67

SCANS

Directions

1. Open **7.63history**, the file you created in Exercise 63, or open **d7.67history** from the Data CD. 
2. Save the file as **7.67history**.
3. Delete the existing page number at the bottom of the page.
4. Insert a header as follows:
   a. Include a centered page number.
   b. Right-align: `by Your Name`
5. Delete each footnote and change them to internal citations (see illustration on page 180).
6. Use widow/orphan control.
7. Hyphenate the document.
8. Preview the document.
9. Print one copy.
10. Save the changes.
11. Compare **7.67history** and **7.63history**, and merge into the current document (**7.67history**).
    Word 2000 Users: Compare **7.67history** and **7.63history**.
12. Print one copy of **7.67history** showing all edits.
    - Compare the printout with the exercise directions to be sure all insertions and deletions were made.
13. Use the reviewing toolbar and accept all changes.
14. Close all files; save the changes.

VOCABULARY

Internal citation

DID YOU KNOW?

Word allows multiple reviewers to make edits on a document, which the author can later choose to accept or reject.

CONCEPT BUILDERS

- Sometimes, you can use an ***internal citation*** in place of a footnote.
- When using an internal citation, only the author's last name and the year of publication are shown.
- When using an internal citation for Web references, the author's last name, Web site, and date of Web posting (if available) are indicated.

Insert AutoText

EXERCISE 88

SCANS

Directions

1. Create a new document.
2. Set 1.25" left and right margins.
3. Begin the report, shown on pages 231 – 232, 2" from the top of the page.
4. Set the title to sans serif, 14 pt, bold.
5. Set the document font to serif, 12 pt.
6. Insert the V and F AutoText entries that you created in the previous exercise wherever they appear in the document.
7. Insert the footer and page numbers, as shown.
8. Correct spelling.
9. Preview the document.
10. Print one copy.
11. Save the file; name it **9.88protect**.

CONCEPT BUILDERS

You can insert AutoText by displaying the AutoText toolbar and selecting the entry you want, or by entering the first few characters of the AutoText name and pressing the F3 key to insert it.

NOTE

- You cannot insert AutoText using the F3 command unless the Show AutoComplete suggestions check box is selected in the AutoText tab in the AutoCorrect dialog box.
- When you insert AutoText, some entries will require you to change the tense of a verb.

A BRIEF HISTORY OF COMPUTERS

Computers are a part of so many aspects of our society today that it is hard to imagine life without them. To understand and appreciate fully the impact that computers have had on our lives, it is important to understand their evolution. What follows is a brief history of the development of computer technology. There are five generations of modern computer history, the first of which was considered to have occurred between 1944 and 1956. Long before the first generation of computers evolved (which was considered to have occurred between 1944 and 1956), computer development was well on its way.

Joseph Jacquard developed a loom for weaving cloth whose operation was controlled by means of cards with holes punched in them. This card laid the foundation for computer development. "In 1886, Herman Hollerith improved on Jacquard's punched card by developing a card that could be used with electrical rather than mechanical equipment. The Hollerith (or IBM) card is still very much in use." (McClung, 1994)

Internal citation

Create an AutoText Entry

EXERCISE 87

SCANS

Directions

1. Create a new document.
2. Use the AutoText feature to create each phrase or word shown.
   a. Save each repetitive text entry using the letter indicated.
   b. Set the text in the font and font sizes as follows:
   - V: serif, 12 pt, italic
   - C: serif, 12 pt
   - D: script, 12 pt
   - F: serif, 12 pt

Name	Text to save
V	*computer virus*
C	Yours truly, Linda Corin Sales Manager lc/yo
D	*Computer Virus Doctor*
F	floppy disk

VOCABULARY

AutoText

CONCEPT BUILDERS

- Creating and inserting an AutoText entry eliminates the need to retype text you use frequently.
- ***AutoText*** is a recorded selection of text that is assigned a unique name and inserted into a document when needed.
- To record an AutoText entry, select the text you want to preserve, click Insert, select AutoText, and click New. Assign a name to the selected text.

Use the Help Index

How Do I...?
Create an AutoText entry

Enter the keyword(s):
AutoText

EXERCISE 68

Display Multiple Documents; Switch Between Open Documents; Copy from One Document to Another

Directions

1. Open **7.62dtp**, the file you created in Exercise 62, or open **d7.68dtp** from the Data CD.
2. Save the file as **7.68dtp**.
3. Set the font for the title and side headings to sans serif, 14 pt, bold, and italic. Move the start line for the title to 2".
4. Set 1" left and right margins.
5. Set line spacing to double.
6. Make the revisions shown on pages 182 – 183.
7. Find each occurrence of "publishing" and replace it with: `Publishing`
8. Change the header to script, 16 pt; set the case to title (upper and lowercase).
9. Justify document text.
10. Use the Thesaurus feature to replace highlighted words.
11. Open **4.37run**, the file you created in Exercise 37, or open **d7.68run** from the Data CD. 
12. Display both documents.
13. Copy the letterhead from **d7.68run** to **7.68dtp**, where shown.
14. Close **d7.68run**.
15. Maximize the **7.68dtp** window.
16. Open **d7.68bp** from the Data CD.
17. Copy the letterhead from **d7.68bp** to **7.68dtp**, where shown.
18. Use widow/orphan control.
19. Make any necessary adjustments to the text.

VOCABULARY

Active document

CONCEPT BUILDERS

A button on the taskbar with the Word icon indicates each open document. When you place the insertion point on a document button, a ScreenTip appears, showing the document name.

The highlighted button indicates the ***active document*** (the document containing the insertion point). To switch between open documents, click the document button on the taskbar, or click Window on the menu, and choose the document you want to display. You can also press the Ctrl + F6 keys to cycle between open documents. **Windows XP Users:** When multiple documents from the same application are open, Windows consolidates all of the files from that application under one button on the taskbar. To switch between these open documents, click the application button on the task bar, which will display a pop-up menu. Then select the document you want to display.

LESSON 9

Work with AutoText and Macros; Merge

EXERCISE 87
Create an AutoText Entry

EXERCISE 88
Insert AutoText

EXERCISE 89
Insert AutoText

EXERCISE 90
Insert AutoText; Find and Replace

EXERCISE 91
Insert a File

EXERCISE 92
Insert a File

EXERCISE 93
Record a Macro; Run/Play a Macro

EXERCISE 94
Skills Review

Directions *continued*

20. Preview the document.

21. Print one copy.

22. Save the changes and close the file.

- When moving text from one page to another within the same document, use the Go To feature to jump quickly to the page you want.
- Hide the toolbars to maximize your document screen when displaying multiple windows.

Using the Help Index

How Do I...?	**Enter the keyword(s):**
Go to another page/place in document quickly	Go to

DESKTOP PUBLISHING

Until recently, graphic design was done by art directors and design professionals whose livelihoods depended on cre-ating effective graphic designs.

Desktop publishing has changed all that.

Desktop publishing has brought graphic design into the office and home. It has enabled people other than art direc-tors to create attractive, effective printed materials, such as newsletters, advertisements, brochures, manuals, and other documents.

Insert A→

EFFECTIVE GRAPHIC DESIGN LEADS TO SUCCESS

Effective graphic design makes it easier for readers to understand the message. If the message is clear and attrac-

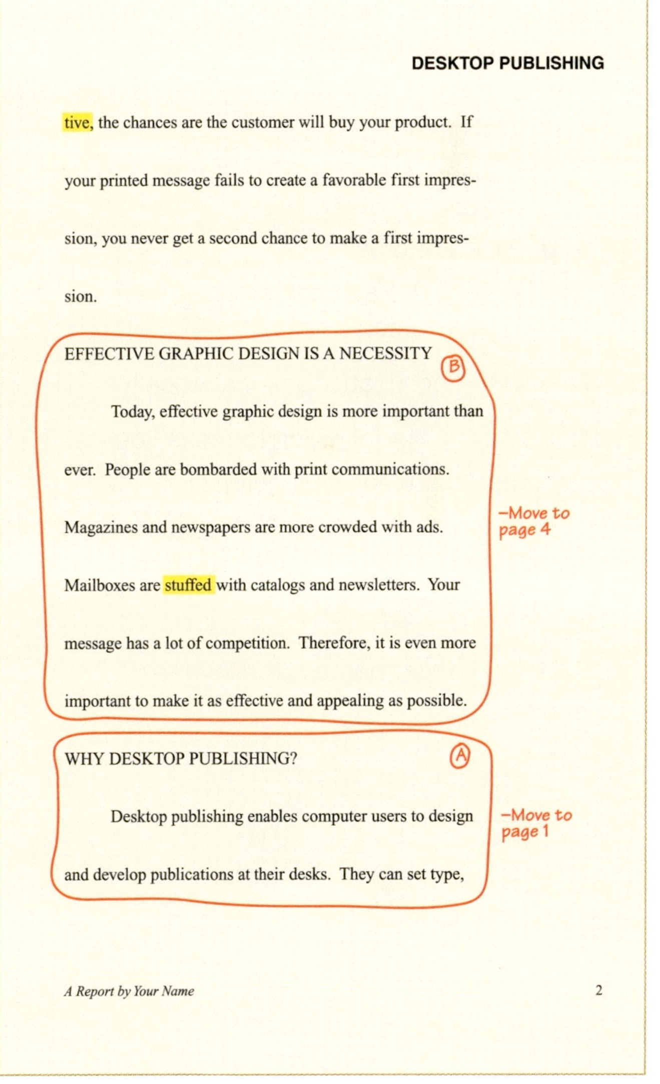

DESKTOP PUBLISHING

tive, the chances are the customer will buy your product. If your printed message fails to create a favorable first impres-sion, you never get a second chance to make a first impres-sion.

EFFECTIVE GRAPHIC DESIGN IS A NECESSITY (B)

Today, effective graphic design is more important than ever. People are bombarded with print communications. Magazines and newspapers are more crowded with ads. Mailboxes are stuffed with catalogs and newsletters. Your message has a lot of competition. Therefore, it is even more important to make it as effective and appealing as possible.

–Move to page 4

WHY DESKTOP PUBLISHING? (A)

Desktop publishing enables computer users to design and develop publications at their desks. They can set type,

–Move to page 1

A Report by Your Name 2

Directions *continued*

4. Use the Internet to research various occupations.
   a. Open your browser. Enter this URL:
      `http://stats.bls.gov`
   b. Click **Occupational Outlook Handbook,** listed under the Publications and Research Papers heading.

5. For each occupation listed in the table, do the following:
   NOTE: *You can either select 10 occupations that interest you and enter the names of those occupations in the first column of your table, or use the occupations that appear in the exercise.*
   a. Click the letter that corresponds to the first letter of the occupation you are researching.
   b. Click **Nature of the Work.**
      - Copy one or two sentences that describe the nature of the work to the appropriate cell in your table.
   c. Click **Job Outlook.**
      - Determine if there is future growth or decline in the occupation.
      - Insert a "+" or "-" in the appropriate cell to identify this trend.
   d. Click **Earnings.**
      - Copy the average starting salary to the appropriate cell in your table.

6. Sort the occupations alphabetically.

7. Do any of the following to make your table more attractive:
   a. Merge and/or split cells.
   b. Use any fonts, font sizes, shading, borders, alignments, or automatic formats that you like.

8. Print one copy.

9. Save the file; name it **8.86careers**.

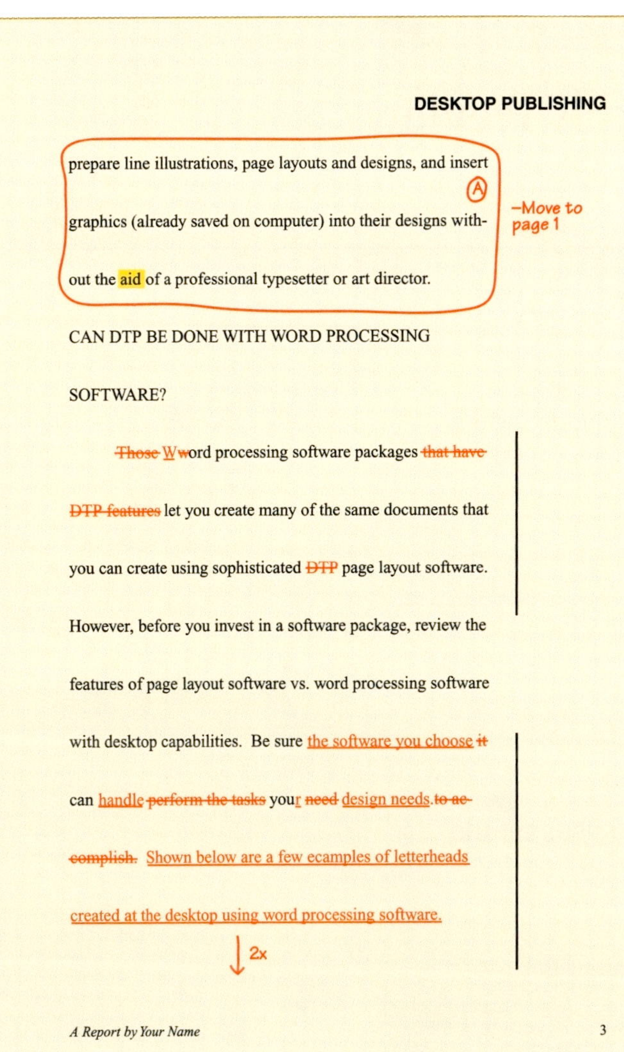

DESKTOP PUBLISHING

prepare line illustrations, page layouts and designs, and insert graphics (already saved on computer) into their designs without the aid of a professional typesetter or art director.

Ⓐ –Move to page 1

CAN DTP BE DONE WITH WORD PROCESSING SOFTWARE?

~~Those~~ Wword processing software packages ~~that have DTP features~~ let you create many of the same documents that you can create using sophisticated ~~DTP~~ page layout software. However, before you invest in a software package, review the features of page layout software vs. word processing software with desktop capabilities. Be sure the software you choose ~~it~~ can handle ~~perform the tasks~~ your ~~need~~ design needs. ~~to accomplish.~~ Shown below are a few ecamples of letterheads created at the desktop using word processing software.

↓ 2x

A Report by Your Name 3

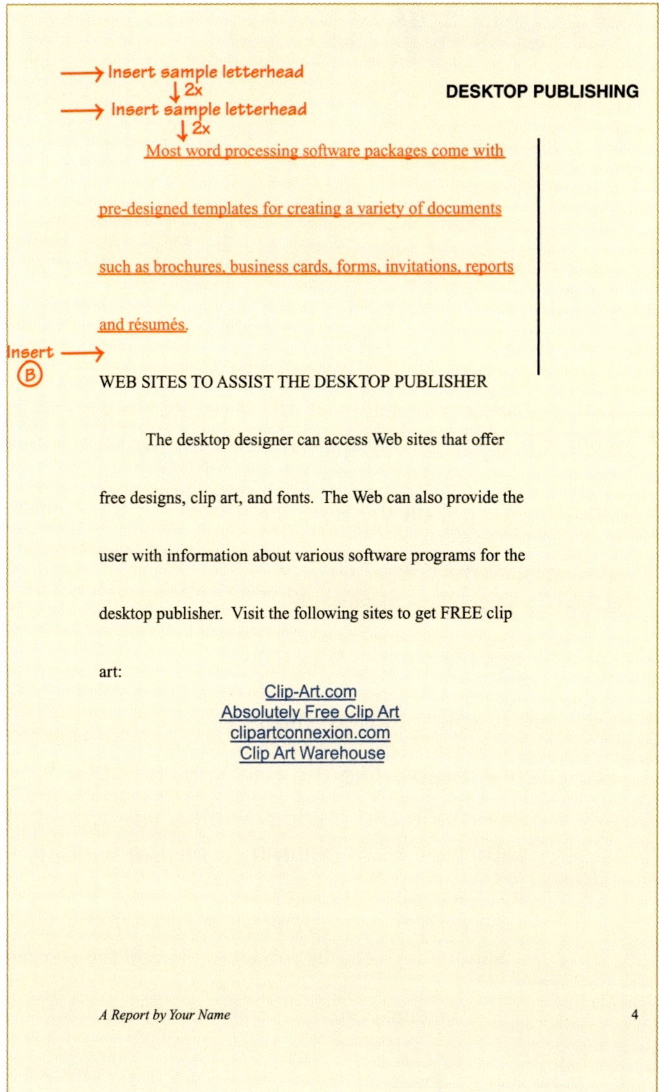

→ Insert sample letterhead
↓ 2x
→ Insert sample letterhead
↓ 2x

DESKTOP PUBLISHING

Most word processing software packages come with pre-designed templates for creating a variety of documents such as brochures, business cards, forms, invitations, reports and résumés.

Insert Ⓑ →

WEB SITES TO ASSIST THE DESKTOP PUBLISHER

The desktop designer can access Web sites that offer free designs, clip art, and fonts. The Web can also provide the user with information about various software programs for the desktop publisher. Visit the following sites to get FREE clip art:

Clip-Art.com
Absolutely Free Clip Art
clipartconnexion.com
Clip Art Warehouse

A Report by Your Name 4

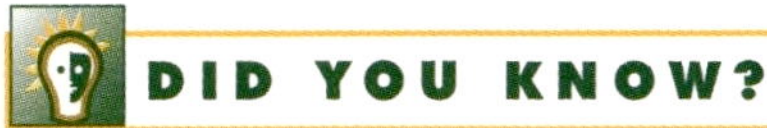

DID YOU KNOW?

Clicking Arrange from the Window menu will display all open documents on screen.

Skills Review

EXERCISE 86

Your guidance counselor has asked you to prepare a table outlining various occupations and noting the nature of the work, the job outlook, and the average starting salary. In order to make this comparison, you will need to conduct research on the Internet.

Directions

SCANS

1. Create a new document.
2. Set 1" left and right margins.
3. Create a table like the one shown below.
   - Determine the column widths you would like to use; set the Nature of Work column to be the widest.

Include this exercise in your portfolio.

POPULAR OCCUPATIONS
Nature of Work, the Job Outlook, and the Average Starting Salary*

	Occupation	Nature of Work	The Job Outlook	Average Starting Salary
Choosing an Occupation	Hotel Manager			
	Aircraft Pilot			
	Architect			
	Broadcast News Analyst			
	Teacher			
	Physician			
	Marketing, Advertising, and Public Relations Manager			
	Computer Programmer			
	Lawyer			
	Accountant			

*Source: U.S. Department of Labor Statistics, *Occupational Outlook Handbook,* (Washington, DC 2002-03)

Display Multiple Documents; Switch Between Open Documents; Copy from One Document to Another

EXERCISE 69

Directions

1. Open **5.50confer**, the file you created in Exercise 50, or open **d7.69confer** from the Data CD. 
2. Save the file as **7.69confer**.
3. Start a new blank document.
4. Display both document windows, as shown in the illustration on page 185.
5. Copy the main title and subtitles in **7.69confer** to the new document. Press the **Enter** key twice.
6. Insert `Brighton College, January 1, 2004` in the new document, as shown in the illustration. Press the **Enter** key three times.
7. Copy the information in **7.69confer** to the new document, as illustrated.
   - Left-align the centered session numbers and titles.
8. Insert Instructor and Room information.
   a. Place Summary description text next to the word "Summary," as shown.
   b. Indent the Summary description text 1" from the left and right margins.
   c. Tab the instructor's name and room number to 1".
   d. Copy the formatting for "Summary" to each occurrence of "Instructor" and "Room."
   e. Press the **Enter** key three times after the information for each session.
9. Close **7.69confer**.
10. Center the new document vertically on the page.
11. Preview the document.

JUMPBALL, INC.

ORDER FORM

SHIP TO:			Invoice #	
Same as billing address? ☐ YES ☐ NO			Invoice Date:	
			Shipping Date:	
			Salesperson:	
			Terms:	
Qty	Item	Description	Price	Total
			$	$
			$	$
			$	$
			$	$
			$	$
			$	$
			$	$
			$	$
			$	$
			$	$
			$	$
			$	$
			$	$
			$	$
NO RISK GUARANTEE			Subtotal	
If for any reason, you are not fully satisfied with an item upon receipt, we will refund your money or replace the item—whichever you prefer.			Tax	
			Shipping	$
			TOTAL	

880 7th Avenue • New York, NY 10106
Phone: 212.555.JUMP • Fax: 212.666.JUMP

Insert drop-down form field with the following names:
Martin Jackson
Ray Landes
Janet Boyle
Renee Cino
Chris Dale

Enter the formula to calculate the subtotal

Enter the formula to calculate the tax

Enter the formula to calculate the total

Directions *continued*

12. Print one copy.

13. Save the new file; name it **7.69conferad**.

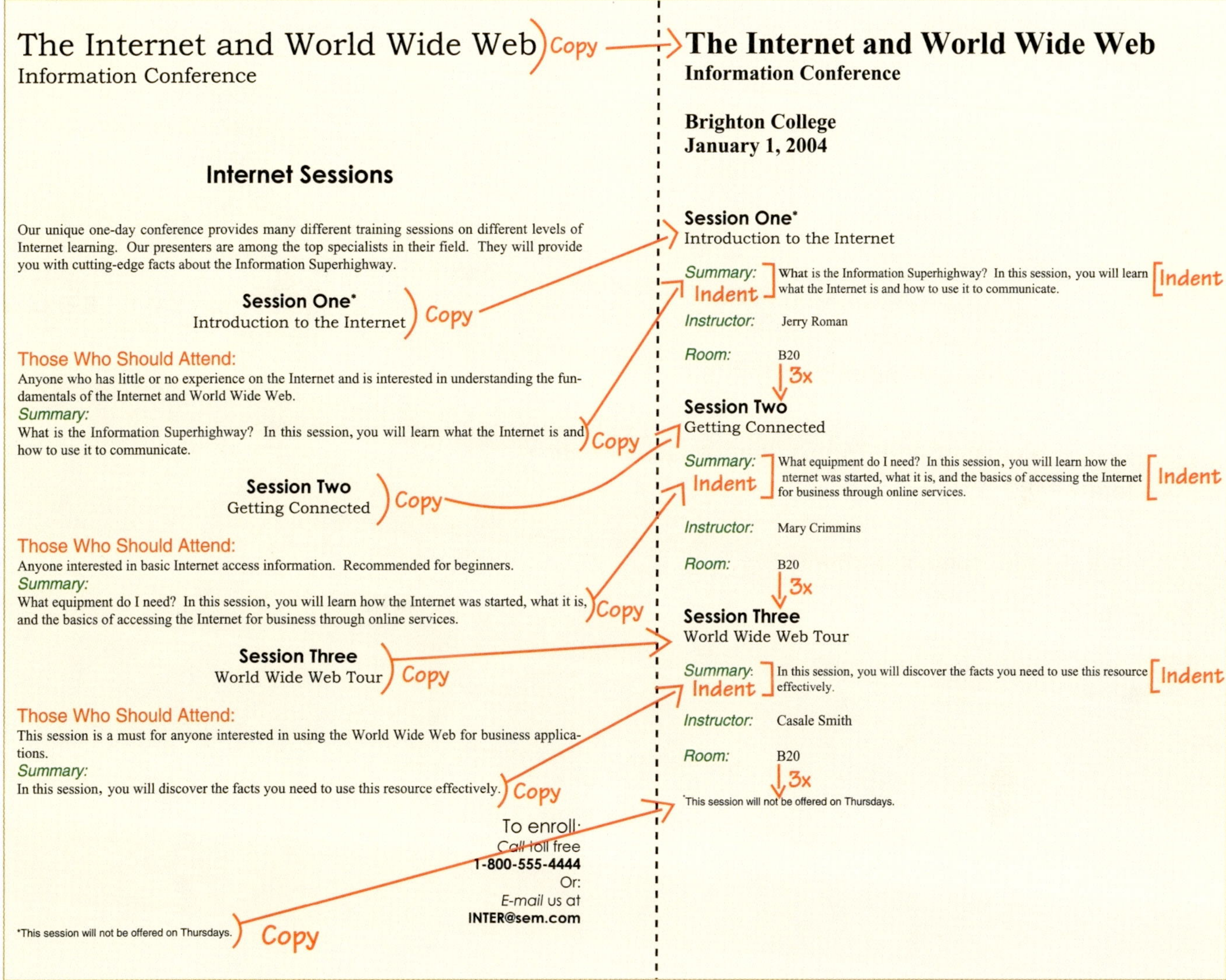

The Internet and World Wide Web
Information Conference

Internet Sessions

Our unique one-day conference provides many different training sessions on different levels of Internet learning. Our presenters are among the top specialists in their field. They will provide you with cutting-edge facts about the Information Superhighway.

Session One*
Introduction to the Internet

Those Who Should Attend:
Anyone who has little or no experience on the Internet and is interested in understanding the fundamentals of the Internet and World Wide Web.
Summary:
What is the Information Superhighway? In this session, you will learn what the Internet is and how to use it to communicate.

Session Two
Getting Connected

Those Who Should Attend:
Anyone interested in basic Internet access information. Recommended for beginners.
Summary:
What equipment do I need? In this session, you will learn how the Internet was started, what it is, and the basics of accessing the Internet for business through online services.

Session Three
World Wide Web Tour

Those Who Should Attend:
This session is a must for anyone interested in using the World Wide Web for business applications.
Summary:
In this session, you will discover the facts you need to use this resource effectively.

To enroll:
Call toll free
1-800-555-4444
Or:
E-mail us at
INTER@sem.com

*This session will not be offered on Thursdays.

The Internet and World Wide Web
Information Conference

Brighton College
January 1, 2004

Session One*
Introduction to the Internet

Summary: What is the Information Superhighway? In this session, you will learn what the Internet is and how to use it to communicate.

Instructor: Jerry Roman

Room: B20

Session Two
Getting Connected

Summary: What equipment do I need? In this session, you will learn how the internet was started, what it is, and the basics of accessing the Internet for business through online services.

Instructor: Mary Crimmins

Room: B20

Session Three
World Wide Web Tour

Summary: In this session, you will discover the facts you need to use this resource effectively.

Instructor: Casale Smith

Room: B20

*This session will not be offered on Thursdays.

Directions *continued*

9. Enter the following information into the order form:

> Sold to:
> Westin Sporting Goods
> 87 Barclay Road
> Palm Beach, FL 33480 (This is also the billing address.)
> Invoice # 1004
> Invoice Date: 6/25/04
> Shipping Date: 6/30/04
> Salesperson: Martin Jackson
> Terms: Net 30
> 3 doz. Rainbow Basketballs (Item B64), $150 dozen.
> Total: $450.00
> 5 doz. JUMPBALL T-shirts (Item S3), $30 dozen.
> Total: $150.00
> 12 The Ultimate Sports Watch (Item W41), $40 each.
> Total: $480.00

10. Save the file; name it **8.85ord1004**.
11. Print one copy.
12. Close the document window.

HOT TIPS

- To calculate the tax, enter the formula =product(above)*.08 in the expression box.
- To calculate the amounts automatically when the insertion point exits the form field, check the Calculate on exit box in the Text Form Field dialog box.

DID YOU KNOW?

Net 30 means that the customer must pay the full amount within 30 days.

Skills Review

EXERCISE 70

In this exercise, you will prepare a report with footnotes and include a header and page number. You will have to search the Internet for information to complete the report. Use the proper report format.

SCANS

Directions

1. Create a new document.
2. Set 1.25" left and right margins.
3. Key in the exercise provided in the illustration on pages 188 – 189.
4. Set the document fonts and sizes as follows:
   - Title: serif, 14 pt, bold, all caps
   - Document: serif, 13 pt
   - Side headings: serif, 14 pt, bold
   - Bulleted headings: serif, 13 pt, small caps
5. Include a right-aligned header on all pages except the first page that reads: `Computing Safely`

   Set it to script, 14 pt.
6. Insert a page number on the bottom right of each page.
7. Use widow/orphan control.
8. Edit the header to read:
   `Computing Safely and Comfortably`
9. Use the Internet to find books on ergonomics as follows:
   a. Open your browser. Enter this URL: `www.bn.com`
   b. Enter `Ergonomics` in the Search textbox and click Search.
   c. Copy five book titles from the Web page to your document, where indicated. Choose books that you feel are interesting and relate to the report.
   NOTE: *Copy all the book information; you can edit it later to include only the information you want.*
   d. Close the browser.

Skills Review

EXERCISE 85

You work for JUMPBALL, Inc., a new company that specializes in selling wholesale basketball-related merchandise. JUMPBALL, Inc. is located at 880 Seventh Avenue, New York, NY 10106, Phone, 212-555-JUMP and Fax 212-666-JUMP, E-mail: jump@spring.com.

Chris Keating, your manager, has asked you to design an order form. He has provided you with a handwritten sketch, shown on page 225.

Use the Table feature to create the order form on the computer. You can use the JUMPBALL logo, which can be found in the **8.76jbminutes** file.

After you have saved the form, enter information for one of the orders that came in today.

Directions

1. Create a new document.
2. Create a table from the information illustrated on page 225.
3. Include the company name, address, and phone/fax information.
4. Enhance the table with borders and shading as you prefer.
5. Add appropriate form fields, as shown in the sketch on page 225.
6. Set the Subtotal, Tax, and Total form fields to calculate the order.
7. Save the file as a template; name it **8.85jborderform**.
8. Print one copy.

SCANS

CONCEPT BUILDERS

- To sum data that has been entered in a form field, do the following:
  - Position the insertion point in the text form field where the answer should appear.
  - Double-click the text form field, which will open the Text Form Field Options dialog box.
  - Click the Type list arrow and select Calculation; enter the formula, =sum(above) in the expression box.
  - Click OK.
- To multiply data that has been entered in a form field, do the following:
  - Position the insertion point in the text form field where the answer should appear.
  - Double-click the text form field, which will open the Text Form Field Options dialog box.
  - Click the Type list arrow and select Calculation; enter the formula, =product(above)**number* in the expression box.
  - Click OK.

Directions *continued*

10. Indent the book information 1" from the left margin. Bullet and single-space each entry.
    - Delete shipping instructions and pricing information after you copy the information.
    - Apply the same document font and font size to the newly copied text.
    - Italicize book titles.
11. Justify document text.
12. Preview the document.
13. Print one copy.
14. Save the file; name it **7.70compute**.

Directions *continued*

17. Click **File, New** to open a new template.

18. Open **8.84application**.

19. Tab through the form and complete the name, address, and education sections.

20. Print one copy of the form.

21. Save the file; name it **8.84myapplication**.

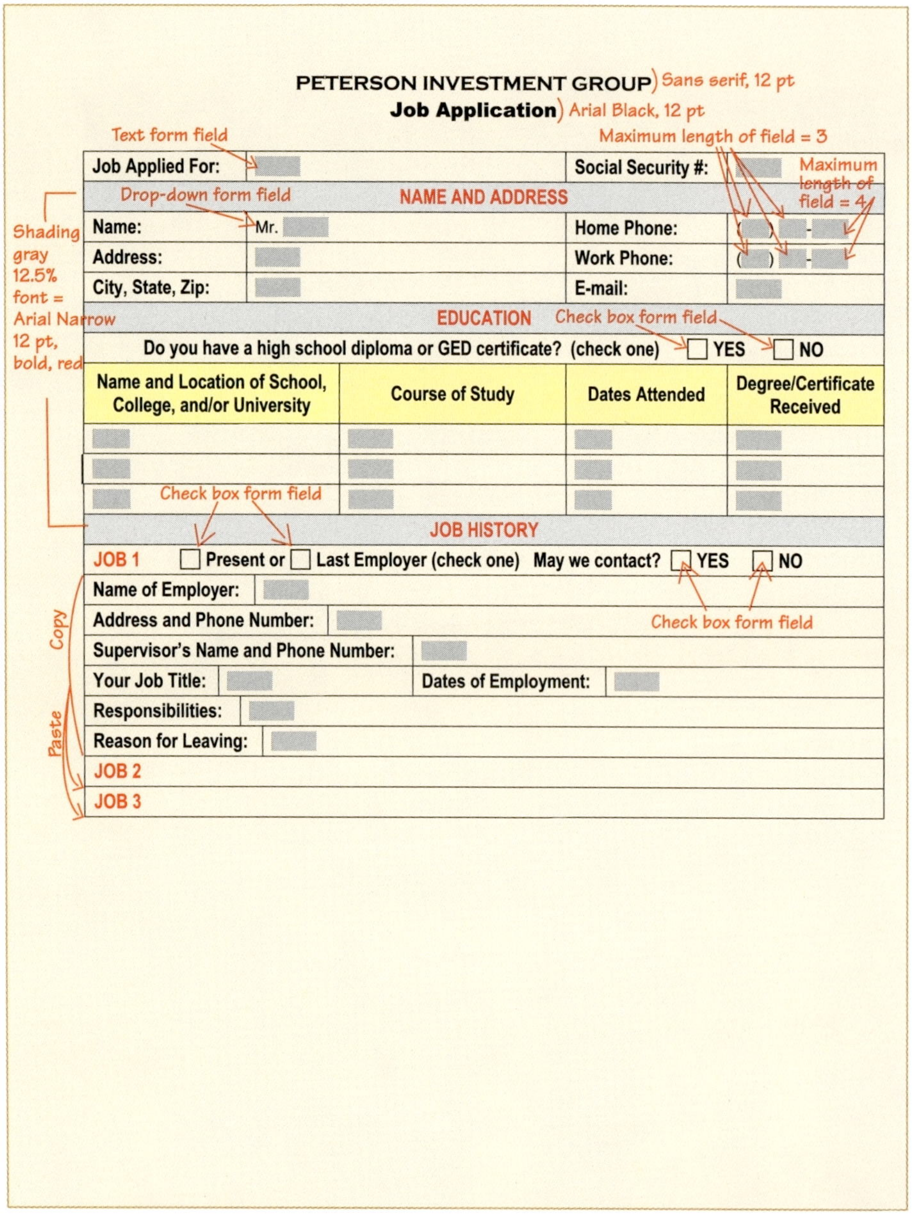

PETERSON INVESTMENT GROUP (Sans serif, 12 pt)

Job Application (Arial Black, 12 pt)

Job Applied For:		Social Security #:	
NAME AND ADDRESS			
Name:	Mr.	Home Phone:	( ) -
Address:		Work Phone:	( ) -
City, State, Zip:		E-mail:	
EDUCATION			
Do you have a high school diploma or GED certificate? (check one) ☐ YES ☐ NO			
Name and Location of School, College, and/or University	Course of Study	Dates Attended	Degree/Certificate Received
JOB HISTORY			
JOB 1 ☐ Present or ☐ Last Employer (check one) May we contact? ☐ YES ☐ NO			
Name of Employer:			
Address and Phone Number:			
Supervisor's Name and Phone Number:			
Your Job Title:		Dates of Employment:	
Responsibilities:			
Reason for Leaving:			
JOB 2			
JOB 3			

HOT TIPS

- It is recommended that you sketch a layout of your form to use as reference during the form-creation process.
- Save your form as a template so that each time you open the template, it is empty and ready for completion.
- To set the length of a text form field, double-click the text form field, which will open the Text Form Field dialog box. Then in the Maximum length box, use the increment arrows to set the length of the field.

NOTE

You cannot test the form until you protect it. Click the Protect Form button and test your fields. Then click the Protect Form button again to unprotect the form and continue editing.

COMPUTING SAFELY AND COMFORTABLY

If you find yourself sitting at the computer for more than a few hours at a time several times each week, then there are a number of good habits you will want to develop and bad habits you'll want to avoid. Bad habits can lead to frequent headaches, back pain, wrist pain, and eye strain. If left uncorrected, these problems can become chronic. To create an environment that ensures maximum comfort and safety, the first thing to do is personalize your workspace.

Ergonomics

Ergonomics is simply the science of fitting the person to his or her working environment. Just because a product may be labeled "ergonomic" does not mean it will be right for you. There are several things to consider for your personal workspace:

• ADJUSTABLE CHAIR. Avoid the use of straight-backed chairs, as they tend to restrict circulation. "Adjustable chairs allow for more movement which can relieve neck and back pressure."[1] Ideally, when sitting at the computer, you should be in a chair that allows you to have your feet flat on the floor (or on a foot rest), back straight, knees slightly higher than the bottom of your chair, eyes slightly higher than your monitor, wrists straight when typing, and forearms parallel to the floor.

• KEYBOARD. Your keyboard should be situated at the proper height from the floor. "If you need to flex your wrists backward as you type, your keyboard is probably too high for you and you may be putting unnecessary pressure on your wrists where they touch the desk."[2] Some ergonomic keyboards are designed with special features that include wrist rests, split keyboards, and adjustable angles to encourage better posture. Good typing skills are also important. By improving your touch-typing, you can avoid the need to bend your head down frequently in order to see the keyboard.

• MONITOR. Your monitor should be adjusted so that your eyes are slightly higher than the computer screen. Ideally, you should be sitting at least two feet away from the screen to avoid unnecessary eye strain. You can minimize glare by making sure your monitor is not directly in front of a window so that the sun is not in your eyes or reflecting off the screen. You will also want to make sure this is true for lamp light. If you still have a glare problem, you may want to get an anti-glare screen for your monitor.

Customizing Your Desktop

A simple way to lessen fatigue and potential health problems, while increasing the pleasure you get out of computing, is by customizing your desktop. Depending on your software, you can organize the desktop items that you use most often and make them readily available. You can customize keyboard

---

[1] Pamela Johnson, *Ergonomics in the Modern Office* (New York: Taylor Publishing Co., 1996), p. 24.
[2] Johnson, *Ergonomics in the Modern Offic*e, p. 84.

Create a Form

EXERCISE 84

SCANS

Directions

1. Create a new document.
2. Set 1" left and right margins, and .5" top and bottom margins.
3. Enter the heading at the top of the screen and set the company name and subheading to the fonts and sizes shown in the illustration on page 222.
4. Create a table with four columns and 21 rows.
5. Merge the cells and adjust column widths, where appropriate, to achieve the results shown.
6. Enter the text in the cells, as indicated, using Arial Narrow, 12 pt, bold. Apply Arial, 10 pt to the empty cells.
7. Set the height of the row shaded yellow to .5"; set all other row heights to .25".
8. Center the text vertically in the cells.
9. Insert text form fields where shown; use the character lengths where indicated.
10. Insert a drop-down form field in the Name cell, which contains the following items: `Mr.`, `Ms.`, and `Dr.` Next to it, insert a text form field for the person's name.
11. Insert check-box form fields where indicated.
12. Copy the cells below Job 1 and paste them below Jobs 2 and 3.
13. Protect the form.
14. Save the file as a template; name it **8.84application**.
15. Print one copy of the form.
16. Close the file.

VOCABULARY

Form
Form fields
Text form field
Drop-down form field

CONCEPT BUILDERS

- A ***form*** is a document that contains fixed text, form fields, and spaces for entering information. You can print and complete forms in ink, or you can open them in Word or online and enter your information.
- The following are some examples of frequently used forms: order form, income tax return, job application, loan application, and college application.
- When you create a form that will be completed online or in Word, you can use ***form fields*** to hold the information provided by the person filling out the form. A ***text form field*** allows the user to enter requested information. A check box allows the user to put a mark in a box if the statement is true. A ***drop-down form field*** allows the user to select an option from a list of choices.
- After creating a form, you must protect it to prevent anyone from changing its contents.

functions, mouse behavior, colors, fonts, sounds, screen savers, and icons. Organize your files carefully and give them descriptive file names so they are easy to find and easy to store. As folders get full, create sub-folders to keep your files easily accessible. By taking the time to set up your desktop according to your needs, you can save yourself lost time and maximize your work or play time at the computer.

Health Concerns

• EYES. You may be experiencing eye strain if you suffer from headaches, dry or tired eyes, blurred vision, increased sensitivity to light, itchy or burning eyes, or difficulties in refocusing. You can decrease eye strain significantly by blinking often or using eye drops, taking frequent breaks – at least 10 to 15 minutes for every hour in front of the computer screen, eliminating glare, and making sure you are not sitting too close to the monitor.

• CARPAL TUNNEL SYNDROME. "Carpal Tunnel Syndrome is a repetitive stress injury to the nerves and tendons in your wrist and hands which results in numbness, tingling, and mild to severe pain in these areas."[3] You can avoid these symptoms by creating an ergonomic environment and taking frequent breaks to stretch and flex your wrists and hands.

• BACK AND NECK PAINS. Poor posture at your workspace can lead to frequent headaches, neck pains, and backaches. Once you have ergonomically adjusted your environment, you can minimize musculoskeletal pains by combining 10 to 15 minute breaks every hour with simple stretching exercises for your back and neck. It is also a good idea to get up each hour you are at the computer and walk around to stimulate the circulation of blood and oxygen throughout your body.

Learning More

Educators, psychologists, managers, and doctors have written books about ergonomic-related issues in the workplace. Every year, companies pay millions of dollars in medical costs for workplace injuries and employees suffer from work-related back pain and other ailments that could have been prevented. The following suggested books will provide you with valuable information about this often overlooked workplace problem.

•
•
•
•
•

Insert book titles, authors, publishers, and date of publication

[3] Peter M. Mason, *Occupational Hazards,* (New Haven: Rally Press, Inc., 1994), p. 81.

(212) 555-5555
E-mail: cc@net.com

Today's date

Ms. Kiku Yuen
Hanover Incorporated
641 Belle Boulevard
New York, NY 10014

Dear Kiku:

RE: New Store Openings

We are pleased to announce the opening of City **Computers** in the metropolitan area. Stores are scheduled to open as follows:

Address	**Borough**	**Date of Opening**
908 Third Avenue	Manhattan	January 19
1401 Broadway	Manhattan	February 18
1070 Richmond Avenue	Richmond	June 2
160 Shore Road	Brooklyn	March 18
409 Pelham Parkway	Bronx	February 21
666 Queens Boulevard	Queens	April 1

As a preferred customer, you are invited to attend our gala opening celebration, which will be held on January 19 at 6:30 p.m. at our soon-to-be-opened Third Avenue location.

I look forward to greeting you personally on January 19.

Sincerely,

James C. McKinley
President

jm/yo

Skills Review

EXERCISE 71

SCANS

You work for D.C. Tours, a travel agency that specializes in tours to Washington, D.C. You have been asked to respond to the letter you received from Helen Wong of Brookvale High School. Ms. Wong, the senior class president, is planning the senior trip to Washington, D.C. She has requested information on hotel accommodations for the students. Beth Friedman in your office wrote a letter to another customer several days ago who had requested the same information. You can use parts of Beth's letter to create a response to Ms. Wong.

To give Ms. Wong the information she needs regarding hotel accommodations, you will have to search the Internet. The class is planning its trip for July 30 of the current year. Each person will have his or her own room and will be staying for two nights.

Prepare a two-page full-block letter. Provide an appropriate salutation and closing. Your title is Travel Consultant.

Directions

1. Open **d7.71dctourlet** from the Data CD. 
2. Save the file as **7.71tour2**.
3. Create a new document on the letterhead page. Set 1.25" left and right margins.
4. Set the document font to serif, 12 pt.
5. Send the letter to:
   Ms. Helen Wong
   Senior Class President
   Brookvale High School
   34 Plains Road
   Arlington, VA 22304
6. Open **6.55tour1**, the file you created in Exercise 55, or open **d7.71tour1** from the Data CD.
7. Save the file as **7.71tour1**.

Create Correspondence with Tables

EXERCISE 83

Directions

SCANS

1. Open **d8.83cclet** from the Data CD.
   Save the file as **8.83newsites**.
2. Set 1" left and right margins and .5" top and bottom margins.
3. Begin the exercise 2.5" down from the top of the page.
4. Set the document font to serif, 12 pt.
5. Create the full-block letter provided in the illustration on page 220 and insert the table shown.
   a. Determine the number of columns and rows needed.
   b. Enter the table data and format it as shown.
   c. Adjust the table size so that it is indented approximately 1" from the left and right margins.
   d. Remove all table borders.
6. Sort the third column so the dates are in chronological order.
7. Correct spelling.
8. Print one copy.
9. Close the file; save the changes.

Directions *continued*

8. Copy the text from **7.71tour1** shown in Illustration A on page 192, to **7.71tour2**, shown in Illustration B on page 193.
9. Copy the company name on the letterhead (D.C.Tours) to become a footer on the second and subsequent pages.
   - Set the font for the footer to 10 pt and center it.
10. Set left-aligned tab stops at .5" and 2.5"; set a right-aligned tab stop at 5".
11. Enter column-head text, as shown in Illustration B.
12. Use the Internet to research hotel rate information as follows:
    a. Open your browser. Enter this URL: `www.hotelaccomodations.com`
    b. Click **Washington, DC** in the United States listing.
    c. Enter appropriate information regarding length of stay and so on, as outlined.
    d. Click the **Check** button to check rates and availability.
    e. Scroll through the list and copy the hotel name and the location for Washington Plaza, Georgetown Suites, Carlyle Suites, and Days Inn Connecticut hotels from the Web site to your document.
    f. Notice the rates for the hotels listed above and enter them into your document.
    g. Print a map of each hotel location.
    h. Close the browser.
13. Make any necessary adjustments to the text.
14. Preview the document.
15. Print one copy of the completed letter.
16. Prepare an envelope. Attach it to the letter.
17. Close all files; save the changes to the **7.71tour2** file.

Directions *continued*

15. Apply italic to Total Cash In and Total Cash Out rows.
16. Adjust the width of Column 1 to approximately .5".
17. Print one copy.
18. Close the file; save the changes.

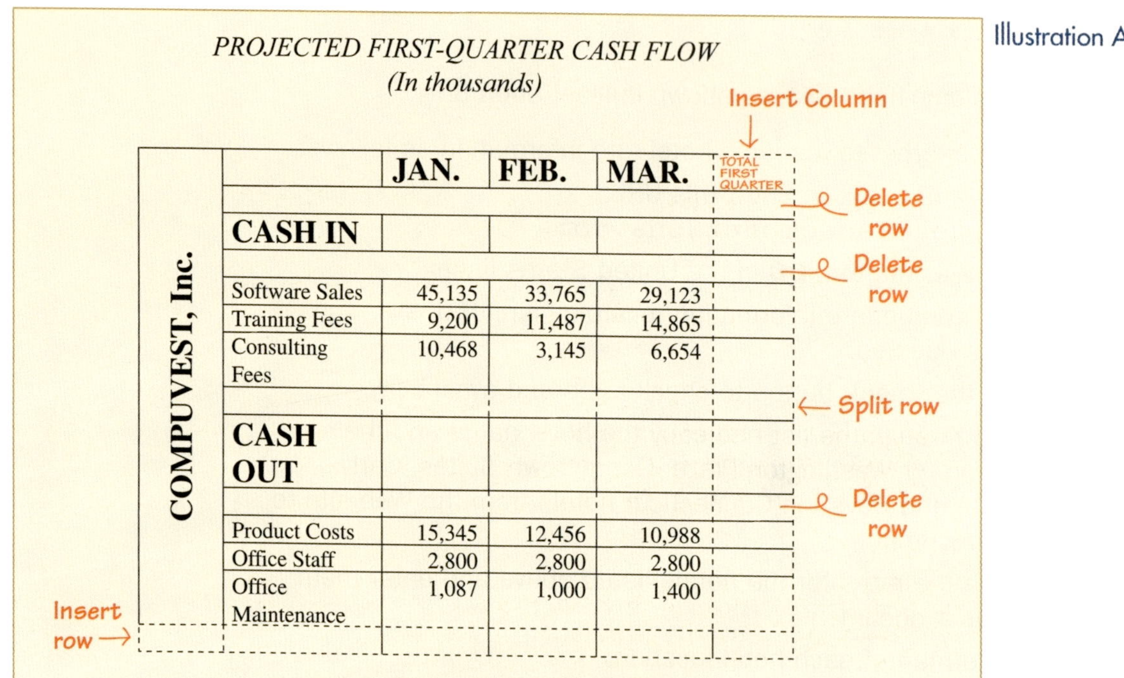

PROJECTED FIRST-QUARTER CASH FLOW
(In thousands)

COMPUVEST, Inc.		JAN.	FEB.	MAR.	TOTAL FIRST QUARTER
	CASH IN				
	Software Sales	45,135	33,765	29,123	
	Training Fees	9,200	11,487	14,865	
	Consulting Fees	10,468	3,145	6,654	
	CASH OUT				
	Product Costs	15,345	12,456	10,988	
	Office Staff	2,800	2,800	2,800	
	Office Maintenance	1,087	1,000	1,400	

Illustration A

PROJECTED FIRST-QUARTER CASH FLOW
(In thousands)

COMPUVEST, Inc.		JAN.	FEB.	MAR.	TOTAL FIRST QUARTER
	CASH IN				
	Software Sales	45,135	33,765	29,123	
	Training Fees	9,200	11,487	14,865	
	Consulting Fees	10,468	3,145	6,654	
	Total Cash In				
	CASH OUT				
	Product Costs	15,345	12,456	10,988	
	Office Staff	2,800	2,800	2,800	
	Office Maintenance	1,087	1,000	1,400	
	Total Cash Out				

Illustration B

D.C. Tours

114 PENNSYLVANIA AVENUE □ WASHINGTON, D.C. 20045
(202) 555-TOUR

April 5, 2004

Ms. Deborah Sprewell
4546 Western Road
Savannah, GA 31405

Dear Ms. Sprewell:

copy — I am glad that you have chosen D.C. Tours to help plan your ~~family's~~ senior trip to Washington, D.C. As you probably know, ~~the spring~~ early summer is an ideal time to visit the nation's capital.

copy — As per your request, below please find information on White House tours, which I found on the official White House Web site, www.whitehouse.gov.

copy —

White House Tours

Tours of the White House have been extended to school-aged youth groups and organized veterans groups in addition to school groups. School groups are defined as students in grades 4 through 12 and who are enrolled in the same school or school district. Group requests may be submitted through one's Member of Congress. These self-guided group tours will be scheduled from 7:45 to 10:30 a.m., Tuesday through Saturday.

copy —

White House Visitor Center

All tours are significantly enhanced if visitors stop by the White House Visitor Center before or after their tour.
The Center is open seven days a week from 7:30 a.m. until 4:00 p.m. and features many aspects of the White House, including its architecture, furnishings, first families, social events, and relations with the press and world leaders, as well as a thirty-minute video. Allow between 20 minutes to 1 1/2 hours to explore the exhibits. The White House Historical Association also sponsors a sales area. Please note that restrooms are available, but food service is not.

In addition to The White House, I highly recommend that you and your family visit the following museums, monuments, and buildings.

Jefferson Memorial	Library of Congress	Lincoln Memorial
National Gallery of Art	Vietnam Veterans Memorial Wall	The Pentagon
Smithsonian	Tomb of the Unknown Soldier	Washington Monument

If there is any additional information that you might need, please call me. I look forward to working with you again soon.

Sincerely,

Beth Friedman
Travel Consultant

bf/yo

Illustration A

EXERCISE 82

Insert and Delete Columns and Rows; Apply Automatic Formats; Calculate; Change Page Orientation

SCANS

Directions

1. Open **8.77cash** or open **d8.82cash** from the Data CD, as shown in Illustration A on page 218.
2. Save the file as **8.82cash**.
3. Change the page orientation to landscape.
4. Insert and delete the columns and rows, as shown in Illustration A.
5. Split the rows where shown.
6. Enter the new column heading: `TOTAL FIRST QUARTER` Press the **Enter** key after each word.
   - Center all column headings.
7. Enter the new row headings, `Total Cash In` and `Total Cash Out`, using serif, 12 pt, bold, and italic, as shown in Illustration B.
8. Calculate FIRST QUARTER totals for each item and format the answers for currency.
9. Calculate totals for JAN., FEB., and MAR. for CASH IN and CASH OUT, and format the answers for currency.
10. Apply shading and borders as shown in Illustration B on page 218.
    a. Apply a 3 pt vertical line between Columns 2 and 3.
    b. Apply a light green shade to the Total Cash In and Total Cash Out rows.
11. Preview the document.
12. Print one copy.
13. Save the changes.
14. Apply an automatic format to the table.

April 22, 2004

Insert inside address

Insert salutation

Copy first, second, third, and fourth paragraphs with indicated changes. (Shown in Illustration A)

Below is a list of recommended hotels, their locations, and rates. These hotels are within walking distance of many sightseeing attractions. We are enclosing an area map for each hotel.

.5"	2.5"	5"
Hotel	***Location***	***Rate Per Night***
Insert hotel information	**xxxxxxx**	**xxxxxxxx**

Since you only have three full days to see the many attractions in our nation's capital, I recommend that you and your classmates visit the following museums, which I know will be most memorable:

- National Gallery of Art
- American History
- Natural History
- Air and Space

Insert paragraphs

As you plan your trip, be sure to check the events, hours, location, and other information about each place you plan to visit. You can do this by visiting www.si.edu/visit/infocenter/mallmap.htm, which provides a map of the mall and allows you to access each of the institutions' Web pages.

Let us know what hotel you want us to book for you and how many will be in your group. The hotel requires that the reservation be held with a credit card.

Insert complimentary close

Insert signature (your name)

Insert title

Enclosures

Illustration B

Illustration A

Insert columns
Delete column
Insert Row
Insert Row

Name	Address	City			Phone	Gender	Contribution
Webster, Bruce	898 Willow Lane	New York			212-555-5555	M	36,000
Pilgrim, Nathan	63 Kirk Blvd	Cedar Rapids			319-777-7777	M	6,100
Blue, Martha	600 Fifth Avenue	New York			212-343-3434	F	500
Sarkov, Lee	3550 Anderson Street	Madison			608-888-8888	F	2,100
Szukics, Frank	100 Lumber Street	Bloomington			847-999-9999	M	15,000
Olson, Judy	10 Hempstead Avenue	Rockville Center			516-888-8888	F	5,700
Brown, Ted	87 Queens Blvd.	Queens			718-999-9999	M	10,000
Hyman Steve	45 East 44 Street	New York			212-111-1111	M	3,000
Elbert, Diane	33 Big Bend Street	St. Louis			314-555-4444	F	400
Frosch, Anne	18 Avenue M	Brooklyn			718-555-3333	F	50
Hickox, Richard	1015 Grand Street	Glendale			818-444-4444	M	100
Apostol, Chris	50 East 60 Street	New York			212-777-7722	M	250
McLaughlin, Laurie	33 Brier Lane	Huntington			516-232-2333	F	50
Yanez, Pat	77 Jay Street	Bronx			212-235-6666	F	100
Rodriguez, Ramon	351 Hudson Avenue	Costa Mesa			714-666-6666	M	1000
Brown, Donna	400 Pearman Road	Anderson			864-666-6000	F	750

Delete row
Insert three rows

Illustration B

Riverbank Run for Children
Contributions List
First Half - 2004

Name	Address	City	State	Zip	Phone	Contribution
Apostol, Chris	50 East 60 Street	New York	NY	10022	212-555-7722	250
Blue, Martha	600 Fifth Avenue	New York	NY	10003	212-555-3434	500
Brown, Donna	400 Pearman Road	Anderson	SC	29622	864-555-6000	750
Brown, Ted	87 Queens Blvd.	Queens	NY	11367	718-555-9999	10,000
Elbert, Diane	33 Big Bend Street	St. Louis	MO	63122	314-555-4444	400
Frosch, Anne	18 Avenue M	Brooklyn	NY	11210	718-555-3333	50
Giles, Van	45 Icon Road	Kearny	NE	68847	308-555-3333	850
Hickox, Richard	1015 Grand Street	Glendale	CA	91200	818-555-4444	100
Jones, Kamisha	890 Summerhill Lane	Medford	NJ	08055	609-555-5555	1,000
McLaughlin, Laurie	33 Brier Lane	Huntington	NY	11556	516-555-2333	50
Olson, Judy	10 Hempstead Avenue	Rockville Center	NY	11510	516-555-8888	5,700
Pilgrim, Nathan	63 Kirk Blvd	Cedar Rapids	IA	52406	319-555-7777	6,100
Rodriguez, Ramon	351 Hudson Avenue	Costa Mesa	CA	91109	714-555-6666	1,000
Sarkov, Lee	3550 Anderson Street	Madison	WI	53704	608-555-8888	2,100
Szukics, Frank	100 Lumber Street	Bloomington	IL	61723	847-555-9999	15,000
Webster, Bruce	898 Willow Lane	New York	NY	10021	212-555-5555	36,000
Yanez, Pat	77 Jay Street	Bronx	NY	11456	212-555-6666	100
					Total	$79,950.00

LESSON 8

Work with Columns, Tables, and Forms

EXERCISE 72
Use Newsletter-Style Columns

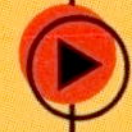
EXERCISE 73
Use Newsletter-Style Columns

EXERCISE 74
Use Columns with Custom Widths

EXERCISE 75
Create a Table; Change Column Width

EXERCISE 76
Create a Table; Change Column Width

EXERCISE 77
Create a Table; Change Column Width; Align Table Data; Merge Cells; Change Text Direction

EXERCISE 78
Create a Table; Change Column Width; Align Table Data; Merge and Split Cells; Change Text Direction

EXERCISE 79
Create a Table; Change Row Height; Apply Borders and Shading

EXERCISE 80
Create a Table; Set Automatic Column Widths; Calculate; Sort

EXERCISE 81
Insert and Delete Columns and Rows; Apply Automatic Formats; Calculate; Sort; Change Page Orientation

EXERCISE 82
Insert and Delete Columns and Rows; Apply Automatic Formats; Calculate; Change Page Orientation

EXERCISE 83
Create Correspondence with Tables

EXERCISE 84
Create a Form

EXERCISE 85
Skills Review

EXERCISE 86
Skills Review

Directions *continued*

11. Align the text, as shown in Illustration B:
   a. Enter and right-align the word `Total` in the last row.
   b. Center all column headings.
   c. Center data in the State column.
   d. Right-align data in the Contribution column.

12. Set column widths to fit the data.

13. Calculate the total contributions and format the answer for currency.

14. Apply an automatic format to the table.

15. Set the font and font size for the column headings to serif, 14 pt, bold.

16. Sort the Name column alphabetically.

17. Center the table horizontally and vertically.

18. Correct spelling.

19. Preview the document.

20. Print one copy.

21. Sort the Contribution column in descending order.

22. Print one copy.

23. Undo the sort.

24. Close the file; save the changes.

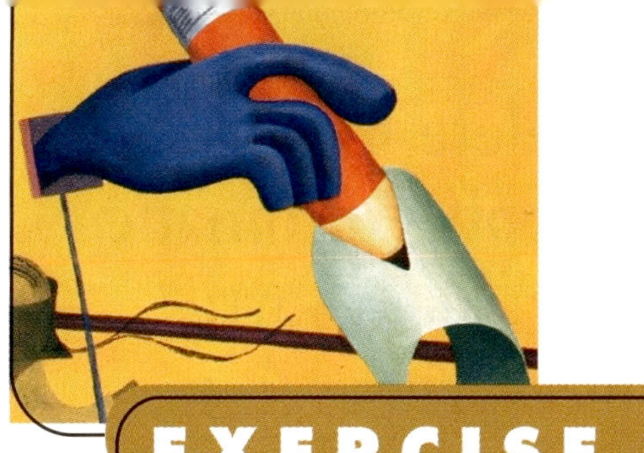

Use Newsletter-Style Columns

EXERCISE 72

SCANS

Directions

1. Create a new document.
2. Set 1.25" left and right margins.
3. Begin the exercise 2" from the top of the page.
4. Create the masthead using the fonts and font sizes shown in the illustration on page 196. Press the **Enter** key three times.
5. Set a two-column, newsletter-style format using the default gutter space to create the newsletter.
6. Center and set the headline text to sans serif, 14 pt, bold.
7. Set the document text to serif, 13 pt.
8. Use any symbol you prefer between the articles, as shown.
9. If necessary, insert nonbreaking spaces to prevent dates and times from breaking during word-wrap.
10. Correct spelling.
11. Preview the document.
12. Print one copy.
13. Save the file; name it **8.72news**.

VOCABULARY

Newsletter
Masthead/nameplate
Contents
Headlines
Body copy
Newsletter-style column
Gutter space

HOT TIPS

To prevent times and dates from breaking during word-wrap, insert nonbreaking spaces between such words. To do so, press Ctrl + Shift + the space bar.

CONCEPT BUILDERS

- A ***newsletter*** is a communication that allows people who share a common interest to exchange ideas, developments, and information on a regular basis.
- Most newsletters contain the following features: masthead or nameplate, contents, headlines, and body copy.
- The ***masthead*** or ***nameplate*** may include the newsletter's title, intended audience, the division or organization publishing the document, and the date of the issue.
- ***Contents*** list the articles or topics featured in the issue.
- ***Headlines*** indicate the contents of the articles.
- ***Body copy*** comprises the text of the articles.
- Text keyed in a ***newsletter-style column*** fills one column and then fills the next column.
- ***Gutter space*** refers to the space between columns.

Insert and Delete Columns and Rows; Apply Automatic Formats; Calculate; Sort; Change Page Orientation

Directions

SCANS

1. Open **d8.81contributions** from the Data CD.  Save the file as **8.81giving**.
2. Set .5" top and bottom margins.
3. Change the page orientation to landscape.
4. Insert the columns and rows as indicated in Illustration A on page 216.
5. Delete the column indicated in Illustration A.
6. Merge the cells in the newly created first and third rows.
   - Center the following titles in the first row and set the font to sans serif, 14 pt, italic:

> Riverbank Run for Children
> Contributions List
> First Half – 2004

7. Enter the new column headings, `State` and `Zip`.
8. Enter State and Zip information, as shown in Illustration B on page 216.
9. Enter the data for the following additional contributors into two of the new rows:

> Giles, Van, 45 Icon Road Kearney, NE 68847 308-555-3333, 850
>
> Jones, Kamisha, 890 Summerhill Lane, Medford, NJ 08055 609-555-5555, 1,000

10. Merge the first six cells in the last row.

VOCABULARY

Portrait
Landscape

CONCEPT BUILDERS

- Word contains automatic formats that you can apply to your table.
- Print orientation indicates how the paper is positioned when it is printed. ***Portrait*** orientation prints pages vertically (81/2" x 11"). ***Landscape*** orientation prints pages horizontally (11" x 81/2").

Use the Help Index

How Do I...?	**Enter the keyword(s):**
Create newsletter-style columns	Newsletter columns

Serif, 22 pt Italic

CABLE*COM* **Company News Briefs** Sans serif, 10 pt, bold

A Monthly Publication of CABLECOM, Inc. Serif, 10 pt

Serif, 10 pt

May, 2004

New Videophone Sales Off to Great Start

CableCom's new Videophone Supreme, just released in March, had a 22% increase in sales during the month of April.

The new Videophone Supreme enables home computer users to send voice and images over standard phone lines or Internet connections (56K modem, ISDN, DSL, cable modem, etc.).

The Videophone Supreme will be featured on CableCom's Web site beginning May 12.

Windows Lunch Hour Workshops

During the month of May, there will be ongoing lunch hour workshops available to all Windows users. Learn new features, keystrokes, and online options with the Microsoft ® Network.

Workshops will be held in the Information Services Conference Room on the 15th floor on Mondays, Wednesdays, and Fridays from 12 noon to 1:00 p.m. There will be a weekly sign-up sheet posted in the 15th floor lobby announcing the focus of each workshop.

Seating is limited to 15 people per workshop, so please sign up early for desired sessions.

CableCom Annual Spring Fling Company Picnic

All CableCom employees and family members are invited to attend this year's Spring Fling Company Picnic.

Festivities will begin at 12 noon on Saturday, June 19 at the South Lawns in Washington Memorial Park. Food and soft drinks will be provided. Bring your gear for softball, Frisbee, and volleyball.

Please RSVP to Karen Watson at extension 44 by Monday, May 17, and let her know how many family members will be attending.

Gutterspace

Directions *continued*

12. Correct spelling.
13. Preview the document.
14. Print one copy.
15. Save the file; name it **8.80payperiod**.

- If your work requires extensive calculations, use spreadsheet software to accomplish the task.
- Save your document before you begin a sort. If your sort produces unexpected results, click Undo.

Use the Help Index

How Do I...?	**Enter the keyword(s):**
Calculate	Calculate
Sort	Sort

			Pay Period		6/5/04-6/13/04	
			Pay Date		June 13, 2004	
			Department		Marketing	
Employee and Hours			**Earnings**			
Name	**Hrly Rate**	**Hrs Worked**	**REG**	**OT**	**Bonus**	**Gross Pay**
Willia, Rich	8.25	41	338.25	41.00	25.00	
Hamm, Steve	7.45	36	268.20		135.00	
Smith, Shirl	5.50	43	236.50	45.00	50.00	
Haris, Jack	7.85	40	314.00	116.00		
Denis, Chris	9.35	45	420.75	10.00		
Totals						

Set a decimal tab

Set a right-aligned tab

Set a decimal tab

Use Newsletter-Style Columns

EXERCISE 73

Directions

1. Create a new document.
2. Set 1" left and right margins.
3. Begin the exercise 2" from the top of the page.
4. Center and set the title using the fonts and font sizes shown in the illustration on page 198. Press the **Enter** key three times.
5. Set a three-column, newsletter-style format using the default gutter space.
6. Set the document text to serif, 13 pt.
7. Enter the column text.
   a. Balance the columns.
   b. Insert a triple space between paragraphs.
8. Hyphenate the document.
9. Correct spelling.
10. Preview the document.
11. Print one copy.
12. Save the file; name it **8.73zoo**.

VOCABULARY

Balanced columns

CONCEPT BUILDERS

Balanced columns is a column style in which text evens out as it is keyed into the columns.

Use the Help Index

How Do I...?	**Enter the keyword(s):**
Balance newsletter-style columns	Balance

Create a Table; Set Automatic Column Widths; Calculate; Sort

EXERCISE 80

Directions

SCANS

1. Create a new document.
2. Set 1" left and right margins.
3. Begin the exercise at the top of the page.
4. Create the table shown in the illustration on page 213.
   - Determine the number of columns and rows needed.
   - Determine the columns and rows to split and/or merge.
5. Enter and align the text as follows:
   a. Set the information in Row 1 to sans serif, 14 pt.
   b. Enter all table data using serif, 12 pt.
   c. Center and bold the column headings.
   d. Set a decimal tab for Columns 2 and 7 and a right-aligned tab for Column 3.
   e. Right-align text in Columns 4–6.
6. Apply shading and borders as follows:
   a. Apply a 3 pt border around Row 3.
   b. Apply a pattern to Row 1, Column 1.
   c. Apply a 95% gray shade to Row 1, Columns 2 and 3.
   d. Apply a 10% gray shade to Rows 4 and 10 as shown.
7. Set column widths to fit the data.
8. Sort the employee names alphabetically (ascending sort).
9. Calculate the columns as follows:
   - Find the Gross Pay for each employee.
   - Find the Total for each column.
10. Format the Gross Pay and Totals for currency.
11. Center the table horizontally and vertically.

VOCABULARY

Ascending
Descending

CONCEPT BUILDERS

- Word can add consecutive numbers in columns or rows.
- You must set a currency format in the appropriate dialog box to include a dollar sign ($) and two decimals.
- Text can be arranged alphabetically or numerically in ***ascending*** order (from A to Z or 1 to 9) or ***descending*** order (Z to A or 9 to 1).
- You can adjust the width of a cell or column to fit the maximum width of text in that cell or column automatically.

DID YOU KNOW?

- Gross pay is the total amount of wages earned before taxes are deducted.
- Net pay is the total amount of wages earned after taxes are deducted.

Discover Wildlife at the Zoo

Script, 36 pt

Decorative, 48 pt

The zoological parks throughout the United States are one of the most popular cultural and recreational attractions in those cities that have them. Visit http://dir.yahoo.com/Science/Biology/Zoology/Zoos for a complete listing of the zoos in the United States and in the world. Below is a highlight of two of the country's most popular zoos, one on the east coast and one on the west coast.

The Bronx Zoo is home to more than 4,000 animals and some of the world's endangered species. The zoo sits on 265 wooded acres. The Children's Zoo allows young visitors to pet and feed domestic animals. The Bronx Zoo is the largest metropolitan wildlife conservation park in the United States.

Now, if you can't visit New York, but want to get acquainted with this zoo, visit the Bronx Zoo Web site at: www.bronxzoo.com

The San Diego Zoo boasts the largest wild animal park and zoo in the country, with over 1,800 acres. The huge enclosures allow animals to roam in their natural environment. Visitors can walk among the colorful Australian parrots in the aviary or head into the backcountry and see elephants, rhinos, and pandas.

The nighttime zoo begins in June and continues until September. Visitors can see their favorite animals move through moonlight and shadows.

While you won't get the sights and smells of the real thing, the San Diego Zoo's Web site will give you a sampling of this world famous west coast attraction. Visit: www.sandiegozoo.org

JUMPBALL,
INC.

Itinerary

FOR: John Ortiz
DATES: July 21-23, 2004

July 21	10:15 a.m.	Depart New York, LaGuardia Airport, Atlantic Airlines, Flight #1817 to Los Angeles
	1:35 p.m.	Arrive Los Angeles Airport Drive-It Rental Car - Confirmation #1294
	3:00 p.m.	*The Palm Hotel* 3653 Hollywood Blvd. Los Angeles, CA 90216 (213) 555-5555
	7:00 p.m.	Dinner Meeting with Jason Crane and Marshal Wittink *Futura Capital Group* *Magnolia Restaurant* 107 Beverly Drive Los Angeles, CA 90214 (213) 555-6666
July 22	10:00 a.m.	Meeting with Shakela Caper and Josh Rodriguez *Rodriguez, & Caper Marketing Group* 3817 Olive Drive Burbank, CA 90036 (818) 555-0093
	7:30 p.m.	Dinner Meeting with Leslie Parker and Sarah Dennis *Runway Licensing & Merchandising Co.* *Da Salvano Restaurant* 888 Almota Street Los Angeles, CA 90211 (213) 555-9999
July 23	12:30 p.m.	Depart, Los Angeles Airport Atlantic Airlines, Flight #11
	9:30 p.m.	Arrive, New York, LaGuardia Airport

Use Columns with Custom Widths

EXERCISE 74

Directions

1. Create a new document.
2. Set 1" left and right margins.
3. Begin the exercise 2" from the top of the page.
4. Center and set the title to the fonts and font sizes shown in the illustration on page 200. Press the **Enter** key four times.
5. Set a two-column, newsletter-style format using the default gutter space to create the announcement.
6. Set the column widths as follows:
   - Column 1: 4.4"
   - Column 2: 1.6"
7. Set the text in Column 1 to sans serif, 12 pt; set the line spacing to double.
8. Set the text in Column 2 to sans serif, 12 pt; set the line spacing to single.
9. Justify and hyphenate the Column 1 text.
   - Be sure that words in all caps are not hyphenated.
10. Correct spelling.
11. Preview the document.
12. Print one copy.
13. Save the file; name it **8.74repair**.

CONCEPT BUILDERS

- To force a new column, you must insert a column break. To do so, click Insert, Break, and select Column.
- You can change column widths by a specific amount in the appropriate dialog box or by dragging the column marker on the ruler.

DID YOU KNOW?

An announcement publicizes an event, occasion, or happening.

Directions *continued*

10. Add shading and borders as follows:
    a. Apply black shading to Column 1. Color the text white.
    b. Apply a 10% gray shading to the three rows shown.
    c. Apply a decorative (or double) line between Columns 3 and 4.
11. Center the table horizontally and vertically.
12. Correct spelling.
13. Preview the document.
14. Print one copy.
15. Save the file; name it **8.79itinerary**.
16. Close **8.76jbminutes**; do not save the changes.

Use the Help Index

How Do I...?	**Enter the keyword(s):**
Change row height	Row height

Serif, 18 pt, bold, italic

Learn to….

Serif, 18 pt, bold

Troubleshoot

and Serif, 12 pt, italic

Serif, 18 pt, bold

Maintain Computers

Have you ever experienced a computer "crash" in the middle of a deadline or spent valuable time trying to recover lost files? If you have been in one of these situations, you know how frustrating and disastrous a computer failure can be.

The **TROUBLESHOOTER WORKSHOP** will provide you with valuable information and equip you with the tools and skills needed to diagnose and repair your computer system when a problem arises. It will also provide you with preventive maintenance techniques you can practice to avoid many common problems before they start. For more information, call 1-800-555-5555 and enroll in the TROUBLESHOOTER WORKSHOP now!

Sans serif, 10 pt, bold

Locations and Dates

Atlantic City, NJ
August 5-6

Cherry Hill, NJ
August 7-8

Edison, NJ
July 16-18

New York, NY
July 8-9

Norwalk, CT
August 15-16

Princeton, NJ
August 17-18

Scranton, PA
August 19-20

Trumbull, CT
August 28-29

Create a Table; Change Row Height; Apply Borders and Shading

EXERCISE 79

Directions

SCANS

1. Create a new document.
2. Set 1" left and right margins and .5" top and bottom margins.
3. Begin the exercise at the top of the page.
4. Create the table shown on page 211.
   a. Determine the number of columns and rows needed.
   b. Determine the columns and rows to split and/or merge.
   c. Set the column widths as follows:
      - Column 1: 1.15"
      - Columns 2 and 3: 1.05"
      - Column 4: 3.75"
   d. Set the height for Row 1 (JUMPBALL, INC) to 1.15"; set the height for Row 2 (FOR: John Ortiz) to .75".
5. Open **8.76jbminutes** (created in Exercise 76).
6. Remove all table borders.
7. Print one copy.
8. Copy the company name from the **8.76jbminutes** file to the first row in the new document and center it.
9. Set the fonts, font sizes, and alignments in each column as follows:
   a. Column 1 ("Itinerary"): center vertically and horizontally within the cell using serif, 48 pt. Rotate the text 90 degrees.
   b. Column 2 (dates): left-align using a sans serif or decorative font in 14 pt.
   c. Column 3 (time): right-align using sans serif, 12 pt.
   d. Column 4 (appointments): left-align using sans serif, 12 pt.

CONCEPT BUILDERS

- Applying borders and shading emphasizes data in a cell. Removing table borders creates another effect.
- When you change the font size, the row height will adjust to accommodate the size of the text. You can change the row height to make text more readable or to add special effects.
- You can change row height by specific amounts in the appropriate dialog box or by dragging on the horizontal line separating the rows to adjust it to the height you want.

HOT TIPS

Display the Tables and Borders toolbar when applying borders and shading to a table.

Create a Table; Change Column Width

EXERCISE 75

SCANS

Directions

1. Create a new document.
2. Set 1.25" left and right margins.
3. Begin the exercise 1" from the top of the page.
4. Center and set the title to serif, 14 pt, bold, as shown in the illustration on page 202. Press the **Enter** key three times.
5. Create a table with two columns and seven rows (or create parallel columns).
   NOTE: *In Word, borders appear as a default setting when creating tables. You will learn to remove them in a later exercise. If you used a parallel column feature, lines will not appear.*
6. Set the column text to serif, 12 pt; apply bold to the column headings.
7. Set the column widths as follows:
   - Column 1: 1.75"
   - Column 2: 4.5"
8. Center the exercise horizontally and vertically.
9. Correct spelling.
10. Preview the document.
11. Print one copy.
12. Save the file; name it **8.75virus**.

VOCABULARY

Parallel columns
Rows
Columns
Cells

CONCEPT BUILDERS

- In ***parallel columns,*** text moves from Column 1 on the first page to Column 1 on the next page instead of flowing automatically to Column 2. Parallel columns are used to create a list, script, itinerary, the minutes of a meeting, or any other document in which text must align horizontally.
- You can create parallel columns using tables. With some software, a parallel column feature is available for creating this format.
- A table consists of ***rows,*** which run horizontally, and ***columns,*** which run vertically. The rows and columns intersect to form boxes called ***cells.***
- As you enter text in a table cell, the cell expands downward to accommodate the text. Pressing the Enter key in a cell extends the cell vertically. It will not advance the insertion point to the next cell. Pressing the Tab key or clicking in the cell advances the insertion point to the next cell.

2001 2002 2003	Riverbank Run for Children **Semi-Annual Contributions**	
Year	**2nd Half**	**1st Half**
2001	22,199.22	123,999.66
2002	115,040.40	22,934.40
2003	51,446.30	79,950.00

Use the Help Index

How Do I...?	**Enter the keyword(s):**
Create a table	Table
Change column width	Column width
Create parallel columns	Parallel columns

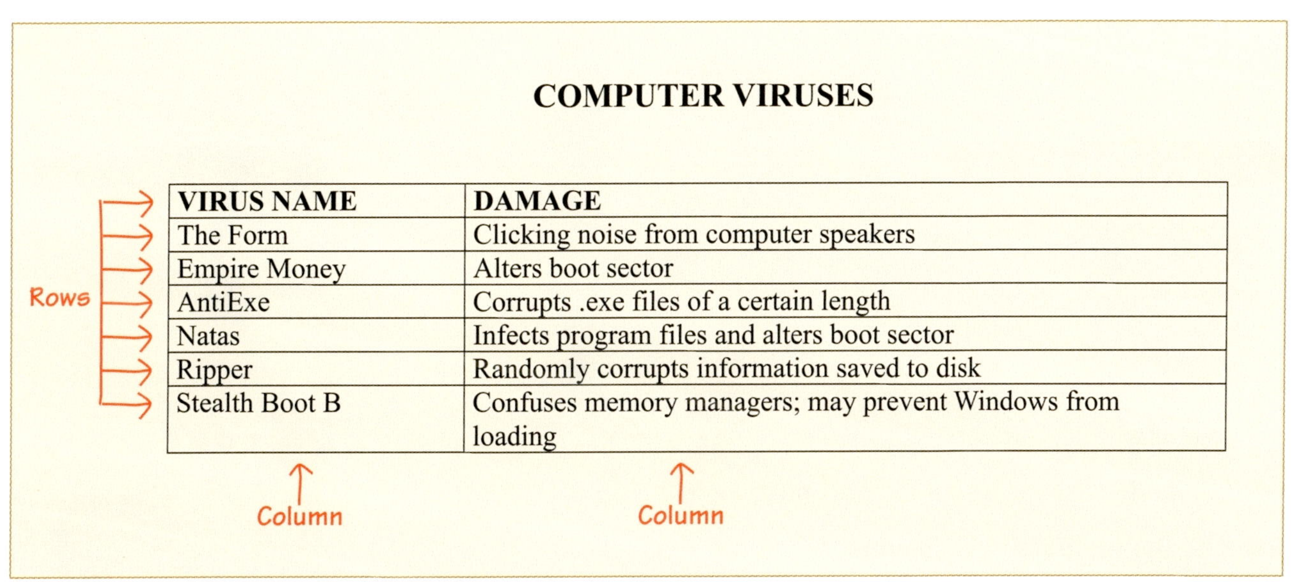

COMPUTER VIRUSES

VIRUS NAME	DAMAGE
The Form	Clicking noise from computer speakers
Empire Money	Alters boot sector
AntiExe	Corrupts .exe files of a certain length
Natas	Infects program files and alters boot sector
Ripper	Randomly corrupts information saved to disk
Stealth Boot B	Confuses memory managers; may prevent Windows from loading

Create a Table; Change Column Width; Align Table Data; Merge and Split Cells; Change Text Direction

EXERCISE 78

SCANS

Directions

1. Create a new document.
2. Set 1.25" left and right margins.
3. Begin the exercise at the top of the page.
4. Create the table using three columns and 6 rows, as shown in the illustration on page 208.
5. Merge Row 1; then split the row into two columns.
6. Set the width of the column for the first row as follows:
   a. Column 1: .75"
   b. Column 2: 5.4"
7. Enter the text in the first row as shown.
   a. Set `2001`, `2002`, and `2003` to serif, 26 pt, bold.
   b. Rotate the text.
   c. Set `Riverbank Run for Children` to sans serif, 14 pt.
   d. Right-align and set `Semi-Annual Contributions` to sans serif, 22 pt.
8. Enter the remaining table data in serif, 12 pt.
   a. Center and bold the column headings.
   b. Center-align text in Column 1.
   c. Decimal-align text in Columns 2 and 3.
9. Center the table horizontally and vertically.
10. Correct spelling.
11. Preview the document.
12. Print one copy.
13. Save the file; name it **8.78donate**.

VOCABULARY

Split cells
Decimal aligned

CONCEPT BUILDERS

- You can divide or ***split cells.*** When you split a cell into multiple cells, you divide the space of a single cell into the specified number of cells.

- When data is ***decimal aligned,*** it is arranged so that the decimal points line up.

Create a Table; Change Column Width

EXERCISE 76

SCANS

Directions

1. Create a new document.
2. Set .75" left and right margins. Set a top margin of 1" and a bottom margin of .8".
3. Begin the exercise 1" from the top of the page.
4. Set the company name to a sans serif or decorative font in the sizes shown in the illustration on page 204.
   - Set the subheading to serif, 12 pt.
5. Create a table with two columns and 15 rows (or create parallel columns).
   NOTE: *You will remove the table borders in a later exercise.*
6. Set the column widths as follows:
   - Column 1: 2.0"
   - Column 2: 4.5"
7. Set the text in Column 1 to sans serif, 10 pt; set the text in Column 2 to serif, 10 pt.
8. Center the exercise horizontally and vertically.
9. Correct spelling.
10. Preview the document.
11. Print one copy.
12. Save the file; name it **8.76jbminutes**.

VOCABULARY

Minutes

CONCEPT BUILDERS

Minutes summarize the discussions of a meeting according to the agenda (the outline) that is established prior to the meeting. The agenda items appear to the left of the discussion points.

Directions *continued*

15. Preview the document.

16. Print one copy.

17. Save the file; name it **8.77cash**.

Use the Help Index

How Do I...?	**Enter the keyword(s):**
Align data within a cell	Align data
Change text direction	Align text
Merge or join cells	Merge cells

PROJECTED FIRST-QUARTER CASH FLOW
(In thousands)

COMPUVEST, Inc.		**JAN.**	**FEB.**	**MAR.**
	CASH IN			
	Software Sales	45,135	33,765	29,123
	Training Fees	9,200	11,487	14,865
	Consulting Fees	10,468	3,145	6,654
	CASH OUT			
	Product Costs	15,345	12,456	10,988
	Office Staff	2,800	2,800	2,800
	Office Maintenance	1,087	1,000	1,400

➢ ➢ MARKETING DEPARTMENT ≺ ≺

Minutes of Meeting

June 10, 2004

PRESENT	Chris Keating, Michelle Richards, David Winter, Janet Boyle, Omar Banks, Lisa Lansky, Peter Bond
ANNOUNCEMENTS	The Sports Merchandising Convention is being held at the Sheraton Hotel on July 15. If you are not yet registered to attend, call David by Friday. The development of a new basketball sneaker just got the green-light from corporate. We will now move forward with our marketing campaign.
Bold → **NEW BUSINESS**	
SWEAT GYM OPENING	A new SWEAT Gym chain is set to open this fall in Chicago and Miami. We have agreed to sponsor the opening events—one in Chicago and one in Miami. We will supply a smaller version of our top-selling gym bag for each attendee. Enclosed in the bag will be a JUMPBALL t-shirt and catalog, from which attendees can order merchandise at a 15% discount. Janet and Omar will be organizing this event and the premium giveaways.
RAINBOW BASKETBALL	Sales of the rainbow basketball for kids have not met expectations. Michelle and Chris have been researching the cause of these faltering sales and have found that we are targeting the wrong demographic. Girls ages 7-12, not boys ages 6-10, prefer the rainbow basketball. They will rewrite a marketing plan to reposition the rainbow basketball and we will discuss the execution of their plan at the next meeting.
SUPER JUMP BASKETBALL SNEAKERS	Our latest product, which will be introduced to the public at the Sports Merchandising Convention next month, is expected to be huge success. Lisa and Peter have been working on a launch campaign for the sneaker. Our target market is males 17-34, who are semi-competitive players. The sneaker is positioned as the one that will give "the extra lift to make the shot you've always dreamed of…" There will be a launch party at the SPORTS VENUE theme restaurant, which will be one of the opening events of the Sports Merchandising Convention.
SPORTS MERCHANDISING CONVENTION	July 15-18. Make sure that you have at least 7 meetings with distributors set-up by July 1. Our focus will be on the following products: Super Jump Basketball Sneaker, The Ultimate Sports Watch, Step and Glow Kids Sneakers and the Rainbow Basketball.
ADJOURNMENT	The meeting was adjourned at 12:30 p.m.

Create a Table; Change Column Width; Align Table Data; Merge Cells; Change Text Direction

EXERCISE 77

SCANS

Directions

1. Create a new document.
2. Set .75" left and right margins.
3. Begin the exercise at the top of the page.
4. Center and set the titles to serif, 12 pt, italic, as shown in the illustration on page 206. Press the **Enter** key three times.
5. Create a table using five columns and 13 rows.
6. Set column widths as follows:
   - Column 1: .5"
   - Column 2: 1.5"
   - Columns 3, 4, and 5: 1"
7. Merge the cells in Column 1.
8. Merge the cells in Rows 2, 4, 8, and 10.
9. Enter the data as shown.
10. Set the fonts and sizes as follows:
    a. Company name to serif, 14 pt, bold.
    b. Column and side headings to serif, 14 pt, bold.
    c. Table data to serif, 10 pt.
11. Rotate the company name as shown.
12. Align table data as follows:
    a. Right-align numerical column data.
    b. Center the company name vertically within the cell.
13. Center the table horizontally and vertically.
14. Correct spelling.

VOCABULARY

Merge cells

CONCEPT BUILDERS

- You can align data within a table cell in various ways during the table creation process or afterward. Data can be left-, center-, right-, decimal-aligned, or justified; it can be vertically centered at the top, bottom, or center; or rotated in 90-degree increments.

Left	Decimal .1 .10 1000.00
Center	Justify Justified text needs more than one line to show its effect.
Right Top Bottom Center	Text rotated 90 degrees

- When you ***merge cells,*** you remove the dividing lines between cells to create a single larger cell.

APPENDIX

APPENDIX A

Microsoft Office Specialist Correlation

MICROSOFT WORD 2002 CORE LEVEL

Standardized Coding Number	Skill Sets and Skills Being Measured	ICV Performance Based?	Unit-Lesson-Exercise			Page Number
W2002-1	**Inserting and Modifying Text**					
W2002-1-1	Insert, modify, and move text and symbols	Yes	2	2	7	53
			2	3	19	76
			2	4	31	100
W2002-1-2	Apply and modify text formats	Yes	2	3	20	78
			2	8	81	214
W2002-1-3	Correct spelling and grammar usage	Yes	2	1	1	43
			2	1	3	45
W2002-1-4	Apply font and text effects	Yes	2	3	18	74
W2002-1-5	Enter and format date and time	Yes	2	2	10	58
W2002-1-6	Apply character styles	Yes	2	5	38	116
W2002-2	**Creating and Modifying Paragraphs**					
W2002-2-1	Modify paragraph formats	Yes	2	4	27	93
W2002-2-2	Set and modify tabs	Yes	2	4	34	106
W2002-2-3	Apply bullet, outline, and numbering format to paragraphs	Yes	2	3	21	81
			2	5	42	124
W2002-2-4	Apply paragraph styles	Yes	2	5	38	116
W2002-3	**Formatting Documents**					
W2002-3-1	Create and modify a header and footer	Yes	2	7	60	158
W2002-3-2	Apply and modify column settings	Yes	2	8	72	195
			2	8	74	199
			2	8	81	214
W2002-3-3	Modify document layout and Page Setup Setup options	Yes	2	3	15	69
			2	4	27	93
			2	4	29	97
W2002-3-4	Create and modify tables	Yes	2	8	75	201
			2	8	76	203
			2	8	77	205
			2	8	78	207
			2	8	79	209
W2002-3-5	Preview and print documents, envelopes, and labels	Yes	2	2	7	53
			2	2	11	60

MICROSOFT WORD 2002 CORE LEVEL *(continued)*

Standardized Coding Number	Skill Sets and Skills Being Measured	ICV Performance Based?	Unit-Lesson-Exercise			Page Number
W2002-4	**Managing Documents**					
W2002-4-1	Manage files and folders for documents	Yes	1	2	6	32
W2002-4-2	Create documents using templates	Yes	2 2	5 5	40 41	120 122
W2002-4-3	Save documents using different names and file formats	Yes	2	2	11	60
W2002-5	**Working with Graphics**					
W2002-5-1	Insert images and graphics		3	1	1	276
W2002-5-2	Create and modify diagrams	Yes	3	1	1	276
W2002-6	**Workgroup Collaboration**					
W2002-6-1	Compare and merge documents	Yes	2	9	94	244
W2002-6-2	Insert, view, and edit comments	Yes	2	2	8	54
W2002-6-3	Convert documents into Web pages	Yes	3	3	24	329

APPENDIX B

Using the Mouse

You must use the mouse to access many software features. You can also access these features using the keyboard, but for most people, using the mouse is easier and more convenient.

When the mouse is rolled on a tabletop, a corresponding movement of the pointer shows on screen. The mouse pointer changes its appearance depending on the software tool in use and the object to which it is pointing.

Most mouse actions require using the left mouse button.

The mouse terms and actions in the table below are commonly used when handling a mouse. If you are using the Microsoft IntelliMouse, notice the terms and actions associated with that device in the table on the right.

Term	***Mouse Actions***
Point	Move the mouse on the tabletop until the pointer is touching a specific item on screen
Click	Press and release the left mouse button
Double-click	Press and release the left mouse button twice in rapid succession
Triple-click	Press and release the left mouse button three times in rapid succession
Right-click	Press and release the right mouse button
Drag	Point and hold down the left mouse button while moving the mouse to a new position; release the mouse button to drop the dragged object (or text) into the new position

Term	***Microsoft IntelliMouse Actions***
Scroll	Rotate the wheel forward or back
Pan up or down	Hold down the wheel while dragging the pointer above or below where you first clicked
AutoScroll	• Click the wheel and the software scrolls down; to scroll up, move the pointer above the starting point on the vertical scroll bar; to cancel AutoScroll, click any mouse button • Click the wheel and word processing software scrolls in the direction you subsequently move the pointer
Zoom in or out	Hold down the Ctrl key as you rotate the wheel; rotating the wheel upward increases the magnification; rotating the wheel downward decreases the magnification

Mouse Pointer Shapes

The following chart illustrates common mouse pointer shapes and a description of what each shape indicates. You can customize mouse pointer shapes by selecting Settings and clicking Control Panel, Mouse from the Start menu. In the Mouse Properties dialog box, as shown in Figure B.1, click the Pointers tab, click the drop-down menu under Scheme, and select any one of the mouse pointer schemes.

You can also change the speed of mouse actions in the Pointer Options tab. Other options are available in the Mouse Properties dialog box.

Pointer Name	Illustration	Description
Normal Select		Used to point to objects and toolbar buttons
Help Select		Used after clicking "What's This?" on the Help menus; when you point and click a window item when this pointer is visible, help on that item appears
Working in Background		Used to indicate that the system is busy
Busy		Indicates the computer is processing a command or working in the background; no other work can be completed while this processing is taking place

Pointer Name	Illustration	Description
Precision Select		Used when drawing objects
Text Select		Used when selecting or inserting text
Vertical Resize		Used to change the vertical size of objects or windows; horizontal and diagonal resize mouse pointers are also available
Move		Used to move objects
Link Select		Used to indicate and select a hyperlink

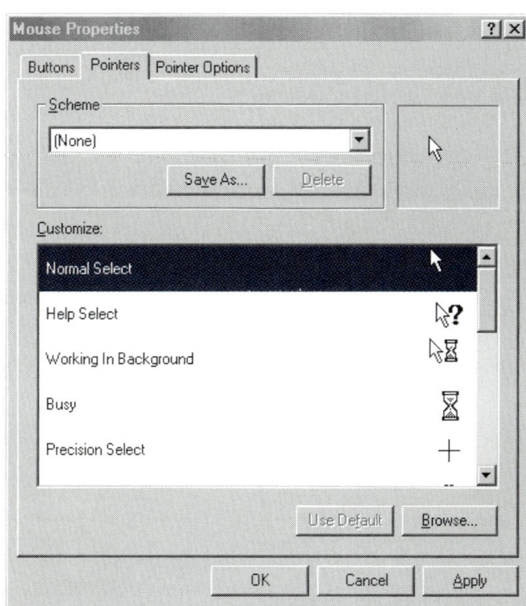

Figure B.1 Mouse Properties dialog box

Toolbars, Menus, and Dialog Boxes

Toolbars

Toolbars throughout Windows applications provide you with quick access to features you use frequently. Using the mouse, point to a toolbar button and click once to access a feature. To learn the toolbar button name (and the feature), position the mouse pointer over the button and a ScreenTip displays its name.

If there are more buttons on the bar than can fit across the screen, you can display the hidden buttons by clicking the Toolbar Options list arrow at the end of the toolbar, as shown in Figure C.1.

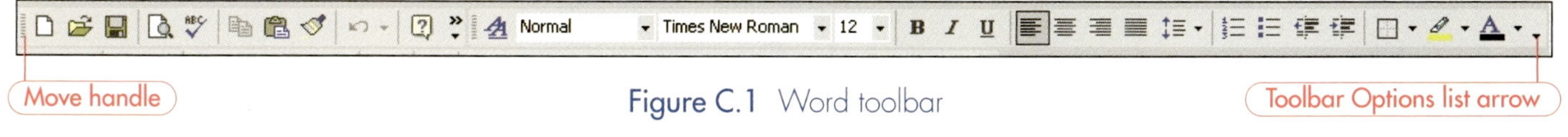

Figure C.1 Word toolbar

Choosing a Toolbar

Most software comes with numerous toolbars from which to choose. You can add buttons to the predefined toolbars, or you can create entirely new toolbars for those features that you use most frequently. To choose a toolbar, select Toolbars on the View menu, as shown in Figure C.2. You can also right-click a displayed toolbar and select a toolbar on the menu that appears. (Word toolbars are illustrated here.)

Positioning the Toolbar

You can move a toolbar to any location on the screen by dragging the move handle on a stationed toolbar to another location (see Figure C.1). You can also drag the title bar on a floating toolbar and position it as you prefer. If you drag the toolbar to the edge of the application window or to a location alongside another stationed toolbar, it becomes a stationed toolbar as well.

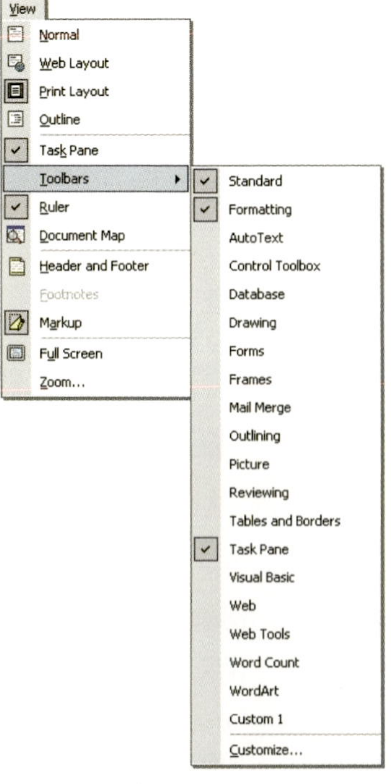

Figure C.2 View menu

Customizing the Toolbar

After using a software package, you will discover which features you use most frequently. You can then customize the toolbars to give yourself quick access to those features, or you can create new toolbars.

To create a new a toolbar in Office, do the following:

1. Click **Tools.**
2. Click **Customize.**
3. Click the **Toolbars** tab.
4. Click **New.**
5. In the **Toolbar** name box, enter the new toolbar name.
6. In the **Make toolbar available to** box, click the template or document in which to save the toolbar.
7. Click the **Commands** tab.
8. In the **Categories** box, click a category for the command.
9. In the **Commands** box, drag the command you want to the toolbar (which is displayed on the screen).
10. Repeat Step 9 until the toolbar is complete.
11. Click **Close.**

To add a toolbar button, do the following:

1. Display the toolbar to which you want to add a button.
2. Click **Tools.**
3. Click **Customize.**
4. Click the **Commands** tab.
5. In the Categories box, click a category for the command you want.
6. Drag the command from the Commands box to the displayed toolbar. Click **Close.**

Or

1. Click the **Toolbar Options** list arrow on the displayed toolbar.
2. Click **Add or Remove Buttons.**
3. Select the check box next to the button you want to add.

To remove a toolbar button, do the following:

1. Display the toolbar you want to change.
2. Hold down the **Alt** key and drag the button off the toolbar.

Menus

Menus throughout Windows applications present you with choices for the commands you want the software to perform. The menu bar displays commands across the top of the application screen. The Word menu bar is shown in Figure C.3.

Figure C.3 Word menu bar

Choosing Menu Commands

You can select menu bar items using the mouse or the keyboard. Using the mouse, point to an item on the menu bar and click once. Using the keyboard, press the Alt key and the underlined letter in the menu name.

When you select a menu bar item, a drop-down submenu appears with additional options. Notice the drop-down submenus that appear when you select Edit in Word, as shown in Figure C.4.

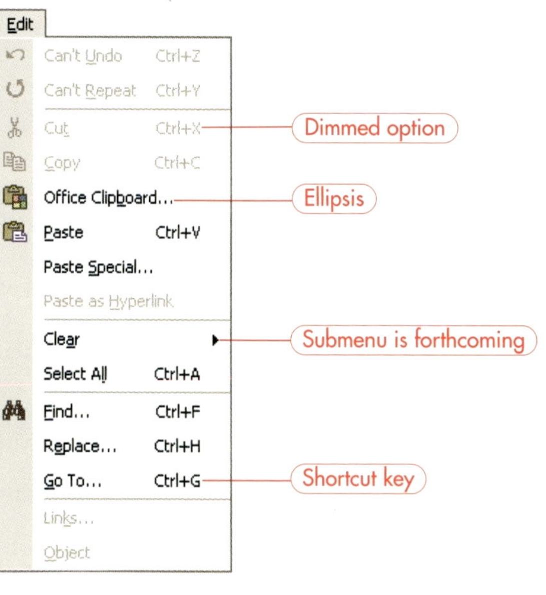

Figure C.4 Edit menu

About Submenus

Notice the following about submenus:

- Some menu options are dimmed, while others appear black. When options are dimmed, they are not available for selection.
- A check mark or bullet next to a drop-down menu item means the option is currently selected.
- Some menu items display shortcut keys that you can use to access a command.
- A menu item followed by ellipsis marks (. . .) indicates that a dialog box, which requires that you provide additional information to complete a command, is forthcoming.
- An arrow next to a menu item means another submenu is forthcoming.

Shortcut Menus

Shortcut menus appear when you click the right mouse button. The menu items that appear vary, depending on where the mouse is pointing and what task you are performing. Notice the shortcut menu that appears, as shown in Figure C.5, when the mouse is pointing to the Document window in Word.

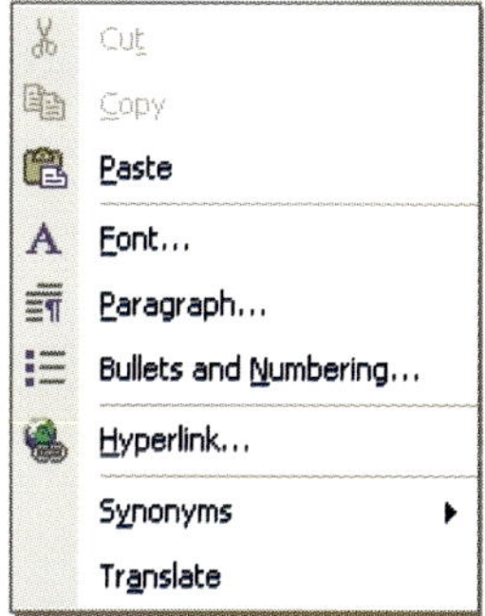

Figure C.5 Shortcut menu

Dialog Boxes

A dialog box presents information about the current settings for a command and allows you to have a "dialog" with it—that is, to change the settings, if necessary. Dialog boxes let you enter information in a variety of ways. Notice the description of each dialog box component in the Word Font and Print dialog boxes shown in Figures C.6 and C.7.

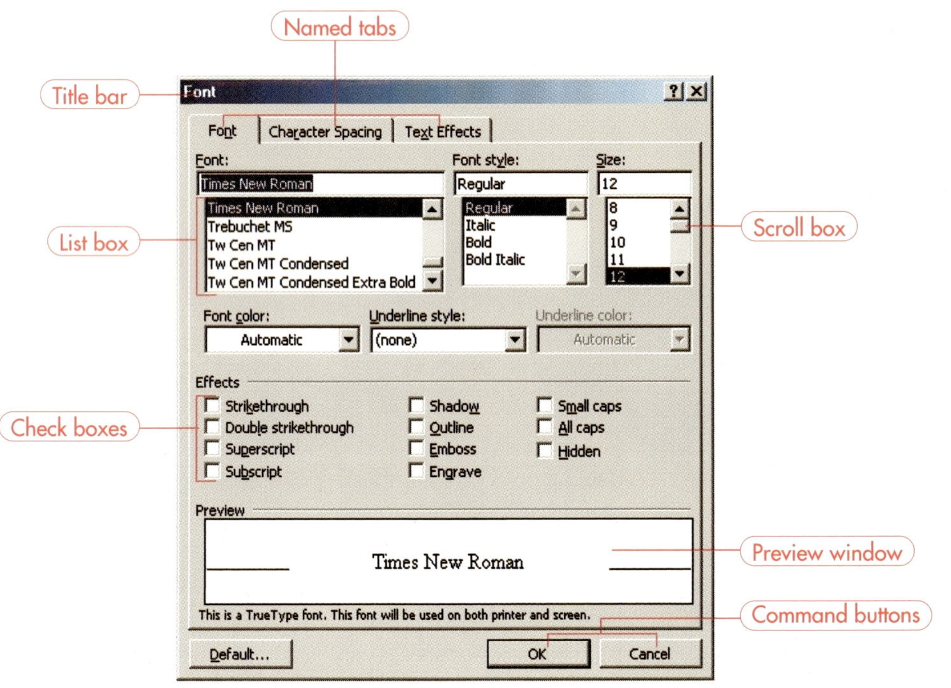

Figure C.6 Font dialog box

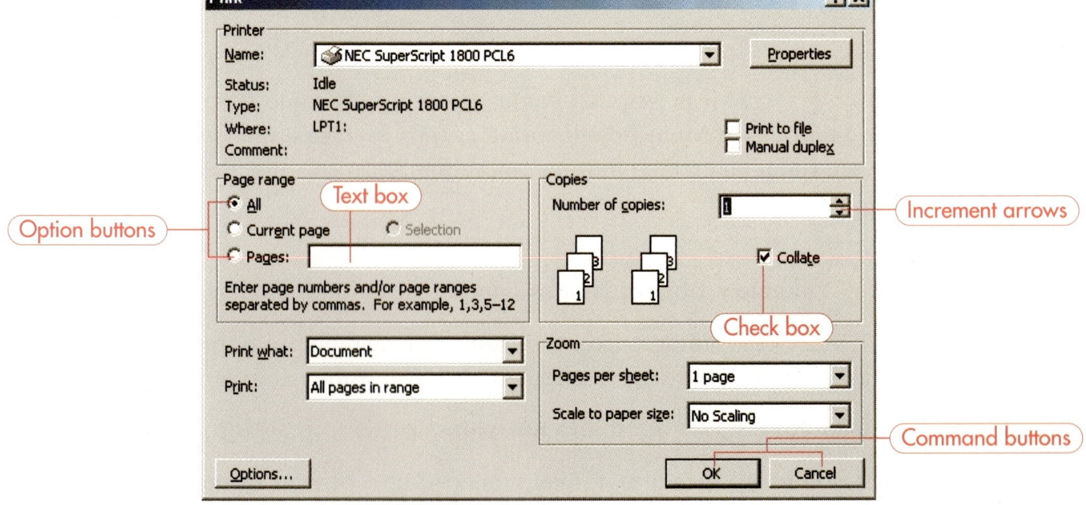

Figure C.7 Print dialog box

- The **title bar** identifies the title of the dialog box.
- A **text box** is a space where you enter information.
- **Command buttons** carry out the actions described on the button.
- An **increment box** provides a space for entering a value. Clicking the up or down arrow (usually to the right of the box) allows you to display the incremental value.
- A **named tab** displays options related to the tab's name in the same dialog box.
- **Option buttons** are small circular buttons marking options in a set. You can choose only one option from the set. A selected option button contains a dark circle.
- A **check box** is a small square box where you can select or deselect an option. A ✓ in the box indicates the option is selected. If several check boxes are offered, you may select more than one.
- A **list box** displays a list of items from which you can make selections. A list box may have a scroll bar that you can use to show hidden items in a list, or the list may be displayed by clicking a down arrow.
- A **scroll bar** is a horizontal or vertical bar containing scroll arrows and a scroll box that you can drag up or down to move through the file quickly.
- A **preview window** allows you to see a sample of the selection you made.

APPENDIX D

Proofreaders' Marks

Symbol	Meaning	Illustration
bf	Boldface	bf Excellent job!
≡	Capitalize	John l. smith
⁀	Close up space	pres entation
	Delete	pagee
ds[	Double-space	ds [This is the first time I have heard about it.
^	Insert	Where will it be?
^,	Insert punctuation	If you are going, I am going too.
'	Insert apostrophe	It was Johns hat.
#	Insert space	I think it will beuseful.
___	Insert underscore	Time Magazine was ordered last week.
	Move as indicated	This table will be omitted. Be sure to remove it from all documents.
[	Move left	[Let's go tomorrow.
]	Move right	] Everything you need is located on the CD.
lc or /	Make lowercase	Her title was Vice President.

Symbol	Meaning	Illustration
¶	New paragraph	It's cold outside. ¶ The forecast for next week
___	Replace word	The mouse ~~may~~ can be used to access many features.
ss[	Single-space	ss[Please be advised that there will be no delivery service next week.
◯	Spell out	(3) years ago
stet or	Let the original stand (ignore correction)	The ~~main~~ building was damaged.
∿	Transpose	This is intreesting material.

Leading and Line Spacing Illustrations

Leading Illustrations

Leading is the vertical spacing between baselines of text, which is measured in points. Leading allows you to adjust spacing in incremental amounts. The amount of leading affects the readability of text.

This is 10 pt Times Roman type with a 10 pt leading. It is called **10/10** and pronounced "10 on 10." Effectively, this means that there is no leading. Notice how close each line is in relation to the others.

This is 10 pt Times Roman type with an 11 pt leading. It is called **10/11.** Compare this spacing to the other examples.

This is 10 pt Times Roman type with a 12 pt leading. It is called **10/12.** This is the default leading in most desktop publishing software.

This is 10 pt Times Roman type with a 14 pt leading. It is called **10/14.** Now notice how unattractive the spread between the lines has become.

This is 10 pt Times Roman type with an 8 pt leading. It is called **10/8.** It is "negative" leading because the lines begin to overlap. It is useful as a special-effect style only.

Line Spacing Illustrations

Line spacing allows you to set the amount of vertical space between lines of text, which is measured in lines.

This is an example of **single spacing.** The amount of actual space varies depending on the font and font size. For the most part, there is no extra space between lines.

This is an example of **1.5 spacing,** in which there is .5 lines of space between the lines of text.

This is an example of **double spacing,** in which one full line of spacing appears between the lines of text.

APPENDIX F

Letter Styles

Letter Styles

Letters can be prepared using various styles. The most widely used **business letter** styles are the **full-block, modified-block,** and **semi-block.** A business letter generally contains a letterhead (information that identifies the company, such as its name, address, phone, fax, e-mail, and Web address of the organization). A **personal business letter** follows the same style guidelines as a business letter; however, the home address of the sender replaces the company letterhead. A brief description and a sample illustration of each style are shown below.

Full-block: All lines begin at the left margin.

Modified-block: All lines begin at the left margin except the date, complimentary close, and signature lines. These begin at approximately 4" from the left edge of the page.

Semi-block: This style is identical to the modified-block letter style, except that the first word of all paragraphs is indented .5" from the left margin.

Today's date

VIA FAX

Mr. Dillon Chasin
34 West End Avenue
New York, NY 10022

Dear Mr. Chasin:

Re: Follow-up to the Business Financing Conference

It was a pleasure meeting you last week at the Business Financing Conference in Las Vegas. I was very impressed with your Cyber Café idea. I would be very interested in meeting with you in Detroit to discuss the small business loan options that the Bank of Michigan has to offer. Our staff of small business advisors is available to consult with you about your venture.

Before we meet, however, you should provide us with a detailed business plan. A business plan is a descriptive report of the business you want to open. It describes the products or services you want to sell and what makes your business unique.

Please call my assistant, Paul Eicher, at (248) 555-5555 to schedule an appointment. We look forward to working with you.

Sincerely,

Tyrone Simmons
Financing Department

ts/yo
enclosure

copy to: J. Haberman
A. Weston

Full-block letter style

Today's date

VIA FAX

Mr. Dillon Chasin
34 West End Avenue
New York, NY 10022

Dear Mr. Chasin:

Re: Follow-up to the Business Financing Conference

It was a pleasure meeting you last week at the Business Financing Conference in Las Vegas. I was very impressed with your Cyber Café idea. I would be very interested in meeting with you in Detroit to discuss the small business loan options that the Bank of Michigan has to offer. Our staff of small business advisors is available to consult with you about your venture.

Before we meet, however, you should provide us with a detailed business plan. A business plan is a descriptive report of the business you want to open. It describes the products or services you want to sell and what makes your business unique.

Please call my assistant, Paul Eicher, at (248) 555-5555 to schedule an appointment. We look forward to working with you.

Sincerely,

Tyrone Simmons
Financing Department

ts/yo
enclosure

copy to: J. Haberman
A. Weston

Modified-block letter style

Today's date

VIA FAX

Mr. Dillon Chasin
34 West End Avenue
New York, NY 10022

Dear Mr. Chasin:

Re: Follow-up to the Business Financing Conference

It was a pleasure meeting you last week at the Business Financing Conference in Las Vegas. I was very impressed with your Cyber Café idea. I would be very interested in meeting with you in Detroit to discuss the small business loan options that the Bank of Michigan has to offer. Our staff of small business advisors is available to consult with you about your venture.

Before we meet, however, you should provide us with a detailed business plan. A business plan is a descriptive report of the business you want to open. It describes the products or services you want to sell and what makes your business unique.

Please call my assistant, Paul Eicher, at (248) 555-5555 to schedule an appointment. We look forward to working with you.

Sincerely,

Tyrone Simmons
Financing Department

ts/yo
enclosure

copy to: J. Haberman
A. Weston

Semi-block letter style

Access provider *See* Internet Service Provider.

Action buttons Ready-made buttons that contain commonly understood symbols indicating specific actions.

Action items Follow-up assignments and due dates.

Active document The document in use.

Address (e-mail) Online code that identifies a user to whom e-mail can be sent.

Address (Web) *See* Uniform Resource Locator.

Align center Text alignment in which text is centered between the margins.

Align left Text alignment in which text is even at the left margin and uneven at the right margin.

Align right Text alignment in which text is uneven at the left margin and even at the right margin.

Alignment The placement of text relative to the margins of a page, a cell, or a column.

American Standard Code of Information Interchange A standard that identifies the letters of the alphabet, numbers, and various symbols by code number for each character in a text document. ASCII is the most common format for text files in computers and on the Internet.

AND A Boolean operator that will display search results that include all the words in a text string.

Application program A specific set of instructions that tells a computer what to do (e.g., word processing, spreadsheets, database).

Ascending A sorting order that organizes text alphabetically from A to Z or numbers/figures from smallest to largest.

ASCII *See* American Standard Code of Information Interchange.

AutoFormat A feature that provides an automatic format to a table.

AutoText Frequently used text, graphics, fields, tables, or bookmarks that are saved as an entry and then inserted into a document when needed.

Balanced columns A column style in which text evens out as it is typed into the columns.

Baud rate A measurement for data transmission speed.

BBS *See* Bulletin board system.

Bibliography Identifies sources used, quoted, or paraphrased within a document.

Bit The smallest unit of measurement for computer data.

Bits per second A measurement used to describe how fast data is transmitted through a modem. This term is synonymous with baud rate.

Body copy Comprises the text of the articles in newsletters.

Bold A text enhancement in which text is darkened.

Bookmark A placeholder that is created to mark specific text on a page in a document or on a Web site so that the user can easily return to that place at a later time.

Boolean operators Words or symbols that modify the search for information on the Web or in a database.

BPS *See* Bits per second.

Bring to front Moves an object to the top of all the other objects in a stack.

Broadcasting The act of sending the same e-mail message to several users at once.

Brochure A small pamphlet, booklet, or manual that provides information about a product line, a place, a service, or an event.

Browser An application program that provides a way to see and hear information on the Web.

Bulleted list A list of items marked by a round dot or other symbol.

Bulletin board system An electronic message system that lets users read, respond to, and post messages.

Byte A group of eight bits that represent one ASCII character. Computer storage is measured in bytes.

Caption Explanatory text appearing above or below an object or chart.

Cathode-Ray tube A vacuum tube in which a hot cathode emits electrons that are accelerated as a beam through a relatively high voltage anode, further focused or deflected electrostatically or electromagnetically, and allowed to fall on a phosphorescent screen.

CD-ROM An acronym that stands for Compact Disc-Read-Only Memory. A CD-ROM disc, which is similar to a floppy disk, can store large amounts of information (moving images, sound, digital programs, and information files).

Center alignment The positioning of text and/or graphics so that it is centered between the left and right margins.

Central processing unit The principal hardware device that controls and regulates the speed and processing of a computer.

Check box A small, square box where you can select or deselect an option.

Citation A reference, usually made in the form of a footnote or endnote, to give credit to the source of any borrowed material used in a document, presentation, or report.

Clip art Pictures and drawings that can be inserted into a document.

Clipboard A memory area of the computer where data is stored temporarily.

Close button A button (represented by an "X") that closes the document or program window.

Closing *See* Complimentary close.

Collapse When working with outlines, this feature hides body text and subheadings under the headings.

Command buttons Carry out the actions described on the button.

Comment Hidden notes or annotations that a user or a reviewer can add to a document.

Complimentary close The closing of a letter, located directly above the signature line.

Computer An electronic device that can perform tasks and calculations to provide logical information based on the instructions that have been given to it.

Contents Lists the articles or topics featured in an issue of a newsletter.

Continuous underline A line that appears below a series of words and the spaces between them.

Copy and paste A method of creating a duplicate of text or a graphic and placing it in another location in a document.

Copy formatting A feature that enables the user to dulpicate formatting (font face, style, and size) from one part of text to another.

CPU *See* Central processing unit.

Crosshair The shape of the mouse pointer when you are drawing lines or objects.

CRT *See* Cathode ray tube.

Custom tabs A feature that allows the user to set special stopping points on the typing line.

Cut and paste A method of moving text or a graphic. The "cut" procedure deletes text from a document and places it on the Clipboard. The "paste" procedure retrieves text from the Clipboard and allows the user to place it in a particular location in a document.

DAT *See* Digital audio tape.

Data Information in the form of numbers or words.

Data entry The process of entering new records.

Data source (document) The document used in the merge process that contains variable information (such as names, addresses, dates, and/or amounts).

Decimal-aligned Data that is arranged so the decimal points line up.

Decimal tab A tab type in which data is aligned at a decimal point.

Default settings A preset condition of the software.

Delivery address The address of the person to whom a letter is written.

Descending A sort order used to organize text alphabetically from Z to A or numbers/figures from largest to smallest.

Desktop An area on the computer screen where the user can work with programs and files.

Desktop publishing Using graphics and page design programs for publishing purposes.

Destination The file that receives the data.

Diagram A visual element that shows process flows and relationships.

Dialog box A box that contains options to carry out a command.

Digital audio tape A standard magnetic medium that has the ability to hold large amounts of information on a tape that is much smaller than an audio cassette.

Digital video disc A new type of CD-ROM that holds a minimum of 4.7 gigabytes, enough for a full-length movie.

Directory Unlike a search engine, a directory depends on people to create its listings.

Display *See* Monitor.

Domain The name given to a computer on the Internet that enables one computer to find another.

Download The process that brings information from a remote computer "down" to your computer.

Drag and drop A method of moving text using the mouse. Text is "dragged" from its original location and "dropped" into its new location.

Drawing canvas A non-printing border with space for drawing.

Drop capital The first letter of a paragraph that is much larger and "drops" several lines below the paragraph text.

Drop-down form field A field in a form that allows the user to select an option from a list of choices.

DVD *See* Digital video disc.

E-mail Electronic messages sent by way of the Internet to another Internet user.

E-mail signature Text and/or pictures that you can automatically insert in an outgoing e-mail message.

Electronic bulletin board *See* Bulletin board system.

Ellipis marks Three periods following a menu item that indicate a dialog box is forthcoming.

Embedded object An object that can be edited using the application in which it was created.

Enclosure notation A notation located at the bottom-left of a letter that indicates that the letter has attachments.

Endnotes A list of citations located at the end of a document.

Eudora An e-mail program.

Expand When working with outlines, this feature displays all levels of text.

Favorites folder A folder that allows the user to record frequently visited Web sites.

Fax A term, derived from the word "facsimile," which means duplicate or copy.

File A collection of information treated as an individual unit by a computer operating system.

File attachment A file appended to an e-mail message.

File extension Three characters that follow a file name and identify the file's type.

File name A name given to saved data.

File server A shared network computer that provides access to files for users in a common environment.

File transfer protocol A set of conventions governing the transfer of files across the Internet.

Find and Replace A feature that scans a document and searches for occurrences of specified text, symbols, or formatting and replaces them with other specified text.

First-line indent A feature that allows you to set the amount of space each paragraph indents.

Floppy disk A removable storage medium, 3.5" or 5.25" in size, that contains up to 1.4 megabytes each.

Font The appearance of a character, as distinguished by typeface and size.

Font face The design for a set of characters. Examples include Times New Roman, Arial, and Helvetica.

Font size The height of the characters, measured in points.

Footer The same text or graphic appearing at the bottom of every page or every other page in a document.

Footnote References that appear at the bottom of a page and give credit to the source of information.

Form In word processing, a document that contains fixed text, form fields, and spaces for entering information.

Form fields Placeholders that hold the information provided by a person filling out a form.

Formatting toolbar Appears in every Office application and contains buttons common to all Office applications as well as application-specific buttons.

Frames Regions of a Web page, which can be sized and made to scroll.

Full-block style letter A letter style in which all parts start at the left margin.

Gigabyte A unit of data that is 1,000 megabytes (or 1,000,000 bytes).

Graphic A line, circle, or box that has been created, or an image or illustration which is imported into a publication.

Grayscale Tones of gray to show the effects of color.

Gridlines Lines that mark the boundaries of columns and rows in a table.

Group In desktop publishing, an option that allows a user to make one object from several selected objects.

Groupware Programming enabling people who are located remotely from each other to work together in a collective effort.

Gutter space The space between columns.

Hacker Slang for an individual who illegally gains access to, and sometimes tampers with, information in a computer system.

Handles Boxes surrounding an object indicating that it has been selected and that it is in an edit mode.

Hanging indent An indentation style in which all lines in a paragraph are indented except the first line.

Hard drive A storage device that usually resides inside the computer and holds huge amounts of information. Also known as a "fixed" disk.

Hard page break A term used to indicate a page break entered manually.

Hardware The actual physical computer and all the wires, cables, and peripheral devices associated with it.

Header The same text appearing at the top of every page or every other page in a document.

Headlines Indicate the contents of articles in a newsletter.

History list A record of Web sites visited.

Hit counter Displays the number of times a Web page has been visited.

Home page The starting page of a Web site.

HTML *See* Hypertext markup language.

HTTP *See* Hypertext transfer protocol.

Hyperlink A connection between two Web documents. Underlined text or a picture defines this connection. Clicking a hyperlink enables the user to jump from one Web site to another.

Hypertext markup language The programming language used to write content for the World Wide Web.

Hypertext transfer protocol (HTTP) The data transmission "rules" governing the transfer of Web documents across the Internet.

Hyphenate The act of breaking up words (by syllable) at the end of a line to produce a tighter right margin.

Hyphenation zone The area at the end of a line of text in which an automatic hyphenation feature will divide words.

Import To use data produced by another application.

Increment box Provides a space for entering a value. Clicking the up or down arrow allows you to display the incremental value.

Inline graphic An imported or drawn graphic that is set in text and functions as a text character.

Indent A feature that sets temporary left, right, or left and right margins for paragraph text.

Index.htm The default name for the home page.

Input devices Transport data into the computer.

Insert mode In this mode, inserted characters will move existing characters to the right of the insertion point.

Insertion point The blinking vertical line that appears in a document window and indicates where the next keyed character will appear.

Inside address The address of the person to whom a letter is written.

Intercasting The ability to surf the Web through the TV.

Integrate The ability to share information between and among software tools.

Internal citation A citation that is indicated directly after the quoted text. Only the author's last name and the year of publication are shown.

Internet A worldwide network of linked computers.

Internet address *See* Internet protocol .

Internet protocol A set of conventions that enables information on the Internet to be routed from one network to another.

Internet protocol address *See* Internet protocol.

Internet Service Provider A company that sells access to the Internet.

Intranet An internal network confined within a specific physical location, usually one particular office or building.

ISP *See* Internet Service Provider.

Italic A text enhancement in which text is slanted to the right.

Justify An alignment option in which text is even at the left and right margins.

Kerning A feature that slightly alters the spacing between pairs of letters.

Kilobyte A unit of data that is 1,024 bytes.

LAN *See* Local area network.

Landscape orientation A paper orientation that is wider than it is tall.

Laptop computers Portable computers, also known as notebooks.

Leader A series of dots that connect one column to another to keep the reader's eye focused.

Leading The vertical line spacing between lines of text or data, measured in points.

Left align To position text along the left margin.

Left indent *See* Indent.

Letter spacing The relative space between characters.

Line space The vertical spacing between lines of text or data.

Link *See* Hyperlink.

Link bar A navigation tool that includes hyperlinks that appear in the same place on every page of a Web site.

Linked object When importing data, any change made to the source file is automatically updated in the destination file.

Linking Connecting data between files so that a change made in one file will automatically update the other.

List box Displays a list of items from which you can make selections.

List serve *See* Broadcasting.

Local area network A computer network that covers a small area.

Logo A symbol, picture, or saying that creates an image of a company.

Macro A symbol, name, or key that represents a list of commands or actions.

Mail merge A word processing and database feature that allows the user to mass-produce letters and other documents so they appear to be personalized.

Main document In the merge process, the document that contains elements that will not change. Sometimes referred to as the "form" document.

Mainframe A computer capable of storing and processing large amounts of data that can have several hundred simultaneous users.

Margins The parameters that are set to position data on a page.

Marquee A scrolling text Web component that can enhance a Web page.

Masthead The information that appears in the top portion of a newsletter and includes the newsletter's intended audience, the division or organization publishing the document, the volume and/or issue number, and the current date of the issue.

Maximize button A button that enlarges a document or application to fill the screen.

Megabyte A unit of data measuring 1,048,576 bytes (equal to about 3,000 pages of information).

Megahertz (MHz) A unit of frequency used to measure the speed of microprocessors.

Memorandum A written communication within a company.

Menu A list of related commands or options.

Merge A feature that combines a data document with a main document to mass-produce personalized letters or other documents.

Merge cells Removing the dividing lines between cells to create a single, larger cell. This is also referred to as "joining" cells.

Merge code Acts as a placeholder in the main document for the variable information that is inserted after a merge.

Minicomputer A type of computer that supports multiple users, each with their own terminal.

Minimize button A button that reduces the window to an icon.

Minutes A summary of the discussions of a meeting.

Modem A device that lets your computer communicate through standard telephone lines with the Internet or other modems and/or communication devices.

Monitor A hardware device that allows the user to view computer information.

Mouse A handheld device that controls the pointer on screen and lets you select options from the screen.

Multimedia Combining text, graphics, video, animation, and sound in computer applications.

Nameplate *See* Masthead.

Navigation Provides a Web site visitor with an easy and consistent way to view a site.

Navigation structure Sets the relationship between the home page and the other pages in a Web site.

Newsletter A communication that allows people who share a common interest to exchange ideas, developments, and information on a regular basis.

Newsletter-style column A column style in which text fills one column and then fills the next column. Also called newspaper-style column.

Network Computers that are connected together. *See* LAN, Internet, or Intranet.

Non-continuous underline When underlining a sentence, this text enhancement underlines only the words, not the spaces between them.

NOT A Boolean operator that will display search results that include only the words preceding the NOT operator.

Numbered list A list of items marked by a number or letter.

Object Item that can be selected and manipulated.

Office Assistant An animated graphic that answers questions, offers suggestions, and provides help unique to the Office program in use.

Office Shortcut Bar Displays buttons for single-click access to the Office features you use most frequently.

Online A computer that is connected to the Internet and ready to receive and/or transmit data.

Operating system The software that controls the operation of a computer and is responsible for the the processing of programs, file management, and the functions of drives, disks, and peripherals.

Option buttons Small, circular butttons that indicate options in a set.

OR A Boolean operator that will display search results that include one of the words in a text string.

Organization chart A diagram that illustrates a company's hierarchy.

Orientation The direction in which text is printed on a page.

Orphan The first line of a paragraph appearing by itself at the bottom of a column or page.

Outline A list of topics and subtopics used to organize information before writing a report or delivering a speech.

Output device A device that allows the user to see or hear the information the computer compiles.

Overtype mode In this mode, new text replaces existing text to the right of the insertion point.

Page banner Any text or graphics that you add to the top of a Web page that usually contains the page's title.

Paragraph spacing A feature that allows the user to insert additional space between paragraphs, headings, or subheadings.

Parallel column A column style in which text moves from the left column to the right column. Parallel columns are used to create a list, a script, an itinerary, the minutes of a meeting, or any other document in which text must be read horizontally.

Password A security code used to keep messages or documents private.

PC (personal computer) Computers small enough to fit on a desk that are relatively inexpensive and are designed for an individual user.

Peripherals All of the associated parts of a computer system that assist in expandability, such as monitors, printers, modems, scanners, removable cartridge drives, and speakers.

Photo gallery A Web page that contains placeholders for graphics, which are arranged in a specific layout.

Pixels A series of dots that make up a computer screen.

Placeholder (Web) A bookmarking procedure that allows the users to record a Web site that they might revisit.

Point size Measures the height of characters. A point is approximately 1/72 of an inch.

Portrait orientation A paper orientation that is taller than it is wide.

Preview window A window within a dialog box that allows the user to see a sample of the selection made.

Programming The act of creating code using a computer language to make application programs.

Protocol The "rules" that must be observed for two electronic devices to communicate with each other.

Pull quote Text art, generally in a box and in a larger size than the surrounding type, that consists of important, interesting, or provocative text from the body copy.

RAM *See* Random access memory.

Random access memory The main memory of the computer.

Re Part of a memorandum heading which means "in reference to" or "subject."

Read-only memory Computer memory on which data has been prerecorded. Once data has been written on a ROM chip, it cannot be removed or altered and can only be read.

Reference initials Appear at the bottom of a letter. The first set of initials belongs to the person who created the document; the second set of initials belongs to the person who typed the document.

Regroup To group objects that had been separated using the Ungroup command.

Resolution Sharpness or depth of detail of an image, usually expressed in dots per inch.

Restore button A button to the right of the title bar that restores the window to its previous size.

Résumé A document that lists one's personal experience, education, skills, and abilities and is used to gain employment.

Return address The address of the person sending a letter.

Reverse text A type style that changes black letters or lines to white.

Right align To position text along the right margin.

Right-aligned tab A tab type in which text is right-aligned at a tab setting.

Right indent *See* Indent.

ROM *See* Read-only memory.

Rotate handle Appears when an object is selected and allows the user to change the angle at which the object appears.

Rules A term used in desktop publishing that refers to the application of lines in a document.

Salutation The opening greeting of a letter (e.g., Dear Ms. Jones:).

Sans serif (typeface) A typeface that is straight-edged.

Scanner A peripheral device that digitizes input.

ScreenTip Pop-up name that appears when the insertion point is positioned over a toolbar button or hyperlink.

Script (typeface) A typeface that resembles handwriting.

Scroll The act of viewing all parts of a document.

Scroll box A box that you can drag to move a precise distance in order to see a different area of a document.

Scroll buttons Buttons with up, down, left, and right arrows used to scroll to different areas of a document.

Scrolling text *See* Marquee.

Search engine A program that searches documents on the Web for specified keywords and returns a list of the documents in which the keywords were found.

Send to back A command that moves an object to the bottom of all the other objects in the stack.

Serif (typeface) A typeface with lines or curves extending from the ends of the letters.

Server A computer that provides common access to files on a computer network.

Shared border A region of a Web page that is common to all pages.

Shortcut menu A menu that appears when you click the right mouse button. The menu items it contains vary, depending on where the mouse is pointing when you click.

Signature line The typed name of the person who has signed a letter. The signature is directly above the signature line.

Sizing handles *See* Handles.

Smart tag A set of buttons that are shared with other Office applications. These buttons provide options for changing a given action or an error.

Soft page break A term used to indicate an automatic new page.

Software The most commonly used term to refer to all application programs.

Software program A detailed set of computer instructions that resides in the computer and tells the computer what to do.

Sort Allows the user to rearrange the order of words or numbers in a list.

Speaker notes The corresponding notes that are written when slides are created in a presentation and help the speaker remember key points during the presentation.

Split cells The action that reverses the merge cells process and returns cells to their normal size.

Split windows The feature that allows the user to divide the window, thus displaying files in separate windows.

Standard toolbar Appears in every Office application and contains common buttons as well as application-specific buttons.

Status bar The area in an application window that displays information about the current status of the document.

Style A set of formatting characteristics that can be applied to a paragraph or selected text.

Subscript Characters that print below a line of type.

Supercomputer The fastest type of computer. It can store data and perform numerous tasks simultaneously. Also, it is used for specialized tasks that require vast amounts of mathematical calculations such as weather forecasting and medical and weapons research.

Superscript Characters that print above a line of type.

Symbol In word processing, an ornamental font or special character.

System software Software that controls the way computer parts work together.

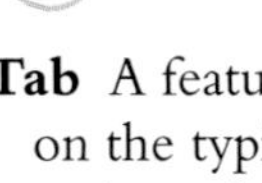

Tab A feature that allows the user to set a stopping point on the typing line. The stop can be set so that text typed at the point will align left, right, center, or on a decimal.

Table A series of columns and rows in which data is entered.

Tabular column Created when text is entered at a tab stop and forms a column of data.

Task pane Appears on the right side of the document/data/slide window and shows options pertinent to the task at hand.

Taskbar The area at the bottom of the Windows screen that allows you to switch easily between applications.

Telecommunications Communications facilitated by the use of a telephone or a computer, modem, and telephone line.

Template A designed and formatted document on which new documents are based.

Text alignments Arranging text along or between the margins on a page. *See* left align, center alignment, right align, or justify.

Text art Graphic elements created from text (e.g., raised or drop capitals, text boxes, or rotated text).

Text box A box that contains text or graphics that can be positioned, sized, and edited.

Text design *See* WordArt.

Text form field A placeholder in a form that allows the user to enter requested information.

Text string A word or words, a phrase, and/or operators that are used to search for documents, data, or other information.

Text wrap An option for controlling whether and how text wraps around a graphic or other object.

Theme A format or design template that can be applied to documents or Web pages.

Thesaurus A feature that provides the user with synonyms for selected words.

Title bar The shaded bar at the top of a dialog box or application window that displays the title of the box, or the name of the file and the application program.

Toolbars A collection of buttons that display icons, which represent various commands.

Transfer connect protocol/Internet protocol A set of communication rules that control the way data is transferred between computers on the Internet.

Type size *See* Font size.

Type style The modification of typefaces to add emphasis or contrast (e.g., bold or italic).

Typeface *See* Font face.

Ungroup The act of separating an object that has been grouped.

Uniform Resource Locator A Web address.

URL *See* Uniform Resource Locator.

VDT *See* Monitor.

Vertical centering Text that is centered between the top and bottom margins.

Video display terminal *See* Monitor.

View modes Options provided in each Office application to display a file on screen.

Virtual reality A computer simulation of three-dimensional, real-world dynamics.

WAN *See* Wide area network.

Watermark Text or graphics used as a background image on printed documents.

Web address *See* Uniform Resource Locator.

Web browser A software program that displays information retrieved from the Internet in a readable format.

Web component Web enhancement that you place on a Web page, such as a photo gallery, a hit counter, and a marquee.

Web page A visual presentation of an idea using text, graphics, sound, and video, that is viewed over the Internet.

Web site A collection of Web pages connected by hyperlinks.

Wide area network A computer network that links computers outside a local area.

Widow The last line of a paragraph appearing by itself at the top of a column or page.

Wildcard A character or symbol used in a search string to substitute for unknown characters.

Windows Explorer A Windows tool that allows the user to view the files and folders on a computer's hard drive.

Windows XP A popular operating system created by Microsoft for PCs.

Word underline A single line that appears below individual words.

Word wrap A feature that automatically advances text to the next line without pressing the Enter key.

WordArt Text created as a graphic image.

World Wide Web An interactive service of the Internet that lets you browse information.

Wrap text A feature in Excel that sends text to a new line within the same cell if the entry exceeds the cell width.

WWW *See* World Wide Web.

Zoom Used to magnify (zoom in) or reduce (zoom out) the size of the document on screen.

Zip disks Larger versions of floppy disks that can hold as much as 80 floppy disks. A Zip disk requires a Zip drive, which can be connected inside or outside of the computer.

INDEX

C

D

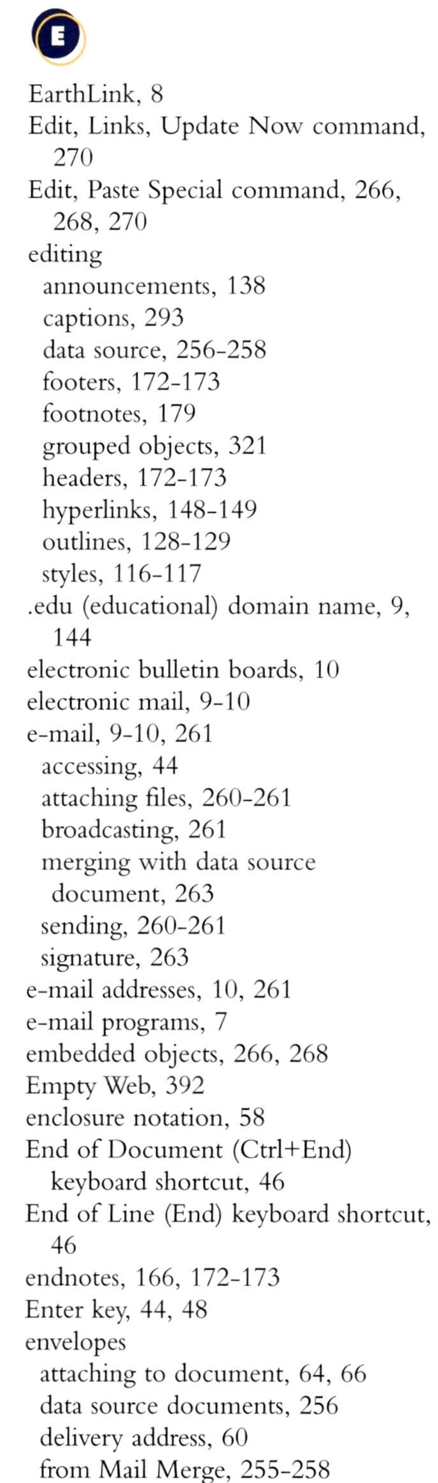

E

F

S